JUDAIC BAPTISM

ΒΑΠΤΙΖΩ

AN INQUIRY INTO THE
MEANING OF THE WORD
AS DETERMINED BY THE USAGE OF
JEWISH AND PATRISTIC WRITERS

BY

James W. Dale

NEW INTRODUCTION
BY
Robert H. Countess

Bolchazy-Carducci Publishers

P&R Publishing Company

Loewe Belfort Projects, Inc.

Cover design
Cynthia Henderson

Reprint of
1869 Edition, Philadelphia
Presbyterian Board of Publication and Sabbath-School Work

Published by:

BOLCHAZY-CARDUCCI PUBLISHERS
1000 Brown Street
Wauconda, IL 60084

ISBN 0-86516-247-6

P&R PUBLISHING
P. O. Box 817
Phillipsburg, NJ 08865

ISBN 0-87552-231-9

LOEWE BELFORT PROJECTS, INC.
Box 25 — 2819 Newby Road SW
Huntsville, AL 35805

Printed in the United States of America

Library of Congress Cataloging-in-Publication Data

Dale, James W. (James Wilkinson), 1812-1881.
Judaic baptism : Baptizō : an inquiry into the meaning of the word as determined by the usage of Jewish and patristic writers / by James W. Dale : new introduction by Robert H. Countess.
p. cm.
Rev. ed of: An Inquiry into the usage of Baptizo and the nature of Judaic baptism as shown by Jewish and patristic writings. 3rd ed. 1869.
Includes index.
1. Baptizein (The Greek word). 2. Baptism—Biblical teaching. 3. Baptism—History—Early church, ca. 30-600. 4. Judaism—Customs and practices. I. Dale, James W. (James Wilkinson), 1812-1881. Inquiry into the usage of Baptizo and the nature of Judaic baptism as shown by Jewish and patristic writings. II. Title. II. Title: Baptizō.
BV811.D33 1991
296.4—dc20 91-22764

INTRODUCTION

Robert H. Countess

THE APPEARANCE of *Classic Baptism* in 1989 anticipated this second volume in the series, which effort is to provide scholars and the general public with the long-out-of-print contribution by Dr. James W. Dale to the settling of the controversy over the *how* of water baptism.

In my lengthy introduction to *Classic Baptism*, I labored to emphasize that there is no longer any need or basis for serious dispute over the mode of water baptism (see pp. 3-15) once one sees that the Greek verb baptizo is a general action verb and lacking in modal specificity. Christians may thus apply water in the ceremony in whatever way they wish *so long as they derive such mode from a context which points to a pouring or a sprinkling or a plunging.*

Since Dr. Dale did not treat the issue of baptizing infants, there is no effort to introduce this doctrinal practice into this or the other volumes of the series. The work he did is primarily philological, not theological, and I see no end in sight for bringing paedobaptism to a peaceful resolution.

In *Judaic Baptism* one finds Dale's remarkable style exhibited as he begins with criticisms against *Classic Baptism*. These alone are a valuable inclusion. Then he examines *baptizo* in the Jewish writers Josephus, Philo, and Jesus the Son of Sirach. Following these are Patristic writers on the Old Testament, then Apocrypha authors, Jewish baptisms in the New Testament, Josephus on Judaic and Johannic baptisms, and lastly Dr. Dale's conclusions based, as always, on *usage*—not dictionaries.

As in the initial volume, he concludes that *bapto* and *baptizo* are not synonyms in their physical or figurative instances of usage. The dogmatism by some writers that *baptizo* has but one clear and constant meaning throughout all history is shown anew to be simply a dogmatic assumption and contrary to usage.

Judaic Baptism therefore goes forth in this reprint as a work that *can* stand alone, but is an integral part of the five-volume set. Special appreciation goes to publishers Bryce Craig and Lou Bolchazy for their continued support in returning this pivotally important work to its rightful place in the English-speaking world.

GENERAL VIEW OF CONTENTS.

BAPTISMS EXAMINED.

JEWISH WRITERS.

Condition of Intusposition and Condition without Intusposition.

Old Testament.

BAPTISMS OF JOSEPHUS, PHILO, AND SON OF SIRACH, CLASSIFIED.

1.

INTUSPOSITION WITHOUT INFLUENCE.

2

INTUSPOSITION WITH INFLUENCE.

3.

INTUSPOSITION FOR INFLUENCE.

4.

FIGURE GROUNDED IN DESTRUCTIVE MERSION.

SECONDARY USE.

1.

BAPTISM WITHOUT MERSION.

2.

APPROPRIATION.

3.

VERBAL FIGURE.

4.

CEREMONIAL PURIFICATION.

BAPTISMS OF SCRIPTURE AND APOCRYPHA.

AGENCIES AND CHANGES OF CONDITION.

WATER BAPTISMS.

WATER ITSELF BAPTIZED.

A New Quality Imparted.

Baptism by Water.

Special Influence Exerted.

Applied to the Body, more or less.

Pouring and Sprinkling.

Baptism by Blood.

Baptism by Fire.

Baptisms Involving Mental and Moral Influence.

Baptism and Miracle.

Baptisms Ceremonially Purifying.

Symbol Baptism.

Ceremonially Purifying Baptism a Symbol of Spiritual Purification.

PATRISTIC INTERPRETERS.

PASSAGES OF SCRIPTURE AND OF THE APOCRYPHA EXAMINED,

WITH THE PAGE WHERE THEY MAY BE FOUND.

JUDAIC BAPTISM.

JUDAIC BAPTISM

CONSIDERED IN ITS NATURE AND AS ILLUSTRATIVE OF THE USAGE OF

ΒΑΠΤΙΖΩ.

JUDAIC BAPTISM properly denotes a baptism which is distinctively Jewish. Under this title, however, will be introduced all baptisms of whatever kind spoken of by Jewish writers, as well as those facts and observances recorded in the Jewish Scriptures, which are declared by Patristic writers, to be baptisms.

The Apostle Paul speaks of a baptism connected with the miraculous division and passage of the Red Sea, although there is no such verbal statement in the original narrative. In like manner, the Patrists speak of many facts in the Jewish history and of many ritual observances in the Jewish ceremonial as baptisms, making interpretation not of words but of things. This course of Paul and of Patrist furnishes us with an exceedingly valuable help to determine the meaning of the Greek word. To many of the Patrists the Greek language was their native tongue. The use of a Greek word, by them, has equal authority for determining its meaning as its use by Plato or Plutarch. There is, also, this vantage-ground secured in the application of the word to Jewish history and ceremonial,—the facts are thoroughly known, and the nature and mode of the ordinances are minutely described. Thus we have no blank to fill up by our preconceptions or fruitful imaginations. We are fast bound by facts.

If this field of inquiry has been explored, to any extent, I am not aware of it. While, therefore, it will have somewhat of freshness, it will, I think, be also found to possess a very clear and imperative authority for determining the meaning of this contested word.

NO DEPARTURE FROM THE RADICAL MEANING.

This investigation will present no antagonism to the radical meaning of βαπτίζω as developed by Classical usage. On the contrary, we shall sternly and always insist on that meaning. The word, carried into the history of God's covenant people, will, indeed, be found in a new atmosphere. And when applied to the pure and purifying rites of revelation, it will be found to assume another coloring from that with which it was invested when found amid the Bacchanalian orgies of heathenism. The radical meaning of the word remains the same; the laws of language development remain the same; and the distinctive result, although without exemplification amid the utterly alien facts of heathenism, has the most absolute indication in the principles and actual developments of Classical usage.

It being, then, very foreign from our purpose to lay a new foundation whereon to establish a Judaic meaning for this word, but proposing to stand squarely on that already laid in the Classics, it will be of interest and not without instruction, to learn what Baptist writers think of that foundation.

Classic Baptism had its severe limitations attached to it, for the purpose of securing the attention of all, and more especially of Baptist scholars, to a single point,—the classical use, and the frank and full expression of sentiment upon it. The result has proved happy, so far as scholars generally are concerned; but only limitedly as relates to the representatives of Baptist sentiment. Among these there has been an unexpected and unwonted reticence. Still, some have spoken, and these sufficiently indicate the course of future sentiment.

As many have not had the opportunity to see the statements of Baptist criticism, who would feel an interest to do so, I will furnish a synopsis of them, as not without value in their bearing on our continued inquiry.

BAPTIST CRITICISMS OF CLASSIC BAPTISM.

THE CHRISTIAN PRESS.

The criticisms, first in order of time, are those of "The Christian Press." I give the remarks of this periodical because Baptists may feel a pride in them, although others may be at a loss to know why. This is their tenor:

1. "The author of the book shows himself to be an ignoramus, to stand up in the face of scholars and say that the classic meaning of the word is to sprinkle and pour."

This statement (aside from the "ignoramus" part of it, which every day makes me feel is too true) bears the most conclusive internal evidence that the writer had never seen even so much as the outside covering of Classic Baptism. He evidently thought with Sydney Smith, that to read a book before criticizing it, was only a hamper to genius.

2. "Professor Stuart, and men of that class, have published to the world, that the classic use of the word *in all cases*, and *in all places* where the Greek word is used, is *to immerse*, *dip*, *overwhelm*." Unwilling to receive the sentiments of my old instructor through this new channel, I turned to Prof. Stuart's treatise, and there found this statement (p. 16), "The words βάπτω and βαπτίζω have, in the Greek classical writers, the sense of *dip*, *plunge*, immerge, sink, &c. *But there are variations* from this prevailing and usual signification." In this statement the meanings of the two verbs are thrown together; the first two belonging to βάπτω, the last two to βαπτίζω. On p. 22, "In *all the derived* and *secondary meanings* of these words, it would seem plain, that the Greek writers made a diverse and distinct use, never confounding them." Then, there are "derived and secondary meanings." And on p. 34, "Both the classic use and that of the Septuagint show, that *washing* and *copious affusion* are sometimes signified by this word. Consequently, the rite of baptism may have been performed in one of these ways." And now let me ask, whether these extracts do not show that the critic had no more seen Prof. Stuart's treatise than he had seen Classic Baptism?

3. "Of what authority is a mere pastor, whose business it is to preach, and especially one whose life has been spent in a small country village"—

It was my lot to hear in a Baptist church, a Baptist preacher advocate a Baptist Bible, on this wise: "I argued in the pulpit of a Baptist minister, not favorable to a new Version, the necessity of a new Translation, because there were words in the old not understood. I quoted, in illustration, 'Jacob sod pottage.' Why, said he, Brother B., I know what that means; I've dug sods many a time! He then pressed his point by appealing to his own case, saying, I was preaching from the text, 'they that are alive shall not prevent them that sleep,' and having some peculiar views on the resurrection, sustained them by 'prevent' in the sense *to hinder*. After service a friend said to me, Brother B., 'prevent' dont mean *to hinder;* but I replied, Think I dont know what prevent means? It does mean to hinder. However, I found out afterward, that prevent does not mean to hinder. So I prove to you we must have a new Version." If these friends of the critic were the kind of men he puffs at, as "mere pastors, whose business is to preach," as it is a family affair, I have nothing to say.

But as this good writer seems to appreciate only a certain style of evidence, and assured that it will make him look with admiration on Classic Baptism, should he ever have the good fortune to see its cover, I will give him the important information, that the "country village" in which the greater part of the life of its author was spent, contains only something less than a million of souls.

4. "It is too late in the day for any upstart with his pedantry"— "We sincerely pity any such pretender, and consider the lunatic asylum more befitting for him." "His words are powerless among all scholars, of all names, and his name is branded for the ignorance and audacity which attach to it."

So endeth the first criticism of the pedantry, and pretence, and lunacy, and ignorance, and presumption, and audacity, and impudence, of the upstart and ignoramus.

The man who writes in this style must look out for the Quaker, who said to the cursing sailor, "That's right, friend, spit it all out; thee can never go to heaven with such trash on thy stomach."

THE NATIONAL BAPTIST.

The tone of this article is, happily, different from that of the preceding. The ignoramus and the upstart, the pedant and pretender, the lunatic and the presumptuous, the audacious and the impudent, becomes converted into "an author of no small ability," whose "work is worthy of careful attention," while "the deliberateness and fulness of the investigation challenge our admiration."

1. Embarrassment is expressed at the statement, "that the word *immerse* expresses not act, but condition. It is a fundamental point with Mr. Dale. We wish we knew more clearly what he means?"

It is with the greatest pleasure that I seek to relieve this embarrassment. It arises from an oversight. The position of Classic Baptism is not adequately stated by the language, "Immerse expresses not act, but condition,"—much less by the statement, "Immerse is a transitive verb, just as the corresponding Greek word is, and it is sheer nonsense to insist that it signifies *only* condition." This statement not only represents inadequately the view of Classic Baptism, but so misrepresents it as, indeed, to convert it into "sheer nonsense." I have not the slightest disposition to charge this to the art of the controversialist, but sincerely believe that it is attributable to oversight, however remarkable that oversight may be. In the paragraph but one preceding this statement, the reviewer quotes this definition: "Baptizo, in primary use, *expresses* condition, characterized by complete intusposition, *without expressing*, and with absolute indifference *to the form* of the act by which such intusposition may be effected, as, also, without other limitations." Surely there is nothing in this definition which "signifies *only* condition." There is act in the verb, but *the form* of the act is not *expressed*, while the condition, effected by the *implied* act, is directly expressed.

Take a parallel word—"*Envelop* the package." The command expresses no *form* of act; it *implies* act, while expressing a condition of covering in which the package is to be put. Envelop, like merse, expresses condition, while the form of the act involved is unexpressed.

This, I am sure, the reviewer will not consider "sheer nonsense;" nor will he feel at liberty to say, "Mr. Dale assures us, that here is a transitive verb which does not and cannot express action, but *only* condition."

2. "Mr. Dale frequently implies, and in more than one instance expresses, a conviction that Baptist writers on this subject are not honest."

This charge is not a matter of indifference to me. It is very painful. I hold the flinging of such charges into the faces of Christian opponents in contemptuous abhorrence. If they appeared in Classic Baptism I would blush to own it as any production of mine. Such utterances betoken weakness and wickedness. When I have to resort to them I will stop writing.

3. "Mr. Dale puts a new meaning on the word *immerse*, and refuses to receive the meaning which dictionaries and all English literature assign to it."

No meaning, new or old, has been put on "immerse." Report has been made of that meaning put on it by "all English literature." Courts of law require, that the best evidence within reach shall be adduced to sustain any cause brought before them, under peril of the conclusion, that if adduced it would be unfavorable. The best evidence within reach, or which can exist, has been adduced,—the usage of accredited writers. If this is not accepted, let it be rebutted by testimony of equal authority.

4. The reviewer thinks it disingenuous to say, "In this definition, by the use of 'to put'—'put into or under'—Dr. Conant gives a greater breadth and freedom to *baptize* than any of his friends who have preceded him. They have insisted that it meant *to dip*, *to plunge*, and nothing else. Dr.

Conant says, (*in this definition by the use of put—put into or under,*) "it no more means *to dip, to plunge*, than does *to put;* that is, it means no such thing." He asks, "Is this fair and honorable dealing? Does Dr. Conant say, 'It no more means *to dip, to plunge*, than does to put?'"

This statement is so plain and so obviously true, that it is hard to imagine how the idea of "disingenuousness" has arisen in the mind of this respected reviewer. If βαπτίζω has a meaning so broad as to be faithfully represented by "put into or under," then, it is simply impossible that it can have the narrow modal meaning "to dip, to plunge, and nothing else." And, thus, Dr. C. says, (by his definition,) "that the word no more means to dip, to plunge, than does *to put.*"

5. After some general remarks, to show that dip and immerse are equivalents, the reviewer answers himself by saying, "We are free to say that Mr. Dale's labors cannot be worthless or unimportant. He has examined the passages in Greek classical authors and classified them, and has established a difference in use between βάπτω and βαπτίζω. His *statement* of that difference seems to us defective, but that there is a difference is evident. He has, also, brought clearly out what our own examination had before proved, that the word βαπτίζω does not of itself involve the lifting out from the fluid of that which is put in. In other words, that it is in that respect exactly equivalent to the English word *immerse.*"

But if *immerse* never takes its object out, and *dip* always takes its object out, how is it possible that they can be "equivalent?" The Baptist view of the word, as heretofore advocated, is not only seriously but fatally erroneous.

EXAMINER AND CHRONICLE.

The critical complaint of this periodical is made on the ground of a lack of submission to dictionaries.

1. "This interchanging of the words dip and plunge and immerse is the common and established use of the words.

The author himself is the transgressor. Standard lexicographers use them to define each other."

To go back to dictionaries in this discussion is to go back to a battle-ground that has been fought over a thousand times without beneficial result.

The critic gives the definition of Webster, "To DIP. To plunge or immerse for a moment or short time." And that of Worcester, "To DIP. To immerse; to plunge into any liquid." Who, now, shall be umpire between Webster, who says *momentary* continuance belongs to this act, and Worcester, who says nothing of any such element?

He, also, gives Webster, "IMMERSE. To put under water or other fluid; to plunge, to dip," and Worcester, "IMMERSE. To put under water or other fluid; to plunge into, to immerge, to overwhelm, to dip."

Suppose, now, I take the general definition, in which there is no form of act and no limitation of time, and insist upon that as the true meaning; while some one else seizes on a particular defining word, *dip*, for example, in which there is both definite form and limited duration, and insists upon that as the true exposition; who shall decide?

Is it not most unreasonable to turn from an inquiry into the meaning of a word, by exhausting the cases of its use, to dictionaries, among whose tens of thousands of words perhaps not one has had its meaning so determined? It is only surprising that dictionaries have that general correctness which they do possess.

Controversial writers who would accurately define the meanings of single words, can never do their work by entering into the labors of the general lexicographer. Baptists have defined the word in question with the severest limitations. And when the supreme authority of usage is shown to condemn such definition, a cry for help is made upon lexicographers.

The statement that dip, and plunge, and immerse, as expressing the same idea, are interchanged in critical, or any other rational writings, is most incorrect. There is such an interchange in Baptist writings, and too much in all writings on the subject of baptism. But there is a special reason for this. It is found, mainly, in the original confounding together of βάπτω and βαπτίζω as absolute equivalents. Thus dipping, and dyeing, and plunging, and mersing, formed an undivided common heritage. When dyeing was claimed, and surrendered, as exclusive property, dip was still left in common. Demand is now made for it as the sole property of βάπτω. When this demand is met. the partnership between these words will be thoroughly dissolved, and βαπτίζω will take its place among that class of verbs to which it belongs, and the mixing up of a definite act of momentary continuance, and of a condition unlimited in continuance, will come to an end. Having tasted of the good wine, we cannot go back to the worse.

2. In a second article this periodical adduces a second objection, which is regarded as of sufficient importance to engross the entire article. It is directed against the final summary statement, and is presented as follows:

"We have reviewed the Rev. Mr. Dale's book, but we refer to it again. The conclusion is this: 'Whatever is capable of changing the character, state, or condition of any object, is capable of baptizing that object; and by such hange of character, state, or condition, does in fact baptize it.'

"A definition is usually made more clear and forcible by examples. The first illustration that occurs to us after reading this definition, is the baptism of gunpowder by a match. How thoroughly the condition of the powder is changed in that case! Was it the Emancipation Proclamation of Mr. Lincoln, or was it the surrender of Lee, that baptized millions of negroes from chattels into freemen? What a famous baptizer the stomach is? How thoroughly it changes the character and condition of meat, fruits, and vegetables! Some baptisms are very gradual. How long it takes, for instance, to baptize an acorn into an oak! The baptism of fire—how plain and pregnant that expression becomes, in the light of Mr. Dale's definition! Yes, fire is a great baptizer. It baptizes water into steam, dough into bread, wood and coal into ashes and smoke. Our fire-places, and stoves, and furnaces, what are they but baptisteries? Our great factories, what unwearied and efficient administrators of baptism they are! What quantities of wool or cotton they baptize into cloth every day! Our chemists and apothecaries, too, what expeditious and thorough baptizers they are!"

The Examiner, no doubt, believes that there is substantial logic under this dash of wit and ridicule, or it would not have put it into type. Classic Baptism must be prepared to stand fire, even though it be "wild fire," which any one may choose to direct against it. Any assault, within the limits of goodbreeding, whether under the mask of Comus or with the open and frowning front of Tragedy, will receive both toleration and welcome from its author.

It is, also, obvious, that "the conclusion" must be shown to be invulnerable to assaults of every character. This is the more important because the aspect of baptism therein presented is not familiar, and, consequently, forms of thought not heretofore regarded as baptisms, or as capable of being thrown into such a form, might be received with embarrassment or be entirely rejected. I will, therefore, resist the temptation to "answer the unwise according to their unwisdom," and will give a sober reply to these suggestions of the Examiner.

1. As to the gunpowder baptism. In so far as this may be spoken of as a baptism, at all, it is nothing more nor less than martyr baptism by fire. The flesh and bones of a "witness" for Jesus subjected to the influence of fire are changed into ashes. Gunpowder subjected to the influence of fire is changed into sulphurous vapor. The baptisms are not distinctively the same. *Martyr* fire effects not merely a destructive baptism, but also, a purifying baptism. A lighted match effects only a destructive baptism.

2. Baptism into freedom. The Examiner ought to be familiar with the historical baptisms of bondsmen, "in the name of a freeman," when about to be released from slavery. And I hope that, before long, it will also understand, that

the millions of Israel were by the proclamation of Jehovah, and the issue of the struggle of the Egyptian hosts in the rushing sea waters, baptized, from a condition of bondage to Pharaoh, into a condition of freedom-subjection to Moses.

3. "What a baptizer the stomach is!" Yes, even beyond what the wit of the Examiner has discovered. (1.) The stomach baptizes pork and cabbage (as the receptacle down into which they are swallowed), as the ship and her crew are baptized, swallowed up, by the gaping mouth of old ocean. This baptism the Examiner does not like; it lasts too long. (2.) The stomach baptizes its contents by thoroughly changing their condition through its peculiar influences, just as ocean by its briny waters disintegrates the oaken timber and iron bolts of the ship, as well as the flesh and bones of her hapless crew. (3.) The stomach, when it fails to baptize pork and cabbage, baptizes the body and the mind through this leaden burden which it carries. It is of escape from this baptism through the stomach, Plutarch says, "A great resource truly for a pleasant day is a good temperament of the body unbaptized and unburdened." (Classic B., p. 338.) Is there more here of stomachic baptism than the Examiner bargained for? "What a famous baptizer the stomach is!"

4. Acorn baptism. "How long it takes to baptize an acorn into an oak!" Yes, quite long; yet not near so long as to baptize "all nations." The Examiner will not deny that a burial is a baptism. An acorn buried in the ground is baptized, then. How long does this baptism last? The burial baptism of the acorn brings with it sweet influences from earth and air and sky, by which it receives a baptism into life, whose new condition is the oak. After all, this baptism is not so funny.

5. "Fire is a great baptizer." A very true statement, and one of which the Examiner will hear more, if Judaic Baptism should be read. Baptism by any influence imports the subjection of the baptized object to the full controlling power of that influence. "There are some things which exert over certain objects a definite and unvarying influence. Whenever, therefore, βαπτίζω is used to express the relation

between such agencies and their objects, it gives development *in the completest manner* to that specific influence." (C. B., p. 316.) The specific influences of fire are: 1. A power to destroy. 2. A power to purify.

When fire is used to bake bread, or to boil the kettle, it is used for the development of neither of these influences. They are not, therefore, cases of baptism. Where fire is used to consume fuel, it is inappropriate to speak of it as a case of baptism by fire, because the object is not to destroy the fuel, but to give warmth to those around it. But if any one chooses to set his woods, or his house, or his bonds and mortgages, on fire, he will secure what the classics would thoroughly understand by a baptism of fire.

It is a blundering use of language, however, to say that the object burned is "baptized *into ashes*." There is neither truth nor sense in saying, that a burned object is "baptized into ashes." "Ashes" constitute the object itself in another form. You cannot put a thing into itself. The proper expression is, as everywhere through the Classics, *baptized by fire*. This carries its own explanation with it. If it is a combustible body, then we know that it is destroyed. If it is a metallic ore, then we know that it is purified from its dross. If it is the "impure lips" of Isaiah, then we know that they are purified from defilement. "Fire is a great baptizer."

6. "Our fire-places, and stoves, and furnaces, what are they all but baptisteries?" But the Examiner is superficial in his examination. Why not complete the catalogue? Let me help the critic by authority more unquestionable than that which has furnished the fire-place, stove, and furnace baptistery.

What are our grog-shops, with their bad whisky, but baptisteries? (C. B., pp. 289, 319.) What are our eating-houses, with tough beef and half-baked pastry, but baptisteries? (C. B., p. 338.) What are our apothecary-shops, with their soporifics, and sedatives, and stimulants, but baptisteries? (C. B., p. 318.) What are our pest-houses, reeking with malaria, but baptisteries? (C. B., p. 304.) What are our fortune-telling establishments, with their lying arts, but baptisteries? (C. B., *idem.*) What are our schools, that "cram" the brain of childhood, but baptisteries? (C. B., p. 308.) What are our college-halls, where hard questions "stump" the modest and "flunk" the Freshman, but baptisteries? (C. B., p. 334.) What—— "*Tene manum,*" do you say? Well, be it so, we will leave the catalogue incomplete; only adding, when the theory of water dipping shall have brought itself into harmony with these classic baptisteries, "the conclusion" will take care of those of the "fire-place, the stove, and the furnace."

7. "Our great factories—Lowell, Lawrence, and Manchester—what baptizers!" These great establishments use altogether too "much water" for Classic Baptism to run them. If the Examiner will put on sufficiently good glasses he will see, that the conversion of cotton and wool, by machinery, into sheeting and broadcloth, neither changes the condition of its object by putting it within a physical element, nor does its work by an *influence.* They, therefore, do not belong to us. We remand these machinery Baptists back to the Examiner's office.

In a third article, the Examiner makes a draft for its criticisms upon

THE NEW ENGLANDER.

The first quotation has reference to figurative use.

1. "The Greek word is used in many cases where there is no literal physical submergence. Mr. Dale has not overlooked these uses; he gives them a great deal of attention; but it is much to be regretted, and it is the great defect of the book, that his treatment of them is, in important respects, unnatural and arbitrary. It may be difficult to determine, in some cases, whether the primary meaning is wholly lost in the secondary, or whether something of the former remains to give picturesqueness and vivacity to the latter. But very few, we think, will agree with the author of this work in the extent to which he assumes a complete obliteration of primary meaning and a consequent loss of figurative character."

I have no novelties to offer on the subject of figurative language. I do not speak *ex cathedra*, but will take my place at the feet of any one who will give me instruction. The subject has its difficulties, as any one will feel who reflects upon it, or who will read those who have done so. But, as to this critic, there seems to be no principle separating us. It is a question of "extent" only. And if this be "the greatest defect of the book," then it will answer very well the purpose for which it was written.

The principles which have governed my interpretation of language not used in physical relations, have been mainly these:

1. Familiar and long-continued use wears out the original physical allusion.

2. Where there is no evidence that the writer has the physical application in his mind, and a meaning is promptly and clearly attained without any such reference, that meaning should be regarded not as borrowed, but as its own; not as figurative, but as literal, secondary.

3. Long absolute use of a word, in like connection, communicates to that word a specific meaning growing out of such relations.

These principles are neither singular nor questionable. Campbell, the Principal of Marischal College, and regarded by Dr. Carson as the Prince of Rhetoricians, says: "And as to ordinary metaphors, or those which have already received the public sanction, and which are commonly very numerous in every tongue, the metaphorical meaning comes to be as really ascertained by custom in the particular language, as the original, or what is called the literal, meaning of the word. . . . One plain consequence of this doctrine is, that there will be in many words a transition, more or less rapid, from their being the figurative, to their being the proper signs of certain ideas. The transition from the figurative to the proper, in regard to such terms as are in daily use, is indeed inevitable. . . . They cannot be considered as genuine metaphors by the rhetorician. I have already assigned the reason. They have nothing of the effect of metaphor upon the hearer. On the contrary, like proper terms, they suggest directly to his mind, without the intervention of any image, the ideas which the speaker proposed to convey by them."

Allow me to call especial attention to the following statement: "Again, it ought to be considered, that many words which must appear as tropical to a learner of a distant age, who acquires the language by the help of grammars and dictionaries, may, through the imperceptible influence of use, have totally lost that appearance to the natives, who considered them purely as proper terms."—*Philosophy of Rhet.*, iii, 1.

In writing Classic Baptism, I had not looked into Campbell; but the views here presented are the same which rule there. I am not aware that they differ from other accredited writers.

Dr. Carson has written a Treatise on the Figures of Speech, to supply "a deficiency in our language to this day." In that work he can find no writer, from Quintillian to Blair, to satisfy him as to the definition of *Figure*. Nor does he know any "author, ancient or modern, that has, with philosophical accuracy, drawn a line of distinction between the territories of common expression and those of figurative language." In his conception of metaphor, he declares his rejection of "the doctrine of Quintillian, Lord Kames, Dr. Campbell, and Dr. Blair." These writers all agree in the definition given by the Roman,—"Metaphor is a shorter similitude." Carson says, "Metaphor always asserts what is manifestly false. Metaphor asserts not only a falsehood, but an absurdity,—that one object is another." He insists upon it, that not a comparison, but a naked declaration, is made in the statement, "Achilles is a lion." He admits likeness to be the ground of the statement, and, therefore, objects to the metaphor, "Steep me in poverty to the very lips," saying, "It is here supposed that there is a likeness between being in great poverty and being steeped in water. We cannot say that the likeness is faint, for there is no likeness at all." Dr. Carson's peculiar ideas led him to put *the man* spoken of, in *water* to the lips; which being done, he found no ground for the figure. And no wonder, for the figure is designed to develop the influence of *poverty* to a degree which shall be only short of destroying life, and to put a man in water to the lips produces no evil influence; but if you will put any *absorbent* into a liquid until it shall become, with a small exception, penetrated by its peculiarities, you will have the basis of the figure. We, then, come back to the man and poverty, and interpret the language as expressive of the influences of poverty in an extreme degree. For the same reason, Dr. C. carries a man baptized by questions, or by sleep, or by wizard arts, *into the water*, with which such a one has nothing to do; but the language is grounded in the resemblance of influence which may be found, not between the man *bewildered*, *sleepy*, or *possessed with the devil*, and a man *under water*, but between such a one as to the controlling influence to which he is subjected, and any object under the influence of a liquid by mersion.

Against *such* interpretations of metaphor Classic Baptism protests. And it may be that it is the unreserved rejection of this "Achilles *is* a lion" metaphor, introducing ever more *picture* figures of dipping men, and cities, and continents, into water, which the New Englander has unwittingly termed "unnatural and arbitrary."

I have spoken to this criticism, because while it is not essential to the issue, yet it has its interest and importance.

I only add a word as to the "extent" to which the denial of figure is carried. 1. It embraces a single class of phrases in which a grammatical form (the dative without a preposition), not found in the other class of baptisms, expresses agency, and in which there is no direct or incidental evidence of a physical scene being present to the mind of the writer. 2. The absolute use of the word in the same repeated connection. This is the "extent" of my offending, no more. And a thorough examination of the merits of the case will, I think, make that extent a vanishing quantity.

2. The Examiner introduces a second criticism from this periodical thus: "Remarking on the assertion that any

thorough change of condition is a baptism, the reviewer observes"—.

Allow me to observe, that this statement makes a perfect metamorphosis of the statement of Classic Baptism. It does not say that "*any* thorough change of condition is a baptism," but, "Whatever" (act or influence) "is capable of thoroughly changing the character, state, or condition of *any object*, is capable of baptizing that object," (according to the nature of the case, if an "act," by putting it into the new condition of intusposition, with or without influence, or, if an "influence," by assimilating its condition to itself by a controlling power.)

"Thorough change of condition" is a genus, with its species and their individuals. Classic Baptism does not treat of the genus, but of species, two, to wit, 1. Such thorough change of condition as results from the intusposition of objects within physical elements; and, 2. Such thorough change of condition as results from a controlling assimilative influence. Wine, opiate, grief, debt, excessive study, &c., &c., controlling the conditions of their objects, so as to bring them into a new condition, assimilated to their several influences.

The two statements, "*any* thorough change of condition," and the thorough change of condition of "*any object*," needs but to be made in order that their utter diversity may be apprehended.

But it is this transference (inadvertent no doubt) of "any," from its true connection with "objects," to a false connection with "condition," which makes the foundation for the "funny" baptism of the Examiner, and the erroneously conceived baptism of the New Englander, now to be noticed.

"He does not say, that a surgeon, who by a successful amputation saves a dying patient, *baptizes* that patient; or that a whetstone, when it makes a dull knife into a sharp one, *baptizes* the knife; or that the sun, when it dries up a stream in summer, *baptizes* the stream. But we are left to suppose that he would regard these and others like these, as natural and appropriate expressions."

If left, heretofore, to such inference, let me try to place an effectual guard against it hereafter.

After what has been already said, this, perhaps, can be best done by a case. A man having a child sick with some internal disease, falls on a medical work treating on this subject, and presenting this conclusion: "A sovereign remedy for this disease, is a thorough drenching with oil and rhubarb. If restive under the application, he must be quieted by tightly twisting the upper lip and nose." Having read "the conclusion," and thus diplomatized for practice, he prepares a bucketful of the mixture, and at the bedside of his child prepares to "drench" him from head to foot. His restiveness is stilled by a tourniquet for lip and nose, but not without outcry. A passer by looks in, to whom the scene is expounded through the disease and "the conclusion." The newcomer turns over the volume and exclaims, "Why, this book treats of the diseases of horses! And it says, that '*to drench*, is to empty a bottle of the stuff down a horse's throat!'" (*Exeunt omnes.*)

If now the Examiner and the New Englander had not hurried into practice on a hasty preparation from "the conclusion," but had taken a full course of reading in the volume, they would have discovered, if not that "drench" is double-faced, yet, that "character, state, or condition," is more than bi-frons, and would have felt it desirable to conform their professional practice to that aspect presented in the book, and not have concluded that "he" meant child, instead of horse, and "drench" meant a dash of a bucketful of the mixture, instead of the swallowing of a cathartic.

If the machinery of Lowell, or the whetstone, or the knife of "the universal whittler" can put forth an "act" introducing its object into a fluid element, then it can perform a baptism of the first class, changing condition by intusposition with or without influence; or, if they are able to send forth "influences" which shall pervade a bale of wool, a mower's scythe, or a bit of shingle, thereby controlling or assimilating them to their own nature, then they can perform baptisms of the second class, changing condition by influence.

"But all this is not stated in 'the conclusion.'" No more is *horse* stated in "the conclusion," and yet "he" is there. And, so, all this, and a great deal more, is in "the conclusion," for the Examiner, says, "It is the conclusion of 354 pages of critical discussion." There are three hundred and fifty-four pages in "the conclusion."

3. The Examiner says, "still more:" and quotes: "The English word *immerse*, according to our author, has nearly the same primary meaning as the Greek βαπτίζω, and it expresses, as Mr. Dale says, 'thorough influence of any kind.'" Let the reader observe the words, "*of any kind*," and say whether we are not authorized to affirm, that "whatever is capable of thoroughly changing the character, state, or condition of any object, is capable of *immersing* that object; and by such change of character, state, or condition, does in fact *immerse* it.' We do not see how this conclusion is to be avoided, though we fear the Baptist enemy may take advantage of it to murmur with the little breath our author has left him: "*Baptizing*, then, is *immersing*, and *immersing is baptizing*."

When I read the statement, "Mr. Dale says immerse expresses influence of any kind. Let the reader observe the words *of any kind*," I said to myself, Well, you have nodded here, if not in the conclusion, and prepared myself to confess, with as good a grace as might be, a slip in the too great breadth of the language. However, on turning to C. B., p. 212, I read, "It expresses *thorough influence* of any kind; the nature determined by the adjunct." I, then, smiled at my fears and sighed over the unreliability of quotations And it becomes my turn to say, "Let the reader observe the words," the nature determined *by the adjunct*. Does not this limit, in the sharpest manner, "any kind of influence?" It can develop no kind of influence, but that which belongs to its "adjunct." And it can have no "adjunct" but what use attaches to it. And use can attach no adjunct to it, but such as may receive appropriate development through the word.

Suppose we laugh at use, and take some of the "funny"

adjuncts to which we have been just introduced, and see how the "any kind" of influence is developed. "A dull knife *immersed in a whetstone* becomes very sharp." "A dying man *immersed in a surgeon's scalpel* springs into life." "A summer pool *immersed in solar beams* scuds through the sky." "A bag of wool *immersed in a power-loom* is influenced into broadcloth!" Whetstones, scalpels, &c., &c., are "funny" adjuncts of *βαπτίζω*.

I believe the statement may stand without the need of pleading for grace. Immerse must have a fit adjunct, and the adjunct determines the nature of the influence.

It is farther to be observed, that the inference from the fact, that because immerse passes through the same general phases of usage, with *βαπτίζω*, it must, therefore, have the same specific meanings, is not well grounded.

Immerse has meanings which the Greek word has not; and the Greek word has meanings which immerse has not.

The grammatical combinations of the two words differ. In secondary use, *immerse in* is the almost invariable form; while in secondary use, *baptize by*, is, so far as I remember, the absolutely invariable form. This diversity of form is indicative of diversity both of conception and of meaning. The difference of conception is ingrained in the terms. The difference of meaning is, sometimes, most obvious. "*Immersed in* business" indicates active, earnest, and constant engagement in business pursuits; while "*baptized by* business" indicates an embarrassed condition resulting from multiplied engagements. "*Immersed in* study" indicates thorough engagedness in student life; while "*baptized by* study" indicates mental prostration as the resultant condition of study. The inference, therefore, of the entire sameness of these words is not correct.

But on the supposition that these words were fac similes in meaning, it would hardly be worth while for "the enemy" to waste their "spent breath" in saying, "immersing is baptizing and baptizing is immersing," inasmuch as "immersing" must first have secured all the meanings shown by Classic Baptism to belong to baptizing, in which case the hard breathing would be wasted on the tautology, "baptizing is baptizing, and baptizing is baptizing."

We cheerfully make over to "the Baptist enemy," (especially as we have not heretofore had much opportunity to show them favor,) all right, title, and privilege, which may appertain to this discovery.

THE RELIGIOUS HERALD.

The book has been reviewed by the Religious Herald, in four consecutive numbers, embracing nine columns. I am indebted to its editors for the privilege of reading those articles, and it is with no ordinary pleasure that I say, that there is no discourteous word in those nine columns. They do not intimate that they have found any such word in Classic Baptism. I have no such words for Christian brethren. With those who use them, I wish to have nothing to do. If there are any whose errors need such chastening, I turn them over to the discipline of others.

The Herald "declines to discuss the meaning of βαπτίζω as to its discriminating meaning, but limits itself to the *argumentum ad hominem* and *reductio ad absurdum*." Any weapon, undipped in poisonous bile, which an opponent thinks best adapted to his purpose, is welcome to the lists.

1. The Herald says, "Baptist writers have maintained, in common with the most distinguished lexicographers and critics, that βαπτίζω signifies *dip*, *plunge*, or *immerse;* that it is a modal term, denoting a specific act, and not an effect resulting from an act: that it has the same meaning as βάπτω, except that of *dye* or *smear*."

To sustain the lexicographical part of this statement, it is said, "Donnegan defines it: To immerse repeatedly into a liquid; to submerge, to soak thoroughly, to saturate; hence to drench with wine, *metaphorically* to confound totally."

Does the Herald, in its gentle courtesy, mean that in exchanging friendly buffets, we should, like Friar Tuck and Richard, take turn about, and therefore quote this definition to give me, too, a chance for the *argumentum ad hominem?*

The Herald says, through Donnegan, that βαπτίζω means "to submerge," in which there is no modal act; yet it says in proper person, it does mean "a modal act;" how is this? The Herald says, through Donnegan, βαπτίζω means "to soak thoroughly," in which there is no specific act; yet it says in proper person, it does mean "a specific act;" how is this? The Herald says, through Donnegan, βαπτίζω means "to saturate," which expresses not an act, but an effect resulting from an act; yet it says in proper person, it does mean "an act, and not an effect proceeding from an act;" how is this?

Was the Herald napping when it wandered into the land of lexicography?

Besides, Donnegan says, βαπτίζω means, *literally*, "to drench with wine," (to make drunk), and also, literally, in secondary (metaphorical) use, "to confound totally."

If a more suicidal blow was ever given to any cause than is given to the Baptist theory by the proffer of this definition, I cannot conceive when, or where, or how, it was done.

This definition suggests the farther remark: to look to dictionaries as authority to settle this controversy is folly.

Will the Herald, or the Baptist world, accept the very first (which ought to be the very best) definition given by this, undoubtedly learned, lexicographer, to wit: "To immerse *repeatedly* into a liquid?" This definition, in common with other errors, as to the meaning of this word, is now rejected by scholars of every name. How idle the complaint, then, that Classic Baptism is not filled with lexicons.

But Classic Baptism has not refused to consider lexical definitions because they were inimical. It is far otherwise.

Every position of Classic Baptism can be deduced from this definition of Donnegan. 1. It utterly rejects modal act as the meaning of the word. 2. It shows, in the most absolute manner, the meaning to be, a condition effected by an unexpressed act. 3. Further, it sustains the distinctions made: (1.) "Intusposition without influence." This is done by the naked *submerge*. (2.) "Intusposition with influence." This is expressed by *to saturate*. (3.) "Intusposition for influence." This is evidently in *to soak thoroughly*. (4.) "Influence without intusposition." This is, as clearly, in *to drench* (make drunk) *with wine*. And (5.) "Influence without intusposition, in the case of elements not physical." This is exemplified by a particular case, *to confound totally;* which is undoubtedly derived from the case of the youth mentioned in Classic Baptism (p. 334), who was baptized, bewildered, "totally confounded" by *questions*. Donnegan and Classic Baptism are in full accord. It is most unaccountable that any one should say, that the Baptist theory of this word and lexical definitions agree together And it is no less groundless to say, that "the views of Classic Baptism are not less opposed to those of lexicographers than they are opposed to those of Baptists."

But the special reason for this quotation from the Herald, is, that the views held by Baptists as to the meaning of this word, ("one meaning, modal term, specific act, same as βάπτω, dyeing excepted,") may be before us on the high authority of the Herald; for respondents are already beginning to deny that such views are held by our Baptist friends. They feel their old ground slipping from under them, and they are casting about for some surer resting-place.

2. *The argumentum ad hominem.*—This is not formally stated, but we are left to conclude, from a supposed warrant in the exhibited use of immerse, that this word has only a literal, primary meaning, and from its (supposed) stated relation to baptize, farther to conclude, that *baptize* has but one, literal, primary meaning throughout its usage.

I would like to state the case in all its strength, but, really, when I attempt to raise it out of the types, it so falls to pieces that I am embarrassed.

"Mr. Dale gives numerous instances of the figurative use of baptize—'baptized by evils, by anger, by misfortune, by wine, by taxes, by midnight, &c.'—In these passages there is not a new meaning assigned to the word, but simply a figurative use of the term, in which it derives all its pertinency and force from the literal and well-known import. . . . Baptize and immerse are similar terms. Every child knows that immerse means *to put into or under* a fluid, and it is impossible by any sophistry or figurative meanings to blind his understanding on the subject. The same sophistry which shows that baptism, mersion, may be effected" (in unphysical matters) "without putting under a fluid, would show that *immersion* may be effected" (in unphysical matters) "without putting under a fluid; while every man, woman, and child in the land, knows immersion means to put under fluid," (in physical elements.)

The language of the Herald is given in a condensed form, and the enclosed words are introduced in order to show, that the reasoning breaks down through the admixture of things unphysical and physical.

To show that "immerse undergoes no change of meaning," the following extracts from Classic Baptism are made:

"'The Secretary of War is immersed in business; immersed in traffic; immersed in calculations; immersed in politics; immersed among worm-eaten folios;'—in these passages the word *immerse* does not change its meaning. It has reference, in every case, to its settled import. There is a resemblance between the condition of an object placed within or under a fluid, and that of the persons said in the above quotations to be immersed. Whether the person using the term figuratively thinks of its tropical" (literal?) "sense, is of no consequence; the analogy is the ground of its use in this application. Does this figurative use of the word cast any doubt on its meaning" (to put in or under a fluid)? "Not the slightest."

The pointblank contradiction in this language is so patent, that it is truly remarkable that it should have escaped the notice of the Herald. We are first told, that "*in these passages immerse* does not change its meaning," *i. e.*, it retains its literal meaning *to put in or under*. Next we are told, "it has *reference* to its settled import." Is a "reference" to a thing the same as the thing itself? And, again, we are told that there is a "resemblance" between, &c. How does the *resemblance* of one thing to another thing make it that thing, or is it consistent with being that thing? In John

Smith, the son, there may be a "reference" to John Smith, the father, because his name is taken from him. But this does not make John Smith, the son, John Smith, the father. There may be a "resemblance" between these parties, in feature, form, size, gait, character, and yet John Smith, the son, is another person from John Smith, the father. Now, there may be a "reference," and a "resemblance," between immerse *figurative* and immerse *literal*, and they not be the same thing; but, on the contrary, because there is a "reference," and a "resemblance," their distinct existence and character is proven beyond all controversy.

We are farther told, that "it is of no consequence whether the person using the term figuratively thinks of its tropical" (literal) "sense; the analogy is the ground of its use." But if the *literal* sense ("tropical," I presume, has slipped in through inadvertence, and would settle the matter by the admission of a "*turned*" sense) is not in the mind of the speaker or writer, then "the ground of the analogy" has vanished, and the residuum left behind is the new meaning cut loose from its literal relationship.

In conformity with this, all writers on figurative language unite in saying, that when the literal use ceases to find any place in the mind, the figurative use has secured a meaning of its own, and thenceforth ceases to be properly designated as figure. Take this illustration: A carpenter in my employ says he has been putting a *bonnet* over my parlor window. The ground of this use is obvious; but that ground had utterly slipped from out of the mind of this uneducated mechanic, and with him, in carpentry, "bonnet" meant directly, and of its own proper force, *a wooden covering to protect a window from sun and rain.*

But the Herald thinks that shame is cast on this doctrine, by every child who knows that immerse has but one literal meaning, and that no sophistry can blind his understanding.

Let us experiment with this child. A parent says to him, "My child, you are entering upon your education, and I wish you to be immersed in your books." On going, subsequently, to this student's room, and calling for him, he is answered from " in and under" spelling books, geographies, grammars, dictionaries, and systems of rhetoric, logic, and philosophy, " Here I am, father." On being asked what he is doing there, he replies, from out of his in-under immersion, " You wished me to be 'immersed in my books,' and here I am in under the pile." " But, my child, do you not know that 'immersed *in books*' means to be thoroughly engaged in their study?" " Oh no, sir! Every child knows that immerse means *put in, under*, and nothing else; for I read it in the Herald, and 'no sophistry can blind my understanding.' " So much for " child" knowledge.

Another test may be applied to the position of the Herald, that immerse, in these relations, undergoes no change of meaning. It is this: the meaning of a word can always be intelligibly substituted, in every use of that word, for the word itself.

Apply this test: " immersed in =*put in or under*" business, traffic, calculations, politics, worm-eaten folios, &c., &c. Does it answer? Is it possible in fact? Is it conceivable in imagination? Try the baptisms by the same test: " baptized by= *thoroughly subject to the influence of* evil, anger, misfortune, wine, taxes, midnight," &c., &c. Could adaptation be more perfect?

In this interpretation the physical investiture is rejected, (as not having the matter of " reference" or " resemblance,") and *thorough subjection to influence*, which has the needed " resemblance," and is the effect of such investiture, is taken.

To insist that a word, which has been used in one class of relations, and has secured a meaning from use in such relations, must carry that meaning into essentially different relations, and maintain it there unchanged by new influences, is to war against the philosophy of language, against facts in every department of the physical, intellectual, moral, and social world, and is, on its face, absurd.

A hundred stones thrown together make, in such relation, *a pile*. The same stones laid in consecutive order make, in such relation, *a line*. When builded together in a half circle they make, in such relation, *an arch*.

The digits, without relation to each other, have an independent value, which value is immediately changed on entering into arithmetical relations. A cipher, which is a nothing, independently, becomes of prodigious value on entering into such relations. It converts a unit (1) into a million (1,000,000). So, by the unity of relationship established by such bonds as these—$(3+3)=6$; $(3-3)=0$; $(3\times3)=9$; $(3\div3)=1$—the same characters, which have a settled independent value, become utterly and diversely changed.

In like manner, every vowel, which has an independent value, has that value changed by entering into relation with other letters, as m*a*r, m*a*p, m*a*n, m*a*te, &c. So, letters, forming words expressive of thought, by a change of relation among themselves, change entirely the thought, *e. g.*, the same letters which, in a certain relation, express *time*, in another relation express *emit*, and in another *item*, and in another *mite*, and in another *I met*, and in yet another *me it*. A simple change of relation produces all these changes of thought.

The same is true in the relation of words. Some of these relations are of simple order, as "he is here," or "here he is," without change of thought; some involve a change in grammatical construction, as "the boy ate the pig," and "the pig ate the boy;" some relations of words are organic, and the several words cannot be interpreted, except in their organic relations to each other, without destroying the life, which is the result of the union.

If a child asks, What is light? and is pointed to the rainbow and told, "Light is red, and orange, and yellow, and green, and blue, and indigo, and violet," has he received a truthful answer? No. Light is neither red, nor orange, nor yellow, nor green, nor blue, nor indigo, nor violet; nor is it red, and orange, and yellow, and green, and blue, and indigo, and violet; but it is a new result from the interaction of these colors when placed in certain relations to each other; each communicating and receiving a modifying influence. So it is with words in organic thought-relations. Independent life is sacrificed to a new organic life.

In the words—"the entire crew were baptized"—there is

no definite, common thought-life. Phraseological combinations of words must not be interpreted disjunctly, but conjunctly. You may galvanize the article and adjective, noun and verb, and you will get no answer. They are dead as to all power to utter any complete thought. It is only the man who knows what "sod" means, because he has "dug sods many a time," that will think otherwise. The sentence must be vitalized by union with an adjunct to the verb. If that adjunct should be—*by a destructive tempest*, then we will have a fearful life imparted to the words. If it should be—*by excessive wine-drinking*, then we should have a very shameful life communicated to them. But whether fearful or shameful, "baptized" cannot be interpreted disjunctly, but must retain its organic union with and receive its life from its adjunct, unless we would stumble over "Jacob sod pottage," or "hinder the resurrection."

The Herald will, I trust, perceive that the condemnatory *ad hominem*, drawn from the representation made by Classic Baptism of *baptize* and *immerse*, has not hurt, and I am sure its esteemed editors will accept the rebounding blow in all good nature.

3. *The argumentum ad absurdum.*—The *ad absurdum* part of the review relates to "the conclusion." It belongs to the same class with the Lowell machinery and whetstone. To these are, however, added "birth" and "a dose of ipecac;" there is not added *a big pinch of snuff*, nor *stumping a sore toe*. Enough has been said of this "absurdity," (mine or theirs,) and I add no more.

I must notice, however, one remarkable error in this connection. It is the idea that literal baptisms are limited to those mentioned on page 235, and are "without influence." The literal baptisms extend through the fifty following pages, and these are all with influence. On this error is based the more important one, "We suppose the author ascribes the power of 'thoroughly changing the character, state, or condition of an object,' *not to literal*, but to figurative baptism." This is very far from being the case. The conclusion embraces both *the acts* of literal baptism and *the influences* of figurative baptism. *All* literal, primary baptisms change the condition of their objects by placing them in a condition of intusposition. Of these baptisms there are two classes: (1.) Such as are not influenced by their intusposition, as a rock. (2.) Such as, in addition to simple intusposition, also, receive influence therefrom, as a sponge, &c.

It is on this latter class of literal baptisms, and, specifically, on the thorough influence proceeding from them, that baptisms of thorough change of condition effected by influence without intusposition, are grounded.

Slips like this, though on a large scale, are readily accounted for by the weekly recurring editorial baptism.

4. *Concessions.*—1. "*It is conceded* that, if 'a state of purification' is baptism, then it is baptism whether induced by sprinkling, magnetism, fire, or anything else. But if it be so, it does not follow that sprinkling is baptism. Baptism, in the case supposed, denotes the effect of sprinkling and not the sprinkling itself."

All of which is most orthodox and quite to the purpose.

2. "*It is conceded* that, figuratively, baptism was employed by Greek authors to denote any strong controlling influence by which an object was mersed or whelmed; or in which there was a resemblance between the object under such influence and an object baptized, *mersed, intusposed.* It does not follow, that because an object under a controlling, transforming, overwhelming influence is said to be *baptized*, that every influence that changes 'character, state, or condition,' baptizes it."

Thank you kindly for this truly welcome aid and comfort. To what class of influences does the "emetic" belong?

3. "*It is conceded* that the Greeks called drunkenness baptism; and in this baptism there was no envelopment. An intoxicated man was baptized by wine. It was not the drinking of wine, nor the operation of it, but the condition—the intoxication resulting from its use—that was called the baptism."

If the author of Classic Baptism be not content with these sweeping concessions, he must be one of the hardest of men to please. They cover, directly or indirectly, all that Classic Baptism was written to establish, and the Baptist theory is, by them, numbered among the things that were.

The Herald concludes, "We can only promise, that should life, strength, and opportunity be allowed us, and should we be able to procure the forthcoming volumes, we will give them a candid notice. Here, for the present, we take respectful leave of Mr. Dale."

THE BAPTIST QUARTERLY.

The Baptist Quarterly for April, 1869, contains an article (27 pp.) entitled "Dale's Classic Baptism. By Prof. A. C. Kendrick, D.D., Rochester, New York."

There may be some who would wish to know what would be said from such a quarter. A theological seminary and its professorate, are naturally suggestive of a pure and loving atmosphere, while a Quarterly lifts up the thoughts to what is weighty with truth and dignified in bearing. How the practical outworking of things harmonizes with their popular estimation, may be learned from the following

QUOTATIONS.

"Philological thimble-rigging, tricks of legerdemain, dexterous, or would-be dexterous manipulation,—of these feats of petty sleight of hand Mr. Dale's book is full; an elaborate and persistent effort to trick *βαπτίζω* out of its honest meaning.—Without learning, without philosophy, and without candor.—As ignorant as if he lived in another planet.—Either ignorance scarcely less than disgraceful, or something less complimentary.—The slenderest acquaintance with critics and commentators.—As barren verbal criticism as it was ever our misfortune to read, or any sensible man to write.—Such pitiful drivel, and the book is plethoric with it.—Phastasmagoria of contradictions.—Strange compound of folly and irreverence.—Incredible puerility.—Is there another living man out of the idiot's asylum.—Impertinent and insulting.—

Spare his scoffings.—Has not taken a single honest step.—Largely false and scientifically worthless.—Pure superfluity and grand impertinence.—Humanity has stood him instead of knowledge.—Sense or nonsense.—Verbal manipulations.—Skilful avoidance of correctness, elegance, and sense.—By such a one as Mr. Dale.—Descend a great many degrees before getting near the level of the expounder of Classic Baptism.—A man who has neither taste nor scholarship.—Dreary and barren criticism.—His feeble ridicule recoils on the captious critic.—Monstrous doctrine.—An absurdity too great to need a moment's argumentation.—Uniform rendering intentionally false, or intentionally unmeaning.—The doctrine is unphilosophical and false.—A spirit of narrow and bitter partisanship.—A scholarly attitude is apparently beyond the conception of Mr. Dale.—His book one half false, one half irrelevant.—Partly false and partly nonsense.—*With his accustomed insolence.*"

It is not necessary to eat an entire joint of meat to learn whether it is tainted or not. These morceaux are enough to test the quality of this "joint." Boiled down they leave this twofold residuum: 1. Mr. Dale is a fool. 2. His book is a lie.

QUOTATIONS IN ANOTHER DIRECTION.

"Nobody doubts that βάπτω may mean *to dip*. Βαπτίζω became naturally applied ordinarily to immersions of a more formal and longer character, while βάπτω ordinarily denoted the lighter and the shorter.—Thus arose the distinction suggested by Dr. Dagg, giving a partial foundation for the dogma of Mr. Dale.—We repeat, none will deny the partial truth of Mr. Dale's distinction.—The submersion of wine (*no matter how*, by pouring, if Mr. Dale pleases) in sea-water.—It is not a dipping that our Lord instituted.—He did not command *to put people into the water and take them out again*, but *to put them under the water*. We repeat, with emphasis, for the consideration of our Baptist brethren: Christian baptism is no mere literal and senseless "dipping," assuring the frightened candidate of a safe exit from the water.—Granting that βάπτω *always* engages to take its subject out of the water (which we do not believe) and that βαπτίζω *never* does engage to take its subject out of the water, (which we readily admit.)—We let βαπτίζω take us into the water, and can trust to men's instinctive love of life, their common sense, their power of volition and normal *muscular* action, to bring them safely out.—The law of God in Revelation sends the Baptist down into the waters of immersion; when it is accomplished, the equally imperative law of *God in nature* brings him safely out."

Subjecting these passages to a sublimation we get this result:

1. "There is an annoying streak of truth (got in there, somehow, by the help of the devil, or of Dr. Dagg), running through 'that lie.'"

2. "Make all haste to square up your notions of baptism by this streak of truth. Baptist brethren! I warn you, once and again, that you must get rid of *dip*. Dip puts into the water and takes out; *baptize never takes out of the water what it once puts in.* Abandon dipping and go down under the water, trusting to 'nature and muscle' to bring you out. Then, when 'this fool' comes along with his thunder we will be ready for him."

One of my theological professors, with whom a universal courtesy was as the breath of his life, once said to me: "If the devil were to pass me and salute me courteously, I would courteously return the salute." He did not say, that if the devil came with horns down, and tail up, and hoof stamping, and breath sulphurous, that he would have any salutation for him. I suppose he would get out of his way. I do not know that I can do better than to follow his example. I have, therefore, no salutation for the "Professor of the Baptist Theological Seminary, of Rochester, New York," (not even "a railing accusation,") but proceed to get out of his way.

Having, therefore, no further need for this double distillation of "Dale's Classic Baptism, by A. C. Kendrick, D.D., Professor of Greek, Baptist Theological Seminary, Rochester, New York,—Philadelphia, American Baptist Publication Society, 530 Arch Street," I make it over, all and particular, to whom it may concern, not forgetting, in especial, "his accustomed insolence."

CRITICISMS FOUNDED IN MISCONCEPTION.

Any one who will look through the criticisms now presented, will perceive, that, so far as they relate to any material point, they are directed not against the positions of Classic Baptism, but against something else widely different from them.

There are controversial artifices for converting granite obstacles into straw figments; but I do not believe that they have been used in this case. Nor will I say, that the misconception is due wholly to others, and in no wise to myself; but to whomsoever it may belong, it is desirable that all ground for its continuance should, if possible, be removed. Let me, then, advert to the more important points, and indicate their true import.

1. It is objected, that βαπτίζω is made to express condition *only*, all act being eliminated.

The true position as taken is, the word expresses condition of intusposition, *involving* some act adequate for its accomplishment, but not expressing or requiring any particular *form* of act. And in this there is no singularity. It is common to all words of the same class.

2. It is objected, that one word has been used to translate βαπτίζω throughout, and therefore, it must have one meaning.

The truth is, that one word is used in all cases where the one Greek word is used, not as its translation, but as its representative. It being distinctly stated, that neither this word (*merse*), nor any other word in the English language, can, in one meaning, translate the Greek word; that this will be manifest to every reader, who will, therefore, be required to modify the meaning of this one word to meet the exigency of the passage, and so, be made to feel that the one Greek word has, in usage, undergone a correspondent change. It was farther stated, that the unusual word "merse" was taken, because it would be more readily susceptible of such modifications than any word already familiar in a fixed meaning. (See pp. 129–134, C. B.)

3. It is objected, that Classic Baptism disregards the generally received interpretation of language, by assigning a direct meaning to phraseology, which should be understood figuratively.

The objection is groundless. There is no departure from the principles laid down by accredited writers on figurative language. Metaphorical language is as truly subject to laws and interpretation as is literal language. It has, also, a meaning as distinct, and as susceptible of development, as language used in physical relations.

In a metaphor there is an untruth stated according to a purely disjunct verbal interpretation. But this mode of interpretation is as false as is the conception deduced by its operation. "Achilles is a lion," is an untrue statement only under an erroneous interpretation. Every metaphor is self-corrective in its terms. Achilles and lion qualify each other. In their relation as the utterance of a sane man to sane men, they say,—The meaning is not that a man is a wild beast; but that there is something in this peerless warrior, which resembles something in this king of the forest; which thing you are to find out and receive as the meaning designed to be conveyed by this language. In the metaphor, "Great Britain has a watery bulwark;" there is an inconsistency between "water" and "bulwark" interpreted independently; but qualified by their relation to Great Britain in its island character, the upraised stone or earth disappears from bulwark, and the residual idea of *protection* remains, and assimilates with flowing water. And the *meaning* of the phrase is, and is nothing else, than that Great Britain has a *protection* in its surrounding seas.

In such language the mind finds pleasure in the boldness of the statement, in being aroused to consider and deduce the truth designed, latent amid incongruities, in its discovery of that sought for, and with its adaptation to the end required.

There is a *conundrum* character belonging to the metaphor, which the hearer or reader is called upon to solve. It may be put in this form: "Why is Achilles like a lion?" "Why may Great Britain be said to have a watery bulwark?" "Why is the London Times the thunderer?" But as every conundrum has a definite solution which is its meaning, so, every metaphor has its solution and definite meaning, which cannot be allowed to evaporate in undefined shadow, or to speak erroneously under a mistaken interpretation. Every metaphor presents to us terms between which there are many incongruities, and one (at least) point of resemblance. The incongruities are to be thrown aside as nothing to the purpose; and the resemblance, alone, to be taken as the residual grain of gold required.

Classic Baptism (pp. 294, 299), refers to the following cases of baptism: "Cnemon, perceiving that he was deeply grieved and baptized by the calamity, and fearing lest he may do himself some injury, removes the sword privately." "The relation of your wanderings, often postponed, as you know, because the casualties still baptized you, you could not keep for a better time than the present."

The objectors say, that these baptisms must be interpreted as figure. Well, Classic Baptism does not say, that they may not be so interpreted, in a common sense way. Its denial is, that any sound interpretation will put *these parties* under water in fact or in figure. It does not deny, that the true meaning of the passage may be reached by tracing a resemblance in some respect, between the condition of an object induced by a state of mersion, and the condition of these persons induced by calamity and casualty.

But in any interpretation, it must be noted at the outset, that these baptized conditions were not transient, but protracted through days, weeks, or months. This settles the matter as to these living men being regarded as being, through these periods, under water, oil, milk, blood, or marsh-mud. The resemblance is between something in their condition *not* thus covered, and something in the condition of an object which is so covered. A farther point settled is, that the resemblance is not to the *covered* condition of a baptized object, for there is no such existent condition effected by calamity. The resemblance, then, must be sought in some *effect* produced by a covered condition, and some *effect* produced in the condition of one affected by calamity.

Now, the specific effects of a covered condition in water, oil, milk, blood, marsh-mud, &c., are various; and as the metaphorical condition is one, the resemblance cannot be to all. It is just as clear, that the reference cannot be to any specific influence; because there is no reference to one more than to another. Neither can the resemblance be to that effect which is common to them all, namely, the suffocation of a human being by protracted mersion; for there is no corresponding suffocation to which such effect should be like.

There is but one other point in which fluids, semi-fluids, and readily penetrable substances, unite in common effect upon enclosed objects, and that is a controlling influence stripped of specialty. Such an effect finds its correspondence in the completest manner in both parties spoken of by Heliodorus. They have long been in a condition induced by the complete influence of "calamity" and "casualty." And baptize is not only not used to express a covered condition, real or imaginary, on the part of these sufferers, but it is not used to express the *covered* condition of the object; the sentiment of the metaphor has nothing to do with covering, but with the effect resulting from such covering.

Thus, if this phraseology be treated as designed figure, we are compelled to cast away everything but controlling influence.

Whether it ought to be so treated, or whether it should be interpreted as directly expressive of influence, is another question.

Some might choose to interpret as metaphor the statements, "A people *enlightened* by education are capable of self-government," "*Established in rectitude* by Christianity, they live in peace." But, I presume, there are not many who would quarrel with those who should prefer to say, metaphor has vanished from such language; and it conveys its sentiment not through a resemblance to sunlight, or a building founded on a rock, but makes direct announcement of the influences of education and Christianity.

There is no more ground for complaint, when it is declared, "baptized by calamity," and "by casualty," &c. &c., express directly, and not merely through resemblance, their legitimate influence.

These were every-day expressions among the Greeks, and we must remember, "There is very little, comparatively, of energy produced by any metaphor that is in common use, and already familiar to the hearer. Indeed, what were originally the boldest metaphors, are become, by long use, virtually, proper terms." (Whately, Rhetoric, p. 195.) "And as to ordinary metaphors, and which are commonly very numerous in every tongue, *the metaphorical meaning* comes to be as really ascertained by custom in the particular language, as the original, or what is called the literal, meaning of the word." "They have nothing of the effect of metaphor upon the hearer. On the contrary, they suggest, like proper terms, directly to the mind, *without the intervention of any image*, the ideas which the speaker intended to convey by them." "The invariable effect of very frequent use being to convert the metaphorical into a proper meaning." (Campbell, Philosophy of Rhetoric, pp. 344, 348.) Campbell farther states, (p. 346,) "It is very remarkable, that the usages in different languages differ, insomuch that the same trope will suggest opposite ideas in different tongues." Now, both the verbal form and thought of the metaphor under consideration differs in the Greek and English languages. "Immersed *in* calamity" makes calamity the element and inness the basis of the thought; but "baptized *by* calamity," makes calamity the agency and controlling power the basis of the sentiment. Inness is neither expressed nor necessarily implied. "Baptized *in* a storm" denotes destruction *during the continuance* of a storm; "baptized *by* a storm" denotes the destructive power of the storm. "Jotapata *baptized in* the departure of Josephus" is nonsense; "*baptized by* the departure of Josephus" expresses the ruinous influence consequent on his departure. The English does not use "*immersed by* calamity" to denote the agency of calamity, but *overwhelmed by.* Nor does it say "*immersed into* calamity;" *in*-mersed expresses position, *into* expresses movement. Their conjunction would be incongruous. The English use of *immerse* and the Greek usage of βαπτίζω are by no means parallel, and "the trope founded on these words has essential difference in the different tongues."

The objection that novelty of principle in the interpretation of figurative language has been introduced into Classic Baptism, is surely without any just foundation.

4. It is objected that "the conclusion" of Classic Baptism is too broad; that there are many things which exert a complete influence in changing condition which could not, properly, be said to baptize.

This objection is grounded both in a failure of comprehension and of discrimination.

There has been a failure to comprehend both acts and influences as causative of changes of condition, and a failure to discriminate between the characteristic differences in the changed conditions, effected, respectively, by act and influence.

The only change of condition effected by "act," with which Classic Baptism has anything to do, is that resulting from an object being intusposed within some readily penetrable medium.

If, now, the act of sharpening a knife by a whetstone changes the condition of the knife *by putting it under the water;* or if a power-loom, by its action, *puts a bale of cotton into the mill-dam,* then they will come within the range of the "conclusion," and may be employed to test its correctness; but not till then.

In like manner "the influences" of Classic Baptism have their limitation. They are not only complete in their controlling power, but they assimilate the condition of the baptized object to their own peculiarities. Thus, an intoxicating influence produces an intoxicated condition; a soporific influence produces a soporific condition; a stupefying influence produces a stupefied condition; an oppressive influence produces an oppressed condition.

If, now, the amputating knife influences the condition of the patient, *assimilating it to the characteristics of the cutting steel*, then it may be employed to test the doctrine whether all influences, like those of which Classic Baptism treats, may be justly said to baptize.

Every conclusion should be broad enough to include all the particulars from which it is deduced; it should not be expected to have greater breadth.

The brevity with which the conclusion of Classic Baptism is stated might render it obscure, or apparently erroneous, to one who had not thoughtfully read the volume on which that conclusion rests; but, none others, I think, would find any embarrassment in its statement.

It might be amplified thus: "Whatever *act* is capable of thoroughly changing the character, state, or condition, of any object, *by placing it in a state of physical intusposition*, is capable of baptizing that object; and whatever *influence* is capable of thoroughly changing the character, state, or condition, of any object, *by pervading it and making it subject to its own characteristic*, is capable of baptizing that object; and by such changes of character, state, or condition, these acts and influences do, in fact, baptize their objects."

There is nothing in this more amplified form, other than what was in contemplation when the briefer form was written, and which is stated everywhere in the preceding pages of the volume.

As there are "acts" which change the condition of their objects without changing it in that way here contemplated, to wit, by placing them in intusposition, and are, therefore, excluded from consideration; so, there are "influences" which change condition, but not after the manner of those with which we have here to do, and are therefore excluded, in like manner.

All the objections offered against the positions and conclusions of Classic Baptism have, now, been presented and considered.

In view of them, we are fully warranted in concluding, that those positions and conclusions are substantially correct.

By them we are led to view the word under an essentially different aspect from which it has, heretofore, been usually considered. Between a word which is expressive of the execution of the mere form of a transitory act, and a word which is expressive of a condition characterized by completeness of envelopment, fulness of influence, and without limitation of continuance, there must be the broadest distinction, not only in primary import, but also in development.

It has appeared to me to be all-essential, that we should reach clearness of views as to the essential character of the disputed word when used in the classics, before entering upon its usage within the sphere of revealed religion.

This, now, has been measurably accomplished. We will, therefore, proceed to follow the word among Jewish writers, and among Jewish ceremonials, to note any modifications which it may undergo, either by limitation, amplification, or specific application.

The separate examination of each case of baptism will necessarily involve a frequent reference to the same principles of exposition and of appeal to the same illustrative facts. There are advantages, however, in this course which greatly counterbalance the disadvantages.

The quotations of Patristic writers are made, almost without exception, from the latest Paris edition, published under the editorial charge of the Abbe Migné.

The quotations are limited, with rare exceptions, to writers of the first four centuries.

JEWISH WRITERS.

JOSEPHUS—PHILO—SON OF SIRACH.

JEWISH writers exhibit the most thorough knowledge of, and the most entire familiarity with, the Greek word *ΒΑΠΤΙΖΩ.*

It is not a little remarkable, considering the limited extent of their writings, that they should furnish an illustration of every phase of usage presented by the Classic Greek writers.

With this complete mastery of the word, we may feel the most entire confidence that, if they carry the word into any field of thought unknown to the Classics, any such new usage or application will be found to be in perfect harmony with the fundamental character of the word.

In order that the identity of conception and usage, as to this word, by Jew and Greek, may be at once obvious, the same classification of passages will be made now, as that which was presented in Classic Baptism.

ΒΑΠΤΙΖΩ.

INTUSPOSITION WITHOUT INFLUENCE.

PRIMARY USE.

Τήν τε δεξιὰν ἀνατείνας, ὡς μηδένα λαθεῖν, ὅλον εἰς τὴν ἑαυτοῦ σφαγὴν ἐβάπτισε τὸ ξίφος.

And stretching out his right hand, so as to escape notice by none, he *mersed* the entire sword into his throat.

Josephus, Jewish War, ii, 18.

This is the case of Simon, a distinguished Jew, who, after he had slain his parents, wife, and children, to prevent their falling into the power of the enemy, committed suicide. All the facts of the case, the act performed, and the issue reached, are well known.

In what aspect is βαπτίζω presented? Does it announce the performance of a definite, modal act? Dr. Conant says yes, and translates *plunge.* This translation his friend Booth would probably accept without feeling that, thereby, "his sentiments were made ridiculous." And he would be right. Baptist sentiments are not made "ridiculous" by speaking of a sword "plunged," instead of a sword "mersed." But the difficulty with "Baptist sentiments" is, that when they once translate a word which has but "one meaning through all Greek literature" by "plunge," its ghost will ever return, unbidden, to trouble them. And this is not only vexatious, but, as the venerable Booth declares, makes their sentiments "ridiculous." It is, also, obvious that, while "plunge" very properly represents *the act* performed in this case, it does not represent βαπτίζω; for if Simon had, after the example of Saul, fixed the hilt of his sword upon the ground, and *fallen upon* it, the sword would have been equally *baptized*—mersed; but the act of "plunging" would have wholly disappeared, and, according to Baptist translation, βαπτίζω would denote the definite act "fall upon." In fact, it expresses neither; while it accepts the one, or the other, or a score beside, as equally competent to meet its demand for a state of intusposition for its object.

It is no less obvious, that this intusposition is without influence upon the sword. Simon is slain; the sword is unaffected. Whether the sword be sheathed in Simon's throat, or in its own scabbard, it is equally unaffected by the mersion. It is important to notice this, because baptisms characterized by influence without envelopment could never originate in such sword baptism, but must originate in another class of baptisms, viz., baptisms attended by influence upon the objects baptized.

INTUSPOSITION WITH INFLUENCE.

1. *Βαπτισθέντος γὰρ ἡμῶν τοῦ πλοίου κατὰ μέσον τὸν Ἀδρίαν.* *Life of Josephus*, § 3.
2. *Οὔπω μέλλοντος βαπτίζεσθαι τοῦ σκάφους.* *Jewish Antiq.*, ix, 10.
3. *Μετέωρος ὑπεραρθεὶς ὁ κλύδων ἐβάπτισεν.* " " iii, 9.
4. *Καὶ σὺν αὐτοῖς ἐβαπτίζοντο σκάφεσι.* " " iii, 10.
5. *Τῶν δὲ βαπτισθέντων τοὺς ἀνανεύοντας.* " " iii, 10.

1. Our vessel having been mersed in the midst of the Adriatic.
2. The vessel being on the point of being mersed.
3. A lofty billow rising above mersed them.
4. And were mersed with their vessels.
5. But of the mersed those rising to the surface.

PARTICULAR CASES EXAMINED.

BAPTISM WITH INFLUENCE.

1. "For our vessel having been mersed in the midst of the Adriatic, being in number about six hundred, we swam through the entire night."

In the transaction here referred to, Josephus was himself a party. The fact is similar to those related in Classic Baptism and described by the same word. A ship is lost at sea and sinks to the bottom, and is said to be baptized—*mersed.* The form of the act involved in this case is invested with no doubt. It is *sinking.* And inasmuch as the form of act in *sinking* is not the same as the form of act in *plunging*, we, at once, see that the attempt to translate *βαπτίζω* by a word expressive of act, definite in form, is a mistake. Conant translates, *submerged.* In doing so, he abandons that modality of form which he had incorporated in his translation of the preceding case, and adopts a word expressive of condition.

It should, also, be noted, that in this baptism there is no recovery of the baptized object. It remains in the Adriatic to this day. The influence attendant upon this baptism was entirely destructive in its character. The facts, throughout, indicate our interpretation of the word, while they are ruinous to "the theory."

2. "The vessel being on the point of being mersed."

Josephus gives an account of Jonah's disobedience, his flight to Joppa, his embarkation on shipboard, the storm which arose during the voyage to Tarsus, and the momently threatened destruction of the ship, which he describes by saying, it was "on the point of being *baptized*."

The storm neither threatened to dip or to plunge the vessel. It did threaten to baptize, to swallow up, to engulf, to merse, to place in a condition within the swelling waves without recovery. Out of this threatened condition, full of destructive influence, the vessel was delivered by the sacrifice of the guilty prophet.

The Baptist theory, as to the meaning of the word, finds no support in this transaction. Intusposition, without limitation of act, or time, or influence, squarely covers the case.

3. "The lofty billow, rising above, mersed them."

The Jews, to escape the Romans, after the capture of Joppa, betook themselves to their vessels, and put out from the shore. A storm, however, arose, which proved very destructive to their shipping. Attempting to escape from the rocky shore, and the certain death which there awaited them, they turned toward the inrolling swell of the sea, and "the lofty billows, rising above their vessels, *mersed* them." The pressure of the storm-driven waves and the weight of the water falling upon their frail boats sank them.

Such cases of baptism make havoc of the Baptist conception of this word, dipping and modal action, while they bring fresh tribute to that idea of its nature which liberates it from all trammels of form, and gives it control over all acts competent to meet its imperious demand, in primary use, for intusposition.

4. "And were mersed with their vessels."

After the capture of Tarichea, the Jews entered the vessels which had been prepared for such an emergency, and engaged in a sea-fight on Lake Genesareth with shipping got ready to attack them by Vespasian.

The lighter vessels of the Jews were crushed by the heavier Roman ships, and "the Jews were *mersed* with their vessels."

Whatever forms of action may be involved in effecting the baptisms, a tempest blast, a swelling billow, the crushing blow of a war-ship, all alike eschew a dipping, while all, with one consent, effect the demanded state of intusposition with its controlling influence.

5. "But of those mersed that rose to the surface, either a dart overtook or a vessel seized upon them."

The occurrence, here referred to, belongs to the same naval engagement. The special point claiming attention is the fact that persons *mersed*, with a sinking ship, may come to the surface again previous to being drowned. Mersion is always unlimited, in itself, as to the time of continuance; but it does not preclude the intervention of other causes to bring it to a termination. In the present case, it was the desire and effort of the Romans to make the mersion permanent; but, not having immediate control of the baptized, they, by their efforts to escape the natural and ordinary consequence of baptism in water of human beings, succeeded in rising to the surface. It can hardly be necessary to call attention to the immense and radical difference between such a baptism and a dipping. A human being baptized into water, and left to the natural force of such baptism, state, or condition, will as certainly and invariably perish as that man was created to live upon the earth and to breathe the atmosphere. A human being dipped into water, and left to the natural force of such dipping, (dipping introduces into no state or condition,) will as certainly and invariably experience no other effect than a superficial wetting, as that dipping carries its object, momentarily, into and recovers it out of water.

Any attempt to unify things so alien in nature as a baptism and dipping must end in the blankest disappointment.

Neither aid nor comfort, then, can be derived from this

transaction to sustain the Baptist theory in the sore extremity to which it is reduced.

Ships baptized (carried to the bottom of the sea) by tempest or naval battle, and human beings baptized (drowned, or a right honest attempt made for it), will indicate βαπτίζω as a word competent to bring its objects into a new state or condition characterized by controlling influence, but they can have neither part nor lot in an effort to fasten upon that word the fiction of a dipping.

INTUSPOSITION FOR INFLUENCE.

1. *Βαροῦντες ἀεὶ καὶ βαπτίζοντες ὡς ἐν παιδιᾷ νηχόμενον.* *Jewish Antiq.*, xv, 3.
2. *Βαπτιζόμενος ἐν κολυμβήθρα, τελευτᾷ.* *Jewish War*, i, 22.
3. *'Εβάπτισεν ἑκὼν τὸ σκάφος.* " " iii, 8.

1. Always pressing down and mersing him, as if in sport, while swimming, they ceased not until they had wholly drowned him.
2. And there, being mersed in the pool by the Galatians according to command, he died.
3. Voluntarily mersed his ship.

PARTICULAR CASES EXAMINED.

BAPTISMS FOR INFLUENCE.

1. "Always pressing down and mersing him, as if in sport, while swimming."

Aristobulus, high priest and of royal blood, greatly beloved by the people, had awakened the suspicion and jealousy of Herod, the reigning monarch, but without claim, by lineal descent, to the throne. Herod, having resolved upon his destruction, allured him to engage in sportive exercise, and when heated thereby, enticed him to a fish-pond, within his palace grounds, to induce him to seek refreshment by bathing in its waters. In the pond were already some of his creatures under pretence of bathing, but really to carry out the murderous intent of the king. Aristobulus having entered the pond, these assassins consummated their purpose by "pressing down and mersing his head while he was swimming, as if in sport." Thus Aristobulus was murdered by being drowned.

The comment of Dr. Carson on this transaction is as follows: "Aristobulus was several times dipped before he was entirely suffocated. If so, the action of the verb was performed on him without destroying him. He might have been saved after having been immersed. It was not the word *baptizo* which destroyed him. It was the keeping him too long under the water after immersion," (p. 263.) In another case of drowning, he says: "The Greek word *baptizo* would not hurt them more than the harmless English word *dip*, were there an immediate emersion; and *dip*, if not followed by an emersion, will be followed by death as its consequence, as well as *baptizo;* and the latter may be followed by emersion as well as the former. The continuation under water is not here expressed by the verb in question," (p. 286.)

Baptists have good reason to do their best with this case, both to get *drowning* out of it and to get *dipping* into it. They could have no bolder or abler representative in making such attempt than Dr. Carson. How has he succeeded? The fact of drowning is so ingrained in the narrative of the baptism, that even a Carson will not attempt to eliminate it. The best that he can do, is to try and divorce it from βαπτίζω. The basis of this endeavor lies in the assumed identification between a baptism and a dipping. This assumption pervades, like a fretting leprosy, all his writings, and utterly vitiates them, notwithstanding much that is true, for the end for which they are designed. In reply to the statement that "Aristobulus was several times *dipped*," we reply, Aristobulus was not "dipped" once. There was no act of "dipping" performed. He was in the water, under the water, except his head. That, his murderers did not *dip*, but "pressed down." The act of pressing down does not nvolve any *raising up;* nor did these murderers volunteer any such addition. It would not have answered their purpose. If the head of Aristobulus ever got, again, above the water, into which it was "pressed down," he must get it there himself as he best could. He will have neither deed nor wish from Herod's assassins to help him. But not only does "pressing down" involve no *taking out*, and is thus alien from dip, neither does it involve any limitation of continuance within the water, and is, thus, again shown to be foreign in its nature from that word. Two things are evident in the narrative. 1. Aristobulus was not "pressed down" sufficiently long, the first time, to suffocate him; this would have betrayed the murderous intent. 2. He was "pressed down" sufficiently deep, and kept under water sufficiently long, to cause partial exhaustion. A repetition of such "sport" (on one who was each time less able to recover himself) soon produced the legitimate effect of a "pressing down" baptism. He was drowned. But, Dr. Carson says, "It was not the word *baptizo* which destroyed him. It was the keeping him too long under the water after immersion." Is it naiveté most charming, or acuteness most marvellous, which makes this suggestion? In whose service and at whose behest is "pressing down" acting? Is it not that of βαπτίζω? When "pressing down" puts the unhappy High Priest under water, does βαπτίζω object? When it keeps him "under water too long" for life, does βαπτίζω object? If the maxim *qui facit per alium facit per se*, be true, this Greek cannot enter the plea—*not guilty.*

"Died from being buried by the fall of a sandbank," says the coroner's jury. "Wrong," says the critic, "'being buried' did not kill him, it was the remaining too long under the sand!" "Guilty of murder by cutting the man's throat," says the verdict. "No," answers the criminal, "cutting the throat does not kill, it is pressing the knife in too deeply!" "Drowned by baptism in a pool," says Josephus. "No," says Carson, "not by baptism, but by being kept too long under water!" Just as though the "keeping under water too long" was not the very alpha and omega of the baptism designed, and as though a baptism was not chosen rather than a dipping, because under the one they could "keep him too long under the water" to live, and by the other they could not.

Dr. Carson adds farther, "Dip, if not followed by an emersion, will cause death as well as *baptize*." The supposition is an impossible one. Emersion belongs to dip as really as immersion. Immersion without emersion is not a dipping. On the other hand, baptism has nothing to do with an emersion. Never since βαπτίζω existed, did it take out of the water what it put into it. In whatever case a baptized object has been removed from a state of baptism, the removal was never effected, directly or indirectly, by βαπτίζω. The assassins baptized Aristobulus. Aristobulus recovered himself out of this state of baptism without help from them. Again they baptized him; and again he recovered himself. At length, too much exhausted to struggle more, he remained in that state of baptism into which he was brought by Herod's command, and perished. Emersion in this case was an accident and foreign to the word; drowning was the natural and necessary consequence, except through foreign intervention to prevent its occurrence. Just as soon as this foreign intervention (the struggles of Aristobulus) ceased, the baptism bore its legitimate fruit, and Herod was a murderer.

Unless Baptists can find some happier case than this by which to convert a baptism into a dipping, their labor will receive but poor reward.

2. "And there, *being mersed* in the pool by the Galatians according to command, he died."

This is a second allusion to this same murder. It differs from the former in omitting to give any form of act by which the baptism was effected. In the absence of such information, imagination might exhaust itself in vain attempts to learn the facts of the case. So far is it from being true, that the Greek word is, in such matter, its own expositor; there is absolutely no help to be derived from it to learn the definite act by which any baptism is secured. Such knowledge must come from other quarters. Had the "Antiquities" of Josephus perished, this statement in his "War" would have left us hopelessly in the dark, as to the act employed by the assassins in the baptism of Aristobulus.

This passage, also, leads to the remark, that Josephus had other ideas than Carson entertained as to the legitimate force of a baptism. The historian says, "being mersed he died." The defender of the Baptist theory says, "*baptize* does not hurt anybody, it is being kept too long under water!" It would seem that Josephus thought that this baptism embraced the "too long under water." Neither Jew nor Greek ever wrote "being *dipped*, he died." This baptism was for the sake of its deadly influence.

3. "As, also, I esteem a pilot most cowardly, who, fearing a storm, should voluntarily *merse* his ship before the tempest came."

This is part of an argument by Josephus against suicide in times of impending peril. He says, that self-murder, to avoid peril, is not manlike, but cowardly, as the action of a pilot who should sink his ship for fear of a storm. As to the particular form of act by which the vessel was to be brought to the bottom of the sea, the Orator gives us no information, any more than he informs us by what form of act the suicide was to kill himself. *To kill*, expresses a very definite result to be accomplished, but does not throw one ray of light on a thousand definite acts equally competent to reach that result. *To merse*, expresses a very definite result to be effected; but it is dumb with silence as to the form of act by which it may be accomplished. We must, then, remain forever in ignorance whether this pilot was to baptize his ship by running her against a rock, by carrying too much sail, by turning her broadside to the rising wave, by unshipping her rudder, by scuttling her, or in whatever other conceivable method the end could be accomplished. Certain is it, we appeal in vain to βαπτίζω to instruct us on this point. Or, if Baptists can extract a definite act from this word, and illuminate the *quo modo* of this pilot baptism, it must be through some secret in philological chemistry to which we have not yet attained.

This comparison by Josephus of a suicide to this mersing pilot may help us to understand some other cases of mersion. The points of comparison pair off thus: self-murderer and pilot; life and ship; suffering and tempest; death and mersion. Does any one doubt, that the point of accord in the first pair is that of *control*, wielded by the suicide over life and by the pilot over his ship; in the second pair, the stakes at issue; in the third pair, the sources of dread; and in the fourth pair, what? a likeness between death and a *dipping?* between death and *enveloping water?* or, between the *destruction* of "life" however effected, and the *destruction* of the "ship" however effected?

Will any one in his sober senses think of bringing into view the means to these ends, a sword in the one case, a watery envelopment in the other? Is not the comparison wholly exclusive of such things, and exhausted by the naked idea of *destruction*, caused in the one case by a sword, and in the other by encompassing waters, and agreeing in nothing but their *power of destruction?* If this be so, then, we may find in other cases, that "mersion" stands neither for envelopment, nor definite act, but as the representative of *destruction.* Certainly this ship-mersion was a baptism for influence.

FIGURE GROUNDED IN DESTRUCTIVE MERSION.

1. *Ὥσπερ βαπτιζομένης νεὼς ἀπενήχοντο τῆς πόλεως.*
   Jewish War, ii, 20.
2. *Τοῦθ ὥσπερ τελευταία θύελλα χειμαζομένους τοὺς νεανίσκους ἐπιβάπτισε.*
   Jewish War, i, 27.

1. As from a ship being mersed, swam away from the city.
2. This, as a last storm, overmersed the tempest-beaten young men.

PARTICULAR CASES EXAMINED.

FIGURE WITH MERSION.

1. "Many of the distinguished Jews, as from a ship being mersed, swam away from the city."

The Romans having raised the siege of Jerusalem and retreated, some of its principal citizens availed themselves of the opportunity to make their escape. The condition of the city, at this time, is represented by the historian as most hopeless, and likened to a ship on the point of being swallowed up in the sea. The comparison thus instituted between the condition of the city being ruined, and the condition of a ship being swallowed up, leads to the use of a word ("to swim away") expressive of method of escape, well adapted to one member of the comparison, a ship, but not appropriate, in its form of movement, to the other, a city.

"To swim" is not limited to application to movement through water,—"She swam across the room." But such smooth, gliding movement is not adapted to express the movement with which men fly from impending ruin. Are we, then, to understand the writer, by the use of this term and by the comparison with a ship, to intend that his readers should conceive of Jerusalem as encompassed by a waste of waters, into which its citizens are leaping and "swimming away?" Is such a picture, drawn by a brush dipped into "swimming away," anything else than most ridiculous? Let us make another application of this method of interpretation. In this same paragraph, this escape from the city is represented as a "flying away." Shall we now, on the strength of this term, make another draft on our imaginations, and taking these eminent citizens from the watery element, substitute *wings* for *fins*, while we gaze in rapt admiration as they launch away from the crumbling battlements, and "fly" to some far-off region of repose? "Ran away" is used to describe this same flight. Does this word shut us up to the spectacle of a race against time, *running* on foot or on horseback? Or, is the wealth of imagination to be displayed by the conception of a picture in which all these features are artistically grouped; having war-shattered Jerusalem for its centre, encompassing waters for its field, citizens "running" through its shallows, citizens "swimming" through its depths, citizens "flying" through the air—is this the picture?

Does this seem to be only an amusing extravagance?

It is a simple representation of Baptist "figure," which demands that a word, not used in its primary sense, should carry with it, in such use, all that pertains to its primary application. Thus, Dr. Carson insists that "figure" shall take up the "baptized coast," and dip it into the sea; for though it is not dipped, yet it must be dipped by imagination, because "the word means dip, and nothing but dip." And the "baptized" drunkard must, by "figure," be put into wine; for although putting into wine won't make anybody drunk, yet "the word means dip, and nothing but dip," and in he must go. And the "baptized" debtor must, by "figure," go into the water, sinking with a load on his shoulders, because "the word means dip, and nothing but dip." Such doctrine, requiring a word to carry everywhere all the features entering into original use, whether applicable or inapplicable, reminds one of the old lady who could not visit her next neighbor without carrying along her "big box and little box, bandbox and bundle." The doctrine of Sir William Hamilton is better conformed to fact and the exigencies of the case,—"All languages, by the same word, express a multitude of thoughts, more or less differing from each other. We are obliged, from the context, from the tenor, and from the general analogy of the discourse, to determine the meaning." Now, when the terms "swim away," "fly away," "run away," each denoting, originally, a definite form of movement, (one through water, one through air, and one over the face of the earth,) are applied to the flight of citizens from an imperilled city, shall we insist on the definite movement of each, or merge them in the idea, *to escape*, which is common to them all? To "swim away" from a ship indicates the use of the last means for safety; to "swim away" from a city suggests, not the modal use of arms and legs, but a resort to extreme means for getting away. So "to fly away," "to run away," do not shut up to mode of departure, but we may take out of both of them the single element of "rapidity of movement," rejecting everything else, and apply it as the case may require.

In the passage before us, the mersion has nothing to do, directly, with the city. The figure centres in the *destruction* common to ship and city, with the anxiety of sailors in the one case, and of citizens in the other, to escape being involved in that destruction; it does not reach either to the nature or the means of the destruction. The figure does not involve the city in any water envelopment. The ship perishes; the city perishes. Ruin, and escape from ruin, begin and end "the figure."

The figure involves a destructive mersion, and, therefore, has nothing in common with a *dipping*.

2. "This, as a last storm, overmersed the tempest-beaten young men."

These young men were the sons of Herod, whom he had long threatened with death, under the idea that they were plotting against him. They had, however, escaped, until accusation was made by Salome, Herod's wife and their mother-in-law, under which, "as a last storm," they lost their lives.

The passage presents, what is rare, a distinct and well-sustained picture figure, with mersion as a leading element. Aristobulus and Alexander, sons of Herod by Mariamne, became, after their mother's death, objects of suspicion, accusations, and plottings, with a view to compass their destruction. Josephus indicates this condition of things, when he speaks of them as tempest-tossed and weather-beaten. They suffered from these influences, but lived. Salome effected their destruction. These facts suggest a resemblance to a ship which has weathered many storms, but, at last, goes down under one of resistless power.

The points of comparison are plain: 1. The young men and ship with her crew. 2. Various evil machinations and frequent storms. 3. Salome's accusation and the final storm. 4. Death and baptism.

What demands attention here, as bearing upon our inquiry, is: 1. The absence of all show of comparison between any *act* on the one hand and on the other. 2. The same lack of comparison between any *condition* on the one side and condition of *envelopment* on the other.

It it be asked, Is there not "envelopment" in *baptism?* I answer, Yes, in every primary baptism; but that does not carry "envelopment" into a comparison. Envelopment may be the *end* of a baptism, as when I put a stone within water, or it may be only a means to an end, as when Aristobulus is put within water by assassins. When, therefore, I use baptism as a comparison, I may use simply the idea of envelopment, or I may reject entirely the envelopment, and limit the comparison to the *result* of envelopment. This has been done in the present case. There is no comparison between the direct means causing the death of these young men, whatever it was, and the direct means causing the destruction of the ship, which was envelopment by water; but the comparison is between the indirect means, namely, Salome's accusation and the final storm. Thus, envelopment is left out of view, and its result—remediless destruction—is brought into the foreground.

As used in this passage, βαπτίζω speaks, directly, of destruction. "This accusation caused these suffering young men *to perish*, as a final storm causes a weather-beaten ship to perish." The *quo modo* of perishing, in the one case or the other, however well they may be understood, are not in the comparison. Figurative use of words often lights up, resplendently, their literal use. We are here, distinctly, taught that βαπτίζω may be used to express, directly, *the result* of mersion.

This is a truth of the first importance, and utterly repudiated by the Baptist theory. To escape it, they prefer to adopt all sorts of grotesque imaginings shrouded in nondescript "figure."

LITERAL, SECONDARY USE.

CONDITION WITHOUT INTUSPOSITION—INFLUENCE PERVADING AND CONTROLLING, UNLIMITED IN FORM, FORCE, OR TIME.

BAPTISM WITHOUT MERSION.

1. Ἐπιβαπτίσειν γὰρ αὐτὸν τὴν πόλιν. *Jewish War*, iii, 7.
2. Οἳ δὴ καὶ δίχα τῆς στάσεως ὕστερον ἐβάπτισαν τὴν πόλιν. *Jewish War*, iv, 3.
3. Ἅτε βαπτιζόμενου τοῖς ἐπιοῦσι τοῦ λογισμοῦ. *Philo, Eusebius.*

1. For he, himself, would overmerse the city.
2. Who, independently of the sedition, afterwards mersed the city.
3. As though the reason were mersed by the things coming upon it.

Baptism of the City of Jotapata.

1. "It did not become him, either to fly from enemies, or to abandon friends; nor to leap off, as from a ship overtaken by a storm, into which he had entered in fair weather; that he would, himself, overmerse the city, as no one would longer dare to make resistance to the enemy when he was gone through whom their courage was sustained."

Josephus, besieged in Jotapata, purposed, after the defence became hopeless, to escape, thinking that he might, on some other field, be of more service to his country. The citizens objected in the language above quoted.

A first glance at the passage might convey the impression that βαπτίζω was used in picture figure. A closer examination would, however, correct such impression. There is, indeed, figure in the passage, but it is limited to a comparison between the city unassailed by enemies (when Josephus came to it) and a ship in a calm, and between the city assailed by enemies (when Josephus talks of leaving) and a ship in a storm. This is all the figure.

The subsequent use of βαπτίζω, most probably, was suggested by this figure; but it is not itself figurative; certainly not in any Baptist sense. It is intolerable to suppose that a city is figured, through the departure of an individual, as dipped into water, immersed in the sea, overwhelmed by a flood, or sunk in the ocean. Such extravagances, in full statement, Baptist writers are careful to keep out of view. They content themselves with a vague reference to the vague term "figure," and then vaguely translate by some word made vague in its import by a double use. Dr. Conant calls it "figure," and translates *overwhelm*. But this word has a double use, in one of which neither water-floods, nor covering can be found.

> "Long beards, long noses, and pale faces,
> They *overwhelm* me with the spleen."

Do "beards," "noses," "faces," let loose water-floods, or *envelop* with anything?

> "Guilty and guiltless find an equal fate,
> And one vast ruin *whelm* the Olympian state."

Can any human device convert "one vast ruin" into a flood of water? Or, can this "Olympian state" be put, by this language, into a state of *envelopment?*

Dr. Conant, theoretically, uses "overwhelm" in one sense; all his readers will understand it in another sense.

Dr. Carson translates "*sink* the city," in flat contradiction of his reiterated and absolutely exclusive definition,—"dip, and nothing but dip." But I must be careful how I call "*dip—sink*," a contradiction, lest I should be sprinkled with "Attic salt."

This is only "figure;" one mode of action put for another! A very convenient figure certainly. And, also, one meaning put for another. For Dr. Carson does not mean that "sink" shall either put the city into the sea or into the earth, but, contrary to theory, is compelled to use it in its secondary sense—*to ruin*. Hear his own language: "He would *sink* or epibaptize the city. His desertion of the city would be the means of its ruin. He is then represented as doing the thing that would be the consequence of his departure," (p.

98.) And this "ruin" is directly, and not figuratively, expressed by βαπτίζω, deriving its power so to do from that destructive influence which is the so-common result of envelopment baptism.

The nut is cracked, the enveloping shell is worse than useless, and thrown aside; while the kernel truth, adapted to the case, is applied.

What these failures of Baptist writers indicate to be true is proved to be so, indeed, by the language of the passage; "He would overmerse—*ruin*—the city, because no one would longer *resist the enemy*." Then the epibaptism was to come from the "enemy," not from an OVER*whelming flood*, nor from the ship-city *sinking in the sea*. Figure would have required their efforts to be made against the *storm*, not against the *Romans*.

The case is one of secondary use,—influence without envelopment. And no abandonment of *dip* for "flood" or "sink" can save the Baptist theory from an epibaptism, as ruinous as that which abandonment by Josephus would have brought on Jotapata.

Baptism of the City of Jerusalem.

2. "Who, independently of the sedition, afterward mersed the city."

During the war between the Jews and the Romans, certain robber chiefs with their bands sought refuge in Jerusalem, where they became the source of turmoil and sedition. But these were not the only evils resulting from their presence. The provisions of the city were limited for a protracted siege, and these plundering and murderous bands, consuming the food which might, otherwise, have sufficed for the defenders of the city, brought on famine, and thus, without sedition, would have baptized—mersed—*ruined*—the city.

Dr. Conant calls this "figure," and says: "This natural and expressive image of trouble and distress occurs often in the Old Testament. For example, Ps. 69 : 2, 'I am come into deep waters, where the floods overflow me.' Verses

14, 15: 'Let me be delivered . . . out of the deep waters; let not the water-flood overflow me.' Ps. 18:16, 17: 'He drew me out of many waters; he delivered me from my strong enemy.' Job's afflictions are expressed under the same image (ch. 22:11): 'The flood of waters covers me.' Compare Ps. 124:4, 5; 144:7; 32:6; Ezek. 26:19."

A grand source of confusion and profitless result in the Baptist controversy has been looseness in the statement of principles, or looseness in the examination of the evidence adduced to support those principles; sometimes looseness in both these particulars.

The Baptist conception of the value of βαπτίζω is a variable quantity of the first degree. There is no harmony in the definition of the word, and there is still less harmony between the definition and the evidence adduced to sustain it.

Consider for a moment the definition of βαπτίζω—"to dip, and nothing but dip"—and then look at these quotations adduced for its support. Is it not a reproach on a man's sanity to ask him to accept the one in proof of the other? If applying their own defining term, *plunge*, (as given on other occasions,) to all cases of usage, makes their sentiments "ridiculous," much more is the definition *dip* made ridiculous in the midst of witnesses like these.

An ass in a lion's skin is a trifle in folly compared with "dip" making *a figure* in the attire of "rushing torrents" and "inundating floods." The zenith and the nadir will come together sooner than such definition and such evidence will be made to harmonize.

Again, there is a looseness in applying these "torrents and floods" to baptism which needs to be corrected. A torrent may effect a baptism, and a flood may effect a baptism; but a torrent may sweep against one, and cause great distress and peril, without causing a baptism; and one may be in the midst of a flood, and be filled with anguish, in view of a baptism within its waters, and yet escape unbaptized. Timon's proposed victim had been swept away by a flood of waters; he was in distress and helpless as he was swept by the torrent toward the bank where stood this hater of his race; but he was not baptized until this man-hater stopped his ears to the cry: "I am come into deep waters;" "Deliver me; let not the water-flood overflow me;" "Draw me out of many waters;" and, with heart which knew no sympathy with his kind, baptized him, pressing his head, never to rise again, beneath the waters. Now, this victim of Timon's went through all the experiences suggested by these quotations of Dr. Conant before his baptism; this imagery of water-floods is no image of baptism, but of peril, distress, and anguish. Water-floods may issue in a baptism; they do not do so necessarily; rushing waters and swelling floods, therefore, are not imagery for baptism, but for troubles and distresses which are *always* their accompaniments. Jonah's ship, assailed by the tempest and the dashing billows, was in distress, in peril, and "ready to be baptized;" so that the cry rang out above the howling of the storm: "Let us be delivered out of the deep waters; let not the water-flood overflow us!" That picture—raging sea, bending masts, tossing ship, praying crew—is the image of distress; it is not the image of a baptism.

Baptism is not an *act* done, nor something *in transitu*, but a result reached; a state or condition accomplished. Herod's sons were many times in peril and distress from plottings and machinations (torrents and floods); but were never baptized until Salome's accusation put them into their graves; their baptisms calmed the troubled waters, as Jonah's baptism stilled the tempest, and brought deliverance to the imperilled ship and crew.

These quotations from the Psalms, therefore, confound things that differ. "Trouble and distress" are no more baptism, than a tempest-tossed ship is a ship lying in the depths of the sea.

If you would have imagery of baptism (in this direction), you must not present imagery of suffering and peril, but of *ruin* and *death*. And this conclusion brings, again, into bold relief the entire incompetency of the Baptist theory to account for the usage of this word.

Let us now look at the passage itself. In doing this we

are struck with the simplicity and straightforwardness of the statement. Nothing could be more naked of all figurative picturing, unless it be found in the naked word βαπτίζω. Baptist writers have long enough assumed the power of "the word to find them water in a desert." They must give some evidence of its power to flood Jerusalem. They will not find such evidence in the passage. These robbers baptized the city, not by letting loose an imaginary flood upon it, but *by eating up its provisions!*

This is Josephus's notion of a baptism, and under its influence the imaginative Baptist soaring on waxen wings is brought back, very summarily, to the regions of common sense. The provisions devoured, then comes famine, then comes feebleness of defenders, then comes conquest, then follows the flaming temple, and stone torn from stone, blank ruin—profoundest baptism.

Most evidently does Josephus take the element of destruction, inhering in so many baptisms, and crowding that idea into every letter of this word, to the rejection of all beside, most directly affirms, that "the robbers, *by inducing a famine*, baptized the city"—brought it into a state of utter ruin!

I affirm baptism in water-floods more strongly than any Baptist writer ever did, or ever can, with any show of consistency with his theory; but I affirm that there is no more water in βαπτίζω, in this passage, than there is *fire*. There is not the remotest hint, in word or thought, that water was present to the mind of the writer. As for the word itself, there is as much *fire* in it as there is water; and Dr. Conant might as well have quoted the fiery baptism of Sodom and Gomorrah, as the water-floods of the Psalms, to meet the demands of the Greek word. Indeed, as there was more fire, under the Roman torch, in the final baptism of Jerusalem, than there was water, baptism by fire would seem to have the right of precedence over water baptism. This is certain, beyond all controversy, that the simple word βαπτίζω gives no authority to introduce water into any baptism; therefore, its introduction in any case, in fact or by imagination, must bring justifying evidence from other source than this word.

In the present case there is not one particle of such evidence. On the other hand, we have the most perfect evidence, from text and context, that utter destruction is the thought in view; while we have no less complete evidence that βαπτίζω is identified with results of destruction most absolute, and is therefore qualified, on the present occasion, to express such destruction. And this duty, we say, it does, in fact, here perform.

Dr. Carson both approves and condemns this conclusion. He says, "The immediate *ruin* of the affairs of the city is the only thing that is asserted. It asserts that the robbers *ruined* or sunk the city." Carson cannot escape acknowledging, that "ruin" is the thing declared. But how can the "ruin" of a great city be got out of *dip?* Why, not at all, as everybody knows, and none better than Dr. C.; "dip, and nothing but dip," must, therefore, be metamorphosed into "sink," a word radically differing both in form and power. Conant translates by "whelm," a word differing essentially from both the others. This difference of translation of a word which is "the most facile in translation of all words, never having but one meaning," arises from a fundamental difference in the interpretation of the passage. Enough has been said of Dr. Conant's view. Carson (p. 84) takes us out to sea, and shows us "a ship sinking from being overburdened and ill-managed in a storm from the dissensions of the crew," and says, see there "a striking and beautiful figure"—of a city *baptized* BY FAMINE!!!

If the pinions of Dr. Carson's imagination had not been sufficiently strong to bear Jerusalem into mid ocean to *sink* it, I have no doubt that he would have taken it to pieces, stone by stone, and *dipped* it in the pool of Bethesda.

This Baptist writer tells us the word, if applied to houses, would show that it did not mean *immerse*, because houses cannot be immersed, (p. 368.) But how so, when he thinks nothing of taking all the houses of Jerusalem and giving them a sinking-dip in a trice? I think we must let Josephus have his own way, and, rejecting flood and storm, accept the robber baptism by famine, bringing the long-prophesied ruin to the city.

Baptism of the Intellect by Gluttony.

3. "One might evidence it also by this,—the sober and content are more intelligent, but those always filled with drink and food are least intelligent, as though the reason were mersed by the things coming upon it."

Philo was a Jew, living in the first century. He contrasts in this passage the intellectual manifestation of those who lead a frugal, with such as lead a gluttonous life,—vigor characterizing the former and imbecility the latter. It is a fact of universal experience, that excessive eating and drinking exerts an unfavorable influence over intellectual development.

Dr. Carson passes over this case. Had he noticed it, we should, no doubt, have been treated to the "beautiful and striking figure" of an overloaded ship sinking in storm or calm; or the glutton, in deep water, sinking under a burden on his shoulders (it may be a wine-skin and a round of beef); thus magnifying the powers of imagination, if not throwing light on the usage of the word.

Dr. Conant translates by "whelm." Whether "the natural and expressive image" of water-floods is to be introduced here, as in the previous case of "whelming," he does not state. What light can be thrown upon the meaning of βαπτίζω by dipping, or sinking, or whelming this glutton, in fact or in figure, I have not enough of imagination to conceive. If no such picturing is to be done, then we must look for the baptism either in a literal envelopment, or give the word direct power to express hurtful influence without envelopment.

Some might plead in favor of the first interpretation, that the meat and drink are represented as "coming upon" the reason. In that case, the reason would have to lie at the bottom of the stomach, while eatables and potables came down upon it. No doubt a baptism could be so effected;

for Dr. Fuller says, a man who lies on the sea-shore will be baptized by the waves "coming upon" him. As to this baptism, I have only to confess that the brains of some people seem to be very closely connected with the epigastric region. My preference, however, is for the other baptism.

I accept the statement as simple and direct in both cases: "The reason is affected beneficially by temperance, while it is baptized—influenced injuriously—by gluttony." Does any one doubt the truth of the sentiment? Does any one doubt that βαπτίζω may, legitimately, acquire such power of utterance from connection with baptisms where hurtful influence has a necessary, yet secondary place (because only a consequence), but now brought forward, in new circumstances, into a primary position?

Such interpretation must stand until the negative of these questions is established.

TO BAPTIZE—TO MAKE DRUNK.

APPROPRIATION.

Οἶδα δέ τινας, οἳ, ἐπειδὰν ακροθώρακες γένωνται, πρὶν τελέως βαπτισθῆναι.

Philo, ii, 478. *On Contemp. Life.*

I know some, who, when they become *slightly intoxicated*, before they become *thoroughly drunk.*

Baptism by Wine-drinking.

"I know some, who, when they become slightly intoxicated, before they become thoroughly drunk, make provision for to-morrow's drinking by contribution and tickets."

Such use of βαπτίζω is to be regarded as proof that this word had secured to itself the power to express, directly, the influence of wine-drinking,—*to make drunk.*

1. The ground of this conclusion is found in prevailing and persistent usage of the same phraseology and with the same application.

In Classic Baptism (p. 317), will be found the following quotations: "You seem to be *made drunk* (baptized) by unmixed wine." "Then *making drunk* (baptizing), he set me free." "Having *made drunk* (baptized), Alexander by much wine." "Wine *makes drunk* (baptizes)." "I am one of those *made drunk* (baptized), yesterday." "*Making themselves drunk* (baptizing), out of great wine-jars." "*Made drunk* (baptized), by yesterday's debauch." "Not yet *made drunk* (baptized)." These quotations are from various writers, separated from each other, geographically, widely, and extending through a space of time exceeding five centuries. In addition to this the fact (drunkenness) to which the word was applied being of daily occurrence, and extending from generation to generation, it could not but be, that any word used to designate it must be in continual use. This is, farther, shown to be true from the form of use. It is employed absolutely, without any helping adjunct, and without the shadow of stated or designed figure. Unless the word was in familiar use, it would be unintelligible when thus thrown upon its power of self-explanation. But it had, most clearly, such self-explaining power. And now, if all other usage of *βαπτίζω* were blotted out of the Greek language, this usage would live, having life in itself, and proclaim from every passage—*make drunk!*

2. Proof of this meaning is found in the fact, that the word is not only self-explanatory, but is capable of being used, in this well-understood sense, in explanation of what was less intelligible.

"When an old man drinks of the fountain, and Silenus takes possession of him, immediately, he is for a long time silent, and resembles one heavy-headed and *drunk* (baptized.)" (Classic Baptism, p. 330.) Here *βαπτίζω* is used by Lucian, as possessed of a meaning so unmistakable, that he considers it quite sufficient, in expounding something not understood, to say, "it resembles one *baptized*." Who will say, this is figure, and means that one who drinks of the Silenic fount is like one dipped in water, whelmed by a water-flood, or sunk in the sea? All retreat under cloudy figure, here, is gone. There is but one meaning possible. The effects of drinking Silenic water are like the effects of drinking wine. The effects of what is not understood are explained by that which is well understood. Let any man who never had explanation of this wonderful fountain, ask Lucian, what is the effect on the drinker? and his answer is,—like that of wine; which makes a man "heavy-headed and *drunk*."

How the theory of "dipping, and nothing but dipping, through all Greek literature," can survive such usage, is for others to determine.

3. Proof of this meaning is found in the meaning of the associated and contrasted word,—ακροθώρακες.

This word, in its philology, has nothing more to do with wine-drinking than has βαπτίζω. It means "slightly armed," or breast armed. Yet, Dr. Conant does not hesitate to translate it—"slightly intoxicated"—while the contrasted word, βαπτίζω, which every rational consideration requires to be translated—*excessively intoxicated*—he beclouds by translating —*whelm*.

If there be one half of the evidence for translating the former of these two words by "slight intoxication," that there is for translating the latter by *excessive intoxication*, I do not know where it is to be found. Reference may be made to Aristotle iii Prob. 2, Erotianus *Onomast.*, Plutarch *Sympos.*, Mercurialis iv 6 Var. Lect., and Clem. Alex. i, 416, in support of the meaning. And there may be other authority; but this is enough. And, if so, why not the more numerous authorities, and the more varied evidence, suffice to establish the meaning of βαπτίζω, however diverse from bare philology? This association of these terms causes them to react, the one upon the other, in confirming to each, respectively, the meaning attributed to it.

4. Proof of this meaning is found in its harmony with the laws of language-development.

Words have a life like that of the vine. They send forth branches, which may be either a simple extension of all the peculiarities of the parent stem, with entire dependence upon it; or, still retaining their connection, they may, like the vine-branch whose extremity is turned down and planted in the ground, make an additional source of life for themselves; or, yet farther, all dependence on the parent stem may be severed, and, rooted in the ground, they make a new and independent source of life for themselves, with peculiarities which may be propagated still farther. When we say, the child grows, the plant grows, the population grows, there is but an extension of the same conception. The man runs, the locomotive runs, the river runs, the steamer runs, the watch runs, the candidate runs, are phrases which show not merely an extension of the original thought, but, also, that each has established a root for itself amid the elements of thought. To dip, *to dye*, shows not merely an extension of the original act, or the formation of an additional root, but the dissolution of all organic relation and the establishment of an independent life with the power of procreation.

Now, as *βάπτω* gave origin *to dye*, through the coloring-vat, so *βαπτίζω* gave origin to *controlling influence*, through mersion of particular objects, and with this new power applied to wine-drinking, it did, by appropriation, advance to the definite and direct expression of such influence in the fullest degree; proclaiming every baptized wine-drinker to be *made drunk.*

5. Proof is found in the impracticability of any rational introduction of figure.

Imagination can do a great deal; but much that it does is without the sanction of right reason. To expound the passage under consideration, Dr. Conant uses the following language: "To overwhelm (figuratively) with an intoxicating liquor, or a stupefying drug, that takes full possession of one's powers, like a resistless flood; or, (as the figure may sometimes be understood,) to steep in, as by immersing in a liquid." In what way, or in what measure, this language throws light upon the case before us, I cannot say; for, to me, it is much less intelligible than what it is intended to expound. Does Dr. Conant mean by "overwhelm, figuratively," that a mental picture is to be sketched of wine-casks, with bursting heads, pouring forth a vinous flood, by which the drunkard is overwhelmed and swept away? Does he mean by a "stupefying drug," a liquid, or a solid? Is stupefaction by "figurative overwhelming," accomplished by *laudanum* as a sweeping torrent, or by *opium* as a falling and crushing mass? Whether Dr. C.'s good sense will repudiate such figuring as this, (in which the luxuriant imaginations of other Baptist writers find delight,) I am quite at a loss to determine from his language.

What is the meaning of "intoxicating liquor or a stupefying drug taking full possession of one's powers, *like a resistless flood*," I am equally at a loss to understand. That "a resistless flood takes possession of one's powers," is a statement of fact that I do not remember ever before to have met with; and if I had, I should still have been "at sea" in attempting to imagine the foundation in nature for such language. Wines and drugs "take possession" of our faculties; overwhelming torrents and floods sweep them away. "To take possession" cannot be likened to "sweeping away." "Wines and drugs," therefore, cannot be likened, in their effects any more than in their forms, to "torrents and floods."

But, Dr. Conant does not seem to be settled in his own mind as to the nature or form of this "figurative overwhelming." We are told that "the figure may sometimes be understood, to steep in, as by immersing in a liquid." Is it intended by the emphatic "steep *in*" and "immerse *in* a *liquid*," to necessitate the imagining of the drunkard put into wine, and of the stupefied put into an opiate? Or, is the reiterated *inness* to be disregarded and effects only to be regarded? But why is the overwhelming limited to a "liquid?" Does Dr. Conant doubt, that a man can be overwhelmed, *baptized*, by chewing solid opium, as well as by drinking its alcoholic extract in the shape of laudanum? In the case of the baptized opium-chewer must we fall back for exposition of this word to "a resistless flood?"

If good sense is too much shocked by such imaginations and such inconsistencies, and affirms, that all that is meant is, *the controlling influence* exerted by wines and opiates on the one side, and floods and torrents on the other, rejecting the *modus*, in the one case and in the other, as having nothing in common, then I ask, whether the Baptist theory has not been rejected, whether it be made to rest on the *sine qua non* of a dipping, or of an intusposition? And I further ask, whether a secondary meaning has not been established—*controlling influence*—with form of act and inness of position, eliminated? And this being granted, what escape is there from the meaning (through appropriation to the influence of wine-drinking) *make drunk?*

The reference to Basil—*Discourse against Drunkards*, iii, p. 452: "So also the souls of these are driven about beneath the waves, being baptized by wine"—is of no value as a model for the interpretation of this and similar passages. If Basil chooses to get up a storm at sea, and depict helpless wretches tossed from billow to billow, while held under their power, unable to escape, to show the miserable results of luxurious living, or of excessive drinking, and to base upon it the conclusion, that no less overmastering and destructive is the power of wine over its votaries, he is at full liberty to do so; but, surely, they have no less liberty who choose to speak in unadorned language, and to declare, without a sea-storm, that wine drunk has the power *to make drunk.* If it should please any one to write, "As the rising sun *enlightens* the world, dissipating the darkness of the night, scattering its morning mists and lighting up its valleys, so education enlightens a people, dispelling the darkness and doubts and errors of ignorance," must we, therefore, find in the sober utterance—"he is *enlightened* by education," all this play of the imagination? Just as much as in the statement, "I was yesterday baptized—*made drunk*—by wine," we must find the sea-storm of Basil, or the dipping, or whelming, or steeping of Baptist interpreters. Basil's figure is Comparison, ours is Metaphor. No picturing can be rationally deduced from such direct and naked statements as those before us.

6. Proof may be found in Baptist translations.

Conant translates,—"Whelm—overwhelm with wine." Both these words are continually used to express *the highest degree of influence* without suggesting or thinking of covering the object. Whether "covering" was in the mind of Dr.

C., or not, I cannot tell; but very few of his readers will feel themselves called upon, by this language, to tax their imaginations to find "covering" for the drunkard. Besides, the phrase "overwhelmed with wine" is incomplete. It is admitted, on all hands, that *drunkenness* is the ultimate thought designed to be expressed. But drunkenness can only be induced in one way—by *drinking;* this, then, being understood, (*ex necessitate rei,*) it is unexpressed, according to the law of ellipsis, which omits that which is most essential, and which, therefore, can never fail to be supplied. If a man is overwhelmed with wine *by drinking*, he is not overwhelmed by it as a *wine* billow. The translation can only express influence, without covering.

But Dr. Carson says, (p. 311,) "The classical meaning of the word is in no instance *overwhelm.*" "Literally it is *immersed in* wine," (p. 79.) Two such combatants as Conant and Carson, the champions of contradictory meanings of βαπτίζω, the one having emblazoned on his shield a rushing torrent for whelming, the other a still pool for dipping, would present a field of contest which, for hard blows, might be expected to compare well with "the gentle passage of arms at Ashby." But Dr. Carson having put the drunkard *in* wine, does, incontinently, take him out, declaring that the point of resemblance is not in the immersion at all, "but between a man completely under the influence of wine, and an object completely subjected to a liquid in which it is wholly immersed," (p. 80.) "There is no likeness between the *action* of drinking and immersion," (p. 79.) "The likeness is between their effects," (p. 272.) Let us bring this likeness to a more definite point. Is wine-influence resembled to the influence exerted by immersion over any particular object,—a stone, a ship, a bag of salt, a human being? As the influence in each of these cases differs, the resemblance cannot be specific; and if you eliminate that which is specific, you have an abstract *controlling influence.* We are, then, under the leadership of these Baptist translators, brought to this conclusion,—that there is a usage of βαπτίζω in which resemblance rejects mode of action, rejects immersion, rejects specific influence, and reveals an abstract controlling influence. Their statement, then, is this: "A man completely under the influence of wine is a *baptized* man, because he is like an object completely subjected to a liquid in which it is wholly immersed—in so far as it is subjected to some *controlling* influence." A rather roundabout way of reaching the truth, but better such way than not at all. Now, this "controlling influence," in its abstract conception, eliminated from the primary use, we say, becomes concrete in a secondary use of βαπτίζω, capable of being conjoined with any word susceptible of exerting such influence, and without carrying with it "form of action," or "intusposition," any more than specific influence, all of which have been sloughed off, when it assumed its abstract garb.

The application of this word, (expressive of such secondary sense,) to a particular case in which the influence was invariably the same, would, necessarily, make it expressive of such influence. The list of influences which are single and invariable is but limited,—joy, grief, riches, poverty, honor, shame, learning, ignorance, and innumerable other sources of influence, do not belong to the list. Wine does; its influence, as a drink, is one and invariable; the controlling influence of wine—to be baptized by wine—therefore, can convey but one meaning,—*to make drunk.*

The examination of this passage has been thus particular, not on its own account, so much, as, being entirely removed from all direct bearing on Christian baptism, it affords a more favorable opportunity for the discussion of principles, than in a case where prejudice might be supposed to disqualify for an impartial examination. Novelties adduced to meet exigencies are suspicious.

BAPTISM BY DRUNKENNESS.

VERBAL FIGURE.

Καὶ βεβαπτισμένον εἰς ἀναισθησίαν καὶ ὕπνον ὑπὸ τῆς μέθης.

Jewish Antiq., x, 9.

And baptized (mersed) by drunkenness into insensibility and sleep.

Baptism into Insensibility and Sleep.

"Seeing him in this state, and baptized into insensibility and sleep by drunkenness, Ishmael leaping up, with his ten friends, slays Gedaliah and those reclining with him in the drinking-party."

Gedaliah was appointed to be governor over the remnant of the Jews after their conquest by the king of Babylon. This office he administered with great consideration for his suffering fellow-countrymen. Ishmael was of the royal family, and had fled from the country during its troubles, but was received with great kindness on his return by Gedaliah. At a banquet, given for the entertainment of himself and companions, he treacherously murdered his confiding benefactor, as related in the extract quoted.

Translation.—Dr. Conant translates, "*plunged* into stupor and sleep." This translation, like that of Baptist writers generally, is not a translation of βαπτίζω, but one made to meet some accident which may pertain, or may be supposed to pertain, to the particular baptism in hand. Thus, a ship baptism is translated *sub*-merge, to meet the idea of going *under;* while some other baptism is translated *over*-whelm, to meet a supposed idea of a flood going *over* the object; and yet another is translated *plunge*, to meet the supposed demand of the preposition εἰς, which is found in the passage; and so on. Now these translations, evidently, neither are nor can be in response to the demand of βαπτίζω, but are modelled after some accidental features of the baptisms; and as these change, so the translations change, the word itself remaining ever the same. For this reason, Dr. Conant, having given us, heretofore, in wine baptisms the translations "whelm and overwhelm," under the imagined presence of a rolling torrent, now introduces "plunge," because of the presence of the preposition, suggesting an act passing into. But this is not to translate βαπτίζω. It has been shown in Classic Baptism (p. 294), that "plunge" is unsuitable to represent the Greek word in the case of a *sleep* baptism.

Peculiarity of the passage: Verbal Figure.—Baptist writers salute our ears at almost every turn with the cry, *Figure!* This is a bottomless abyss, into which all difficulties about dipping are cast and buried out of sight. Not content with such use of the term as would enable them to say, that in such and such cases, the word was *troped*, turned from its primary sense to meet a special application, they convert "figure" into a limner with brush and pallet and *water* colors, ever ready to sketch some marine view, enlivened by a tempest, or made picturesque by a company engaged in "performing the act," without which, neither literality nor figure has any being. If there is a baptism by grief, the exposition is by a dipping into water; a baptism by study, is resolved by going under water; a baptism by perplexing questions, is met by an onrolling flood of waters; a baptism by famine, is illuminated by a trip to the sea and a sinking into its waters; a baptism by wine, is expounded by an immersion under the water. What magical and infinitely varied virtue has *water*, that it can, on demand, equally portray grief baptism, study baptism, question baptism, sleep baptism, wine baptism, famine baptism, woe of spirit, unnerved intellect, bewildered faculties, profound repose, utter destruction, and so on, even *ad infinitum!* Did ever conception bear, more boldly written upon its front, "*vagary of the imagination?*"

The patent character of this error is made manifest in another direction. Its advocates are compelled to apply this florid picturing to one-half the cases in which the word is found in the Greek Classics. Was there ever a word in any language which, through centuries of use, presented an equally divided usage of literality and highly-wrought picturing? There is no overboldness in saying that there never was, and there never will be, any such word.

Baptist theorists must pardon us for keeping green in their recollection the similar attempt to divide the domain of βάπτω into equal parts of literality and figure, filling the Greek language with figurative vat-dippings as they now would fill it with figurative water-dippings. But these rhetorical dippings have, at last, with one consent, been numbered with commonplace literalities. Where, now, is βάπτω used in figure? It is extremely doubtful whether, in the primary sense of dipping, enough cases can be found in all Classic literature to require one-half the digits for their computation. If the same shall not be found true of the Classic use of βαπτίζω, in its primary sense, there will be a close approximation to it.

The passage before us not only overthrows the Baptist theory for figurative exposition, by torrents and floods, and dippings and plungings, but establishes the true form and nature of a figurative use of βαπτίζω. In every literal, primary, baptism there is a baptizing power, a baptized object, and a receiving element. But in literal, primary, baptism we have seen that it is a matter of indifference whether the object is moved to secure intusposition, or whether the element is moved to embrace its object. In figurative baptism, therefore, phraseology may be adopted which shall be based on the one or the other of these means to a result. But whichever form be selected, as these baptisms are for influential, and not for physical results, there will be neither movement nor investment in either case, but simply a development of controlling influence, the character of which must be derived from the elements which enter into any particular baptism.

The phraseology of the baptism before us is based on the language which is appropriate to the movement of an object, in order to its being enclosed in the receiving element. Inasmuch as this is the first baptism, expressed in verbal figure, that we have encountered, (Classic Baptism presents no such case,) it has a just claim to our very special attention.

'ΕΙΣ—its translation.—Let us first determine what should be the translation of the preposition εἰς, which must control the form of the thought.

This preposition may denote a demand for inness of position, by passing into, or it may indicate the point toward which movement or thought tends, and at which it rests. Associated with verbs expressive of movement, or which make demand for inness of position, this preposition must be translated by *into*, unless imperative reasons can be shown for translating it *to*, *unto*, or *for*.

That it should be translated *into* in this passage, we consider to be conclusively established:

1. Because of the nature of the verb with which it is associated. That βαπτίζω makes demand for intusposition, in primary use, is in proof. It does not indicate movement *toward*, or rest *at*, a point. The association of this preposition with such a word, therefore, forbids a merely *telic* character being attributed to it, and positively requires intusposition.

2. Because the association of kindred verbs with this preposition does, admittedly, produce this result. Take, for example, the following: Εἰς ὕπνον καταπεσόντων—"Having fallen *into* sleep" (*Clem. Rom.*)—not *unto*, nor *for*, sleep. Παραπεσοῦσα εἰς μέθην—"The feast passing *into*, not *unto*, nor *for*, drunkenness." (*Clem. Alex.*) Εἰς ἀναισθησίαν ὑποφερομένη—"Carrying down *into*, not *unto*, nor *for*, insensibility." (*Clem. Alex.*) "In novam legem inducti sunt. In Evangelium inducti sunt. Inducted *into*, not unto, nor for, the new law," &c. (*Ambrose.*)

Because another translation than *into* may make good sense, or declare a true sentiment, gives no sufficient proof that it is accordant with the form of the phraseology, or is reached by the route which the phraseology suggests. These figurative phrases are founded in literal use. Καταποντισθῆναι εἰς θαλάσσαν—"To be swallowed down *into* the sea, not *unto*, nor *for*, the sea." (*Clem. Alex.*) "Emergere in lucem—to emerge *into*, not *unto*, nor *for*, the light." (*Tertull.*)

In every case of baptism, the baptized object passes *out of* one position or condition, and passes *into* another. Sometimes both of these (always implied) are expressly stated—

ἐκ σωφροσύνης εἰς πορνείαν βαπτίζουσι—"They baptize *out of* temperance *into* fornication." (*Clem. Alex.*) So, literally, *μετάξεις ἐκ τόπου εἰς τόπον*—"You may lead our bodies *out of* one place *into* another place." (*Clem. Alex.*)

These quotations are sufficient to bring into view the fact, that the translation contended for rests on established usage in kindred phrases, as also in the nature of things. Unnecessary departure from this usage and requirement is without apology.

3. Because the laws of language require, that in the transference of words from literal to ideal relations, verbally correspondent, for the purpose of deducing a new sentiment from these new relations, the words must be used, individually, in their ordinary signification; the thought being evolved from the incongruous combination.

In such phrases—as dipping *into* mathematics; wallowing *in* vice; petrified *with* horror; troubles rolling *over* us; rising *to* the occasion; sinking *unto* despair—there is verbal figure; that is to say, the phraseology presents the figure or form of a literal transaction. Each word, also, presents itself in its own, and not in a borrowed character. Interpreting on this basis, we soon encounter "a fault;" dipping will not carry us "into" *mathematics;* incongruous materials have been brought together, and are insusceptible of adjustment without some modification. Where shall it be made? Let us resolve the phrase into its elements, and examine them separately. "Dip into" group together, and "mathematics" stands alone. Can this word be modified? It cannot be changed into *geography*, or *grammar*, or *philosophy*, for this would not modify the statement, but convert it into something wholly diverse. But cannot it be imagined to be water, or oil, or milk, or soft clay? Not rationally; "dipping into" any of these things would throw no light on dipping into *mathematics;* such imaginations would be labor lost; you must convert them back again into the reality. But would it not help to solve the meaning of such associations of words? Not at all; "mathematics" (or whatever else in like phraseological combinations may take its place) is a fixed quantity; it allows of no modification; and, because it does not, we are struck with the incongruous materials brought together, and we seek for explanation in the other member of the phrase.

And, here, in "dip into," we find an every-day acquaintance, belonging to the water, or other easily penetrable substance, to which we, thus, have ready access without any metamorphosis of "mathematics." Understanding the function of "dip" to be to place its object, by a slight force, for a slight period of time, slightly beneath the surface, we now reject the idea of the fluid element and the form of action, as not suited to the case, and carry back "dip into" to its novel relation, cheerfully assuming the character—*to engage slightly in;* and, in this new character, "mathematics" promptly affiliates with this verb, and its satellitic preposition. The form of verbal figure remains, and, through that form, the meaning may be traced by the uninformed of every generation; but to say that I must go through this process every time I meet with such a phrase, is to talk most irrationally; the meaning being once established, it becomes the meaning of the phrase, and thenceforth gives direct expression to the thought. The members are no longer *disjecta membra*, but established in organic union with a newly developed life. And it is the freshness of this new life, like the sparkle of newly opened wine, which gives the figure its power, and leads Carson to say, "the first use of the figure is the best."

All the other phrases are to be expounded in a similar manner. "Vice" is not, by the force of imagination, to be converted into a *mudhole;* but from the associate member, through its physical relations, we adduce the idea of a *bestial practice* of vice. "Horror" is not to be changed by the force of imagination into a liquid *holding some mineral in solution*, but from "petrify," in physics, we eliminate the idea of "*incapacity to use our faculties*." It is at war with our consciousness, and with the laws of mind, to suppose that familiar combinations of this character are, or can be, treated as unknown quantities needing to be resolved and reduced to an intelligible proposition every time they are met with.

When Josephus associates together "baptize (merse) into," and "insensibility and sleep," he brings together incongruous materials, quite insusceptible of combination under a literal interpretation of individual words. But it is to be presumed that Josephus writes rationally; and that there was a rational combination of these materials in his mind. Seeking to discover what this was, we find the phrase made up of a variable and a fixed element. "Insensibility and sleep" are fixed quantities in their own nature, and must remain as they are, or the life of the passage perish. "Baptize (merse) into" is a variable quantity: 1. As to form of action; 2. As to the nature of the enclosing element; 3. As to the character of its objects; 4. As to influences consequent. Here is a wide field from which to select, or out of which to construct some modifying element. In seeking for such element we are led to reject, 1. Any definite form of action; 2. To reject the idea of intusposition, (1), because it is impossible to apply it actually; (2) because it is just as impossible to conceive of it imaginatively; (3) because intusposition in any liquid would be destructive to a human being; therefore the historian did not conceive of Gedaliah as put within either "insensibility or sleep" conceived of as liquids; (4) because any such conception is as unnecessary as it is inconsistent with the nature of things.

But while we reject intusposition as inapplicable in any form to "insensibility and sleep," we accept it as inherent in the phrase "baptize (merse) into," and we look on while it executes its functions upon a *flint rock*, and we say, that will not answer; here is intusposition without influence, but the relations in the passage exhibit influence without intusposition. We look on upon a second baptism, and witness a *ship and crew* go down into the sea. Here is both intusposition and influence, yet it is not the kind of influence; this is destructive, that of the passage is not. We become spectators of a third baptism, that of a porous body put into oil and remaining there for an indefinite period; when brought out it is neither like the "flint," impervious and uninfluenced; nor like "the ship and crew," destroyed; but it is penetrated and pervaded and brought thoroughly under the peculiar oily character of the material within which it has been placed. We have, at last, what the passage demands; rejecting the means by which the result has been secured (intusposition), as having no footing in the case, we have left *controlling influence*, which meets all the exigencies of the passage, rendering its elements congruous and its sentiment appropriate.

From all which we draw these conclusions: 1. Βαπτίζω εἰς, when used in relations not admitting of intusposition, but of influence, drops the former idea and expresses directly the idea of *controlling influence.* 2. Intusposition is limited to the verb and its preposition, and is to be applied (1) To their physical relations, that out of it may be extracted the thought demanded by the passage; and (2) As suggesting, by their verbal form and present relations, the source and character of the developed influence. 3. The conversion of these terms, expressive of influence endlessly varied, into one imaginary fluid, is absurd, because one fluid could not express varied influences; to convert them into diverse fluids is no less absurd, because no fluids could express the distinctive character of the influences. 4. The term expressive of the source and nature of the influence to be expressed, must remain without change. Its duty is exhausted when, at the demand of βαπτίζω εἰς, it communicates its distinctive influence in all the fulness of its power.

When Gedaliah was "baptized (mersed) into insensibility and sleep," he was, according to the legitimate and only rational interpretation of the verbal figure, *brought under the controlling influence of insensibility and sleep.*

4. *Why employ verbal figure?* Not merely, or mainly, for rhetorical embellishment, but to limit, and define with precision, the thought intended to be conveyed. Βαπτίζω expresses, definitely, the condition of intusposition; but the effects of intusposition are various, and it cannot express these influences distinctively; it takes, therefore, secondarily, that which is common to all these influences, namely, *con-*

trolling power. When the word is used in this sense, it takes its coloring from its adjunct. Sometimes, as already stated, this is single and invariable, (as in the direct influence of wine,) in which case it becomes the absolute measure and representative of that particular influence. But where diverse influences proceed from the same source, it is not sufficiently explicit to speak of a baptism from that source while wishing to express some one of its influences. This can only be done by express statement, which will take the form in the passage under consideration—verbal figure—εἰς being employed, with the proper word, to denote the source and specific character of the influence desired. Thus, while the influence of *wine* is specific, that of *drunkenness* is diversified. It may baptize into shame, or poverty, or crime, or many other things. Josephus wished to express a specific result of this baptism; therefore, he says, not merely, "baptized by drunkenness," but "baptized by drunkenness into *insensibility* and *sleep*." The passage is important as being rare in its form, (never met with in the classics,) and now first appearing. It is, also, eminently instructive, throwing its light both backward and forward, along the path of this inquiry. We shall meet with it again, under noticeable circumstances, before we get through. It expresses influence in the most specific manner and in the most perfect measure.

CEREMONIAL PURIFICATION.

BAPTISM BY SPRINKLING HEIFER ASHES.

Τοὺς οὖν ἀπὸ νεκροῦ μεμιασμένους, τῆς τέφρας ὀλίγον εἰς πηγὴν ἐνιέντες καὶ ὕσσωπον, βαπτίσαντες τε καὶ τῆς τέφρας ταύτης εἰς πηγὴν, ἔρραινον τρίτῃ καὶ ἑβδόμῃ τῶν ἡμερῶν. *Jewish Antiq.*, iv, 4.

"Those, therefore, defiled by a dead body, introducing a little of the ashes and hyssop-branch into a spring, and baptizing of this ashes (introduced) into the spring, they sprinkled both on the third and seventh of the days."

APPROPRIATION.

The ritual observance referred to in this extract, is described in the book of Numbers, chap. xix. "He that toucheth a dead body shall be unclean seven days. He shall purify himself with it (the heifer ashes) on the third day, and on the seventh day he shall be clean. . . . This is the law. . . . They shall take of the ashes of the burnt heifer of purification for sin, and running water shall be put thereto in a vessel: And a clean person shall take hyssop, and dip it in the water, and sprinkle it upon him that toucheth one dead. . . . But the man that shall be unclean, and shall not purify himself, that soul shall be cut off from the congregation, because the water of purification has not been sprinkled upon him; he is unclean."

Reference is made to this rite, as to its nature, purpose, and mode of performance, in Hebrews, 9:13. "For if . . . the ashes of a heifer, sprinkling the unclean, sanctifieth to the purifying of the flesh." . . .

The occasion which induced the historian to refer to the rite, was the purification of the people consequent upon the death of Miriam, sister of Moses. Philo, the Jew, quoted by President Beecher, also refers to this rite in the following language: "Moses does this philosophically, for most others are sprinkled with unmixed water, some with sea or river water, others with water drawn from the fountains. But Moses employed ashes for this purpose. Then, as to the manner, they put them into a vessel, pour on water, then moisten branches of hyssop with the mixture, then sprinkle it upon those who are to be purified."

These quotations from Moses, and Paul, and Philo, and Josephus, place this ordinance before us in all its characteristics, in the clearest manner. It is an ordinance which contemplates persons as being in a certain state, or condition, and proposes to take them out of that state, or condition, and to put them into another; or, to speak more definitely, it regards persons as being in a state of ceremonial defilement, and proposes to change that state by the application of a peculiar purifying influence, and so bring them into a state of ceremonial purity.

The elements, then, which claim attention are, 1. A state of ceremonial defilement; 2. A state of ceremonial purification; 3. Ashes, (mixed with spring-water as a vehicle,) the purifying agency; 4. Sprinkling, the mode of applying.

By the ordinance, possessed of such features, a baptism was effected, according to the declaration of Josephus, "baptizing them of ashes by sprinkling." The task before us is to harmonize the use of *baptize* with "ashes," (when no envelopment and consequent smothering takes place,) and with "sprinkling," with which it is said to be irreconcilable. The discussion, herein involved, demands, first of all, the determination of the fundamental character of the Greek word.

If this word does express "a definite act, dip, and nothing but dip, and has no other meaning through all Greek literature," then our task is ended before commenced; for no one, not moonstruck, would attempt to perform the act of *dipping* by the help of "ashes," or the modal act of dipping, by the alien modal act of sprinkling. If, however, this word is no more a word modally executive than darkness is light, but demands for its object *state*, or *condition*, characterized, primarily, by envelopment, subject to development under the laws of language, and modification under the exigencies of usage, like all other words, then, it will hardly be regarded as proof of hopeless lunacy to attempt to show, that a man *brought into a thoroughly changed state* by the sprinkling of ashes-water, may be called a "baptized" man.

The true import of this word has been discussed, at large, in Classic Baptism. For the conclusions there reached, so far as they are my own, I ask no deference to be paid by any Baptist scholar; but inasmuch as many of the first scholars of the country have made these conclusions their own, by a cordial approval, I feel bound to affirm their judgment, and to say, that *it is a settled point*, that βαπτίζω does not belong to the class of verbs which expresses modal action, but to the class of verbs making demand for *state*, or *condition*.

It has been shown that the characteristic state, or condition, secured for its object by βαπτίζω, was one calculated to exert over such object the most thorough, penetrating, pervading, and controlling influence; and that, as a matter of fact, it did (exceptional cases aside) exert such influence.

It has been shown that these resultant influences varied greatly in their character, according to the nature of the object and of the investing element, while they retained the common feature as to the measure of influence, namely, *controlling* power.

It has, also, been shown, and it is a vital point, determining the whole usage of the word, that to this state, or condition induced, there is no limitation of time; the object may be taken out of such condition, but only by a force counteracting and overcoming the work of βαπτίζω.

Such are the outstanding features in the physical history of this word.

To bring this word of great power, of wide range, and of facile adaptation, out of the world of physics, and to introduce it into the wider realm of metaphysics—of mind and morals—as applicable to the many and varied cases of controlling influence there to be met with, required only an extension of the manner in which the influence should be exerted. That is to say, when the intellectual or moral condition of persons or things was to be changed by any influence competent to exert a controlling power, but not adapted to influence through envelopment, or the object not adapted to receive influence through such method of operation, then such change of condition, however effected, should be equally expressed by that same word which, in physics, expressed thorough change of condition, through envelopment. Baptist writers do not deny the extension of the word beyond physics; but they say the meaning of the word remains unchanged.

The domain of error is a wide one, and furnishes many roads along which its subjects may travel. Our Baptist friends having laid down a principle, rather to burden others than to govern themselves, show neither agreement nor consistency in maintaining it. Those who insist that the word means modal act should, in obedience to their principle, carry a *dipping* through all the metaphysical usage of the word. Dr. Carson attempts it; but even his courage fails, and after appealing, most unreasonably, to figure for aid, gives up, times without number, and asks, "Is not the resemblance between *the effects?*" Those who insist on modal act, (but inconsistently allow of half a dozen,) run through the catalogue, dipping, plunging, sinking, whelming, submerging, and overwhelming, mind and spirit; yet all will not do; they, too, have to fall back on *results*, to the abandonment of *acts*. Some, in their extremity, when hard pressed summon "intusposition" to their aid; but if the word is expressive of an *act*, it is not expressive of intusposition,—a condition; and an appeal to this, is abandonment of "one meaning" alike in physics and in metaphysics. Nor am I alone in making this affirmation. Hear the language of a tried friend: "The baptism" (dipping) "and the state that follows have no necessary connection." (*Carson*, p. 287.)

"Nothing can exceed the absurdity of supposing that the word should designate both the immersion," (*dipping*, in Dr. C.'s vocabulary,) "and the state after immersion." (*Carson*, p. 283.) Baptists, then, must make their choice (their great controversialist being judge,) between act and state; but if they choose "act" for physics, and insist on the same meaning (only in figure), through all metaphysical usage, they must not slip in "absurdity," *state*, to help them out of a dilemma. If they choose "state," then they must abandon "act," as also the theory on which they have builded up their system, and reconstruct it after another model.

From the utter failure of Baptist writers to carry "the same meaning" from physical to metaphysical relations (when the life of their most cherished theory depended on its being done), we may draw the conclusion, that the demand that this should be done is a false and impracticable one.

We doing avowedly and of free will what they do covertly and compulsorily, occupy the vantage-ground of harmony with the laws of language-development, generally, and in the most eminent manner, with that closely related word βάπτω, which expressing originally *dipping*, (with coloring as a result,) subsequently expresses *coloring* without the dipping.

So, βαπτίζω, originally expressing in physics, intusposition (having influence as a result); passing into another realm, where intusposition has no place, expresses change of condition from influence without the intusposition. Therefore, in the application of this word to mental and moral relations, we say, that the idea of a condition unlimited as to duration and controlling influence, is retained, while the form of that condition, causative of controlling influence, is dropped: 1. Because there is no possibility for it as a reality; 2. Because the imagination must fail in its efforts to invest with any suitable medium, and would only perpetrate a great folly if it could; 3. Because the conceit which would invest spiritual objects with physical elements, in order to exhibit influence exerted over them, is an absurdity.

With this general idea of the meaning of the word, and of the method by which that meaning is reached, it becomes our duty to show that the word is used in such meaning in the passage before us.

Translation.—"Baptizing of (by) this ashes (introduced) into the spring, they sprinkled (the defiled)."

"Baptizing," denotes here, as everywhere, the bringing into a new state or condition, which may be with or without intusposition. In this case without intusposition. The object has been in a state of ceremonial impurity; it is brought into a state of ceremonial purity. This translation agrees with our definition, is indicated by more than a score of cases in Classic Baptism, is in full sympathy with the scope of the passage, accords with the grammatical structure, and is demanded by the exigency of the case.

"Ashes" constitute the instrumental agency of the baptism. Ashes are capable of constituting a physical envelopment, as Herculaneum and Pompeii abundantly testify; but what then? Does the passage require or allow of such envelopment? Just as much as many other envelopments which we are called upon to tax our imaginations to picture. Wine baptizes, and wine is capable of enveloping as well as water; but does wine, where it effects a drunken baptism, envelop its object? Is it not absurd to conceive of it as so doing, inasmuch as it would destroy the baptism contemplated, and effect another, wholly different,—a drowning baptism? Wine envelopment (as in the case of the Duke of Clarence), kills; and ashes envelopment (as in the case of Pompeii), kills. Wine drank, baptizes by bringing into a condition of intoxication. Heifer ashes sprinkled, baptize by bringing into a condition of purification.

Ashes are as competent to baptize, all Greek writers bearing witness, as are the mountain billows of the ocean. The nature of the baptisms differ; but so do baptisms of "armor in marshes," of "a bag of salt" in water, and of a man who swallows "an opiate." If it will give any aid or comfort to friends of "the theory," they are welcome to bring imagination into full play, and to "figure" these falling drops of the watery mixture, into the peltings of a storm, or the rushing of a torrent, or the dashing of bursting billows, and so form, according to the established mode, a well-approved "whelming;" only, after this play of ideality, come back to the sober confession, that heifer ashes do baptize. "Whatever influence is capable of thoroughly changing the character, state, or condition of an object, controlling and conforming it to its own characteristics, is capable of baptizing that object." (Classic Baptism, p. 354.) Heifer ashes are capable of effecting such change in the condition of a ceremonially unclean man, and is, therefore, capable of baptizing such man.

"Sprinkling" this ashes is as competent to baptize into ceremonial purity, as *drinking* wine is capable of baptizing into drunkenness, or *eating* opium into sleep, or the falls of Niagara into their seething depths. The right arm of Baptist argumentation against "sprinkling," is, here, broken. We know nothing of "one definite *act*," or "many definite *acts*," or "some general *act*;" we make demand for *condition*, and, by that badge, as the servitors of *βαπτίζω*, every act, modal or immodal, few or many, as well as sweeping torrents, falling billows, rising floods, sprinkling drops, in short, whatever is capable of *thoroughly changing condition.*

The amount of influence which shall belong to this baptizing agency, and the form through which that influence shall find development, belong solely to the will of Him who has established the rite. Under his appointment "sprinkling" is as competent and as every way adapted, to exhaust the divinely ordained influence, and convey it to the defiled object, and to change its condition by accomplishing the most thorough purification, as any other conceivable mode.

Ashes, then, are the baptizing agency, the sole agency; the spring-water was not used as an auxiliary in effecting the baptism, but merely as a vehicle for the transmission of the ashes; Philo, and Josephus, and Paul, speak of nothing but "the ashes." *Sprinkling* is the mode through which, by divine appointment, the baptizing agency operates. And *ceremonial purification* is the changed condition, state, baptism, accomplished.

I only add here another remark. The use of βαπτίζω to develop and express the power of these sprinkled heifer ashes, places it in a relation so identical in its features with that which it occupies when expounding the power of wine-drinking, that the influence exerted over the word must be the same in both cases. Each of these agencies exerts a specific influence, also, a single, invariable, and controlling influence; now, when, βαπτίζω is employed to express the changed condition effected by wine-drinking, (which condition was of frequent occurrence and invariably the same,) it could not be without a miracle, but that it must become identified with the specialty of that condition, and secure the meaning,—*to make drunk.* In like manner, used to expound the changed condition effected by this purifying rite,—specific in its character, and frequent in its occurrence,—a miracle, only, could prevent its absorbing that peculiarity, and expressing directly,—*to make ceremonially pure.*

Thus these two meanings, *to make drunk* and *to make pure*, so widely diverse in their nature, would, as legitimately as certainly, attach themselves to this word in these varying spheres of usage.

FRIENDS OF "THE THEORY" NOT SATISFIED.

Unimpeachable as this exposition may appear, it would be strange if it should be acceptable to the friends of the Baptist theory. Its acceptance would as hopelessly baptize their system, as the departure of Josephus would have baptized Jotapata, and with the same kind of ruinous baptism.

Let us look at their objections.

1. *As to the text.* It is said to be corrupted. Bonfrer suggests the omission of, τε καὶ τῆς τέφρας ταύτης εἰς πηγήν. This suggestion is accepted by Bekker and the text of his edition made to conform to it. Dr. Conant, also, adopts this reading. Hudson, Principal of St. Mary's Hall, Oxford, and a critical editor of Josephus, refers to this criticism, but retains the passage. He farther states, that some copies have μετά after βαπτίσαντες. The ground of this supposed corruption, as stated, is, "the evident repetition of some words." But where a good reason exists for the repetition of words, there is no just ground furnished for the notion of corruption. Any appearance of such words not being needed may arise from a misconception of the passage.

The reading alluded to by Hudson is opposed to the idea of any needed omission. A proper translation may relieve the passage of any apparent incumbrance. The introduction of ταύτης, shows not mere repetition, but gives proof of design. This textual difficulty brings to mind another case of embarrassment, in which relief was sought by complaint of the text. I refer to the passage in Plutarch, Life of Alexander, lxvii, in which the drunken revelry of the army is described. (Classic Baptism, p. 335.) Du Soul, under the idea that a dipping must be got out of βαπτίζω, questions the reading,—βαπτίζοντες ἐκ πίθων; but it would have been better, in view of the syntax, to have questioned the correctness of the meaning attached to the word. Coray proposes to let the text stand and to interpret by the help of figure. The construction of the two passages is similar,—the verb with the genitive. It would be not a little remarkable under these circumstances, that the text, both of Plutarch and Josephus, should have been corrupted and after precisely the same style. The baptizing influence proceeds out of the wine in the one case, and out of the ashes in the other case.

The evidence for corruption, certainly, is not very impressive.

Punctuation.—But fault is found not merely with the words of the passage, but, also, with the punctuation. Carson (p. 288–9) says, "The punctuation of Josephus is evidently wrong. . . The comma ought to be before *hyssop.*" He translates, "Having cast a little of the ashes into the fountain, and having *dipped* a branch of hyssop and also a little of the same ashes into," &c. Having denied that ενιέντες could immerse (dip) the ashes, both because of its own nature, being a "generic term," and because of the nature of ashes, which "cast" into water floats on the surface; and having translated βαπτίσαντες dipping, according to the demand of theory, (notwithstanding that "ashes floats on the surface,") he makes provision to help this latter word to do what the other could not do (dip ashes), by putting them, first, "into a bag, as in cookery." Surely this "dipping" is a thorny road to travel. First, it denies the laws of language-development; then, it fills Greek literature with imaginary dippings and whelmings, torrents and floods; then, it affirms corruption of text; then, errors of punctuation; and, last of all, requires the manufacture of a bag to be filled with ashes, in order that it may be dipped, like a pudding in cookery! Could any testimony be more conclusive that there is no dipping in the case, than the necessity for resorting to such a method in order to secure its introduction? But not only does this passage, in particular, reject a dipping, but there is no authority, in the general usage of the word, for transmuting βαπτίζω into βάπτω. The word and the construction alike protest against such an abuse. It puts, most lawlessly, words and syntax to the rack. The received text and punctuation may stand, unaltered, under a proper conception and translation of the passage.

Translation.—While Carson retains the common text, and runs into the extravagances just indicated, Conant adopts the modification proposed, and, by an altered punctuation, unites grammatically, ὕσσωπον βαπτίσαντες, dipping the hyssop-branch. Provision has been already made for putting the hyssop into the ashes-water; therefore, this new arrangement is uncalled for. There is no authority, but it is against all authority, to make βαπτίζω perform the office of a dipper either of wine-cups or of hyssop-branches. Besides, it is an axiom with all Baptists, that a baptized object must be wholly covered; but there is no evidence, and it is contrary to reason and the use to which it was to be put, to suppose that this branch was put into, so as to be wholly covered by the mixture, whether made in a vessel, as stated by the Scriptures, or in a spring, as supposed to be stated by Josephus. The translation—"Introducing a little of the ashes and the hyssop into spring-water, then baptizing (purifying) by this ashes (put) into spring-water, they sprinkled the defiled"—not only does not betray any excess of words, but those repeated words, standing in an entirely new relation and expressing a wholly different truth, do, and are used in order to, give fulness and precision to the explanation of the rite. The facts stated are, 1. The mixture of ashes and spring-water; 2. The dipping of a hyssop-branch into this mixture; 3. The purification of the people by the ashes, which imparted their virtue to the water; 4. The mode of applying the ashes to the people by sprinkling.

The very pith and point of the passage lies precisely in those very words which are to be "improved" out of the text. Josephus states that the purifying (baptizing) was "*by the ashes*." The very point on which Philo, as well as a greater than Philo or Josephus, even Paul himself, insists. It is "*the ashes* of a heifer sprinkling the unclean, which sanctifieth to the purifying of the flesh." (Heb. 9:13.) As to the translation of βαπτίζω, *to purify ceremonially*, let me again, most pointedly, state, that it is no nameless foundling brought forward for the nonce, to lay claim, under false pretences, to a heritage in which it has no right; but it is the offspring of lawful wedlock, with title to legitimacy running back through all Classic records, until, in deep antiquity, it meets the ancient βαπτίζω yet in his bachelor days. The genealogical tree is deposited in court and open to the examination of all comers.

If the view now presented be correct, there is deep significance in the words of Carson (p. 62): "The language of no writer can have more authority on this subject than that of Josephus. A Jew, who wrote in the Greek language in the apostolic age, must be the best judge of the meaning of Greek words employed by Jews in his own time." That sounds like the truth. And we are here introduced, by a competent witness, to the Jewish usage of βαπτίζω, by one who has shown himself to be the perfect master of its Classic usage through all its modifications. This witness testifies, that the Jews used βαπτίζω to express the *baptism* (purification) *by heifer ashes*, of defiled persons, by sprinkling it upon them, thus bringing them into *a state of ceremonial purification;* and excluding, most absolutely, all idea of a dipping or a covering. As a seal to this interpretation I close with the following quotation from Cyril of Alexandria on Isaiah 4 : 4, "βεβαπτίσμεθα μὲν γὰρ οὐκ ἐν ὕδατι γύμνῳ, ἀλλ' οὐδὲ σποδῷ δαμάλεως, *We have been* BAPTIZED not with bare water, nor yet BY THE ASHES OF A HEIFER."

This settles the attempt to "correct the text," by settling the sufficiency of heifer ashes to baptize. Inasmuch as there was not to be any Pompeii baptism (deadly suffocation under ashes sprinkled "long enough to cover"), there was no intusposition in this baptism; and as the only other baptism within the competency of these sprinkled ashes, was a baptism of ceremonial purification, we must even be satisfied with this, theories notwithstanding.

BAPTISM BY HEIFER ASHES.

Βαπτιζόμενος ἀπὸ νεκροῦ καὶ πάλιν ἁπτόμενος αὐτου, τί ὠφέλησεν τῷ λουτρῷ αὐτοῦ. *Sirach*, 34 : 30.

Being baptized from a dead body, and touching it again, what is he benefited by his cleansing?

Baptism from the Dead.

The phraseology of this passage differs, materially, from the preceding. It is, in itself considered, much less definite. The word βαπτίζω never declares the performance of any definite act, and not being limited to physical results, it cannot, alone, declare any definite result. The phrase βαπτιζόμενος ἀπὸ νεκροῦ cannot, without knowledge derived from other sources, convey any definite and complete idea. This is proved from the insuperable difficulty attending the interpretation of the phrase, βαπτιζόμενοι ὑπὲρ τῶν νεκρῶν (1 Cor. 15 : 28). The phrase not being self-explanatory, and the context not clearly indicating the bearing designed by the Apostle, and the possible interpretations being legion, no exposition has been given, or perhaps, can be given, which will command assent. The verbal resemblance to the passage before us is striking, and it is within the range of possibility, that both refer to the same thing; but this is not very probable. Clear knowledge outside of the passage, is now, perhaps, beyond our reach. This embarrassment, however, is eminently instructive. The Greek word, of itself, is dumb with silence to any inquiry as to its relations to physics or metaphysics; and as in both these relations it is controlled in specialties of form and effect, by things outside of itself, it is absolutely necessary, in the interpretation of any given case, to know, 1. In general, whether the baptism belongs to the real or the ideal. 2. And, in special, what is the baptizing agency or element. Without such knowledge no baptism can receive intelligent interpretation. But this baptism of the Son of Sirach presents no embarrassment, because, while his own language does not give the needful information, we can get it from other sources. By a comparison with Numbers xix, we learn that the baptism is connected with a particular rite for purification; by a reference to Josephus, (J. A. iv, 4,) we learn that the agency in this baptism was heifer ashes, and the mode of its use was sprinkling; by a reference to Josephus, (J. A. x, 9,) we farther learn, by analogy, that the verbal element of such baptism is καθαρισμόν; as drunkenness baptizes into a state of insensibility, so heifer ashes baptize into a state of ceremonial purity.

Thus we have all the materials requisite for the most precise determination of this baptism,—"being baptized from the defilement of a dead body," by heifer ashes, into a state of ceremonial purity.

As to the absolute use of βαπτίζω, (agency and element eliminated,) and the value to be attached to it in such use, we receive all needed information by turning to analogous cases. Such is that in Classic Baptism, p. 331,—"I am one of those yesterday baptized." Here, there is not a ray of light thrown on the nature of the baptism, beyond the fact that it was not destructive of life; with this limitation imagination may range *ad libitum* among pools, torrents, and floods, on the one hand, and states of insensibility, sleep, and purification, on the other. The context, however, clips these pinions by revealing a wine-influence—baptism into a state of drunkenness by wine-drinking—and, thus, we learn that the frequent use of this marked word, in connection with intoxication, rendered unnecessary the constant repetition of the verbal element, or the agency, but that both were absorbed in and expressed by the, now, enriched and pregnant word βαπτίζω,—"I was yesterday baptized=*made drunk.*" In like manner, under a similar condition of things, arising from the use of this word in this religious rite, it absorbs the verbal element, (purification,) and the baptizing agency, (heifer ashes,) and out of this fulness is enabled, in absolute use, to give a new utterance,—"being baptized=*made ceremonially pure* from a dead body."

Thus, in this abbreviated, absolute use, we have the most conclusive evidence for the familiar, long-continued, and well-understood use of βαπτίζω in connection with purifying rites, and coming to express directly, without any aid, the end of such rites, namely, *to make ceremonially pure.* This usage, and this its necessary result, is confirmed by the historical fact, that between the Son of Sirach and Josephus, was a period of some two hundred years, and between Josephus and Cyril of Alexandria, (who, as we have seen, employs the word in the same manner,) there is an interval of twice two hundred years. Familiar and long-continued usage made the word, without adjunct, plain.

The absorption of one or more phrases by a single word, which thenceforward becomes the representative and spokesman of all, is a common development of language. "He *drinks*," was once but a member of the sentence,—"He drinks *intoxicating liquors to drunkenness*," but, "to drunkenness" was first dropped as sufficiently expressed in,—"He drinks *intoxicating* liquors;" after a long familiarity with this abbreviation, it became possible to make farther abbreviation, and, "He *drinks*," became perfectly competent to express the whole sentence, and did, absolutely used, express,—*He makes himself drunk.*

When, therefore, we say that βαπτιζόμενος, in this passage is a pregnant word, has put on a new character, has attained a secondary meaning, we set up no new statute, but are overshadowed by the protecting and vindicating power of common law. It may be used alone="being purified," or with the cause of purification—"being purified by *heifer ashes*," or with the addition of the special cause of defilement—"being purified by heifer ashes from a dead body." In this there is no figure. Verbal figure would require a recasting of the phrase, thus: "being baptized (mersed) by heifer ashes, from a dead body into purification;" thus we return to primary signification, and "baptize (merse)" is employed to develop the full influence of "purification;" when "into purification" is dropped, "baptize" becomes impregnated with its influence, gives direct expression to it, and all appearance of figure has disappeared. "Words which must appear as tropical to a learner of a distant age, who acquires the language by the help of grammars and dictionaries, may have totally lost that appearance to the natives."

Λουτρῷ.

There is one feature of this passage which is not exhibited by that in Josephus. It is found in the introduction of *λουτρῷ*, in connection with this baptism. On the ground of the use of this word, and the appointment of a washing (Numbers, 19:19) subsequent to the purification by sprinkling "the water of separation," Baptist writers have claimed that there was a *dipping* in the rite, and that, on the ground of this feature, the word "baptize" is used to describe it by Josephus and others.

This position requires us to examine, 1. Whether there was any "dipping" in the law of the rite. 2. Whether there is any "dipping" in the word which originates this interpretation.

In answer to the first of these points, it may be declared, in the most unqualified manner, that *no dipping is required by the law of the rite.* There is none in the original text, nor is there any in the Septuagint translation. The English translation, "*bathe in* water," is greatly more limited in mode and measure of using the water, than is that of the Septuagint, *λούσεται ὕδατι*, (*wash with* water;) and in so far as it straitens, directly, or by implication, the manner of using the water, or gives definiteness to the quantity to be employed, it departs from the original. The evidence for this so utterly excludes all other view, that the friends of "the theory" do not, directly, deny it; but content themselves with saying, that "a washing" may be effected by a *dipping.* Suppose this to be true, of what avail is it to explain the presence of "baptize?" If a dipping may be a "washing;" the *act* of dipping can never be metamorphosed into the *state* of baptism. As there is no "dipping" in the Jewish law, so there is none in the allusions, by Jews, to the fulfilment of the law. Philo says nothing of "dipping" in speaking of the rite, but refers, exclusively, to the sprinkled ashes.

Josephus g ves no hint of a "dipping," but ascribes the

purification exclusively to the ashes sprinkled. Cyril, (not a Jew, but a student of the law,) says nothing of a "dipping." Must it not betoken great extremity when, under such circumstances, this modal act is attempted to be fastened on the rite, and not only so, but to subject all other features so absolutely as to subordinate them to itself, and obliterate the divinely appointed title, "*sprinkling* the water of separation," and substitute in its stead *dipping* into water, of a wholly different character? Can "the theory" carry its votaries any farther?

But, let us inquire more closely into this "washing." Was it any constituent, at all, in the purification from defilement contracted by "touching a dead body?" We say not: 1. Because the priest who prepared the ashes was required "to wash his clothes and flesh with water and be unclean till even." He had not touched the dead body. 2. He that burned the heifer was required "to wash his clothes and flesh with water and be unclean till the even." He had not touched the dead body. 3. He that gathered the ashes was required, "to wash his clothes and be unclean until the even." He had not touched the dead body. 4. He that sprinkled the water of separation was required "to wash his clothes, and he that toucheth the water of separation shall be unclean till even." Neither of these had touched the dead body. When, now, he who had touched a dead body, and had received the appointed means of purification, (the sprinkling of the ashes,) was subsequently required, (in common with all others who had been employed in preparing and dispensing, or accidentally touching this ashes,) "to wash his clothes and flesh," is it not most irrational to consider this as any element in "the purification *from a dead body*," since it was common to all others, with himself, who had not touched a dead body?

The truth is, that while "the water of separation" had the power "to purify from a dead body," yet in another aspect it had itself the power to make unclean; and therefore, while cleansing from one impurity, its very application made another, and wholly different, cleansing necessary.

That the sole cleansing power "from a dead body" belonged to the heifer ashes, is evident from Hebrews, 9:13, 14, "For if the blood of bulls and of goats, and the ashes of a heifer sprinkling the unclean, sanctifieth to the purifying of the flesh; how much more shall the blood of Christ . . . purge your conscience from dead works." The blood of sacrificial victims and the ashes of a blood-red heifer symbolized the blood of Christ; the one cleansed ceremonially and typically, the other cleansed spiritually and efficiently; neither required supplementary aid for the perfect accomplishment of their allotted functions. It is, then, an incidental washing, not pertaining to the purification effected by the sprinkling, which Baptist interpreters would introduce into the rite, giving to it a name which converts the law-appointed baptism by sprinkled ashes into a lawless dipping into water. Dr. Carson has but little countenance from the law and testimony for his translation,—"He that *dippeth* or *baptizeth* himself, because of a dead body, and toucheth it again, what availeth his *dipping* or *baptism?*" (p. 66.) He not only falls into the philological heresy which confounds "baptizing" and "dipping," but extends it to *λούω*, making it, by a double error, first a *dipping*, then a *baptism*.

If the view now presented be correct, all attempt to exclude the baptism as contained in and effected by the ashes, and to transfer it to the appended "washing," falls to the ground; because it was but a sequence to the purifying baptism by sprinkling, and not a part of the rite; it was something to be done after, and as a consequence of the baptism, and consequently can bear no part in its explanation.

Λουτρόν—dipping. But let us more particularly examine this word, which is said so distinctly to proclaim a dipping.

Dr. Gale says, "The Hebrew word expressing the washing required, 'always includes dipping, and never signifies less.'" Dr. Carson says, "The Greek word translating the Hebrew, requires an immersion of its object—complete covering by the fluid."

The rash and erroneous statements made, by those who should know better, touching vital points of this controversy, are most remarkable.

The statement by Gale, respecting the Hebrew word for washing, is without any adequate foundation. In many cases, the manner of washing is not indicated by circumstances, and the word itself, not expressing mode, we cannot have any certain knowledge in regard to the mode. Others are more explicit, either from the nature of the case, or from circumstances mentioned.

In Gen. 43 : 31, Joseph is said to have " washed his face," after weeping. If this was done by *dipping*, he was, most probably, the only one in Egypt who followed that mode of face washing. It is, indeed, possible to dip the face and thus wash it; and it is possible to dip the beard and *dye* it; but Dr. Carson thinks this so unreasonable, while not impossible, that he makes it a ground for affirming a secondary meaning of βάπτω. Here the improbability is just as great, and yet, to help on " the theory," we are asked to believe that an immodal verb has become modal, and forced the great ruler of Egypt *to dip* his face to wash off the tear-marks. This abuse in the interpretation of the word, is made more evident in the translation of the Septuagint, where it is represented by νίπτω; a word which Dr. Carson says, " does not mean *to dip*."

In Deut. 21 : 6, certain persons are directed to " wash their hands over the heifer." When we remember that Elisha " poured water on the hands of Elijah," and that here, too, the Septuagint translates by νίπτω, there is but little encouragement given to a " dipping." In 1 Kings 22 : 38, the armor of Ahab, after battle, being stained with blood, was washed. Is it so necessary and so universal a custom *to dip armor*, in order to wash blood off from it, that this modal act must be accepted without questioning?

When such cases are of every-day occurrence, why is it that Dr. Gale ventures to lay down such a proposition,—*this washing always includes dipping?*

Dr. Carson's claim, that the Greek word requires always, " an immersion "—" a complete covering " of the object—is not more accurate.

In Acts 9 : 37, the body of Dorcas, after death, was " washed and laid in an upper chamber." Was this a case of "immersion and complete covering?" In Acts 16 : 33, the jailor took Paul and Silas and "washed their stripes." If this was by "dipping," it may be put alongside of the dipping of Joseph's face; being modelled after the same manner of good sense, only on a larger scale. Origen, (iv, 241,) speaks of the bullock on the altar needing cleansing—δεόμενα λουτροῦ, which was done not by dipping, but by pouring, as we are expressly told.

To make good his position, Dr. C. refers to the use of this word in cases of bathing. This reference assumes, does not prove, that "bathing," in the times alluded to, was by immersion and complete covering. This assumption has no better foundation than many others which form corner-stones to "the theory."

There are some bold and unquestionable facts in this direction, which, both because of present and general bearing, demand distinct presentation.

Few persons, since the fall of man, have equalled Dr. Carson in self-confidence. When such men err they err prodigiously and persistently; for nobody is good enough to teach them. "If the angel Gabriel" were to differ from them, they would, (as this wise and learned Doctor says he would,) "send him to school," where they taught the primer and held the birch. Some of these errors of Dr. C. have been already pointed out, others remain to be indicated.

In discussion with President Beecher, this writer had affirmed that "λούω, like our word bathe, applied to animal bodies only." This position, having been refuted by an amount of evidence which could not be gainsayed, was withdrawn, and this new position taken,—"But none of the examples prove that the thing so washed was not *covered with the water;* this is all we want."

Everything cannot be disproved at once. And when Baptist writers flee from their present falling house, to some other refuge, and cry, "But you have not shaken down this," we can only answer, Get fixed in your new quarters and wait your turn.

This Greek verb Carson has translated, in the same passage, *dip*, and *bathe*, and *wash*, and *immerse*, and now exults in there being, at all events, "a covering with water, which is all we want." This position must take its turn, and bide the decision of a court of last resort.

The challenge thrown out is this: "All cases of bathing described by this word (λοῦω) among Greeks and Scythians, Egyptians and Indians, were cases of bathing by immersion."

In testing the defensive merits of this new position, we present, first, the following extract from Professor Wilson, occupying the Chair of Biblical Literature, Belfast, Ireland, contained in his work on Baptism (pp. 156–168): "In the age of Homer, the vessel for bathing went by the name of ἀσαμίνθος, and among Greeks, of a somewhat later age, it was called πύελος. Dr. W. Smith, in his Dictionary of Greek and Roman Antiquities, in the article on *Baths*, presents us with the following clear and important statement respecting the mode of using the ἀσαμίνθος: 'It would appear, from the description of the bath administered to Ulysses in the palace of Circe, that this vessel *did not contain water itself*, but was only used for the bather to sit in while the warm *water was poured over him*, which was heated in a large caldron or tripod, under which the fire was placed, and when sufficiently warmed was taken out in other vessels, and poured over the head and shoulders of the person who sat in the ἀσαμίνθος.' From this pregnant instance the advocate for dipping may learn an instructive lesson. It is no proof of immersion, that a party is represented as *going into* the bath, and *coming out of* the bath.

"In the case of Ulysses, the descent and the ascent are both distinctly recorded; while the author expressly informs us, that the ablution was performed by *pouring* or *affusion*, and not by immersion. This testimony must tell on every discerning mind. Dr. Smith farther says: 'On ancient vases, on which persons are represented bathing, *we never find anything corresponding to a modern bath, in which persons can stand or sit;* but there is always a round or oval basin, resting on a stand, by the side of which those who are bathing are represented standing undressed, and washing themselves.'

"This was one of the ordinary public baths of Greece. Where is the 'immersion?' These basins were called λουτῆρες, as also similar basins at the porticos of Christian churches, in the earlier centuries, for washing the hands.

"It is not, then, a matter of fact, though Dr. Carson has stated it in strong and unequivocal terms, 'that *immersion* is almost always the way of *bathing*.' It may be so in our own age and country, and if this furnished the standard of comparison, no doubt his cause would be triumphant. But, in regard to the baths of the ancient Greeks, his statement utterly fails, and, failing in that quarter, it is nothing to his purpose.

"The common practice of Greece is incidentally, but very strikingly, referred to by Plutarch, in his Ethical Treatise against Colotes. After stating that you may see some persons using the warm-bath, others the cold, he adds: 'Οι μέν γαρ ψυχρὸν όι δὲ θερμον ἐπιβάλλειν κελεύουσι: 'For some give orders to apply it cold, others hot.' The force of ἐπιβάλλειν strongly corroborates the views which we advocate, and indeed constitutes an independent attestation. The value of this testimony is greatly enhanced by its exact correspondence with the representations on the Greek vases. The ordinary system of bathing in ancient Greece *knew no immersion*, and *embraced no covering of the body with water.*

"Among the paintings in an ancient tomb at Thebes is one containing a representation of a lady enjoying the luxury of a bath, and attended by four domestic servants. This precious relic of former art is thus described by Sir J. Gardner Wilkinson, in his elaborate work on The Manners and Customs of the Ancient Egyptians, iii, 338: 'One attendant removes the jewelry and clothes she has taken off, or suspends them to a stand in the apartment; another *pours water from a vase over her head*, as the third rubs her arms and body with her open hands; and a fourth, seated near her, holds a sweet-scented flower to her nose, and supports her as she sits (on a carpet or mat).'

"'The same subject,' Wilkinson adds, 'is treated nearly in the same manner, on some of the Greek vases, *the water being poured over the bather*, who kneels or is seated on the ground.' The mode of bathing in Egypt is thus identified with that of ancient Greece. This course of research will convince those who prosecute it, that their understandings are trifled with, and that speech is abused, when *pouring water on the bather*, the mode practised in the public baths of Greece, is referred to merely as a *possible* way of bathing."

How evidently and how fatally these *facts* penetrate the centre of the "new position" needs no supplementary words to indicate. The evidence, however, might be much extended, did it not seem like inviting the remark,—"And thrice he slew the slain." Still, one more fact, developing, in the most unmistakable and instructive manner, the mode of bathing by a people widely separated, geographically, from those hitherto spoken of, may be adduced. Facts, like diamond points, will make their mark when all else fails. Dr. Carson refers to the bathing of the East Indians as supporting an "immersion" bath. The following statement of fact by the Rev. Mr. Löwenthal, missionary in India, is conclusive, in more than one direction, against unqualified assertions based on absolute assumptions. This missionary (eminent for talent, learning, and devotion, murdered at his post) says,—"The Hindoos use a small urn, called *lota*, with which they bathe at the river, *pouring water over the body*." How often have we been told, that when a man "goes to a river," to bathe or to baptize, idiocy only could deny that he must go for an "immersion." And yet here is the practice of a people (appealed to for the purpose of sustaining an immersion bath) who do not only bathe by "pouring water over the body," like Greeks and Egyptians, but who "*go to the river*" for this purpose, taking up the water by means of a "small urn." Assertions and assumptions should have a very small place in controversial writings. Having no knowledge of the Sanscrit, I rely upon others, when I say, *Allava*, in that language, means *to bathe, to wash*. *Lota*, the vessel used in bathing, would seem to stand in the same relation to *allava* as λουτήρ to λούω, and laver to lave (*lavo*); and that *lota*, λουτήρ, and *laver* were vessels not for bathing in, but for holding the water with which, when poured out or drawn out, the bathing or washing might be effected.

The Septuagint uses the term λουτήρ for the brazen laver placed in the tabernacle for ritual purification. There was no immersion in this laver. It contained water with which, when drawn out, the hands and feet of the priests were washed; thus fulfilling the same office as the λουτήρ of the Grecian baths, from which water was taken to be poured over the bathers, as also that of the "lota" of the Hindoos. The Scripture direction is,—"Aaron and his sons shall wash their hands and their feet, with water, out of it"—Καὶ νίψεται Ἀαρὼν καὶ οἱ υἱοι αὐτοῦ ἐξ αὐτοῦ τὰς χεῖρας, καὶ τοὺς πόδας ὕδατι. (Exod. 30:19.)

I add but one more fact on this subject of Indian bathing. The Rev. Charles Stewart, chaplain U. S. N., (who was on board the man-of-war appointed to convey back to their country the Japanese ambassadors to the United States government,) states, that the mode of bathing by these ambassadors, on board the ship, was by having water taken out of a small vessel, and *spirted* over them by an attendant, while they were seated on the floor.

The fixedness of Eastern customs carries these modes of bathing, on the river-bank and in mid-ocean, by "pouring" and by "spirting," far back to the ages of Grecian vases, and Egyptian paintings, and Mosaic institutions.

If ever a crushing blow was delivered, such facts go right through the assertion, that λούω, λουτρόν, *washing*, *bathing*, require the "immersion or the complete covering" of the object.

Cleansing.—But we may go farther and say, λούω is used when water is not employed at all, or not employed to effect any physical washing; the effect contemplated being one cleansing in its nature.

It is thus used both in the Septuagint and New Testament. When Isaiah says, "Wash (λούω) you, make you clean, put away the evil of your doings, cease to do evil, learn to do well," he issues no command for the use of water, much less for its modal use by "immersion, complete covering." He contemplates a result (cleansing), and the mode for its accomplishment he expressly states, "cease to do evil, learn to do well." If, after being thus cleansed, they should return to their evil-doing, the prophet might well ask, in the language of the Son of Sirach, "Of what profit was your cleansing or 'washing?'"

In the New Testament, the redeemed are said to be "washed" (λούω) by the blood of the crucified Saviour. The only definite mode in which Christ's blood is represented as applied to his people is that of *sprinkling*, the same as that in which the typical ashes were applied. Now, the least particle of these ashes had all the cleansing power belonging to the entire mass. The same is true of the blood of the slain Lamb. This great truth (antagonistic to the notion of a greater good in quantity) is implied in the mode of use employed—by "sprinkling."

Inasmuch as these sprinklings were competent to produce the most absolute cleansing, (ceremonial and typical in the one case, spiritual and real in the other,) there is the most entire propriety in representing such sprinklings as washings=*thorough cleansings.* And if the sprinkling of the blood of Christ is spoken of as a "washing," why not the typical sprinkling of the ashes, also, be spoken of as a washing (λουτρῷ)? Is it not entirely gratuitous to disconnect this term from the purifying effect of the ashes, in order to bring in a sequent washing, having nothing to do with the distinctive purification of the rite? If λουτρῷ *may be* applied to the ashes purification, we say it *must not* be applied to anything else.

It is in proof that βαπτίζω refers to the state of purification induced not by water, but by ashes; and this being so, there is a logical necessity that λουτρῷ should refer to the same state of purification.

Dr. Carson endeavors to show, that "sprinkling" and "washing," as applied to the blood of Christ, denote two modes of its use; the one for sprinkling, and the other for *immersion.* But there is no ground whatever, in Scripture, for the idea that one soul is "immersed" in the blood of the Lamb, much less the universal church of all ages. There are few, outside of the theorists, who will not be intellectually and morally shocked in attempting to give embodiment to such a conception. If it were necessary, under such circumstances, to go to the literal application of the word, Dr. C. and his friends ought to know, right well, that the washing with water of a very limited part of the body was sufficient to purify the whole; and that touching with blood the tip of the ear, the thumb, and the toe, had efficacious cleansing power extending to the whole body, without "immersion" in blood. But it is not necessary to go back to the primary use of the word.

In such cases, the idea of cleansing is directly conveyed, without regard to the extent or the manner of application. The efficacy of the blood of Christ depends on neither quantity nor mode. And when the terms *sprinkle* and *wash* are applied to it, distinction of mode is not to be pressed, but that in which they agree, namely,—*power to cleanse.* "Washed by his blood,"—"blood of sprinkling," call our attention not to modes of operation, but to efficacious influence.

That λουτρῷ may be used, in the passage under consideration, as expressive of the result reached by *sprinkling*, is made certain by its use, with the purification of Ariantheus, by sprinkling, on his dying-bed, who, *thus*, was baptized "with the *bath*, *washing*, *cleansing*—λουτρῷ—of regeneration." (*Basil*, iv, 1001.) This death-bed sprinkling, Basil being witness, effected a "washing." The sprinkling of the blood of Christ effects a washing. The sprinkling of heifer ashes effected a washing in precisely the same general sense,—*a cleansing from impurity.* Now, shall we adopt this well-established interpretation, meeting all the features of the case, or shall we leave out the sprinkling and the ashes, (the alpha and the omega of the rite,) and introduce "immersion" and "bathing," (not a syllable for which can be found in the law,) on the ground that "superstition" may have introduced them (Carson)? Ambrose (ii, 1583) speaks of a washing, cleansing, ablution without water, indeed of water itself,—"*ablutæ per carnem Christi.*" If the "flesh" of Christ can wash, *ashes*, representing the blood of Christ, can "wash." And this "washing" is a *cleansing* from which water has disappeared, not only as to "covering," but in every other form.

Syntax.—The syntax of this passage is unusual and claims attention. Any essential change of syntax in the structure of a sentence is admitted to be evidence of some change of thought and of the meaning of words.

President Halley, of England, adduces the phrase δι τὴν πορφύραν βάπτοντες—"those dyeing the purple"—as conclusive evidence of a change of meaning in βάπτω. "The syntax is so varied as to make not the thing colored, but the color itself, the object of the verb; the secondary sense has renounced all dependence on the primary, and established itself by a new law of syntax, enacted by usage to secure its undisturbed possession."

Professor Wilson, of Belfast, after examining and rejecting the explanations of Gale and Carson on Daniel 4:30, ἀπὸ τῆς δρόσου—ἐβάφη, "wet from the dew," based on the primary meaning—*dip*, says: "The construction with ἀπὸ is inexplicable on the principle of a literal, primary interpretation. But if the verb, divorced from mode, takes the meaning *to wet*, then a literal exegesis is both practicable and natural."

Professor Stuart, of our country, quotes a similarly constructed passage from Leviticus 4:17, καὶ βάψει ὁ ἱερεὺς τὸν δάκτυλον ἀπὸ τοῦ αἵματος—"And the priest shall *moisten* or *smear over* his finger from the blood," as indicating, by its change of syntax, a change in the meaning of the verb.

Precisely the same syntactical form, as in the last two passages, occurs in the passage under consideration—βαπτιζόμενος ἀπὸ νεκροῦ, "being baptized from the dead;" there can be no translation of this passage, as it stands, on the basis of a *dip ping*, an *immersing*, or a *covering over;* but if we adopt that meaning which has been shown to be the legitimate production of the laws of language—*to make pure*—the translation is direct and facile, "*being purified* from a dead body." And just as "dye" and "wet" are the natural advance meanings of *dip*, so "to purify" is the natural advance meaning of βαπτίζω in religious rites.

Thus the result of language-development is sustained by modified form in the relation of words to meet modified meaning of words.

When we come to usage like this, we feel the necessity, in writings intended for general circulation, to introduce a second word in translation.

The Greeks employed βάπτω to denote *a dipping*, and also the far-off idea of *a bloodied face.* They reached this second meaning legitimately, but our language has not travelled in that direction, certainly not to that point, and probably never will; if, therefore, we wish to translate from the Greek anything respecting "a bloodied face," (or "bloodied finger,") we will use some other word than *dip*.

The Greeks also used βαπτίζω to express *to merse*, and also the far-removed idea *to make drunk*, reached, however, by methods most legitimate; but we have no such usage, and therefore, to be intelligible, must use a second word. The Jews used βαπτίζω, like the Greeks, in the sense *to merse*, and (by a development which the Greeks had not followed out, but on the same principles which they had followed to other issues) they used it to express the idea *to make ceremonially pure.* We have nothing to do with Jewish or any other ceremonial purity, and have no such meaning attached or readily attachable to the word, and, consequently, are under obligation to use another word, or introduce some *caveat* against misconception. The Jew would have been no less embarrassed, in speaking of the Duke of Wellington and of Nelson's *flag-ship*, by the same designation—ἀνὴρ πολεμιστής. Having such phrase rigidly fixed to express the warlike character of a David or a Goliah, and having no counterpart to the "Victory" and her thundering cannon, (any more than we have to Jewish defilements and ritual purifications,) they would not be likely to engraft upon their language by a literal translation, "man-of-war" for a fighting-ship, but would give it expression by some word or phrase in harmony with their own use of language.

In Classic Baptism, having represented the one Greek word βαπτίζω by the one word *merse*, (indicating, in other ways than by the translation, the differences of meaning, and pointing out their legitimate outgrowth from the radical idea,) I will no longer do violence to our very different language position by retaining always the same verbal form.

Feeling justified in believing that proof has been adduced that the Classic Baptism, *par eminence*, was a state of intoxication, and that, by like eminence, *a state of ceremonial purification* was Judaic Baptism, I shall feel at perfect liberty to translate and to speak accordingly.

Much attention has been given to this passage because of its importance, both direct and indirect. When it shall have been closely compared with the ritual law; with Josephus, Philo, and Cyril; with the usage of λούω in the Septuagint and New Testament; with the classical development of βαπτίζω; and when the absolute use of βαπτιζόμενος, and its peculiar syntax shall have been duly considered; I think that there will be few who will not admit it as proving, that the sprinkling of heifer ashes reveals the agency and the mode by which this baptism was effected, and that the resultant condition—*ceremonial purification, was* JUDAIC BAPTISM.

Abundant evidence confirmatory of this conclusion will be, hereafter, met with.

OLD TESTAMENT BAPTISMS.

PATRISTIC INTERPRETATION

OF

PASSAGES IN THE OLD TESTAMENT,

EXPOUNDED AS

JUDAIC BAPTISMS AND FIGURES OF CHRISTIAN BAPTISM,

SHOWING THEIR CONCEPTION OF

ΒΑΠΤΙΖΩ.

The passages taken from the Old Testament Scriptures, now about to be examined, do not, of course, exhibit the Greek word in the original (Hebrew) text; nor is this word often found in the Greek (Septuagint) translation. This, however, far from being a disadvantage, is a manifest advantage. The use of a word belonging to one language as the equivalent of a word in another language, or as expository of an idea resultant from many words, or as declarative of an effect accomplished by an act or combination of acts and influences, all sharply defined and well understood, leaves but little material to be desired for a proper understanding of such word.

The propriety and the value of such usage find their vindication in the employment by the inspired Apostle of *βαπτίζω* to describe the relation established between the Israelites and Moses by the miraculous passage of the Red Sea. In the Hebrew text there is no verbal form which is represented by the Greek—*εἰς τὸν Μωσῆν ἐβαπτίσαντο*; it is no translation, but an independent, authoritative statement or interpretation, which may or may not be found in the narrative by Moses.

But whether in the verbal record as originally made through the Holy Ghost, or not, it was in the transaction. The historical narrative of occurring events may be varied, but the events themselves cannot be changed. Paul's statement, if not found among the words of Moses, will be found among the facts of the transaction or their outwrought results. The record by Moses and by Paul has equally the stamp of divine authority. Justly expounded, the different forms of phraseology will give welcome and valuable aid in reaching the meaning of words, and a fuller understanding of the transaction. When Patristic writers, not professing to translate the Hebrew text, but to expound the nature of minutely described rites, or the results of historically detailed transactions, pronounce them *baptisms*, their statement has no divine authority, as has Paul's, but it has the highest human authority.

These writers had, unquestionably, a perfect knowledge of the Greek word, as classically used, as also of its capabilities for development, and the laws of the Greek language, under which such development should be made. Their authority for the use of a Greek word is as unimpeachable as is that of Homer or of Xenophon, so far as meaning and fitness of application are concerned.

The exposition of the Old Testament, in reference to baptism by Patrists, must be made from their own standpoint, as to the nature of Christian and Judaic Baptism; and, in interpreting their interpretation, we must occupy the same position. They may err in their understanding of the nature of these baptisms, but they cannot err in their understanding of the nature, abstractly, of a baptism.

When they say that the nature or value, intrinsic or relative, of Judaic Baptism, of John's Baptism, of Christian Baptism, was this or that, they may be right or wrong, and are subject to peremptory challenge; but when they say that a certain rite, by means of a drop of water falling from the finger's tip, effects a baptism; or, that the act by which the hand of the priest is laid upon the head, effects a baptism; or, that influence, proceeding from any source, without contact, effects a baptism, they are beyond impeachment from us. They are arbiters, without appeal, as to the capability of the word for such usage. Such use, is, in itself, a final decree in the case.

Again, when these writers declare of certain transactions, that they are "figures" of baptism, we are at liberty to question whether there was any such "figure" designed by the inspired writer; or we may question the soundness of judgment which finds such figure; or we may challenge on the ground of the abstract merits of the case; but it is beyond our province to raise a question as to the existence of resemblance to baptism, as it has become concrete in the minds of these writers. Whenever they put their finger upon a fact, or indicate a conception, and say "that resembles baptism," we have nothing to do but to accept such fact or conception as an image in the glass shadowing forth the reality in their minds. The great value of these "figures" and "images" is that they are fixed quantities, not like the ever-varying "figures"—trope, and metaphor, and hyperbole, and catachresis, and metonomy, and synecdoche—which wait, as an ever-ready band of servitors, upon the theory; nor like the pictures of "pools, and floods, and torrents," into which debtors and tax-payers are dipped, or by which ships and cities are whelmed. Such things may give exercise to the imagination, but will furnish very little satisfaction to thoughtful men, as introduced into this subject by Baptist writers.

If, in the examination of the many and varied appeals to "figure," by Patristic writers, we do not find one instance of "a dipping," one instance of "a torrent," one instance of "a covering over," as exhibiting a resemblance to baptism, but, on the contrary, find constant reference to resemblances in things which are as far removed from *dippings*, *whelmings*, *coverings*, as is the east removed from the west, what must we conclude to be the Patristic estimation of the theory which makes baptism "a dipping, and nothing but a dipping, through all Greek literature?"

If there were no other ruinous evidence against the dipping theory than that furnished by these Old Testament baptisms and figures of baptism, brought to view by Patristic writers, this alone would be sufficient to insure its death and burial, without hope of resurrection.

Let us now look at some of them.

BAPTISM OF THE WATERS BY QUALITY IMPARTED.

GENESIS 1 : 2.

"And the Spirit of God moved upon the face of the waters."

Baptism of the Waters by the Spirit of God.

"Sed ea satis præcerpsisse, in quibus et ratio Baptismi recognoscitur prima illa, qua jam tunc etiam ipso habitu prænotabatur ad Baptismi figuram, Dei Spiritum, qui ab initio supervectabatur super aquas, intinctos reformaturum. Sanctum autem utique super sanctum ferebatur; aut ab eo quod superferebatur, id quod ferebat, sancitatem mutuabatur. Quoniam subjecta quæque materia, ejus quæ desuper imminet, qualitatem rapiat necesse est, maxime corporalis spiritalem, et penetrare et insidere facilem per substantiæ suæ subtilitatem. Ita de sancto sanctificatæ natura aquarum, et ipsæ sanctificare concepit."

"But it is sufficient to have premised these things, whereby also may be recognized that prime nature of baptism, by which, even then, by its very dress, was foreshown by a figure of baptism, that the Spirit of God, which from the beginning was upborne above the waters, would transform the imbued. But, indeed, the holy was borne above the holy, or that which bore received sanctity from that upborne. Since whatever substance is beneath, receives, of necessity, character from that which rests above, especially is a physical substance pervaded by a spiritual, through the subtlety of its nature. So the nature of the waters was sanctified by the Holy, and itself received the power to sanctify."—*Tertullian*, i, 1203.

Didymus Alexandrinus (692), speaks of this passage in terms so closely resembling those of Tertullian, that they almost appear to be a translation.

Ἡ ἀδιαίρετος καὶ ἄῤῥητος Τριὰς, προορῶσα ἐξ αἰῶνος τοῦ ἀνθρωπίνου βίου τὰ ὀλισθηρὰ, ἅματῷ παραγαγεῖν ἐκ μὴ ὄντων τὴν ὑγρὰν οὐσίαν, ηὐτρέπισεν ἀνθρωποις τὴν ἐν τοῖς ὕδασιν ἴασιν. Τοιγάρτοι τῇ ἑαυτοῦ ἐπιφορᾷ τὸ ἅγιον Πνεῦμα ἐκ τότε ἁγιάσαν αὐτὰ, κάὶ ζωογόνον ἀποτελέσαν φαίνεται. Παντὶ γὰρ πρόδηλον ὑπάρχει, ὡς καὶ τὸ ὑπερκείμενον τῷ ὑπερκειμένῳ τῆς οἰκείας μεταδίδωσιν, ἵν' οὕτως εἴπω, ποιότητος, καὶ πᾶσα ὑποκειμένη ὕλη, τῆς τοῦ ἐπικειμένου φιλεῖ πως ἁρπάζειν ἰδιότητος. Ὅθεν ἀδιακρίτως παντὶ ὕδατι, . . . βάπτισμα γίνεται. ("Baptism is *effected by* every water indiscriminately.")

EXPOSITION.

This is not a case of Judaic Baptism; but a "figure" of Patristic Baptism as conceived of, taught, and practised, by Tertullian and others.

It is not a little remarkable that in the first chapter of the Old Testament, and, almost, in its first verse, there should be found a "figure of baptism," susceptible, under any appliances of imagination, of developing nearly all the salient points of baptism as it lay in the Patrist mind. Whether their views were right or wrong is not, now, any inquiry of ours. We have to do with philology, not with theology. A heathen Greek or a Patristic errorist can, here, give sound instruction as to the usage of words.

It would not be proper to consider in detail, the peculiarities of Patristic baptism; but they form so completely the web and woof of their interpretations of these Old Testament baptisms, that it becomes essential to give them some attention. The present is a favorable opportunity to do so, as they cluster around the exposition of this passage in an unusual degree.

"*Figure of Baptism.*"—In this figure of baptism presented before us by Tertullian there are but two elements,—*the Holy Spirit and water.* Our business is to discover the justifying ground for affirming that these elements, in themselves, or in their relations to each other, or by their influence over each other, exhibit "the figure," form, or character of a baptism. A "figure" must contain a resemblance to the reality figured. Baptists have maintained, with the most cast iron rigidity, that baptism consists of "mode, and nothing but mode," and that a discussion of the mode of baptism is as great a blunder as to discuss the mode of dipping, whose form is a fixed unity. Try this theory by "the figure of baptism" before us. Is there anything in it which resembles *a dipping?* I need hardly say that there is no such thing.

We have, then, a figure of baptism, with the baptism part left out.

But the more sober-minded Baptists are beginning to shrink from this position, to which they so long demanded the obedience of the Christian world under penalty of disloyalty to God, and are substituting liberty in the act, yet requiring completeness in the covering. Is there any completeness of covering in this "figure?" There is none whatever. Again, then, we have a house built with the foundation forgotten. The Baptist theory, whether represented in its rigidity by Carson, or in its laxity by Conant, utterly fails to expound this "figure of baptism."

Submit, now, to the same test the conclusion to which we have been brought by an examination of the usage of classic writers,—a conclusion which denies that the essence of *βαπτίζω* is to be found in *action*, definite or indefinite; and affirms that it is to be found in change of *condition:* 1. To place an object in a condition of physical intusposition subject to all the controlling influences of such condition. 2. To change controllingly and after its own nature the condition of an object, without intusposition, by any influence competent to effect such change.

Does this definition find its shadow in "the figure of baptism" before us? So complete is the resemblance that we are tempted to believe that the one was directly sketched from the other. This is not so; they were not taken, the one from the other, but both were taken from one original,—the Classic writers. Hence the perfect resemblance between "the figure" of Tertullian and "the conclusion" of Classic Baptism. We originate no novelty in the ecclesiastical usage of this word. We rest squarely on the Classic foundation. The only novelty is in the application of the word to a class of things with which heathen writers had no acquaintance; thus increasing its domain without changing its principle. The "figure" resemblance, in this case, consists in *the change of condition* in the waters, by the new "quality" imparted to them through the influence of the Holy Spirit. This was itself *a* baptism, yet, only, a figure of *the* baptism. The lamb slain on Abel's altar was *a* sacrifice, yet, only a figure of *the* sacrifice of the Lamb of God slain on Calvary.

The Agent.—The agent in this baptism was the Holy Spirit. The *quo modo* of any baptism is never governed by the word. The mode, by which the baptism was effected in this case, Tertullian is very particular in stating was neither by "dipping," nor by any act "effecting a complete covering;" but by "moving above" and "resting upon." He lays it down as a received axiom that "the decumbent must receive the quality of the superincumbent." Thus the waters were penetrated and pervaded by a holy quality received from the incumbent Holy Spirit; and, still more, were endued with the power to communicate such quality; in other words became capable of baptizing—changing condition by imparting the quality of sanctity. Without bearing in mind this new power claimed to be conferred on the waters, Patristic baptism can never be understood.

The Object.—The object in this baptism was "the waters." Dr. Carson insists that a dipping must be impossible before a secondary meaning can have any hearing. Will those who have fallen heirs to his sentiments, tell us where the possibility of a dipping is to be found here? Gale could hyperbolize the waters of a lake into the scanty pool of a frog's blood; but where is the hyperbole to come from, or where is the tiny pool to be found, when the object for dipping is "the waters" swathing the globe, before "the dry land was made to appear?"

But while "the waters" are the object of baptism in this case, they stand in another relation, entirely, in *the* baptism. They there become *the agent* in baptism, and execute the function for which they are now qualified—"*sanctified and with power to sanctify.*" That water is *an agency* in baptism, exercising a positive power, controlling the moral condition of those subject to its influence, is another Patristic idea, without whose aid their baptism cannot be rightly interpreted.

Intinctos.—The friends of the theory may here smile and say, "At last we have a dip." We could almost wish that it were so, they have been so often and so sorely disappointed; but it is not a very hopeful case. Let us suppose, however, that Tertullian does, here, speak of "the dipped," what is the precise value of the statement? Is it replied: "It teaches that when men were baptized they were 'dipped,' and therefore to baptize is to dip?" *Festina lente;* do not draw conclusions too fast. Cloth is dyed by dipping, therefore to dye means to dip! Is that the logic? Has it not been settled, even to Dr. Carson's satisfaction, that *dyeing* is not dipping, and *dipping* is not dyeing? And has it not been settled, on yet stronger evidence, that "baptizing is not dipping, and dipping is not baptizing?" Whatever place, then, dipping might have in a baptism, it cannot represent βαπτίζω. This inquiry, then, is not affected if "intinctos" should be written down "dipped." But before that is done, let us reflect on some things which otherwise might require it to be undone. Does not *tingo* mean *to dye?* "Certainly." And does not *tingo*, also, cease to express color and declare *a quality* (as of honesty, justice,) without color? "But, what has that to do with 'intinctos' applied to *water?*" Just this: the water of Patristic baptism is "*sanctified*" water, and is capable of "sanctifying" that which is dipped into it, or that which is sprinkled by it; therefore the sanctified or baptized condition induced by this water-agency is no more the dipping which puts the object into it, than is the dyed condition of the cloth the dipping which put it into the coloring-tub.

That Tertullian had no idea of limiting this word to the action of dipping, is manifest by its adjunct, "intinctos *reformaturum.*" Were "the dipped" to be "made over again," by the act of dipping into simple water? Did Tertullian believe any such thing? Did any Patristic writer believe any such thing? Did not he, and others, believe that men dipped into water, "penetrated and pervaded with a quality communicated by the Holy Spirit," were, by this "quality," "reformed," regenerated, *intincted* with a divine influence? And did they not believe that this "quality" was able (Dr. Carson to the contrary notwithstanding) *to baptize, to intinct,* to regenerate, to purify from sin, to save, *to change the condition of the soul,* by *sprinkling* as well as by dipping? No man, who will take the trouble to read the testimony on these points, will think of denying this. An intelligent apprehension of all the features of the case, will place a very imperative *veto* on the confounding of the "intinctos" with the merely dipped, or a dipping with a baptism.

I should have preferred saying nothing, at present, on these features of Patristic baptism, had not the case, as presented, seemed to make it imperative. I only add a testimony or two from the Classics, to show that water may be "intincted," have quality without color imparted to it: Et incerto fontem medicamine *tinxit.—Metamorph.*, iv, 388. "Tincted or infected the fountain with a doubtful drug."

> An quia cunctarum contraria semina rerum
> Sunt duo, discordes ignis et unda Dei,
> Junxerunt elementa patres: aptumque putarunt
> Ignibus et *sparsa* TINGERE corpus *aqua?*
>
> *Fastorum*, iv, 787–790.

Here is the body *tincted* without being colored, by "*sprinkled water,*" used in religious rites. It is perilous for controversialists to stake their all on naked words. Verbal alliances constitute a new power which will make itself to be felt. Chemical elements, in combination, lose their isolated character. Individuals, in social organization, give up old rights and secure new ones. Words, in organic phrases, modify their individuality, by giving to and receiving from associate words. *Tingo* cannot put on an abstract unchangeability, but must submit to universal law, and take character from the company it keeps.

The views of Tertullian on this passage are not peculiar, but fairly represent the views of his times. This will sufficiently appear from one or two quotations.

Jerome ii, 161. " Quomodo antiquis sordibus anima purgatur, quæ sanctum non habet Spiritum? Neque enim aqua lavat animam, sed prius lavatur a Spiritu, ut alios lavare spiritualiter possit. *Spiritus*, inquit Moyses, *Domini ferebatur super aquas.* (Gen. 1, 2.) Ex quo apparet baptisma non esse sine Spiritu sancto. Bethesda lacus Judææ, nisi per adventum Angeli, debilitata corporaliter membra sanare non poterat: et tu mihi aqua simplici, quasi de balneo animam lotam producis?"

This passage brings into bold relief the following points:

1. Simple water, however used, by dipping, covering, sprinkling, pouring, or with whatsoever formularies, however orthodox, associated, cannot effect Jerome's baptism.

2. In Jerome's baptism the soul is "washed,"=cleansed, (antiquis sordibus purgatur,) *changed in condition.*

3. To effect this change of condition in the soul, the water itself must first be changed by a new quality imparted to it by the Holy Spirit.

4. In proof that such change in the water is effected, he quotes Genesis 1 : 2: " *The Spirit of the Lord was borne above the waters.*"

As the Classics teach us that there are two baptisms of wine, most absolutely distinct in nature, the one resulting from its mersing quality, the other from its intoxicating quality; so Jerome teaches that there are two baptisms of water, as absolutely distinct in nature; the one due to its mersing quality, the other due to its soul-sanctifying quality, imparted by the Holy Spirit. The first of these wine baptisms is exemplified by Richard drowning Clarence; the second by Thebe intoxicating Alexander. The first of these water baptisms is that of Arian, who uses simple water because "he has not the Holy Spirit." The second is that of Jerome, who employs water having a sanctifying quality able "to change the condition of the soul."

The limitation of baptism to a dipping or a covering, is a thought nowhere to be found among Classics or Patrists. To bring such a conception to expound the subject of baptisms, is like using a dark lantern to illumine the realms of

Erebus. The mode of baptism employed by Arian and by Jerome, may have been the same. Both may have dipped their disciples; but those of Arian came out of their dipping unbaptized, and those of Jerome came out of their dipping baptized, for precisely the same reason that cloth dipped into mere water comes forth *uncolored*, and dipped into dye-water, comes forth *colored.* Jerome knew nothing of the theory that "baptizing is dipping, and dipping is baptizing."

A passage of like import may be found in Ambrose, ii, 1583: "*Baptizatus est* ergo Dominus non mundari volens, sed mundare aquas; ut ablutæ per carnem Christi, quæ peccatum non cognovit, baptismatis jus haberent."

Here we have inculcated: 1. That a divine influence was exerted over the waters. 2. That, by virtue of this divine influence, the waters were invested with the POWER *of baptism.*

If, now, it be a token of lunacy to deny that water has, of essence, and not by accident, "the power" to receive any object dipped into it; and if Ambrose denies that water has, by its essential nature, the "JUS *baptismatis*," and only possesses it through a special quality, extraordinarily conferred, then, either Ambrose was a lunatic, or "jus baptismatis" means something else than a quality making competent for a *dipping.* All, not inextricably involved in the theory, will be likely to conclude that Ambrose was of a sound mind, and that "the *power* of baptism," divinely conferred, was the power to change the condition of the soul by spiritual cleansing.

Tertullian, Jerome, Ambrose, and a great cloud of associates, knew nothing of a baptism characterized by definite action. Their baptism was, and was only, one of changed condition, however effected. *Patristic* baptism was a changed condition of the soul, effected by the influence of water, through a quality specially and divinely imparted to it.

Allow me to conclude by giving a definition of baptism from Basil Magnus, iii, 736:

'Τίς ὁ λόγος ἤ ἡ δύναμις τοῦ βαπτίσματος; Τὸ ἀλλοιωθῆναι τὸν βαπτιζόμενον κατά τε νοῦν, καὶ λόγον, καὶ πρᾶξιν, καὶ γενέσθαι εκεῖνο κατὰ τὴν δοθεῖσαν δύναμιν, ὅπερ ἐστι τὸ ἐξ οὗ ἐγενήθη.

"What is the purport and the power of baptism? That the baptized be changed as to thought, word, and act, and become, through the power conferred, the same as that of which he is born."

I present this definition, 1. Because the Latin translation —"Quæ sit *ratio* aut vis baptismatis?"—presents "*ratio*" in the same relation to baptism (ratio baptismi) as does the extract from Tertullian.

2. Because of the identity of conception between this definition of baptism, as given by Basil, and that given in "the conclusion" of Classic Baptism.

"The conclusion" is more comprehensive than the definition of Basil, because made to comprise all baptisms, while his contemplates the class of baptisms effected by influential agencies.

Compare "the conclusion," as explained, p. 57: "Whatever *influence* is capable of thoroughly changing the character, state, or condition of any object, *by pervading it and making it subject to its own characteristic*, is capable of baptizing that object," with the definition of Basil, "That the baptized be changed, as to thought, word, and act, and become, through the power conferred, the same as that of which he is born."

"The conclusion" was deduced from a collation of all the passages relating to baptism in Greek classic writings, and the definition of Basil was derived from immediate personal knowledge of the usage of his native tongue.

"The conclusion" and the definition, weighed over against each other, do not differ so much as by the weight of the dust in the balances.

Tertullian, also, and Basil, are in perfect accord on this subject.

It is a hopeless task, then, to look any longer for a "dipping" in this "figure of baptism."

Reference may be had to the following, among many other passages:

Peccata enim purgare et hominem sanctificare aqua sola non potest nisi habeat et Spiritum sanctum.—*Tertullian*, iii, 1132.

Aqua opus est, operatio Spiritus sancti est. Non sanat aqua, nisi Spiritus descenderit.—*Ambrose*, iii, 422.

Et bene in exordio creaturæ baptismi figura signatur, per quod haberit creatura mundari. (743.)

Plurima baptismatum genera præmissa sunt, quia secutum erat verum illud unum. (1248.)

As illustrative of "*intinctos*," the following has special value:

Πρὶν ἤ τοὶνυν ἐπελθεῖν τὴν ἀληθῆ τοῦ Πνεύματος βαφὴν, ἐξάλειψον τας χακῶς ἐντεθεἰσας σοι συνηθείας.—*Chrysostom*, ii, 235.

Any overbold man, offering this passage to Dr. Carson to prove that *βαφὴν* meant something else than *a dipping*, must expect a plentiful sprinkling of his characteristic "Attic salt." Yet, after all, the xlvii Prop. of Euclid does not challenge more absolute assent to its Q. E. D., than does this passage and its context demand assent to the clearness of its representation, as exhibiting the Holy Spirit removing sin-spots from the soul, as a painter imperfect colors from a picture, and using the waters of baptism, not for a dipping, but, as a painter, his last choicest colors, for tincting the soul and bringing it into a changed, spotless condition.

Carson's demand for the "impossibility" of *dipping*, is here met four-square.

BAPTISM OF A FOUNTAIN BY A TREE.

EXODUS 15 : 23-25.

"And when they came to Marah they could not drink of the waters of Marah, for they were bitter; therefore the name of it was called Marah.

"And the people murmured against Moses, saying, What shall we drink?

"And he cried unto the Lord; and the Lord showed him a tree, which when he had cast into the waters, the waters were made sweet."

Multa sunt genera baptismatum, sed unum baptisma, clamat Apostolus. (Eph. 4 : 5.) Quare? Sunt baptismata gentium, sed non sunt baptismata. Lavacra sunt, baptismata esse non possunt. Caro lavatur, non culpa diluitur; immo in illo lavacro contrahitur. Erant autem baptismata Judæorum (Mark 7:8), alia superflua, alia in figura. Et figura ipsa nobis proficit, quia veritatis est nuncia.—*Ambrose*, iii, 424.

Aliud (genus baptismatis) etsi non ordinem tenemus .·. . Moyses misit lignum in fontem, et cœpit aqua quæ antea erat amara, dulcescere. Quid significat, nisi quia omnis creatura corruptelæ obnoxia, aqua amara est omnibus . . . amara est quæ non potest auferre peccatum. Amara ergo aqua: sed ubi crucem Christi, ubi acceperis cœleste sacramentum, incipit esse dulcis et suavis: et merito dulcis, in qua culpa revocatur. Ergo si in figura tantum valuerunt baptismata, quanto amplius valet baptisma in veritate? iii, 427.

Sicut ergo in illum fontem Moyses misit lignum, hoc est propheta; ita et in hunc fontem sacerdos prædicationem Dominicæ crucis mittit, et aqua fit dulcis ad gratiam. (iii, 393.) . . . et amaritudinem suam aquarum natura deposuit, quam infusa subito gratia temperavit. (406.) . . . non utique dubitandum est quod superveniens (Spiritus sanctus) in fontem, vel super eos qui baptismum consequuntur, veritatem regenerationis operetur. (410.)

Myrrhæ fontis amaritudine per ligni gratiam temperata, cognoscimus esse mundatos.—*Ambrose*, ii, 1434.

Οὐκ ἀπὸ ξύλου ἐγλυκάνθη ὕδωρ, ἐις τὸ γνωσθῆναι τὴν ἰσχὺν ἀυτοῦ.

Wisdom of Sirach, 38:5.

OLD QUALITY CHANGED AND NEW QUALITY IMPARTED.

PATRISTIC INTERPRETATION.

"There are many kinds of baptisms, but the Apostle announces *one* baptism. Why? There are baptisms of the Gentiles, but they are not baptisms. They are washings, they cannot be baptisms. The body is washed; sin is not washed away: nay by that washing it is contracted. But there were baptisms of the Jews (Mark 7:8), some unnecessary, others in figure. And the very figure is profitable to us, because it is the messenger of truth."—*Ambrose*, iii, 424.

"There is another kind of baptism, although we do not preserve the order. . . . Moses cast the wood into the fountain, and the water which before was bitter grew sweet. What does this signify, except that every creature liable to corruption, the water is bitter to all . . . . that is bitter which cannot take away sin. Water, therefore, is bitter; but when thou shalt have received the cross of Christ and the heavenly sacrament, it becomes sweet and pleasant: and that is with reason sweet, by which sin is revoked. Therefore, if in figure merely baptisms were so powerful, how much more powerful is baptism in reality? (427.)

"As, therefore, Moses cast the wood into the fountain, this is prophetic; so, also, does the priest cast the proclamation of the Lord's cross into this fountain and the water is made sweet for grace. (393.) . . . the waters lay aside their natural bitterness, which infused grace has quickly attempered. (406.) . . . and certainly it is not to be doubted that the Holy Spirit coming over upon the fountain, or over those who obtain baptism, effects true regeneration. (410.)

"The bitterness of the fountain of Myrrhæ being attempered by the grace of the wood, we know that they were made pure (baptized)."—*Ambrose*, ii, 1434.

"Was not the water made sweet by wood, in order that its power might be made known?"—*Wisdom of Sirach*, 38:5.

Points claiming attention.

The substantial resemblance between the baptism of this fountain by "wood," (symbol of the Cross,) changing its condition of bitterness, and the baptism of the waters by the incumbent Spirit changing their condition by imparting a new quality, is too evident, and sufficiently explained by remarks on the latter baptism, to require more than the calling attention, briefly, to some additional points.

1. "*There are many kinds of baptisms.*" This is a flat contradiction of the theory that tells us, whether it be of a world or a flea's foot, whether of saint or of sinner, whether in heathendom or in christendom, whether in fact or in figure, a baptism is an unalterable unity; "a definite act;" "a mode, and nothing but mode;" a change in it is a destruction of it. Over against this theory, which has nothing to sustain

it but self-assertion, Ambrose writes: "There are *many* kinds of baptisms."

Inasmuch as we have seen this statement emphatically sustained by the facts of "Classic Baptism," we take sides with the Milanese Bishop.

2. "*There are baptisms of the Gentiles, but they are not baptisms.*" If those who have a right to write authoritatively on the subject, had never written anything else but this sentence and context, it would be enough to establish a twofold meaning of the word "baptism," and to overturn the theory which contradicts it.

Ambrose does not commit the absurdity of saying that the Gentiles have *no* baptisms; no *secular* baptisms. He is discoursing on religion, and he asserts that, in their religious rites, they have nothing which can be called "baptism," in the sense in which he uses that term, because they have no use of water under any form of "washing," which is capable of changing the condition of the soul, by taking away sin. "Washings," by sprinkling, pouring, dipping, covering, they have for the body; "baptisms," which cleanse the soul, they have not. In the vocabulary of Ambrose, "baptism" did not mean a definite act; it did mean a change of condition in the soul, through the influence of a quality divinely communicated to the water.

3. "*There is another kind of baptism.*" Having referred to a baptism in connection with the axe lost in the Jordan, (which we will meet with hereafter,) Ambrose says: "There is *another kind* of baptism;" and then states that of the fountain of Myrrha, which is before us. If these baptisms strike any one as novelties, let them remember the conclusions reached in "Classic Baptism," and reflect whether the two be not in the most perfect harmony. The theory insists that there can be but "one baptism." Unfortunately our theorists have confounded *a dipping* and *a baptism*, and have thereby got into a world of trouble. They can only escape by getting rid of this sad error—*fons et origo malorum.*

As Tertullian declares that "the waters" were baptized, changed in condition, by a new quality imparted to them by the influence of the Holy Spirit, so Ambrose declares that this fountain of water was baptized, changed in condition, by the removal of a quality, through the influence of a tree, symbolizing the cross of Christ.

4. "*That is bitter which cannot take away sin.*" This water, made sweet, and impregnated with the influence of this symbol tree, was able "to take away sin;"=to baptize; "cognoscimus esse mundatos." If any one asks *how?* I answer, *by drinking.* For the principle involved—baptism by *drinking*—we have abundance of authority, not only in wine-drinking baptism, and in opiate-drinking baptism, but in baptism by drinking at a fountain. If the fountain of Silenus was capable of baptizing after that "kind of baptism" appropriate to its peculiar quality, why should not the fountain of Myrrha baptize those who drank of it, after that "kind of baptism" appropriate to the new quality with which it had become impregnated?

Ambrose is as classically orthodox in his mode of baptizing, as he is in the nature of his baptism. His theology is another matter.

5. "*If baptisms in figure are so powerful.*" It should be written deeply on every mind, that this Myrrha, and other kindred transactions, are declared, in absolute terms, to be "baptisms." They are not something else, in fact, and only entitled *quasi* baptisms by a theological fiction. They are "baptisms" in their own right, and "powerful" baptisms, too. As such, they "figure" another baptism higher and mightier than themselves. This is the doctrine of Ambrose. Dipping finds no more countenance in this Myrrha baptism of the Patrists, effected by wood thrown into it, than by the wine-baptism of the Classics, effected by water poured into it.

The quotation from Ecclesiasticus shows the controlling power of the wood over the water, rendering it competent to thoroughly change its condition. Classic Baptism has shown that the development of such a power constitutes a baptism. And we have that conclusion reiterated by Ambrose, in declaring that the changed condition of the fountain of Myrrha was a baptism.

So Ovid says of the fountain Salmacis, "*vis est notissima fontis, . . . et incerto fontem medicamine tinxit.*" If *tingo* can express a quality imparted to the fountain Salmacis, why may not βαπτίζω be used to express a quality imparted to the fountain Myrrha? The change from the primary meaning, is no greater in one case than in the other. The evidence that such change does take place, in fact, is as great in the latter case as in the former.

BAPTISMS BY WATER.

CHANGE OF CONDITION THROUGH INFLUENCE.

DELUGE PURIFICATION.

GENESIS 6 : 13; 7 : 1, 18, 22.

1. And God said unto Noah, The end of all flesh is come before me; for the earth is filled with violence through them; and behold I will destroy them with the earth.

7 : 1. And the Lord said unto Noah, Come thou, and all thy house, into the ark; for thee have I seen righteous before me in this generation.

V. 18. And the waters prevailed, and were increased greatly upon the earth; and the ark went upon the face of the waters.

V. 22. All in whose nostrils was the breath of life, of all that was in the dry land, died.

Interpretation.

Quemadmodum enim post aquas diluvii, quibus iniquitas antiqua purgata est, post Baptismum (ut ita dixerim) mundi.—*Tertullian*, i, 1209.

Nam ut in illo mundi baptismo, quo iniquitas antiqua purgata est, qui in arca Noe non fuit non potuit per aquam salvatus fieri; ita nec nunc potest per baptismum salvatus videri qui baptizatus in Ecclesia non est.—*Cyprian*, 1136.

In diluvio quoque figuram baptismatis præcessisse hesterno cœpimus disputare. Quid est diluvium, nisi in quo justus ad seminarium justitiæ reservatur, peccatum moritur? . . . Nonne hoc et diluvium, quod est baptismum; quo peccata omnia diluuntur, sola justi mens et gratia resuscitatur?—*Ambrose*, iii, 423.

Non tam diluvium quam baptismum contigisse. Baptismus plane fuit, per quod in peccatoribus iniquitas sublata est, Noe justitia conservata.—iv, 650.

Τὴν οὖν τοῦ βαπτίσματος χάριν κατακλυσμὸν ὀνομάζει.—*Basil*, i, 304.

Καὶ ὁ κατακλυσμὸς . . . προεφήτευεν . . . τῶν ἁμαρτιῶν καθαρισμόν.—*Didymus Alex.*, 696.

Translation.

"For as after the waters of the deluge, by which the old iniquity was purged, after the baptism (as I might have said) of the world."—*Tertullian*, i, 1209.

"For as in that baptism of the world, by which the old iniquity was purged, he who was not in the ark of Noah, could not be saved, so, now, neither can he be saved who is not baptized in the church."—*Cyprian*, 1136.

"That a figure of baptism, in the deluge, also went before, we began to argue yesterday. What is the deluge, but that by which the righteous is preserved as a seed of righteousness, while sin perishes? . . . . Is not this deluge the same as baptism, by which all sins are washed away, and the soul of the righteous, and grace alone, preserved?"—*Ambrose*, iii, 423.

"Not so much a deluge, as a baptism, occurred. Baptism it clearly was, because, with sinners, iniquity was taken away; with Noah, righteousness was preserved."—iv, 650.

"'*The Lord inhabiteth the flood.*' (Ps. 28:10.) A flood is an overflow of water, covering all that is under it, and purifying every defilement. *Therefore he calls the grace of baptism a flood;* so that the soul washed from sin, and cleansed from the old man, may be, afterwards, a fit habitation of God, by his Spirit."—*Basil*, i, 304.

"The deluge foretold the purification of sins."—*Didy. Al.*, 696.

MUCH WATER AND THE THEORY.

Here is an abundance of water. What will the friends of the theory do with it? There is "a complete covering." Will that answer the purpose? Dr. Carson thinks that he can get a dipping out of this deluge, by the help of *figure*. But, observe, his figure is a very different affair from that of Patrist exposition. They make one baptism, by its essential nature, to figure another baptism to which it is generically related; but Carson calls on figure to help him make a baptism. As the facts of the deluge stand, outtopping the highest mountains by fifteen cubits, there is no dipping, and therefore (according to the theory) no baptism, for "baptism is dipping, and dipping is baptism." Now, Carson calls on figure to help him to change the facts, and claims a transaction—whose record contradicts his theory—as all on his side, after it has been made something else than it is.

This ever recurring demand on figure to help a false theory out of trouble, reminds us of the constant necessity of the old astronomers to add cycle and epicycle to work on with their mistaken conception. There is difference, however, in the two cases; the astronomer hung appendages to his theory, to meet the facts, while the Baptist hangs appendages to the facts, to meet his theory.

This flood of waters, covering its object for a large portion of a year, lends but little comfort to those who accept some modification of the action, yet insist on a momentary covering. The subject of baptism can no more be mastered with "momentary covering" for a starting-point, than can unshorn Samson be bound with seven green withes. Baptist argumentation is not susceptible of being amended. It must go back and start, *ab initio*, with a new element of thought, and follow it through its developments. Old facts will, then, assume new aspects, and this deluge baptism will be quite intelligible. Figure and epicycle, alike, may be thrown aside when the true central thought has been secured.

Besides the dipping of the world into the flood, by the help of figure, Carson speaks, repeatedly, throughout his book, of the baptism of Noah in the flood. This is his language: "What! Noah not immersed, when buried in the waters of the flood? Are there no bounds to perverseness? Will men say everything rather than admit *the mode* of an ordinance of Christ, which is contrary to the commandments of men?" (p. 388.) "What could be a more expressive burial in water than to be in the ark, when it was floating? As well might it be said that a person is not buried in earth, when lying in his coffin covered with earth.

May not a person in a ship be said *figuratively* to be buried in the sea? They who were in the ark were deeply immersed." (p. 413.) "Noah and his family were saved by being buried in the water of the flood; and after the flood they emerged as rising from the grave." (p. 462.)

Will any one expect a sober answer to erratic imaginings like these? The expositor who is willing to follow a rigid theory to issues like these, and indorse to bankruptcy its demands on common sense, must look for the issuing, at the next session of the court, of a writ *de lunatico inquirendo*. "Much *theory* doth make thee mad," honest though not courteous, truth-loving though not sober-minded, Carson!

It is a reproach to truth to admit the claims of so poor a counterfeit, even to a hearing. "Noah and his family" (beasts, birds, and creeping things,) "buried in the flood and emerging" (on the summit of Ararat) "as from the grave!" What next?

SPECIAL VALUE.

There is an especial value in this case of Deluge Baptism as enabling us to point out, within itself, some of the "many kinds of baptisms."

1. If we regard the earth merely as a physical body and the water as encompassing it, we have an illustration of a simple mersion (baptism) *without* influence.

2. If we regard the earth as having cultivated fields, houses, cities, works of art, then this universal deluge becomes a mersion (baptism) *with* influence, ruinous in its character.

3. If we take into view men, inhabiting the world and unrepenting sinners against God, for whose punishment this flood of waters was sent, then, it becomes a mersion (baptism) *for* influence, designed to destroy—to drown men.

4. But neither of these is the baptism contemplated, and drawn out from the case, by the Patrists. They regarded the earth as defiled and needing to be purified—O aqua, quæ humano aspersum sanguine, ut præsentium lavacrorum figura præcederet, orbem terrarum lavisti! (*Ambrose*, ii, 1815.) The world is here represented as polluted by murder,

being "sprinkled with human blood," and as cleansed by being "washed" by the deluge waters. This, then, was conceived of, not as a physical mersion, but as a baptism for religious purification, accomplished by water through its quality, divinely communicated, to purge and sanctify.

But it may be asked, Was not the water, in fact, used in the form of mersion? Undoubtedly, yet not as a necessity, but accident, which may or may not be in such baptism. Cloth *dyed* (βάπτω) may be dyed by *dipping* (βάπτω): yet "dipping" is not an essential to "dyeing," but an accident which may or may not be present. In a baptism *for purification*, mersion, in like manner, may or may not be present. And whenever present it is not to be regarded as a feature, much less the feature of the baptism; any more than *dipping*, when it chances to be the form, is to be regarded as the *dyeing*. Proof of this may be found in a perfectly analogous case from *Chrysostom*, ii, 409.

Ἐπειδὴ πᾶσα ἡ γῆ τότε ἀκάθαρτος ἦν ἀπὸ τοῦ καπνοῦ, καὶ τῆς κνίσσης, καὶ τῶν εἰδωλικῶν αἱμάτων, καὶ τῶν ἄλλων μολυσμῶν τῶν Ἑλληνικῶν.

"When the whole earth was, then, defiled by the smoke, and fume, and blood of idol sacrifices, and other pollutions. . . . But Christ having come, and having suffered without the city, he purified the whole earth (πᾶσαν τὴν γῆν ἐκάθηρε)." How this was done is stated, more definitely, in a few lines preceding:

Ἔσταξε γὰρ τὸ αἷμα ἀπὸ τῆς πλευρᾶς ἐπὶ τὴν γῆν, καὶ τὸν μολυσμὸν αὐτῆς ἅπαντα ἐξεκάθηρεν.

"For the blood from his side dropped upon the earth, and thoroughly purged away the pollution."

We have, here, evidence that a world may be defiled by all manner of pollution, and instead of a necessity for a mersion in water, outtopping all mountain tops, in order to its purification, *drops of blood falling from the spear-pierced side* are adequate for the purification of all the earth.

To the objection that the word "baptism" is not used in this latter case, it may be replied, 1. All the facts—condition to be removed, pollution; mode of remedy, dropping blood; condition effected, purification; as well as all the terms employed, are identical with the facts and terms in other cases to which the title of "baptism" is given. 2. A secondary use of "baptism" covering this case is in proof. 3. We shall yet have overwhelming evidence establishing the same point. 4. A mersion baptism is distinctly repudiated in the present case, and a baptism for purification is presented.

"The old *iniquity was purged* by the waters of the deluge," therefore, (not because of the covering,) it is called "a baptism of the world." "The deluge is the same as baptism"—Why? Because they both "wash sins away." The dropping blood from the Redeemer's side is the same as baptism—Why? Because it "washes sin away." "Not so much a deluge as a baptism." What does this mean? Not so much a deluge as a *dipping*, an *immersion*, a *covering?* Is not this an utterly impossible, absurd, interpretation? Is it not expressly said,—"because sin was removed and righteousness established?" Could there be a more explicit distinction between a deluge and a baptism? And so, *Basil*, i, 304, "A flood is an overflow of water, covering all that is under it and purifying every defilement." Therefore he calls the *grace* of baptism a flood, ('*the Lord inhabiteth the flood,*' Ps. 28:10,) because it cleanses the soul. A flood covers to baptize, to cleanse physically; it can only cleanse what it covers; but "grace" baptizes (cleanses) the soul, and "redeeming blood" baptizes (cleanses) the world, without covering it.

While, therefore, the Deluge presents an example of primary baptism in which the earth is mersed, by the varied acts of water *falling* from heaven's windows and *rising* from the bursting fountains of the deep, and kept for most of a year in this state; still, it is a patent fact, that this baptism is not regarded in the reference to the transaction in the passages before us; but another, and wholly different baptism, namely, a *purification* by these waters, irrespective of the form of their operation, in which they see a figure of that baptism which is the highest and fullest of all purifications.

If such a case as this fails to lend help to the theory, where will it look for succor?

CHANGE OF CONDITION THROUGH SPECIAL INFLUENCE DIVINELY IMPARTED.

JORDAN HEALING.

II Kings 5 : 14.

"Then went he down and dipped himself seven times in Jordan, according to the saying of the man of God: and his flesh came again like unto the flesh of a little child, and he was clean."

Septuagint.

Καὶ κατέβη Ναιμὰν καὶ ἐβαπτίσατο ἐν τῷ Ἰορδάνῃ ἑπτάκις κατὰ τὸ ῥῆμα Ἐλισαιέ; καὶ ἐπέστρεψεν ἡ σὰρξ ἀυτου ὡς σὰρξ παιδαρίου μικροῦ, καὶ ἐκαθαρίσθη.

"And Naaman went down and baptized (purified) himself in the Jordan seven times, according to the word of Elisha; and his flesh came again like the flesh of a little child, and he was made pure."

Examination.

All trespassers are warned from this ground as belonging by unquestionable right to friends of the theory. A mere claim of ownership will hardly pass unchallenged. All ground which is covered by fair title-deeds, or all that has been won by sword and spear, in fair conflict, we will cheerfully yield. Let us see how the documents read, and under what right possession is claimed.

Baptist Claim for a Dipping.

Carson (pp. 59–61, 313–317) vindicates the claim of the theory with a force and positiveness not excelled, certainly, by any other Baptist writer. His points are the following:

1. "The word occurs in the Greek translation of the Old Testament, and is faithfully rendered *dip* in our version.—II Kings 5 : 14." (p. 59.)

2. "That the Greek word signifies *dip*, is clear from the fact that this is the meaning of the word in the original."

3. "He did what was commanded. It is described as an

immersion. He bathed, and consequently he immersed. That Naaman was immersed is as certain as that the word of God speaks truth. He was enjoined to *bathe.* Was not his *dipping* a fulfilment of the command to bathe?"

4. "If a word is proved to dip one object, it may dip another. Naaman went down and dipped himself seven times."

Carson's Points Examined.—1. "The word (βαπτίζω) in the Greek translation (II Kings 5 : 14) is faithfully rendered *dip* in our version." If any one else had made such a statement, he would have been bespattered with "Attic salt." None knows better than Dr. C., that "our version" is not made from the Septuagint, and therefore could not have translated this Greek word—"*dip.*"

2. "The Greek word means dip, because the Hebrew word means dip." Such a position has no reliable foundation. Of a similar position taken by an opponent—that βαπτίζω must mean *wash,* because it fulfils a command given by λούω, which means to wash—he says (p. 61): "Lexicographers, critics, and commentators, receive this as a first principle, but are imposed on by a mere figment." Again, of a writer who takes identically the same position as to the translation of Isaiah 21 : 4, which Dr. C. takes as to II Kings 5 : 14—namely, that the Greek word of the Septuagint must mean the same as the Hebrew word translated—he says: "Were this the assertion of all the lexicographers in existence, it is false and extravagantly foolish." (p. 315.) That is to say, when Dr. C. thinks that a translating word is of the same precise value as the translated word, the principle which would make the translation measure the height, and depth, and length, and breadth of the original, is true and surpassingly wise; but, when he thinks differently, then the principle becomes "false and extravagantly foolish." It is certainly a very admirable thing to have an autocratic critic, who can never err, even when he utters contradictions. On this general subject, of exact correspondence between the Septuagint and the Hebrew text, Principal Fairbairn says: "The Septuagint is far from being a close translation. They who always expect to find in it the key to the exact mean-

ing of particular words and phrases, are by no means to be trusted." (*Herman. Man.*, p. 62.)

As illustrative of the correctness of this remark, and, at the same time, exhibiting a parallelism with the passage under consideration, we may refer to Psalm 50 : 9. Here, for the Hebrew text, (which signifies *to purify*, by using a religious rite, without expressing any definite action,) the Septuagint substitutes the sharply definite act, *sprinkle*, by which the purification was accomplished. The principle is the same in II Kings, only its development is reversed. In the Hebrew we have a word expressive of definite act, and, in the translation, we have *a condition*, which includes that, and many other acts, which may be causative of such condition. The Hebrew, "*purify* with hyssop," (which, on the face of it, involves sprinkling, since "hyssop" was only used for this mode of purifying,) the Septuagint translates, "*sprinkle* with hyssop." In like manner βαπτίζω includes sprinkling as one of many modes by which its demanded Judaic purification may be met. And this purification may be, was, termed a washing. Both these points are exhibited in the passage from the Son of Sirach, already considered.

How ungrounded is Dr. Carson's conclusion as to the meaning of the Greek word, from the meaning (real or supposed) of the Hebrew word, I need not farther say.

3. "*He was enjoined to bathe.*" He was not enjoined to bathe. To wash and to bathe are not measures of each other. "*He bathed in fact.*" There is no sure evidence of such fact. "*He dipped himself.*" Satisfying evidence is wanting. "*He immersed himself.*" Where is the proof?

In justification of the rejection of these statements, I appeal to the usage both of the Hebrew and Greek words in question. Neither the Hebrew nor the Greek word, for *wash*, requires a *dipping*, or an *immersion*, or a *bathing*, in the more common sense of that word, covering the body in water. They are used where the washings are local, and where the water is applied to the body, and the body is not put into the water.

The Hebrew word, which is translated *dip*, has, undoubtedly, "to dip" as its primary meaning; but this does not justify Dr. C. in the dogmatic assertion, based on the word, that a dipping of Naaman took place on this occasion. The word has other meanings. It answers to βάπτω in Greek, and *tingo* in Latin. Like these words, it has the twofold radical application, *to dip* and *to dye*, with subordinate modifications springing out of both these meanings. A glance into the Concordance of Buxtorf or of Fürst, particularly the former, will show that טָבַל and טָבַע, in Hebrew, correspond with βάπτω and βαπτίζω in Greek, *tingo* and *mergo* in Latin, and dip and immerse in English. Hebrew literature being comparatively limited, we cannot expect to find as many illustrations of varied use, as in other languages. But that the Hebrew word does not necessarily mean to dip, covering completely, or to dip at all, is shown by its use in Genesis 37 : 31, of which the translation by the Septuagint is—καὶ ἐμόλυναν τὸν χιτῶνα τῷ αἵματι—"and they *stained* the coat (Joseph's) with the blood." Our Version is, "they dipped the coat in the blood." Whichever translation be preferred, two things are certain: 1. The Greek translators believed that the Hebrew word had more than one meaning. 2. The object of the verb is not necessarily covered by the action of the verb, and therefore no immersion, no baptism takes place. Joseph's coat could not be covered by the blood of a kid, any more than the lake by the blood of a frog. An immersion of the whole body is not necessarily got out of a dipping. The word, of itself, neither dips nor covers Naaman.

But still farther. In I Chronicles 26 : 11, we find this Hebrew word in combination with that of Jehovah, as a proper name, the import of which, as given by Gesenius, is, "Whom Jehovah has immersed, *i. e.*, HAS PURIFIED." Now, inasmuch as this eminent Hebraist finds the meaning of *purification* growing out of this modal verb, used in ritual purification; and inasmuch as the Greek translators (in Ps. 50 : 9) find the modal verb *sprinkle*, expressive of purification; and inasmuch as the correspondent Latin modal verb *tingo*—sparsa aqua *tingere* corpus—is used to express purification; and inasmuch as, in this passage, the Greek translators have represented this modal verb by a word which has been proven to express purification in connection with Jewish rites, is he not a bold man who will affirm that this word could not have secured to itself the idea of purification, but must signify a naked dipping?

But Dr. Carson is not satisfied with assertion which makes nothing of facts like these. He must make the divine veracity depend upon his judgment of a Hebrew word. "That Naaman was immersed, is as certain as the word of God speaks truth." When the theorists make the "Christian honesty" of the general church to kick the beam, weighed against their knowledge of a Greek word, I have nothing to say. When the Tubbermore Theorist birches "the angel Gabriel," and "sends him to school" for ignorantly differing from him in matters of exegesis, I am quite satisfied that they should settle their own quarrel. But when any man makes God's truthfulness to depend on his Hebrew knowledge, or any other knowledge, then I indignantly fling in his face those words which the Holy Ghost teacheth, "*Let God be true, but every man a liar!*"

4. But one other point remains to be considered. "If a word is proved to dip one object, it may dip another," (provided it is of a like character.) I can readily understand what is done when it is said, "He dips his pen in the ink;" "He dips his hand in the water;" but when it is said, "Naaman dipped himself in the water," I confess that I do not find, in the words, any such distinct statement as to what was done. Can a man dip himself as he dips his hand? Can you possibly tell from the Hebrew word what was done in a self-dipping? If, in effecting a self-dipping, the whole transaction must be modified in comparison with the dipping of anything else, may it not be true that there is such a modification of meaning that there is no dipping at all? May not the object of the verb be something else than the person of Naaman? Is it not unusual to employ this word in connection with a dipping of the whole person? Is there any other case of the kind in the Bible? Is it not unusual in any other language to use this word to express a dipping

of the entire person? Is not, strictly speaking, self-dipping an impossibility? Is there not strong reason to believe that this disease was local? (See v. 11.) May not this diseased spot (well understood between the prophet and Naaman, and therefore not mentioned) have been the object of the verb, both in the command and in the execution of the command?

But farther. He was to dip "seven times;" and Carson says, "from head to foot." Did he come out of the water each time, and go in afresh, until the seventh time? Or, having gone into the water, and having dipped what was out of water, more or less, did he, remaining in the water, dip again and again, head, &c., seven times? If this was the process, then it must be admitted that he did not dip himself, "from head to foot," *seven times*, and that, after all, this dipping was but that of a part of the person.

When we examine this case, interpreted as self-dipping, there is much about it which the theory leaves unillumined.

There may have been good reason why the translators rejected the simply modal character of the word, and gave, as its representative, one which never means "dip," but is always expressive of condition, and, Judaically, of a purified condition, which is just what the case demands.

But Dr. Carson objects: "If βαπτίζω here expresses purification, then there were *seven* purifications." A reference to Psalm 12:7, "The words of the Lord are pure, ... as silver *purified seven times*," will show that such conjunction of words is allowable. Tertullian, ii, 575, is not alarmed by *seven* purifications. He represents the case as showing forth power to cleanse the seven capital sins of the Gentile nations: "Idololatria, blasphemia, homicidio, adulterio, stupro, falso testimonio, fraude. Quapropter septies quasi per singulos titulos in Jordane lavit, simul et ut totius hebdomadis caperet expiationem; quia unius lavacri vis et plenitudo Christo soli dicabatur." "Wherefore he washes" (not dips) "in the Jordan seven times, as if for the several sins, and that he might receive expiation from all seven at once; for the power and fulness of one washing belonged to Christ alone."

Dr. Fuller, justly honored with high position among his brethren, has written on baptism, and examined this particular passage. He thus pleads for fair dealing: "Should any one review this argument, I only ask that he will quote me fairly, and show me as a brother where the flaw is, and I will confess it." I cannot review his book, but will try to quote "fairly" his words. To prove the facility and accuracy with which βαπτίζω can be translated he says: "In short, *the translators of our Bible have, themselves, exposed the pretext that there is any difficulty as to the word baptizo.* In the case of Naaman, the Septuagint uses baptizo, and the translation renders it 'dip.' Then went he down and dipped (ebaptisato)" (p. 11). The italics are Dr. Fuller's. I have read this statement over once, twice, thrice, and twice thrice, feeling that it could not possibly mean, what on its face it seemed to mean; but there were the staring words charging a band of men, "of whom the world was not worthy," with coldly planned hypocrisy, and basing that charge upon the statement of a fact, not one syllable of which, as relating to those men, was true. As to the first of these charges—"*pretext of difficulty in translating baptizo*"—I will quote the words of a Baptist scholar (after reading Classic Baptism), whom Dr. Fuller would cheerfully confess to have but few peers among Baptist scholars; they are as follows: "*You have certainly shown* HOW DIFFICULT *it is to frame a definition of the act of baptism, that shall be free from objection, and satisfactory even to Baptists themselves.*" If this authority is not sufficient to suffuse with shame the charge of "pretext of difficulty," then let me refer Dr. F. to Classic Baptism, (pp. 242–4,) where he will find sufficiently "exposed" the pretext that there is *no* difficulty in translating βαπτίζω, in the case of the Rev. Richard Fuller, D.D. As to the second statement: that "dip" in II Kings 5:14, is a translation of βαπτίζω, out of the Septuagint; a statement made in, and for, an important issue, it is simply shocking. Dr. Carson knew that it was not true. Dr. Fuller knew that it was not true. Did they, then, design to sustain their cause by a designed appeal to an untruth? By no means. The case is illustrative of the ruinous effects of assumption and presumption. These writers assume identity of value between the Hebrew word and the Greek word, and then presume that it is of no consequence whether they speak of the translation of one word or the other. The assumption is false; the presumption is monstrous. I am sorry to say, that this style of argumentation by friends of the theory is not limited to the present case. They write as though they were absolved from all the laws of language which interfere with their idolized theory, and not satisfied with saying that "idiocy" and "childhood" confess the truth of their principles, go on to proclaim, that if men, and angels, aye, and the Deity, too, do not say "*it is so*," it is because there is no truth in them!

I do not present this error of fact as a "flaw in the argument;" it is a bottomless pit, down into which the whole statement plunges out of sight.

This case is resumed (p. **38**) thus: "The instance where it occurs literally is in the history of Naaman. . . . Here, in a work known by Jesus, and cited by him, we find *baptizo*, and it is admitted on all hands to mean *immerse*. Jesus uses the same word, and thus commands the very same act. 'Naaman went down and dipped himself seven times (ebaptizato) in the Jordan.' All concede that this was immersion. Now Jesus commands this very act. . . . The Septuagint says, Naaman 'ebaptisato en to Iordane.' . . . In Matthew 3:6 we are told that the people, 'ebaptizonto en to Iordane,' the very same expression."

Review of argument.—**1**. When Dr. Fuller says, "it occurs literally," *i. e.* in primary physical sense, he ASSUMES a vital point. It is in proof that the word is used otherwise. The *assumption* of a particular use, determinative of the question, is "flaw" number one.

2. "It is admitted on all hands to mean immerse." It is not admitted to mean "immerse" in the sense *to dip*. It is not admitted to mean "immerse" as representing any definite act. It is not admitted to mean "immerse," only, or, at all, in the Baptist use of that word. This second assumption is "flaw" number two.

3. "Jesus uses the same word, and thus commands the very same act." The *assumption* that the use of the same word must convey the same idea, embodying the *assumption* that the word did convey but one idea in the days of the Septuagint translators, and the farther *assumption* that it did continue for centuries after to convey but one idea, is "flaw" number *three.* "Commands the very same act." The *assumption* that any form of act was ever commanded, being utterly groundless, is "flaw" number *four*, Dr. Fuller being himself judge; for (p. 29) he tells us, no form of act is commanded, "it matters not how the immersion is effected."

4. "All concede that this was immersion." The *assumption* of such concession being without foundation, constitutes "flaw" number *five.*

5. "Now Jesus commands this very act." The *assumption* in this assertion placing Dr. F., again, in antagonism with Dr. F., as well as with the anti-theorists, we have "flaw" number *six.*

6. "The Septuagint says, 'baptized en to Iordane;' the New Testament says, 'baptized en to Iordane;' the very same expression." The *assumption* that the same expression in a limited phrase, carries with it sameness in all governing particulars, though the usage be separated by centuries, is without warrant in common sense or exegetical law.

"The wool was BAPTED *in the dyehouse* to free it from all greasy quality." "The wool was BAPTED *in the dyehouse* a scarlet color." Dr. Fuller will admit that the same phrase, here, does not carry with it the same meaning. To assume that "baptized in the Jordan" in connection with a miraculous cure of leprosy, must mean the same thing when used generations after, under another dispensation, and in connection with a religious rite, is "flaw" number *seven.*

Perhaps we ought to thank Dr. Fuller that he has not taken under his patronage—"*went down* and dipped seven times in Jordan," (as assumption number eight,) the usual argument of his friends—"went down *into the water*," and thus proved (?) a dipping.

This sevenfold dipping baptism suggests the following

problem: If Naaman was baptized seven times in the Jordan and benefited by it, how many times must Aristobulus have been baptized in the fish-pool to have been drowned by it? We commit this question to the charge of the arithmetical section of the friends of the theory.

Jewish translators.—Having looked at this passage from the Baptist point of view, one that turns on the performance of an act, I now remark that it is of importance to bear in mind that the translators of the Septuagint were Jews. The Jews used the word βαπτίζω in their religious rites to express, as has been proved, *a change of condition* irrespective of the performance of any particular act. Now, in this transaction we have a change of condition identical with that, removal of leprosy, secured by some of their religious rites; and for such change of condition the ordinary use of βαπτίζω, expressing a purified condition, is appropriate. It is proper to attribute its appearance in the passage to such national use, rather than to make it the translation of a word, with which, in its primary meaning, it is never, in the Septuagint nor in the Classics, used as an equivalent.

Patrists.—The Patristic view of the passage sustains this conclusion. Ambrose (ii, 426,) says: Diximus figuram præcessisse in Jordane, quando Naaman leprosus ille *mundatus* est. . . . Ergo habes unum baptisma. "We have said that a figure of baptism preceded in the Jordan, when Naaman, that leper, was cleansed. . . . Thus you have one kind of baptism." The baptism is made to centre in the changed condition,—the healing and consequent cleansing. And this changed condition is attributed to a peculiar power of the water, and not to the manner of using it. Quid ergo significat? Vidisti aquam; sed non aqua omnis sanat; sed aqua sanat, quæ habet gratiam Christi. (422.) "What, then, does it signify? Thou hast seen the water; but all water does not heal, but that water heals which has the grace of Christ." The healing of Naaman did not depend upon the manner of his using the waters of the Jordan, but upon the divinely imparted power. The prophet specified no form of use. In whatever form he used them, had he used them in a different form, they would have been equally efficacious. The Patrists make the baptism consist in the effect produced, not in the manner of use, and thus agree with the Septuagint translators. Mode of use being neither enjoined nor of controlling value. We conclude then; if there was any dipping in this case, it belongs exclusively to the Hebrew word; which word no more controls the meaning of βαπτίζω, than does βάπτω to which, and not to βαπτίζω, it is related in all its Hebrew use.

DISEASED CONDITION CHANGED TO CONDITION OF HEALTH.

BETHESDA HEALING.

John 5:4.

"For an angel went down at a certain season into the pool and troubled the water; whosoever then first after the troubling of the water stepped in was made whole of whatsoever disease he had."

Ὁ οὖν πρῶτος ἐμβὰς μετὰ τὴν ταραχὴν τοῦ ὕδατος ὑγιὴς ἐγίνετο.

Figure of Baptism.

Tunc curabatur unus, nunc omnes sanantur. Non sanat baptismus perfidorum, non mundat, sed polluit.

Ergo et illa piscina in figura: ut credas quia in hunc fontem vis divina descendit.

Habes quartum genus (baptismatis) in piscina, quando movebatur aqua.—*Ambrose*, iii, 395, 426.

"Then one was cured, now all are healed. The baptism of the unbelieving does not heal, it does not cleanse, but pollutes."

"Then, that pool is for a figure: that you may believe that a divine power descends into this fountain."

"You have a fourth kind of baptism in the pool, when the water was troubled."—*Ambrose*, iii, 395, 426.

BAPTISM BY THE POOL OF BETHESDA.

Although this transaction is recorded in the New Testament, it belongs to the Jewish economy and not to the

Christian. It is introduced here because of its essential unity with that class of baptisms now under consideration. A purgative power, beyond that merely physically washing quality which belongs to all water, was attributed to the Deluge. To the Jordan water, as used by Naaman, was communicated a curative power, not belonging to Arbana or Pharpar, or inherently to the Jordan itself. The same is true with regard to the waters of Bethesda. The usual qualities of water belonged to them at all times; but "at a certain season" an additional quality was divinely imparted to them, by means of which they exercised a controlling influence over any disease subjected to their power, relieving the sufferer and restoring him to perfect soundness of body.

Special Points.—1. If there is anything determined beyond controversy, as to this pool, it is that *its power to baptize was limited to a certain time.* Ambrose is entirely explicit on this point: "You have a fourth kind of baptism in the pool, *when the water was troubled.*" Now there was not one particle of water added to the contents of the pool at the time of this troubling. Its capability for baptism, therefore, did not arise from increased depth of water. If it had capacity for physical mersion at this time, it had the same capacity every day in the year. But it could baptize at this time, and it could not baptize at any other time. No water being added in the one case, and none being subtracted in the other, it follows, therefore, with the same rigid necessity, as does the conclusion in any demonstrated mathematical proposition, that *the baptism spoken of cannot be a physical mersion.*

2. This conclusion is sealed by fact, superadded to logic, showing that no physical mersion took place when this solitary baptism took place. The baptism was effected, neither by the party dipping himself, nor by being dipped by any one else, but by "stepping in" (ἐμ βὰς) the troubled water. Whether these waters reached to "the ankles," or to "the knees," or to "the loins," as in Ezekiel's vision, we are not told; but we are told that, *entering in*—though it wet but the soles of the feet, as of the priests bearing the ark through Jordan—effected a baptism, thoroughly changed the dis-

eased condition, and brought into a condition of health. But some earnest friend of the theory may cry: "Hold! No dipping? Why, for what else did he 'enter in' the water, but for a dipping? Could he not have been *sprinkled* out of the water? And, as for one to do the dipping, where was the angel? Did not he, too, 'go down into the water'—both the angel and the sick man—and why, if not to dip into the water? No dipping! What but 'a lack of Christian honesty' could resist such convincing evidence?" Well, I will concede this much: the evidence for this angel dipping, is quite as convincing as in some other cases, which we may look at by and by.

3. A third point, claiming to be brought into bolder relief by distinct mention, is the presence, in this transaction, of a *thorough change of condition.* Proof is needless. It is the *sine qua non* feature of the whole affair, as it is also of every baptism. Its presence is full justification for Ambrose in calling it "a fourth kind of baptism."

4. The position occupied by this "troubled" water, in relation to the baptism, is that of efficient agency, and not of a receiving element.

If this point be established, the theory at once vanishes into thin air. In every primary physical mersion, there are always present a baptizer, or a baptizing agency, a baptized object, and a receiving element, within which the baptized object finds its rest, and enters upon its changed condition. The Baptist theory affirms that βαπτίζω represents nothing but a definite form of action, carrying its object within the element, and, without resting there, bringing it out again. This notion has been so utterly ground into impalpable powder, between the millstones of facts, that we may let it go, for the present, to the winds. But some theorist may say: "Suppose the definite act be abandoned as an error, still there remains a *covering over*, and here, as our final refuge, we fight our last battle." To this we reply: It is necessary to determine whether this "covering over" is essentially transient or of indefinite continuance. If the former, then we are brought back to *a dipping* under another name. If the latter, then all the radical results flowing from this new position, must be accepted. But, whether accepted or not, as we aim, not merely at the overthrow of a mistaken theory of a word, but to establish truth, we proceed to show that a baptism is not limited, as the amended theory would affirm, to the enclosure of an object within a fluid, but that a fluid, present in a baptism, may be there, not as a receiving element, but as an efficient agency, effecting a baptism—change of condition without any enclosure.

In support of this position, I appeal, 1. To those multiplied cases adduced in Classic Baptism, in which *study*, *grief*, *questions*, *disease*, are represented as agencies in effecting baptisms, where physical covering is impossible, and where imaginary covering is never stated nor intimated. 2. To those cases mentioned in Classic Baptism, where a *fluid* element is employed as the agency in effecting the baptism, without any covering. (1.) *Hot* iron, baptized by water, as agency, without covering, bringing it into a cold condition (p. 325). (2.) Intoxicating wine, baptized by water, as agency, not covering it, but mixed through it, and bringing it into an unintoxicating condition (p. 339). (3.) Water, itself, impregnated with an intoxicating principle, and baptizing, as an agency, by drinking, bringing into a changed condition, resembling that of a drunken man (p. 330). (4.) Wine, as an agency, baptizing men by its intoxicating quality without covering, by drinking, bringing into a condition of drunkenness (pp. 316–342). 3. To the case in hand, where the water is impregnated, not with an intoxicating principle, but with a sanative power, the influence of which was to be developed, not by drinking, but by contact. A baptism is effected; the condition of the diseased man is thoroughly changed; there is no "covering over;" the result is not due to water as a fluid, but as a vehicle through which divine power is communicated, which divine power is exerted without calling into exercise the covering quality of water.

If these facts do not establish the position, that water, wine, or any other fluid, (possessed of a quality *capable of controlling condition* without mersion,) is capable of baptizing as an agency, without acting as a receiving element, then evidence has lost its power to control conclusions. But if they do suffice to establish this position, then, the amended theory, "covering over"—last refuge of its friends—perishes without remedy.

5. This baptism *by*—not dipping *in*, nor covered *with*—Bethesda water, proves that Naaman was baptized *by* the influence communicated through the water of Jordan, and that his baptism consisted in his changed bodily condition as to the leprosy, and not in his dipping—supposing that to have been present in the transaction. The same is true as to the baptism of the world *by* the deluge water. There was a baptism here of the world *in* the waters; but it is not that baptism to which attention is directed, but the cleansing of the world from its sin-defilements, by the agency of these world-embracing waters. Therefore Ambrose (iii, 426) groups them all together: "Ergo habes *unum* baptisma (quando Naaman leprosus ille mundatus est), *aliud* in diluvio, habes *tertium* genus, quando in mari Rubro baptizati sunt patres, habes *quartum* genus in piscina, quando movebatur aqua." All these are baptisms by changes of condition, through water as the agency, and not as a receiving element. And they are of "one," and "another," and a "third," and a "fourth" *genus* of baptism. "*Multa sunt genera baptismatum.*"

6. We have the clearest proof that the ground on which Ambrose rests, in calling all these cases baptisms, is the change of condition, which is the central truth presented in each. And it is this feature of their baptism—a thoroughly changed condition—which, in Ambrose's view, qualifies a purified world, a purified Israel, a purified Naaman, a purified Bethesdaite, to be a "figure" of that higher, holier, perfect baptism, effected through the water impregnated with the purifying and soul-regenerating influences of the Holy Spirit, in which he and other Patrists so fully believed.

WATER APPLIED TO THE BODY WITH DIVERSITY OF FORM AND EXTENT.

BAPTISM BY WASHING.

LEVITICUS 15:5.

"And whosoever toucheth his bed, shall cleanse his clothes and wash himself with water, and be unclean until the even."

Interpretation.

Τίνος δὲ ἕνεκεν ἐπὶ τὸ βάπτισμα ἔρχεται ὁ Χριστὸς ἀναγκαῖον εἰπεῖν, καὶ ἐπὶ ποῖον ἔρχεται βάπτισμα . . . . Βάπτισμα ἦν τὸ Ἰουδαϊκον, τὸ ῥύπων σωματικῶν ἀπαλλάττον, ὀυ τῶν κατὰ τὸ συνειδὸς ἁμαρτημάτων . . . . Λούσεται γὰρ τὸ σῶμα αὐτοῦ ὕδατι καθαρῷ.

"But it is necessary to say why Christ comes for baptism, and *for what baptism* he comes. For this is as necessary to know as that. And it is necessary to teach your love the latter first, because from the latter you may learn the former. *The baptism was Judaic;* that which takes away bodily defilement; not that which takes away sins of conscience. For if one should commit adultery, or be guilty of theft, or should transgress in any such way, it would not take away his guilt; but if any one should touch the bones of the dead, if any one should taste food not appointed by the law, if any should be near corruption, if any one was in company with lepers, he washed and was unclean until evening, and then was clean. For it is said, 'He shall wash his body with pure water, and shall be unclean till evening, and then he shall be clean.'" (Lev. 15:5, seqq.)—*Chrysostom*, ii, 366.

Οὐδὲ μὴν τὸν ἀπὸ τῆς κατὰ συζυγίαν κοίτης, ὁμοίως ὡς πάλαι, βαπτίζεσθαι καὶ νῦν προστάσσει ἡ θεία διὰ Κυρίου πρόνοια . . . . τὰ πολλὰ Μωῦσέως δι ἑνὸς περιλαβὼν βαπτίσματος.

"Divine providence, through the Lord, does not now, as formerly, command to be baptized from the conjugal bed . . . embracing, by one baptism, the many baptisms of Moses."—*Clemens Alex.*, i, 1184.

JUDAIC BAPTISM—BAPTISM FROM THE BED.

"*For what baptism he comes.*" This statement implies a diversity of nature in baptisms. Ambrose, as we have seen, expressly affirms this: "*Multa sunt genera baptismatum.*" There are many kinds of baptisms. Chrysostom tells us "what kind" of baptism this was, and says, that "the kind of baptism" which the Saviour received, will explain why he received baptism at all. The nature of some baptisms was such as to cause embarrassment at the thought of the Saviour receiving them. Such a baptism was that by which "sins of conscience" were taken away; and this was the baptism claimed to be administered in Chrysostom's day. But the Saviour had no such sins to take away. How then could he receive this kind of baptism; and, if he did not receive this kind of baptism, what kind did he receive? Such difficulties and queries could not but arise under Patristic teaching, and "the Golden Mouth" Bishop sets himself to answer them. In doing so, he declares that the baptism which Christ received was not Christian baptism, nor Johannic baptism, nor Classic baptism, but "*Judaic* baptism." He then expounds the distinguishing peculiarity of this kind of baptism. He does not make the difference to lie in dipping forward, or backward, or sideways, or standing, or kneeling; nor yet in being "wholly covered" by a sweeping torrent, or rising flood, or falling wave. Fortunately, or unfortunately, this modern theory of diverse baptism was unknown to this eloquent and learned Grecian. His explanation turns on the different influences possessed, and the different conditions, ceremonial and spiritual, induced by the elements operative in Judaic and Patristic baptism. The former takes away "bodily defilement," the latter takes away "sins of conscience."

"But we can escape this difficulty," exclaims the theorist. "When Ambrose and Chrysostom say there are '*many* kinds of baptisms,' they do not mean what they say; they mean that there is but *one* kind. They speak figuratively of different effects under one cause, or the diversities of a whole are embraced in the use of one of its parts." But the text does not speak of *a dipping* being in "the whole" as a part. "Very true; but we escape that difficulty, too, by 'figure.' Washing is the requirement, and as dipping is one mode of washing, and the greater includes the lesser, a dipping must be included in the washing." Certainly, the theory does cut quite a figure in its exposition, especially as being received on sufferance into the home of washing, like the pleading wolf into the home of the lamb, it incontinently devours its confiding host.

After all, we prefer believing that Chrysostom means what he says, that baptisms differ, though dippings do not, and that Judaic baptism changes the condition of the body by removing ceremonial defilement, while Patristic baptism was imagined to change the condition of the soul, by removing "sins of conscience." The baptism of Christ was (as taught) "*Judaic* baptism."

As to the manner of using the water for this washing, there is no intimation, whatever, of any particular mode. It is admitted that the word (λούω) carries no one mode with it, nor do any incidental directions or circumstances point to any modal use.

It is not necessary that the object washed should be in the water. This has been proved. And it is in proof, in respect to this particular washing, that neither the Septuagint nor Chrysostom believed that the body was required to be dipped in, or put in the water in any way, for the language they employ—λούσεται ὕδατι—allows the body to be washed out of the water as well as in the water, the requirement being to wash *with* water. This Judaic baptism of ceremonial purification, no more self-evidences the *quo modo* of its execution by dipping, pouring, or sprinkling, than does the Classic baptism of intoxication give its own proof as to the mode in which the wine was received—at one draught, by frequent sipping, or by sucking through a straw.

Clement.—The extract from Clement shows that this was one, only, of the "many baptisms" of Moses. It also exhibits two points irreconcilable with the theory.

1 The greater power of Patristic over Judaic baptism, and
2. The phraseology, "baptized *from* the conjugal bed."

As to the first of these points, Clement is in accord with other Patrists in attributing greater power to Christian baptism, over all other baptisms; but if baptism was understood by them to mean a dipping, no "power" can be attributed to one dipping over any other dipping. If baptism is expressive of condition, then there is fitness in saying that a Jewish or Christian rite had more or less power to produce a given effect.

In relation to the second point, it is obvious that "dipping *from*" defilement, is not such form of language as we would expect, while "to purify from," harmonizes with the idea. This form of expression we have met with before under similar circumstances—"baptizing *from* a dead body"—and we shall meet with it again. Such established usage can only be satisfactorily explained by the propriety of its form to express the nature of a baptism—purification from defilement.

BAPTISM BY WASHING.

Ezekiel 16 : 4, 9.

"And as for thy nativity, in the day thou wast born . . . thou wast not washed in water. Then washed I thee with water."

Septuagint.

Καὶ ἐν ὕδατι οὐκ ἐλούσθης . . . . καὶ ἐλουσά σε ἐν ὕδατι καὶ ἔχρισά σε ἐν ἐλαίῳ.

Interpretation.

"Cruenta infantium corpora, statim ut emittuntur ex utero lavari solent; ita et generatio spiritualis lavacro indiget salutari. . . . Multaque sunt lavacra quæ Ethnici in mysteriis suis pollicentur; qui omnes lavant: sed non lavant in salutem. Quod quidem non solum de hæreticis, sed de Ecclesiasticis intelligi potest, qui non plena fide accipiunt baptismum salutare. Dequibus dicendum est, quod acciperint aquam, sed non acciperint

Spiritum; sicut et Simon ille Magus, qui pecunia volebat redimere gratiam Dei, baptizatus quidem in aqua, sed nequaquam baptizatus est in salutem."

"(*Verse* 9.) 'Et lavi te aqua . . . . et unxi te oleo.' . . . . "Et lavi te, inquit, aqua baptismi salutaris. . . . de quo baptismate et Isaias loquitur, dicens: Lavabit Dominus sordes filiorum et filiarum Sion."—*Jerome*, v, 127, 131.

"The bodies of infants, stained with blood, are washed as soon as born. So, also, spiritual birth needs the salutary washing. The heathen practise many washings in their mysteries; who wash all; but they do not wash into salvation. Which indeed may be understood not only of heretics, but of those connected with the church, who do not receive with full faith the salutary baptism. Of whom it may be said, they receive the water, but do not receive the spirit; as also, Simon, the Magician, who wished to purchase the grace of God with money, was baptized, indeed, with water, but by no means, baptized into salvation."

Verse 9. "And I washed thee with water . . . . and I anointed thee with oil."

"And I washed thee," he says, "with the water of salutary baptism. . . . Concerning which baptism, Isaiah, also, speaks: The Lord will wash the uncleanness of the sons and daughters of Zion."—*Jerome*, v, 127, 131.

SPECIAL POINTS.

1. *Infant washing.*—Not one new-born babe in a million is put under the water in washing. But the theory says: "Under the water, baptism; not under the water, no baptism."

2. *Washing is baptism.*—No new-born babe was ever washed by a simple dipping into or covering with water. Birth impurity is not thus cleansed. Soul impurity is not to be washed away by a mere dipping into simple water. Washing and baptism are, both, more than a dipping. Washing is baptism because it is more than a dipping. Baptism is washing because it is more than a dipping. Dipping is neither a washing nor a baptism, because it is nothing but a dipping. Washing is more than (and may be performed without) either sprinkling, or pouring, or *dipping*. Dr. Fuller

(p. 15), says: "A command to wash is a command to wash, and nothing else." Doubtless Naaman thought so too.

3. *Salutary washing.*—That washing which is more than a dipping, yet no dipping, frees the new-born babe from its impurities, and brings it into a salutary, healthful condition. That washing which the Holy Spirit effects through power imparted to the water, frees the soul from its impurities and brings it into a salutary condition—one of spiritual health and salvation—baptizes "into salvation." So Patrists thought.

4. *Simple water cannot baptize.*—Simon Magus was baptized, (*dipped* Jerome, probably, supposed,) yet was not baptized. Just as Ambrose says: "Baptismata sunt gentium, sed non sunt baptismata." It may be called a baptism because avowedly a religious purification; but it was no baptism, in fact, because no purification of the soul took place, the power of the Holy Spirit not being incorporated with the water. He received the water; he did not receive the Spirit. No change of condition took place. He did not pass out of a state of impurity and condemnation, into a state of purity and salvation; therefore no baptism took place.

5. *This washing was* WITH *water and not* IN *water.*—It is true that the Septuagint introduces the preposition with the dative; but it is hardly necessary to say, that this is done, almost times without number, with instrumentality as well as locality. That it should be so regarded in this passage is shown, 1. By the fact that the preposition is omitted in Jerome's version. 2. That the preposition is used in the same verse, by the Septuagint with "*oil*," where inness is out of the question,—"I anointed thee *with*, not *in*, oil." In which case, also, Jerome omits the preposition. 3. In describing the use of oil, immediately after, he expresses the mode of use, by *pouring—olei infusione* linivit. The use of water, in the same baptism, both as instrumental means and receiving element, is as impossible as to use wine at the same time for baptizing one by making him drunk by drinking, and for drowning by putting him in it. The theory can find neither aid nor comfort in this washing.

BAPTISM BY WASHING THE HANDS AND FEET.

EXODUS 40 : 30–33.

(Exodus 29 : 4; 30 : 18–20.) (Numb. 8 : 5; 19 : 20.)

"And he set the laver between the tent of the congregation and the altar, and put water there to wash withal.

"And Moses and Aaron and his sons washed their hands and their feet thereat.

"When they went into the tent of the congregation, and when they came near unto the altar they washed; as the Lord commanded Moses."

Septuagint.

Ποίησον λουτῆρα χαλκοῦν—ὥστε νίπτεσθαι—καὶ ἐκχεῖς εἰς αὐτὸν ὕδωρ. Καὶ νίψεται Ἀαρὼν καὶ οἱ υἱοὶ αὐτοῦ ἐξ αὐτοῦ τὰς χεῖρας, καὶ τοὺς πόδας ὕδατι. (Ex. 30 : 18, 19.)

. . . . *καὶ λούσεις αὐτοὺς ὕδατι.* (Ex. 40 : 12.)

Interpretation.

Πρῶτον ὁ ἀρχιερεὺς λούεται, εἶτα θυμιᾷ . . . . πῶς γὰρ ἐνεχώρει τῶν ἄλλων ὑπερεύχεσθαι; τὸν δι' ὕδατος ὄυπω κεκαθαρισμένον; καὶ σύμβολον ἔκειτο τοῦ βαπτίσματος, λουτὴρ ἔνδον ἀποκείμενος τῆς σκηνῆς.

"The high priest first washes, then sacrifices; for Aaron was first washed, then became high priest. For how could be be permitted to pray for others who was not first cleansed by water? And the laver placed within the tent was a symbol of baptism."—*Cyril of Jerusalem*, 433.

"Interanea sane cum pedibus aqua dilui jubet sermo præcepti, sacramentum baptismi sub figurali prædicatione denuntians.

"Igitur sacrificium, pro quo hæc omnia sacrificia in typo et figura præcesserant, unum et perfectum, immolatus est Christus."

"The word of the precept, truly, with the feet, orders the washing with internal water, announcing, figuratively, the sacrament of baptism.

"Therefore Christ was sacrificed, the one perfect sacrifice, for which all these sacrifices in type and figure went before."—*Origen*, ii, 410, 442.

Ἁγνεία δὲ ἐστι φρονεῖν ὅσια· καὶ δὴ καὶ ἡ εἰκὼν τοῦ βαπτίσματος εἴη ἂν καὶ ἡ ἐκ Μωϋσέως παραδεδομένη τοῖς ποιηταῖς ὧδέ πως.

Ἡ δ' ὑδρηναμένη καθαρὰ χροῒ εἵματα ἔχουσα,
Ἡ Πενελόπη ἐπὶ τὴν εὐχὴν ἔρχεται.

Τηλέμαχος δὲ, ...
Χεῖρας νιψάμενος πολιῆς ἁλὸς, εὔχετ' Ἀθήνῃ.

Ἔθος τοῦτο Ἰουδαίων, ὡς καὶ τὸ πολλάκις ἐπὶ κοίτῃ βαπτίζεσθαι.
Εὖ γοῦν κἀκεῖνο εἴρηται·

Ἴσθι μὴ λουτρῷ, ἀλλὰ νόῳ καθαρός.

Clem. Alex., i, 1352.

"Purity is to think purely. An image of this baptism was communicated to the poets, from Moses, thus—

'Having washed, and being clothed with clean vestments,
Penelope comes to prayer.'

'But Telemachus, ...
Having washed his hands of the hoary sea, prays to Minerva.'

"This is a custom of the Jews to baptize often upon the couch. Therefore, it is well said,

'Be pure, not by washing, but by thinking.'"

Clemens Alex., i, 1352.

BAPTISM OF THE WHOLE BODY BY WASHING A PART.

Washing.—Dr. Carson insists that if these washings are called baptisms, they must have been "immersions." At the same time he says, "That the word (*λούω*) does not necessarily express mode, I readily admit. This must be determined by circumstances. All I contend for from this word is, that the object to which it is applied is covered with the water. The application of this word to baptism shows that the rite was a bathing of the whole body; and as immersion is the usual way of bathing, baptism must have been an immersion." (p. 486.) Dr. C. here distinguishes between "bathing" and "immersion," yet insists that in either case, equally, the object bathed or immersed shall be "covered with the water." There is such a careless and groundless mixing up of important words, having essentially diverse meanings, by this writer, that one cannot tell what he means. Does he mean that an object not in water, but rubbed by a wetted hand or cloth, is "bathed," "covered with water?" He speaks of the wounded thigh of Adonis being bathed, covered with water. If he was not "immersed," which is not said, how else could his wounded thigh have been "bathed" but by rubbing with the hand? So, unquestionably, the stripes of Paul and Silas were washed—bathed. But if this is the "covering with water" which Dr. C. contends for, what becomes of his conclusion of immersion-dipping when this Greek word is used?

The fullest proof has been adduced to show that λούω, lavo, wash, bathe, do not require their objects to be in the water. And as to the mode of applying the water, Carson (p. 493) admits—"the water might be applied by sprinkling, or by pouring, or in any way." Tertullian speaks of one as exposed "lavacro Jovis," to "the washing of Jupiter," effected "imbribus et pluviis," by "showers and rains." Would this meet the idea of "bathing and covering with water?" A line of poetry reads, "The rose had been washed, just washed in *a shower;*" is this washing, bathing, covering, by *sprinkling?* If this is his meaning, I do not know who will find much fault, unless it be the friends of the theory. And with this meaning, what becomes of the logic which *infers* these washings into immersions? And why is not Calvin (Harm. of Pent. ii, 210) justified, not merely by the merits of the case, but by Carson himself, in saying,—"Moses, before he consecrates the priests,. *washes* them *by the sprinkling* of water?" Carson says, (p. 471,) "A purification performed by pouring or sprinkling a few drops of water, would not be a *loutron.*" This statement overlooked the truth that religious purification does not depend for its extent on the extent of the application of the purifying element. The purification effected may embrace the entire person, although but a few drops of the purifying element may fall on the body. It is to this complete purification that the term λουτρόν, washing, is applied.

Thus Chrysostom speaks of martyrs "washed (λούονται) by

their own blood." And Origen speaks of be.ng "washed (loti) by our own blood." Blood, of itself, has no "washing" quality; it defiles. It is not used, here, for washing physically any part. Sacrificial blood cleanses the whole of that to which it is applied, irrespective of the extent of its application. This was martyr blood, and it washed the whole man—body and soul—though applied but in sprinkled drops. It is to this universal cleansing, this condition of purity, to which λουτρόν is applied, and applied without any possibility of just questioning. And Calvin is right in saying, (ii, p. 186,) "The washing of the hands and feet denoted that all parts of the body were infected with uncleanness; for since Scripture often uses the word 'hands' for the actions of life, and compares the whole course of life to a way or journey, it is very suitable to say, by synecdoche, that all impurity is purged away by the washing of the hands and feet."

Dr. Carson's plea for immersions because of washings, (baptisms,) is all in the air.

The brazen laver.—This laver, Cyril tells us, was "the symbol of baptism." It was not the symbol of dipping. Aaron and his sons did not wash *in* this vessel. Would not a command for several persons to wash their hands and feet in the same vessel, be, at any time, incredible? Would it not be pre-eminently incredible, that after one had washed his *feet* in a vessel of water, another should be required to wash his *hands* in the same vessel for a religious purification? But we are not left to reject, by inference, this singular conception; we are most distinctly told that the water was to be taken out of the laver—ἐξ ἀυτοῦ—ὕδατι—"wash with water out of it." But Dr. Carson would immerse the priests in the brazen sea, (p. 444,)—"Such things as they offered for burnt offering, they washed in them; *but the sea was for the priests to wash in.* Are not these immersions? Are not these different immersions even in the temple?" That is to say, he would make the priests climb up over these "twelve oxen," and then climb up five cubits higher, and plunge into twenty thousand gallons of water to wash! How many times a day this was done; or, how many this water purified before it became impure, and had to be drawn off, and supplied with twenty thousand gallons of fresh water, we are not told.

The theory needs a courageous advocate, and it has one in Dr. Carson. But "the sea" will not serve for immersion. The Hebrew uses two words (neither of modal act) to express these laver and sea washings. The Septuagint employs three words—πλύνω, περικλύζω, νίπτω—the last (applied to *hand* and *feet* washings) denoting the washing of the priests. Thus, the highest testimony, that of Jews who had full knowledge of the facts, denies an immersion in the "sea."

Baptism in Figure.—When Cyril speaks of the laver, at which the hands and feet were washed, as "a symbol of baptism;" and when Origen speaks of feet-washing as "baptism in figure;" and when Clement speaks of the washing of hands as an "image of baptism," they all mean to declare that these washings were baptisms, without any regard to the modal action by which the washing was effected. There is no hint as to the manner of the washing. It is said, (by the use of δὶα with the genitive, and by the use of ὕδατι without a preposition,) that the water was used as *a means* to effect the baptism, and not as an element to receive an object put into it. The baptism effected was one in fact, and not of mere imagination. It was not the absurdity of a physical baptism of a hand or a foot. How would such a baptism fit the priest for his duties? It is not his hands or his feet that he needs to be made pure, but his entire person. And this is accomplished by applying water, merely, to the hands and feet. This baptizes the whole person; brings the whole man into a condition of ceremonial purity, which is the baptism. This change of condition, from impurity into purity, is a fact, as truly as is the change of condition in a mass of lead passing from the atmosphere into the depths of the sea. This change, in the ceremonial condition of the whole man, by the local application of water, is called symbol of, figure of, image of, baptism, because it is a baptism which resembles some other baptism, and is intended so to resemble it.

As these symbols, figures, images, are connected with a

great variety of modes in the use of the agency in the baptism—water, blood, ashes, &c.—it is important to establish the fact that, under all these forms, they are not merely called, for some known or unknown reason, but truly are *bona fide* baptisms. For this purpose I call attention to the use of the same terms, "type and figure," in the extract from Origen, in reference to sacrifices which preceded "the one and perfect sacrifice." Although these sacrifices differed greatly among themselves, and still more from the "perfect sacrifice," still, they agreed generically among themselves, and in their resemblance to "the one sacrifice," in this, namely: that, in every case, there was a substitutionary victim. With great variety in the victims, and in the modal arrangements, they were all true sacrifices, "typifying and figuring" one which was like, and infinitely unlike. These baptisms, amid diversity of object and modal execution, were as real baptisms as these sacrifices were real. As Origen says, there were many sacrifices, yet only "one sacrifice." So Ambrose says: "Multa sunt genera baptismatum sed unum baptisma." Let no one suppose that the terms "symbol, figure, image," detract, in any wise, from the substantive character of these baptisms.

Jewish Custom.—Clement had been engaged in a discussion designed to enforce the great superiority of mental purity—right thinking—over ceremonial purity, water-washing. This leads him to speak of baptism, water-washing, as practised by Jew and Gentile. He supposes that the heathen poets may have received "the image of baptism" from Moses. Among the baptisms enjoined by Moses, he appears to have had especially in mind the washing of hands, as he quotes a case of this kind as practised by Telemachus; and also refers to the Jewish custom of washing hands at meals, "upon the couch." And in view of this widespread water-washing, and its ceremonial purity, presses, again, the great superiority of a pure mind over a ceremonial washing. To fasten this truth in the mind, is his single and earnest purpose.

Inasmuch as dipp'ng into water, or covering over with

water—one reclining upon a dining-couch—would be both untimely and embarrassing, Baptist writers have sought to introduce quite another scene. Thus Dr. Carson (p. 492) says: "The passage refers to the nightly pollutions, after which bathing was prescribed by the law of Moses. They were immersed on accout of the bed; that is, pollutions contracted there." (Levit. 15 : 16–48.)

This is only another of those extravagances of interpretation, constantly exhibited in the attempt to sustain a groundless theory, by cutting off and stretching out the facts of usage.

The interpretation is extravagant, 1. Because there is not a single point of contact between it and the context. There is neither statement of, nor hint at, sexual intercourse, in the remarks of Clement. Such conception cannot be made to mingle with the train of thought, any more than oil with water. It is an alien thing. 2. It is ridiculously absurd to suppose that "the poets" would learn "the image of baptism" from post-concubital washings! 3. It is a gross impeachment of Clement, to suppose that he would place, in juxtaposition, the purifications for prayer by Penelope and Telemachus, with sexual uncleanness. 4. It is an extravagance, most extravagant, to suppose that, out of the multiplied washings of the Jews, Clement would select a washing of this class, to hold it up before the world as illustrative of Jewish "custom."

What is the ground on which this interpretation is based? 1. The assumption that κοίτη must mean a sleeping couch. 2. The assumption that reference is made to Leviticus 15 : 16–18, and its remarkable washing. 3. The assumption that this washing was by "immersion." 4. The assumption that ἐπὶ has an unusual meaning. Not one of these assumptions has been proved, or can be proved. As to the first, it is disproved by President Beecher, most conclusively:—"Xenophon, in his Memorabilia, authorizes the usage (dinner-couch). Speaking of the marks of honor due from the younger to the elder, he mentions 'rising up in their presence, honoring them with a soft couch—κοίτῃ μαλακῇ—and giving them the precedence in speech.' This interpretation is sustained by Struzius, in his Lexicon Xenophonteum, who describes it as 'lectus quietis et convivii,' a couch of repose and feasting. Morell, in his Lexicon Prosodaicum, gives κλίνη and κοίτη as synonyms."

The comment of Hervetus, a translator of Clement, on this passage, is: "The Jews washed themselves, not only at sacrifices, but also at feasts, and this is the reason why Clement says that they were purified or washed upon a couch, that is, a dining-couch or triclinium. To this Mark refers, ch. vii, and Matt., ch. xv. Tertullian also refers to it when he says, Judæus Israel quotidie lavat."

The second assumption is sufficiently refuted when confronted with the passage. We may add, however, additional disproof, taken from Clement himself. He does refer to the washing in Levit. 15, in i, 1184, but in very different terms: ἀπὸ τῆς κατὰ συζυγίαν κοίτης—βαπτίζεσθαι. Now, can any one, when Clement has described this baptism in such unmistakable terms, claim a right to confound with it a baptism described in terms so diverse, and belonging to such diverse circumstances? The diversity of these passages does not consist merely, or mainly, in the presence of συζυγίαν, in the one case, and in its absence in the other, but in the presence of ἀπὸ in the first passage, and the use of ἐπὶ in the latter. The use of ἀπὸ, with the noun indicating the source of defilement, from which cleansing has been effected, is established usage; thus, we have "baptized from (ἀπὸ) a dead body," "from (ἀπὸ) the market," "from (ἀπὸ) an evil conscience." The use of ἐπὶ, under such circumstances, is unheard of. If, then, συζυγίαν might be omitted, ἀπὸ would, in its absence, be most imperatively required to be retained, in a reference to the baptism contemplated. Its absence, alone, is disproof of the assumed reference.

The third assumption has been met with so frequently, heretofore, and is in such constant demand as a staff on which the theory may lean, that no, present, formal disproof is needed.

The fourth assumption is dismissed by the truth, that no

unusual meaning can take the place of a usual meaning, when that meaning fully meets the exigencies of the case. The usual meaning meets all the demands of the present passage, most perfectly. It is in proof, that the washing of hands constituted a baptism of the entire person. It is in proof, that the washing of hands did take place, for the purification of the person, at meals. It is, therefore, in proof, that baptisms might take place, as Clement affirms, "*upon* the couch." And, this being in proof, the theory is again disproved, for hand-*dipping*, as a door of retreat, is both locked and bolted. The hands were no more defiled than any other part of the body, and if the purifying influence of the water extended no farther than its physical application, then the man, hands excepted, remained in all his impurity. But the man was purified, and consequently the purifying influence of the water extended beyond its application. Wine, drank, does not baptize—*make drunk*—merely the mouth, and throat, and stomach, which the liquid touches, but the whole man, from head to foot. So, purifying water does not merely baptize—*make pure*—the hands and the feet, with which it comes into contact, but the entire person, reached through these members of the body. When we meet with a heathen or a Jew, who believes that that part only of the body is baptized to which the water or the ashes is applied, we will listen to a hand-baptism as being something else than a baptism of the entire person. Hand-washing, "*upon* the couch," however effected, was no *dipping* of the person into water, but it was a *baptism* of the entire man.

There is strong reason to believe that Clement, instead of referring to Leviticus 15, had his eye on Mark 7 : 2, 3. In addition to general considerations, very strong special evidence for this may be found in the use of πολλάκις. It is well known that the use of πυγμῇ, in Mark, has been a cause of embarrassment to translators. The Vulgate, Luther, and the English Bible, translate "*frequently*," "many times," "often," and it is quite probable that Clement obtained his "frequently" from the same source. Certainly the word has thus a reason for its use, while, on the Baptist hypothesis, it must be confessed that it is a very remarkable addendum.

Alex. D. Le Nourry (Dissert. ii, in Clementem) makes the following remark on the passage under consideration: "Nostri porro sacri baptismatis imaginem non solum apud Judæos, sed etiam Gentiles fuisse Clemens noster ostendit. Et apud Gentiles quidem in eo, quod de Penelope et Telemacho cecinit Homerus *Odyss.* A′ et Δ′. Apud Judæos autem, quia mos eorum erat, ut sæpe in lecto *tingerentur*. Sed scite Clemens monet hæc plane imperfecta fuisse baptismata quandoquidem non lavacro, sed animo mundi purique esse debemus."

On this passage we may ask: 1. Can the irrationality of theory go beyond the making washing *post concubitum*, the image "*nostri sacri baptismatis?*" 2. When the theory insists that *tingo*, used with baptism, proves *a dipping*, how does it manage to effect a dipping "*in lecto?*"

Clement, a native of Athens, knew somewhat of Greek, but clearly he knew nothing of the dipping theory.

BAPTISM BY SPRINKLING.

Leviticus 14:4–7.

"Then shall the priest command to take for him that is to be cleansed, two birds alive and clean, and cedar wood, and scarlet, and hyssop:

"And the priest shall command that one of the birds be killed in an earthen vessel over running water.

"As for the living bird, he shall take it, and the cedar wood, and the scarlet, and the hyssop, and shall dip them and the living bird in the blood of the bird that was killed over the running water:

"And he shall sprinkle upon him that is to be cleansed from the leprosy seven times, and shall pronounce him clean, and shall let the living bird loose in the field."

Septuagint.

Καὶ περιῤῥανεῖ ἐπὶ τὸν καθαρισθέντα ἀπὸ τῆς λέπρας ἑπτάκις καὶ καθαρὸς ἔσται.

Interpretation.

. . . . "Et intingens passerem vivum in aquas, in quibus sanguinem immolati passeris decurrere fecerat, cum ligno cedrino, lana coccinea, et hyssopo aspergeret septies leprosum, et tunc rite mundaretur. . . . Per lignum vero cedrinum Pater, per hyssopum Filius; per lanam autem coccineam, quæ fulgorem ignis habet, Spiritus sanctus designatur. Iis tribus, qui rite mundari volebat, aspergebatur; quia nullus per aquam baptismatis a lepra peccatorum mundari potest, nisi sub invocatione Patris, et Filii, et Spiritus sancti. . . . Nosque a peccatis nostris, qui per leprosum designamur, per eorum invocationem, et per aquam baptismatis abluit."

"The Lord also commanded Moses that if any leprous person would be cleansed, he should come to the priest and offer two sparrows to the priest. Of which he killing one should make its blood flow into living water, and dipping the living sparrow into the water in which he had made the blood of the slain sparrow to flow, with cedar wood, scarlet wool and hyssop, he should sprinkle seven times the leprous person, and then he would be properly cleansed. . . .

"But by the cedar wood the Father, by the hyssop the Son, but by the scarlet wool, which has the brightness of fire, the Holy Spirit is designated. Whoever wished to be cleansed in proper form was sprinkled by these three; because no one can be cleansed from the leprosy of sin by the water of baptism, except under the invocation of the Father, and of the Son, and of the Holy Ghost. . . . And he cleanses us, who are designated by the leper, by their invocation and by the water of baptism."
—*Ambrose*, iv, 829.

BAPTISM BY SPRINKLING.

Ambrose, here, draws out in minute detail the points of resemblance between the figure baptism and the figured baptism.

The resemblances are 1. The leper and the sinner. 2. Leprosy and sin. 3. The mingled water and blood, and the water of baptism. 4. The cedar wood, the hyssop, and the scarlet wool, designating the Father, Son, and Holy Ghost.

5. The removal of the leprosy and the purification of the soul from sin.

Where these elements were present, the cleansing, the baptism, was duly performed. But the theory cries out, "Stop, where is *the dipping?*" Alas, here as everywhere else, it is lacking. The fact is that all through the Patristic interpretations of Jewish baptisms, it is written in characters so plain, that "a wayfaring man, though a fool, need not err therein," that a dipping or a covering with water never enters into their thoughts as a requisite for baptism.

And this, not because they did not know that βαπτίζω had power to effect a physical intusposition unlimited by form of act, or time of duration, thus essentially changing the condition of its object; but because they knew this well, and because they knew more, namely, that this word was able to throw aside this limited application to a condition of physical investment, and to advance into a broader and nobler field, indicative of thorough change of condition under any competent influence. This places the Patrists in full accord with the Classics, and expounds with the most entire facility, all their language. These Jewish baptisms have nothing to do with physical investments. They belong to baptisms whose change of condition is due to influences which do not invest externally, but pervade internally. Hence this baptism was by sprinkling, and it operated as an agency controlling the condition of the sprinkled object; as Ambrose says, "by (*per*) the water of baptism." Ambrose believed in *baptism* by sprinkling, though not in *dipping* by sprinkling.

BAPTISM BY WASHING AND SPRINKLING.

PSALM 51:2, 7.

"Wash me thoroughly from my iniquity, and cleanse me from my sin.

"Purge me with hyssop, and I shall be clean: wash me, and I shall be whiter than snow."

Septuagint.

Ἐπιπλεῖον πλῦνόν με ἀπὸ τῆς ἀνομίας μου, καὶ ἀπὸ τῆς ἁμαρτίας μου καθάρισον με.

Ῥαντιεῖς με ὑσσώπῳ καὶ καθαρισθήσομαι, πλυνεῖς με καὶ ὑπὲρ χιόνα λευκὰν θήσομαι. (*Ps.* 50:4, 9.)

Interpretation.

"Renovamur enim per lavacri regenerationem; renovamur per Spiritus sancti effusionem; renovamur etiam per resurrectionem. . . . Quomodo renovemur, audi: *Asperges me hyssopo, et mundabor.* (Ps. 50:9.) . . . Recte renovatur qui de tenebris peccatorum in lucem virtutum mutatur et gratiam.—*Ambrose*, i, 827.

"Non tam sæpius quam plenius lavari petit, ut conceptam sordem possit eluere. Noverat secundum legem pleraque mundandi esse subsidia, sed nullum plenum et perfectum. Ad illud ergo perfectum tota intentione festinat, quo justitia omnis impletur, quod est baptismatis sacramentum, sicut ipse docet Dominus Jesus (Matt. 3:15). i, 867.

"Qui enim baptizatur, et secundum Legem et secundum Evangelium videtur esse mundatus; secundum legem, quia hyssopi fasciculo Moyses aspergebat sanguinem agni: secundum Evangelium, quia Christi erant candida vestimenta sicut nix, cum resurrectionis suæ gloriam in Evangelio demonstraret. Super nivem ergo dealbitur cui culpa dimittitur. (iii, 399.)

" Per hyssopi fasciculum aspergebatur agni sanguine qui mundari volebat typico baptismate."—*Ambrose*, i, 875.

— διὰ τοὺς μέλλοντας ὑσσώπῳ ῥαντίζεσθαι, καὶ καθαρίζεσθαι ὑσσώπῳ τῷ νοητῷ τῇ δυνάμει τοῦ κατὰ τὸ πάθος ὑσσώπῳ καὶ καλάμῳ ποτισθέντος.—*Cyril*, 425.

Βαπτισθῶμεν οὖν, ἵνα νικήσωμεν· μετάσχωμεν καθαρσίων ὕδατων, ὑσσώπου ῥυπτικωτέρων, αἵματος νομικοῦ καθαρωτέρων, σποδοῦ δαμάλεως ἱερωτερων ῥαντιζούσης τοὺς κεκοινωμένους, καὶ πρόσκαιρον ἐχούσης σώματος κάθαρσιν, οὐ παντελῆ τῆς ἁμαρτίας ἀναίρεσιν.—*Gregory Nazianzen*, 372.

"We are renewed by the regeneration of washing; we are renewed by the effusion of the Holy Spirit; we are renewed, also, by the resurrection. How we must be renewed, hear: 'Thou shalt sprinkle me with hyssop, and I shall be clean.'

He is rightly renewed who is changed from the darkness of sin into the light of virtue and grace."—*Ambrose*, i, 827.

"He does not desire so much to be washed frequently as thoroughly, that contracted defilement may be washed away. He knew that, according to the law, there were many means of cleansing, but none full and perfect. To that perfect one, therefore, he hastens with full purpose, by which all righteousness may be fulfilled, which is the sacrament of baptism, as the Lord Jesus himself testifies (Matt. 3:15)." i, 867.

"He who wished to be cleansed by typical baptism, was sprinkled with the blood of the lamb by a bunch of hyssop." i, 875.

"He who is baptized, whether in conformity with the Law or in conformity with the Gospel, is cleansed; in conformity with the Law, because Moses sprinkled the blood of the lamb with a bunch of hyssop." . . . . iii, 399.

"Rejoice, O heavens, and be glad, O earth, because of those who are about to be sprinkled with hyssop, and to be purified by the spiritual hyssop, through the power of him who drank, in his suffering, from the hyssop and the reed."—*Cyril*, 425.

"Therefore let us be baptized, that we may overcome; let us partake of the purifying waters, more purging than hyssop, more purifying than the blood of the Law, more sanctifying than the ashes of a heifer sprinkling the unclean, and having, for the time, power for the purification of the body, but not for the complete removal of sin."—*Gregory Nazianzen*, 372.

Sprinkling Water, Blood, or Ashes, Effects a Baptism.

POINTS.

1. *Washing, sprinkling; a means toward Baptism.*—Ambrose teaches, in the first extract, that we are renewed by the regenerative power of washing; that the mode of the washing effecting this renewal, is by "sprinkling with hyssop;" and, farther, that what is meant by "renewal" is a change of condition, passing out of a state of moral darkness into a state of moral light. This new condition, effected by sprinkling-washing, is baptism.

Is this the doctrine (not theological but philological) of the theory? Is it not the identical philological conclusion to which we were brought by the Classics, viz., a thorough change of condition, effected by an influence, is a baptism?

2. *Baptism under the Law not of full power.*—Ambrose had before told us that there were "many baptisms;" he now tells us that "not one of these was perfect." He does not mean to deny that any or all were perfect baptisms, considered in themselves, but that they were relatively imperfect; the power effecting the baptism,—the changed condition, was not adequate to meet all the necessities of men. In like manner John's baptism was "imperfect," and for the same reason. The theorists will not deny that John's baptism was perfect as a baptism considered in itself; nor can they deny that the Patrists regarded John's baptism as "imperfect" as respects its power to change the condition of those receiving it. The "imperfection" of legal baptisms by sprinkling, considered as carrying with them "the fulfilment of all righteousness," does not affect their being true and perfect baptisms in themselves. This idea of perfectness of power in a baptism, is proof that form of *act* had nothing to do with it; fulness of result was the issue in contemplation.

3. *Legal sprinklings Baptize.*—In the third extract he declares, as plainly as it can be expressed in language, that baptism under the Law and baptism under the Gospel, are on a perfect equality as baptisms; that they are, also, on an equality as to the effecting a change of condition from impurity to purity; but as to the measure of that change they differed. He, also, tells us, in terms so explicit as to admit of no addition, that the mode of baptism "according to the Law" was by *sprinkling*,—"*Moses sprinkled the blood of the Lamb upon him who was baptized according to the law.*"

4. *Type Baptism.*—In the last extract this truth is reaffirmed with a vividness and force which writes as with a pen of iron in the rock forever, that *sprinkling the blood of the Lamb baptizes*,—brings the impure out of their condition of impurity into a condition of purity. And this baptism is a "type" of that one, full, and perfect baptism by the Lamb of God, according to the Gospel.

Against this identification of sprinkling and baptism Dr. Carson lifts up a cry of indignation and rebuke. And well he may; for if Ambrose is right Carson is wrong, all wrong, and the theory,—"dip and nothing but dip through all Greek literature," as also its amendment, "at least a complete covering,"—perishes without hope.

On this point Carson thus speaks (p. 369): "To what purpose is it to refer us to the sprinkling of Aaron and his sons with blood, with other sprinklings? These were *divers purifications*, but they were not *divers baptisms*. Yet, after enumerating these sprinklings, he gravely tells us: 'Now these are the divers baptisms of which the apostle speaks.' Who told him this? The passage does not say so; we have not even the authority of a dream. Nothing but assumption, assumption, assumption. Why does he not identify these sprinklings with the baptisms? This has never been effected; this cannot be effected. . . . There is here nothing that looks like an identification of the sprinklings under the law, with the baptisms under the law." Then let us try again: "'Qui enim baptizatur, . . secundum Legem . . Moyses aspergebat,'—For he who *is baptized* according to the law, Moses *sprinkled*." Does this look more like identification? "Aspergebatur agni sanguine qui mundari volebat typico baptismate,—He was *sprinkled* with the blood of the lamb who wished to be cleansed with *typical baptism*." Is this any more satisfactory? We hand over the charge of triple assumption to its proper ownership, the theory. Sunshine does not more surely reveal shadow as attendant upon substance, than does history show assumption to wait on the theory. Now, that Ambrose calls the sprinkling of the blood of the lamb a baptism, human wit can neither evade nor deny; but troubled theorists may seek to escape on the ground that it is only a *typical* baptism.

To this we answer: 1. These sprinklings are called baptisms scores of times, without any limiting adjunct. 2. They are here called baptisms, regarded in their own nature, and *typical* baptisms, because they have such a nature as to resemble some other baptism to which reference is made.

3. Whatever may have been the conception of Ambrose as to the antitype baptism, he must have seen that conception shadowed forth in the type baptism. 4. If Ambrose believed that a dipping or a covering was the alpha and the omega of a baptism, as the theorists believe, and as they affirm that Ambrose believed, then a dipping or a covering must have been seen by this Patrist in whatever he called a "*typical* baptism." That this is true, and is felt to be an absolute necessity under the theory, by its friends, a glance at facts will abundantly prove. 1. In the battle of the Frogs and the Mice, Gale, who had assumed the identity of βάπτω and βαπτίζω, (the one in a short coat, the other in a long coat,) and had remorselessly shut up both to a dipping, felt bound by his theory to effect, against the outcry of common sense, the dipping of a lake into the blood of a frog. Carson having assumed that βαπτίζω means "dip, and nothing but dip," feels bound, against staring fact, to transmute the *flowing* of the tide into a *dipping* of the coast into the sea. Dr. Fuller, having assumed that it means at least "a complete covering," felt compelled, even while gazing upon the *pouring* water and the *uncovered* altar, to declare, though it is not covered, yet *it means that it is covered.* The whole company of theorists feel bound to uncover the shame of their assumption, by declaring that the Apostles were dipped in—or at least covered by—the wind, at Pentecost. This class of facts shows how dire is the necessity, under the theory, to find a dipping or a covering wherever the word baptism is used. 2. Another class of facts reveals the same truth. Whenever the Classics show us a baptized drunken man, or a baptized sick man, or a baptized studious man, or a baptized business man, or a baptized bewildered man, or a baptized sleeping man, the theorist feels bound, and does, pitilessly, put them all under the water. 3. The same development is exhibited under another class of facts. Noah is regarded as having received a *typical* baptism. And the theorists feel themselves bound to show "a dipping, or at least a complete covering." Consequently we have learned men exposing the nakedness of their wisdom to the pity or

the derision, as the case may be, of every passer by, by talking about Noah buried in the waters, and emerging from his grave on Ararat. Again; it is believed that Israel received a *typical* baptism at the Red Sea. And, at once, with all alacrity, as an obligation which admits of neither controversy nor escape, they set about the discovery of "a dipping, or at least a complete covering." With what success this effort is made, we will soon consider in detail. It is sufficient now to point out the fact that a *typical* baptism is recognized as embodying the *sine qua non* feature of the theory. 4. Once more. What is that baptism which is now practised by the theorists, according to their claim, but a *typical* baptism, throwing backward its resemblance shadow, as the Flood and the Red Sea threw theirs forward? If anything can be settled under the theory, it is, that every baptism must have within itself "a dipping, or at least a complete covering;" and especially is this true of every *typical* baptism. Now, Ambrose furnishes us with a "typical baptism," and tells us most explicitly how it was effected, namely, by "the *sprinkling* of the blood of the lamb." Will some friends of the theory do us the favor to hunt up "a dipping, or at least a complete covering," in this baptism? If it is there, it can be pointed out, and then we will give up our argument. If it is not there, then either Ambrose did not know what constituted a baptism, or the friends of the theory do not. But they admit that Ambrose did well know all that entered into the nature of a baptism, *therefore* the theory, &c.——. But, apart from this short-hand reasoning, let us look back from the standpoint to which we are brought, along the line of the theory, to note the make-up of the dippings and coverings for their baptisms. And, in doing so, we are struck with the fact, that the dipping, got out of the frog's blood, by Gale, is laughed at by Carson; while the dipping which Carson gets out of the rising tide, by the invocation of *catachresis*, Fuller, considerately, rejects with the *unuttered* remark, "the less said about such a dipping the better;" Fuller, himself, warned by the Scylla which had ruined one of his friends, and alarmed by the Charybdis which had destroyed another, abandons the dipping, and patronizes "at least a complete covering;" and, after quite reluctantly ascending Carmel to witness the baptism there, declares, as he looks upon the poured-out water, that "if the altar is not covered, it ought to be, for the sake of a very dear theory, and, in fact, is, by a most appropriate flood of rhetoric." I need but glance at the violence done to sound reason by the endless dippings of individuals, and of communities, of cities and nations, as shown in the misinterpretations of Classic baptisms. Nor need I dwell upon the feats of imagination, by which Noah is dipped into the flood, Israel into the Red Sea, and the Apostles into the wind. The theorist who can accept and intellectually digest trifles like these, may smile at the tenpenny nails and flint stones which enter into the commissariat of the Bird of the Desert.

We choose to cast in our lot with Ambrose as the faithful expositor of Classic baptism, which repudiates the presence of a dipping or a covering in baptisms of influence, while declaring, that the changed condition effected by the sprinkling of the sacrificial lamb is a baptism typical of another condition, more full and more perfect.

CYRIL.

In addressing candidates for baptism, Cyril calls upon the heavens to rejoice, and the earth to be glad, "because of those who are about to be sprinkled with hyssop, and to be purified with the spiritual hyssop, by the power of Him who drank from the hyssop and the reed." He, thus, brings together the type baptism and the antitype baptism. I do not adduce this fact to prove that Cyril baptized by sprinkling (undoubtedly he oftentimes did so), but to show, 1. That it never entered into his mind to question that baptism might be effected by sprinkling with hyssop. 2. That he had no hesitation, however he may, usually, have administered the rite of baptism, to speak of it by the same terms which described the typical baptism; but inasmuch as the typical baptism by hyssop was never administered otherwise than by "sprinkling," while the Patristic baptism was usually administered in a different form, it follows, inevitably, that Cyril did not regard the mode of administering baptism as involved in the type or in the nature of a baptism. In other words, Cyril believed that baptism was a change of condition, effected by any competent influence, and that it never involved the question as to mode of accomplishment; consequently he does not hesitate to bring baptism, by sprinkling, face to face with baptism administered in any other mode, and even to call it by the modal word (" sprinkle ") by which the type baptism was accomplished. 3. That Cyril believed that both the blood used by Moses in sprinkling, and the water used by himself after another fashion, were used as *means*, having a power of influence to effect baptisms independently of their character as fluids. Thus he says (429): "Do not regard this washing (τῷ λουτρῷ) as by simple water, but by the spiritual grace given with the water . . . —by invocation it acquires the power of holiness—(δύναμιν ἁγιότητος ἐπικτᾶται)." This truth, overlooked by its friends, takes the ground from underneath the feet of the theory, and it sinks out of sight. Cyril adds: "As man is twofold, purification is twofold; that which is spiritual by the spiritual, that which is physical by the physical; water purifies the body, the Spirit seals the soul; sprinkled, as to the heart, by the Spirit, and washed, as to the body, by pure water, we come to God." Sprinkling and washing are instrumental means to effect a change of condition.

GREGORY NAZIANZEN.

The testimony of Gregory N., as to the two points: 1. That the sprinklings under the law were baptisms. 2. That the water used in Patristic baptism had a baptizing *power* communicated to it, and on that account, and on that account only, was capable of baptizing, is the same as the testimony of Cyril and Ambrose. 1. On the first point we have not the direct use of the word baptism, but it would be the veriest despair which would rest an argument on the absence of a word in the presence of the thing. 2. Catechumens are invited to come to baptism, and to partake of the purifying power of the water, which is extolled as transcending that belonging to all the other agencies employed under the law for effecting baptism. There was power in hyssop to baptize (change the condition); there was power in sacrificial blood to baptize (change the condition); there was power in the ashes of the heifer, sprinkling the unclean, to baptize (change the condition); but there is "a power of baptism" in Patristical water, which far excels all these, according to Gregory. These baptisms of sacrificial blood and heifer ashes could not perfectly take away sin, but Patristic baptism could take away every sin; therefore these imperfect baptisms were only types of that perfect baptism which thoroughly changes the moral condition of body and soul.

This view of baptism (effected by any influence competent to make a thorough change of condition, irrespective of form of operation) is identical with the view presented by the Classics; it has nothing in common with the theory.

BAPTISM BY POURING AND SPRINKLING.

EZEKIEL 36 : 25, 26.

"Then will I sprinkle clean water upon you and ye shall be clean; from all your filthiness and from all your idols will I cleanse you.

"A new heart, also, will I give you, and a new spirit will I put within you."

Septuagint.

Καὶ ῥανῶ ἐφ' ὑμᾶς καθαρὸν ὕδωρ, καὶ καθαρισθήσεσθε ἀπὸ πασῶν τῶν ἀκαθαρσιῶν ὑμῶν, καὶ ἀπὸ πάντων τῶν εἰδώλων ὑμῶν, καὶ καθαρῶ ὑμᾶς, καὶ δώσω ὑμῖν καρδίαν καινὴν, καί πνεῦμα καινὸν δώσω ἐν ὑμῖν.

Interpretation.

"Et effundam (sive aspergam) super vos aquam mundam . . . . ita ut super credentes, et ab errore conversos, effunderem aquam mundam baptismi salutaris, et mundarem eos ab abominationibus suis . . . . et darem eis cor novum ut crederent in Filium Dei, et spiritum novum, de quibus David loquitur: Cor mundum crea in me, Deus, et spiritum rectum innova in viscribus meis (Ps. 50 : 21). Et considerandum, quod cor novum, et spiritus novus detur per effusionem et aspersionem aquæ."

"And I will pour out (or sprinkle) upon you clean water . . . . so that upon the believing and those converted, I will pour out the clean water of saving baptism, and I will cleanse them from their abominations and from all their errors, with which they have been possessed, and I will give to them a new heart, that they may believe upon the Son of God, and a new spirit, of which David speaks: Create in me a clean heart and renew a right spirit within me (Ps. 50 : 21). And it is to be observed, that a new heart and a new spirit may be given *by the pouring and sprinkling of water.*"—*Jerome*, v, 341, 342.

"Adspersio autem secundum legem emundatio peccatorum erat, per fidem populum sanguinis adspersione purificans (Ps. 50 : 9); sacramentum futuræ ex Domini sanguine adspersionis, fide interim legis sanguine holocaustomatum repensante."—*Hilary*, i, 238.

"But sprinkling according to the law was the cleansing of sin, through faith purifying the people by the sprinkling of blood (Ps. 50 : 9); a sacrament of the future sprinkling by the blood of the Lord, faith, meanwhile, supplementing the blood of the legal sacrifice."—*Hilary*, i, 238.

Καὶ ἡ εἰκὼν αὐτὴ τοῦ βαπτίσματος ἐφώτιζεν τε πάντοτε πάντας τοὺς κατ' ἐκεινον τὸν καιρὸν 'Ισραηλίτας καὶ ἔσωζεν—ὡς Παῦλος ἔγραφεν (1 Cor. 10 : 1, 2): *Καὶ ὡς προφητεύουσιν, 'Ιεζεκιήλ*—(36 : 25) *'Ρανῶ ἐφ' ὑμας ὕδωρ καθαρὸν. . . . Δαυϊδ δέ 'Ραντιεῖς με ὑσσώπῳ.*

"And the very image of baptism both continually illuminated and saved all Israel at that time—as Paul wrote (1 Cor. 10 : 1, 2): and as prophesied Ezekiel, 36 : 25, 'I will sprinkle clean water upon you, and you shall be clean from all your sins;' and David (Ps. 50 : 9): 'Sprinkle me with hyssop and I shall be clean.'"—*Didymus Alex.*, 713.

Βλέπεις τοῦ βαπτίσματος τὴν δύναμιν. . . . . Θάρσει, 'Ιερουσαλὴμ,—'Ραντιεῖ ἐφ' ὑμᾶς ὕδωρ καθαρὸν.

"Thou seest the power of baptism.—Be of good courage, O

Jerusalem, the Lord will take away all thy iniqu.ties. The Lord will wash away the uncleanness of his sons and daughters by the spirit of judgment and the spirit of burning. He will sprinkle upon you clean water and ye shall be purified from all your sin."—*Cyril of Jerusalem*, 418.

"Ut inde exeamus loti sanguine nostro. Baptisma enim sanguinis solum est quod nos puriores reddat, quam aquæ baptismus reddidit. . . . Mihi si concederet Deus ut proprio sanguine diluerer, ut baptismum secundum morte pro Christo suscepta perciperem. . . . Post istud baptisma."

"That we may leave this world washed by our own blood. For it is only the baptism of blood which can make us more pure than the baptism of water made us. . . . If God would grant to me that I might be cleansed by my own blood, that I might attain that second baptism, dying for Christ, I would depart out of this world secure. . . . After this baptism."—*Origen*, ii, 980.

"Neque enim spiritus sine aqua operari potest, neque aqua sine spiritu.—For neither can the Spirit operate without water, nor water without Spirit."—*Cyprian*, 1057.

Δεῖ δέ καθαρίζεσθαι καὶ ἁγιάζεσθαι τὸ ὕδωρ πρῶτον τοῦ ἱέρεως, ἵνα δυνηθῇ τῷ ἰδίῳ βαπτίσματι τὰς ἁμαρτίας τοῦ βαπτιζομένου ἀνθρώπου ἀποσμῦζαι Διά τε 'Ιεζεκιήλ.—36 : 25.

"But it is necessary that the water be first purified and sanctified by the priest, that it may be able by its own baptism to wipe off the sins of the baptized man. And through Ezekiel, the prophet, the Lord says: 'And I will sprinkle you with pure water.'"—*Cyprian*, 1082.

"Ezek. 36 : 25; Numb. 19 : 13; 8 : 7; 19 : 9.—Unde apparet aspersionem quoque aquæ instar salutaris lavacri obtinere."

"Whence it appears that the sprinkling of water, also, like the saving washing, obtains divine grace."—*Cyprian*, 1148.

Καὶ τοῖς δάκρυσι βαπτιζόμενος ἐκ δευτέρου.—"Baptized a second time by tears."—*Clemens Alex.*, ii, 649.

JEROME.

The "clean water of saving baptism," Jerome declares is communicated by "pouring or sprinkling." The effect of pouring or sprinkling this clean water is a baptism exhibited in "a new heart and a new spirit." This is, indeed, a thoroughly changed condition without dipping or covering.

Jerome thinks that this baptism (changed condition), through the power of "clean water" sprinkled or poured, is so remarkable that he attaches to it a *nota bene:* "A new heart and a new spirit may be given by the *pouring* or *sprinkling* of water."

This eminent scholar, then, is to be added to the list of those who believed that baptism was a changed condition induced by a powerful influence imparted to the water, and through it to those who received it in the ritual ordinance. Jerome never thought of such a thing as a Judaic or a Patristic baptism being a dipping or a covering, any more than Classic writers thought of a baptism by wine-drinking being a dipping or a covering.

HILARY.

The *power* of blood sprinkling, under the law, to change the condition of the soul, when assisted by faith, Hilary, also, teaches. He declares this blood sprinkling to have been a typical sacrament. The only one which it could represent was that of baptism. According to his view, the sin-remitting power of the blood of Christ was exerted through the Sacrament of Baptism. And the mode of application is represented as by "sprinkling." Let no one imagine that I represent the (common) mode of baptism by Patrists to have been by sprinkling. I do no such thing. I do what is more to my purpose. I show that their view of baptism was such, that in the very act of administering it in a manner the farthest possible removed from sprinkling, they still felt that there was no possible reason why they might not speak in the freest manner of baptism by sprinkling. That they did so speak under such circumstances, is just as certain as that we have their writings. Either these men knew nothing of the dipping, covering theory, or they were all, and several, bereft of their senses when they wrote the books which have come down to us.

DIDYMUS ALEXANDRINUS.

This distinguished Greek scholar tells us that "the image of baptism" was ever with the Jews in its instructive and saving power.

Can imagination conceive of any greater contrast than that presented by Dr. Carson, in his conception of baptism as a dipping of pots and cups and of the legs and shoulders of sacrificial victims, and that of Didymus, as a source of illumination and salvation?

But worse, if possible, than this. Didymus places the theorists in the very sharpest of dilemmas. He tells us that this "image of baptism" is exemplified in the passage of Paul, 1 Cor. 10: 1, 2, and of Ezekiel 36: 25, and David, Ps. 50: 9. Every theorist accepts the first as an undoubted and most charming "image of baptism." "What could be more clear, or more striking, or more demonstrative of the truthfulness of the theory, than (the dipping?) the covering, by the cloud and the water walls, of those in the depths of the sea?" May be nothing; at least we have nothing, just now, to say against it. But what of that other "image of baptism?" What of that "sprinkling with clean water" of Ezekiel, and that "sprinkling with hyssop" of David? Please point out to us the overhanging cloud, the congealed waters, the cavernous depths which "dip, or at least completely cover," in this case? Or, not to stand on particulars, substitute for these items aught else, though they should "shadow forth" the theory as "dimly" as the mythic burial and resurrection of Noah. If time is wanted for imagination to work up the case, we will not press the solution. In the meanwhile we present this dilemma on behalf of the Alexandrine Greek, viz.: Reject the Red Sea transaction as an "image of baptism," or accept the sprinkling of Ezekiel and David as equally an "image of baptism." There is a baptism in each, in the one no more, no less, than the other, or Didymus did not understand Greek. This alternative, to be sure, would cause but little embarrassment to Carson; there is probably room enough for Didymus in that same school to which this never erring theorist proposes to send the Angel Gabriel.

CYRIL OF JERUSALEM.

Our attention is again called, 1. To the *power* of baptism, —*τοῦ βαπτίσματος*. 2. To the fact that this power is developed by "the sprinkling of pure water." If "line upon line" will establish as truth that these baptisms were not dippings, but the result of a divine power exerted through water, and that sprinklings of this water were baptisms, then the truth is established.

ORIGEN.

1. The use of "loti," *washed*, claims attention. It shows the groundless character of the claim set up by Dr. Carson, that *λούω*, or *lavo*, when no part is specified, shall put the whole man into water or in some way *cover* him with it. This demand overlooks the fact that in religious washings no mere physical cleansing is contemplated. And, consequently, a man may be completely washed, religiously, by the application of a cleansing element to a very limited part of the body. And that in such cases "washing" does not refer to the local effect of the application, but to the nature and extent of its religious influence. These things are clearly shown by the present case. No one could be so irrational as to suppose that this refers to a physical washing. None, surely could be so infatuated by theory as to imagine that Origen represents the martyrs as "covered" in their blood. Yet they are represented as washed by blood, completely washed from head to foot, thoroughly washed body and soul. How is this? Because there is a virtue, influence, power ("jus," "vis," "*δυναμις*,") in martyr blood, which takes away sin and thus cleanses; and this cleansing is called a washing, which in no wise depends on the extent to which the blood is applied. When Dr. Carson would make two kinds of cleansing out of *sprinkling* and *washing* by the blood of Christ, (making the latter to cover,) he does that which is, absolutely, without foundation. The same thing is indicated by either

phraseology; in the former the modal application is stated, and in the other the result of the application. The same is true with regard to purifying water or any other purifying agency; no conclusion can be drawn as to the mode or extent of use, because the result is, religiously, a universal washing.—Martyr blood, not one drop of which falls upon the person, "washes" the whole man. The remembrance of this usage would have saved from some great errors. Sprinkling can wash from impurity, or from sin, as well as a deluge of waters; and therefore may baptize, as Origen declares martyr blood does.

2. *Baptisma sanguinis.*—Baptism of blood, is phraseology demanding consideration. This use of the genitive joins with the simple ablative ("proprio sanguine"), as well as with the exigencies of the case, to make imperative the conclusion, that in this baptism *blood* is the *source whence* comes the causative influence inducing the baptism, and is not the element *in which* an object is to be mersed, dipped, or covered. To discriminate between the agency effecting a baptism, and the element within which the baptized object is placed (when such element exists), is of vital importance. This is especially true where a fluid is the agency causative of the baptism; because a fluid is the natural element within which a baptism takes place, and therefore, offers a special facility for the deception, by ourselves or others, which would rob it of its true position as an agency and convert it into the wholly distinct office of a receiving element. The case before us is such as not only to assist in reaching, but to compel the adoption of a true conclusion. The use of the cases, as just indicated, would be enough for the scholar; but, possibly, not enough for the controversialist. But even controversialists, generally at least, will hold their peace in view of the *impossibility* of a martyr being either dipped or covered *in his own blood.*

Dr. Carson ought here, on his own principles, to run up the white flag. He says, that in any case of use where a primary meaning is impossible, there a secondary meaning finds credentials of legitimate birth. Now, it is absolutely impossible for a martyr to be baptized, *dipped*, *covered* in his blood, which Dr. C. says is primary baptism; but Origen says that their own blood does baptize all Christian martyrs; therefore, Origen must use "baptize" in a different sense from the primary "dipping, covering."

This is logic, and common sense, and consistency, but, alas! rhetoric slays them all. *Hyperbole* can expand "the blood of a frog" to the dimensions of an ocean, and "dip a lake" into it; and why should its magical arts prove incompetent to fill a baptistery with the blood-drops of martyrdom and dip "the witness" into it?

The theory has executed feats as difficult as this, and we have not much hope of the controversialist. But we ask the attention of all others to the fact, that Origen declares that their own blood baptizes martyrs, and that he wished thus to be baptized himself, *not to come out of a bloody pool all dripping with gore*, but that *his condition as a sinner might be thoroughly changed*, and his soul pass, washed from all sin, into the presence of God!

3. *Baptismum secundum.*—This blood baptism was a "second baptism;" what was the first? *Water* baptism. Now, observe that between these two baptisms, as to their general nature or modal execution, Origen does not make the slightest distinction. In so far as they were baptisms there was none to be made. They were of the same general nature, having power to cleanse from sin; and as to modal execution, such a thing was never known since the Greek was a language, so far as the word was concerned. While, therefore, the mode of executing the first baptism (by water) may have differed from the mode of executing the second baptism (by blood), this difference no more controls nor belongs to the baptism, than does the mode of martyrdom, by beheading or crucifixion, affect the making or unmaking of a blood baptism.

Water-baptism and blood-baptism are identified as baptisms of like reality and character, (differing only in the measure of their value,) by being termed, without qualification, a first and a second baptism. But we have farther evidence. They not only stand on the most absolute equality as baptisms, but the water and the blood stands each, to its own baptism, in precisely the same relation, namely, that of an *agency*. As "baptisma sanguinis" indicates blood to be the source of this baptism, so, "aquæ baptismus" indicates water as the source of that baptism. Neither water nor blood —not water any more than blood—is represented as a *receiving* element; they are alike agencies. In full accord with this grammatical testimony, is the unbroken Patristic testimony, which ascribes to water a "power" to baptize, wholly independent of its natural qualities as a fluid, which "power," and not fluidity, is the pivot on which turns all their interpretations of Judaic baptisms and of images of "the perfect baptism."

Now, it is a matter of infinite indifference in what manner the water was employed in this first baptism. Employ it as you will, by sprinkling, by pouring, by dipping into it, by walking into it to such a depth, or such a depth, and dipping so much as may be left above the water, or by any other simple or complex movements imaginable, and after all is done, Origen declares that the water is an *agency* to purify from sin, and that the baptism is a changed condition, produced by this "power," independent of any modal use. A baptism *in* water (drowning or covering indefinitely) has no more to do with the "baptism *of* water" of Origen, than a baptism *in* wine (drowning or covering indefinitely) has to do with a baptism *of* wine (making thoroughly drunk). Water and wine, as fluids, have a quality of nature adapting them to receive and envelop objects placed within them, and this is called a baptism of those objects. Wine has a quality of nature (intoxicating) which develops itself, not when objects are put into it, but when drunk. And the development of this influence by drinking, is called a baptism. These two baptisms, *in* wine, as a receiving fluid, and *of* wine, as an intoxicating fluid, have this in common, that they both exhibit their objects under a thoroughly changed condition; but as to the nature of the condition, and as to the mode of effecting the condition, the differences are such as to present nothing in common. Patristic water has a "power," not intoxicating, but spiritually purifying; not of nature, but by special divine communication; which "power," like that of wine, is capable of baptizing. Its development is effected by sprinkling, by pouring, and by washing. A man baptized *by* this "power" of water, differs from a man baptized *in* "simple" water, just as a soul *without a sin-spot* differs from a man who is—*very wet.* Origen's philology is unimpeachable; his theology is not so good.

CYPRIAN.

Cyprian offers the same testimony as that already considered.

1. Water has a power to baptize. But this power is not a quality inherent. "The Spirit cannot baptize without water, nor can water baptize without the Spirit." How absurdly untrue would this be if the writer referred to water as capable of *receiving* an object within itself. This, surely, it can do without the special intervention of the Holy Spirit. In this respect the heathen had baptisms; yet they were not baptisms, because the water was used without the Spirit, and no baptism was effected; the condition of the soul remained unchanged.

2. Therefore, Cyprian says: "The water itself must be first purified, sanctified, baptized, that it may by its own baptism wipe off the sins of the baptized man." So Tertullian says: "Ita de sancto sanctificata natura aquarum, et ipsa sanctificare concepit." Is it not surprising that the friends of the theory should have overlooked the great gulf which separates baptisms *by* such water, from baptisms *in* water, through a natural enveloping quality?

3. Cyprian quotes the text under consideration, to show that these peculiar baptisms were effected by the "sprinkling" of this pure water.

How marvellously inept is the objection that sprinkling cannot baptize by the "power" of this water! Go tell the old Greeks that drinking cannot baptize by the power of wine, that hearing cannot baptize by the power of bewildering questions, and they will tell you that your Greek sounds very "modern" in their ears. "But these were cases of 'figure.'" Yes, very much such "figure" as that of Gale, which made Carson laugh; and very much such "figure" as that of Carson, which might well make Fuller smile; and very much such "figure" as that of Fuller, at which some friend, who comes after him, will yet kindly smile; while all the world will laugh at a theory which fills the Classics with figure-pools and torrents, and empties the treasury of rhetoric to meet the exhaustive demand from Patrists for a dipping ornamentation.

4. Cyprian quotes, besides this passage of Ezekiel, those in Numb. 19:13; Numb. 8:7; Numb. 19:19; for the express purpose of showing that the baptizing power of water is developed by sprinkling, as truly as by any other mode.

CLEMENS ALEXANDRINUS.

This learned Greek declares that a second baptism may be *by tears*, as the learned Origen had declared that it might be by martyr-blood. Shall this baptism, by sprinkling tears, give origin to another figure—*hyperbolic?* Well, I suppose that is the best disposition which the theory can make of it.

Alongside of these clear and reiterated statements of baptisms by sprinkling of water, blood, and tears, look at these statements of Dr. Carson: "Sprinkling cannot be called baptism with more propriety than sand can be called water. This I do not leave as an inference from my doctrines: I wish to proclaim it to all my brethren." (p. 392.) This is undoubtedly true on Dr. C.'s theory as to the meaning of the word, viz., "dip, and nothing but dip, through all Greek literature." But to make good this theory, it will be necessary to enlarge the school-house at Tubbermore, and provide primers for all the old Greeks, and the whole army of Patrists, that they may learn anew their native tongue.

Again (p. 400): "If one instance of sprinkling was called immersion, I would give up the point of univocal meaning."

Let us see: "Qui enim baptizatur . . . Moyses aspergebat." According to Carson, "baptize" always means *immerse;* then Ambrose says, "He who was *immersed* . . Moses sprinkled." Again: "He was sprinkled with the blood of the lamb, who wished to be cleansed with typical *immersion* (baptism)." Is this the lightning which Dr. Carson called for to smite his univocalism? And (p. 401): "A people who called a purifying, by sprinkling or pouring, *a baptism!!!* Where is such a people? Not under the heavens. The facts alleged to prove this, are all mere assumptions." Pretty substantial assumptions. And with Clement, and Cyprian, and Origen, and Cyril, and Didymus, and Hilary, and Jerome, as representatives of "the people who call purifying, by pouring or sprinkling, a baptism," the neighborhood "where such people may be found," is, at least, proximately answered.

The Greeks, or the theorists certainly are in trouble as to what constitutes a baptism. The theorists say that angels and inspired men are wrong if they do not agree with them, and I suppose we may as well throw in the Greeks (Classics and Patrists) into the bargain.

CIRCUMCISION BAPTISM.

BAPTISM BY CIRCUMCISION.

JOSHUA 5: 3, 9.

"And Joshua made him sharp knives, and circumcised the children of Israel, at the hill, of the foreskins.

"And the Lord said unto Joshua, This day have I rolled away the reproach of Egypt from off you."

Interpretation.

Τίς οὖν ἔτι μοι περιτομῆς λόγος ὑπὸ τοῦ Θεοῦ μαρτυρηθέντι. Τίς ἐκείνου τοῦ βαπτίσματος χρεία ἁγίῳ πνεύματι βεβαπτισμένῳ.

"What, then, is the word of circumcision to me, having received testimony from God? What need is there of that baptism to one baptized by the Holy Spirit?"

Ἐκεῖνος λέγεται δευτέραν περιτομὴν . . . . ἧς περιέτεμεν ἡμᾶς αὐτος Ἰησοῦς Χριστὸς.

"He is said to have circumcised the people with a second circumcision, by stony knives, which was an announcement of this circumcision with which Jesus Christ himself circumcises us from stones and other idols."—*Justin Martyr*, 437, 757.

Περιτομὴ, τυπικὴ οὖσα σφραγὶς.

"For it is better to be sanctified unconsciously, than to depart unsealed and imperfect. And the evidence to us, of this, is circumcision on the eighth day, being a typical seal, and administered to those without intelligence."—*Gregory Nazianzen*, ii, 400.

Τὴν πνευματικὴν λαμβάνομεν σφραγῖδα ἁγίῳ Πνεύματι διὰ τοῦ λουτροῦ περιτεμνόμενοι. . . . Ἐν τῇ περιτομῇ τοῦ Χριστοῦ.

"Therefore, by the likeness of the faith of Abraham, we come into adoption. And, then, after faith, like to him, we receive the spiritual seal, being circumcised through washing by the Holy Spirit. . . . By the circumcision of Christ, being buried with him by baptism."—*Cyril*, 513.

"Videamus tamen quale sit hoc ipsum quod dicitur, quia hodie abstuli opprobrium a filiis Israel. Omnes homines etiamsi ex lege veniant, etiamsi per Moyses eruditi sint, habent tamen opprobrium Ægypti in semet ipsis, opprobrium peccatorum. . . . Sed ex quo venit Christus, et dedit nobis secundam circumcisionem per baptismum regenerationis, et purgavit animas nostras, abjecimus hæc omnia, et pro iis assumpsimus conscientiæ bonæ astipulationem in Domino. Tunc per secundam circumcisionem ablata sunt nobis opprobria Ægypti, et purgata sunt vitia peccatorum. . . . Audis quia hodie abstulit a te opprobrium Ægypti."

"We may see, however, what means that saying: 'To-day, I have taken away reproach from the children of Israel.' All men, even though they may come from the law, even though they may have been taught by Moses, have, notwithstanding, in themselves, the reproach of Egypt, the reproach of sins. . . . But since Christ came and gave to us the second circumcision by the baptism of regeneration, and purged our souls, we have cast away all these things, and in their stead have received the answer of a good conscience in the Lord. Then, by the second circumcision the reproaches of Egypt have been taken away from us, and the vices of our sins have been purged. Thou hearest that to-day he takes from thee the reproach of Egypt." —*Origen*, ii, 850, 852.

Circumcision is a Baptism.

JUSTIN MARTYR.

Justin Martyr explicitly declares that circumcision is a baptism. This declaration is marked neither by hesitation nor by qualification. He makes no explanation of the use as though it were unusual and needed apology; but simply and absolutely, as though well understood, he speaks, *currente verbo*, of circumcision as a baptism.

This use of the word is too palpable to be denied. Is, then, univocalism abandoned? The promise was that it would be when one case of sprinkling was called baptism. Such case has been adduced, and now we present another quite as far removed from a *dipping* as is sprinkling. Dr. Carson boasts that "no case has been adduced where the word *must* have any other meaning than dipping." Does circumcision mean dipping?

But what does Dr. Carson say of this case? This (p. 490): "He sometimes, also, speaks of circumcision as a baptism, or agreeing in the emblem, though altogether different in the things and in the words that designate them. Study this, and it will show how the Fathers can call various things by the name of baptism, without importing that they are included in the meaning of the word."

"Study this," the Doctor says. Another development of his *penchant* for sending folks "to school." But some things cannot be studied out, in school, without the help of "the master," and this Delphic utterance is, surely, one of them.

Dr. Carson has written a book of half a thousand pages, to prove that baptism is a modal act—and nothing but a modal act, and claims that if there is any truth in axioms he has settled such to be its meaning; and yet, a case, admittedly called "baptism" by a highly cultivated Greek philosopher, in which the act done differs from the act claimed to be proved by axioms, as far as pole from pole, and as absolutely as a straight line from a circle, is dismissed in five *sphynxic* lines thrown out for "study!" Every defeated leader has a right to choose his own method and line of retreat. It is generally done under the cover of thick darkness; and so it is here.

While I do not understand these lines and give up their "study," there are some things in them and about them of which we may speak.

1. "He sometimes speaks of *cutting around* (circumcision) as *a dipping* (baptism)." Does any one believe that Justin Martyr ever spoke of the act of "cutting around" as an act of "dipping?" Has such a statement, enunciated by any one, a claim to anything but silent incredulity?

2. Where does Dr. C. get that *addendum*—"or agreeing in the emblem?" There is not one syllable of it in the words of Justin; nor one to justify its introduction. Justin calls circumcision *a baptism*, and baptism it must remain in spite of any attempt by light-handedness to change it into something else.

3. But what is meant by—"or agreeing in the emblem?" It, of course, flatly denies that circumcision is a baptism; which Justin had straitly affirmed; but, apart from this, after the Martyr's statement has been murdered, what usurper is appointed to its place? On this same page we are told that the converted Greek philosopher believed that baptism was immersion, and that he believed that immersion was emblematical of death, burial, and resurrection; now does circumcision agree with immersion as an emblem of death, burial, and resurrection?

Dr. Carson might say in unravelling—"study this"—certainly this is its emblem: the flesh cut off dies; who can deny that it was buried? The burden of proof does not lie with me; that it *may be* buried is enough for my purpose; proof after so many ages cannot be asked; and, as for resurrection, "who that has a soul" cannot see it in the life of the babe, beautifully developing after the "death" and "burial" of its own flesh! Or, with less of rhetoric, but more of learning, the "student" might be instructed thus: "Circum" means *around;* and, if dimly yet beautifully, shadows forth the waters which are *around* every immersed disciple; while the act of "scision" cannot go "around" without first descending and then ascending, and as a downward movement and an upward movement are involved in every case of "dipping," what could be a more beautiful emblem of this act? Circum-cision, therefore, is a beautiful emblem of dipping and surrounding with water! Undoubtedly. How surprising that things made palpable, under a competent teacher, by a few luminous words, should otherwise remain hid for ages! Why this, before incomprehensible emblem of death, burial, and resurrection in circumcision, is, now, just as plain as the death, burial, and resurrection of Noah in the flood, of Israel walking between the water-walls, and of the disciples in the wind! "Not so much light as Christian honesty," must be wanting in the man who cannot see a demonstration so plain as this!

Having sufficiently admired at these profundities in the school of Tubbermore, let us now turn in another direction.

4. Admitting, or certainly not questioning, the exegesis to which we have just attended, we are under the necessity of putting its remarkable light "under a bushel," inasmuch as there is no "emblem" in, nor introducible into, the statement of Justin. This is absolutely certain. This attempt to ally the circumcision baptism of Justin with the ritual baptism of the theory, is all in the air. It is as foundationless as a dream of the night. The statement is: "Of what use to me is circumcision baptism, having been baptized *by the Holy Spirit?*" What "emblem" is there here? What room is there for its introduction by the most heated imagination? Is there any death, burial, resurrection, or dipping, in "baptism by the Holy Spirit?" Is not the statement simply and clearly this: Having received a perfect baptism, what need have I of an imperfect baptism?

Dr. Carson, instead of raising the question, "May I not have mistaken the nature of a baptism?" when he meets with the word in circumstances irreconcilable with his conception of it, sets to work to cloud the inconsistency, so that its rude outlines may be as little repulsive as possible. I do not say that he does this consciously, to evade truth; for I believe that his ideas upon this subject were so fully regarded as absolute truth, that he would, in very deed as he says that he would, have told the Angel Gabriel, denying it, to sit down at his feet and "study this."

This writer, after affirming with all the emphasis of which language is capable, that "baptize" must always, everywhere, mean *dip;* and after resorting to all sorts of figures to bring it "dimly" out, where it confessedly was not, in fact; and after subjecting common sense to torture, (so that with its dislocated members it was no longer recognizable,) in order to secure some cry that might sound like "dip," is now compelled to admit, that here is a case in which there is no dipping, in which figure can form no shadow of dipping, and in which common sense presents no bone unbroken by which, on the rack, a groan might be extorted to save a dipping. We leave the case, *in extremis*, to be medicated by any heroic remedies which the wit of the fast friends of the theory may suggest. In the meanwhile we seek an exposition of the passage under other auspices.

Justin was a Greek. He spoke and wrote the language of Homer and Plato. He had the knowledge to speak it correctly; he had the right to use it with the same breadth of freedom; and he has authority in his usage equal to that of any Classic. Classic usage has been examined. It has been proved to the satisfaction of Greek scholars, (between whose attainments, and those of Dr. Carson, I wish not to make invidious comparisons,) that βαπτίζω does not make demand for a definite act, as Dr. C. declares, but for *condition:* 1. With inness of position. 2. Condition, controlled by influence, without intusposition. Or, stated in terms sufficiently comprehensive to embrace both classes: "Whatever act or influence is capable of thoroughly changing the character, state, or condition of an object, is capable of baptizing that object, and by such change of character, state, or condition, assimilating that condition to itself, does in fact, baptize it."

Classic usage presents such an endless variety in the forms of action and in the natures of condition, that no limitation can be assigned to either, beyond that in the statement now made.

Apply, now, that result reached, by a detailed study of every known case of Classic Baptism, to the case in hand. Is it capable of expounding it? If not, there must be error or imperfection, for a complete definition must fairly cover every case of usage, without exception. In reply, we may pass by the *form* of the act, for with this baptism has nothing to do, and limit our evidence to the competency of the act or influence to thoroughly change the condition of its object. This, then, is the determining question: "Does circumcision change the character, state, or condition of the circumcised person?" Can the most devoted friend of the theory answer this question in the negative? Is not every circumcised person, man or babe, taken by circumcision out of an uncovenanted condition, and brought into a covenanted condition? It is not necessary to raise here the question as to the nature of this covenant, whether it embraced spiritual blessings, or was limited to those which were temporal; either answers our purpose perfectly well. The condition demanded by the word requires nothing beyond completeness and assimilation. Circumcision, as a covenant seal, brings into a new condition as to the promises of God, whatever the character of those promises may be.

If there is any authority in Classic usage, Justin is overshadowed by all the fulness of that authority, when he calls circumcision a baptism. One square foot does not more fully cover another square foot than does the definition cover this case of usage. Consider, now, the defiance which it offers to all the manipulations of the theory, to bring it under the control of its errors, and can there be any doubt as to the answer which should be given to the inquiry, "What is truth?" The theory is bankrupt.

Circumcision by Stony Knives.—Carson says: "In like manner Justin speaks of Christians as having the spiritual circumcision of which Greeks, and those like him, were partakers, *though they had nothing that literally resembled what was imported by the word.*" This admission springs a mine beneath the Doctor's theorizing, which makes it a hopeless wreck. In scores of cases, in Classic usage, he has attempted to find out a resemblance—where there was none—to the literal meaning of the word, as claimed by him. Thus he hunts up some figure by which he can convert the covered and uncovered sea-shore into a beautiful case of "dipping." "In like manner" water poured upon an altar is converted into a dipping. "In like manner" drunkenness becomes a dipping, sleep becomes a dipping, sickness becomes a dipping, magical arts become a dipping, hard study becomes a dipping, an overloaded stomach becomes a dipping, &c., &c., &c. And for what is all this irrational procedure? Why, in good sooth, to establish a philological miracle; to show that a word of physical form of act (so claimed) carries that form of act with it out of the physical into the metaphysical world, and where the act is *drinking*, *hearing*, *seeing*, *eating*, *thinking*, still it is "dipping!" Can the history of philology parallel so wild an assumption of the infinite credulity of men? And all this rather than accept that so universal principle, of a secondary meaning to words, as applicable to this word.

But after trampling under foot confessedly contradictory facts, and transmuting, by some Rosicrucian principle, "one form of act into another form of act;" and after ransacking imagination to discover "a resemblance" to the physical form, or, at least, some shadowy picture, we have at last the confession, that a word which literally expresses a definite form of action, may be applied to cases in which there is "nothing that literally resembles what was imported by the word." It is hardly necessary to say, that under such circumstances either the word has lost all meaning, or it has acquired a secondary meaning.

But while Dr. Carson abandons, incontinently, all attempt to discover a "cutting around," real or pictured, in the circumcision *by Christ* received by Justin, he challenges angels and men to deny that there was a "dipping," in the baptism *by the Holy Spirit*, received by this same Justin. If it should be said, that the admission of Dr. Carson that circumcision has lost its form of act, does not imply that baptism has lost its form of act, I answer: 1. There is no form of act in baptism, to lose. 2. Any one who admits that "circumcision" has lost its form of act in circumcision *by Christ*, and denies that "baptism" has lost its form of act in baptism *by the Holy Spirit*, has certainly lost his reason.

This rejection of what is vital to a word in its primary use, and the adoption of some associated idea in secondary use, is of constant development. "I am an American," means, primarily, I am *born* on American soil. But one born on the other side of the globe may say, "I am an American," rejecting claim to birth, and claiming to hold *the principles* which distinguish American citizens. Paul says of uncircumcised Christians, ye are the circumcision, because they held *the principles* which appertained to circumcision; and he denies that the circumcised Jew was of the circumcision, because they rejected those principles. The same thing is exhibited in the declaration, "They are not all Israel which are of Israel." In such usage there is a modification of the primary meaning, and the development of a conception which was subordinately in the primary meaning, or which had become an outgrowth of it, or an accretion around it. So βαπτίζω rejects the form of condition belonging to its literal, primary use, and develops the idea of *controlling influence*, growing out of such form of condition.

Justin's baptism "by the Holy Spirit" rejects form of condition and expresses the controlling influence of the Divine Spirit; just as "circumcision by Christ" rejects the form of act and confers the reality exhibited by that act.

I do not enter upon any detailed examination of "baptism by the Holy Spirit," as here spoken of, (it will come up in its place,) but merely remark, that as there is no more of dipping or covering in this baptism than there is in baptism by circumcision; so, if the theory stumbles at the one, it ought to fall down discomfited before the other.

GREGORY NAZIANZEN.

Circumcision, typical Baptism.—This writer teaches that circumcision was a typical seal or baptism; and as this type baptism was administered to infants eight days old, when intelligence was yet undeveloped, so the antitype seal, or baptism should be administered to those who were in danger of dying, whether infants or adults, as was the common practice. It should be observed, that while Justin speaks of baptism by circumcision, he contrasts it, as to efficacy, with baptism by the Holy Spirit, while Gregory makes circumcision baptism a type of ritual baptism. If the Fathers had regarded Christian baptism as only a type or symbol baptism, they could not have made these Judaic baptisms types of it, for there cannot be a type of a type; but they believed it to be an efficacious baptism, one of divine power over the condition of the soul, and therefore, could, consistently, make it the antitype of Old Testament typical purifications. Justin Martyr was more orthodox than those that came after him, and he refers type baptism to baptism by the Holy Spirit, without the intervention of water.

CYRIL.

Circumcised by Washing.—"Circumcised by the Holy Spirit through washing." In this circumcision, the prime, efficient agent is the Holy Spirit, the efficient, instrumental agency is "the washing," and the result is an unfleshly, spiritual nature.

We have here, proof, 1. Of the type character of circumcision; that it was a purification of the flesh, and therefore was called a baptism which was suitable to foreshadow that spiritual purification which cleansed the soul, and was the work of the Holy Spirit. 2. The Holy Spirit operated through the water to take away sin.

Mem.—Cyril, Gregory, and Justin forgot to point out the resemblance to death, burial, and resurrection, in this type baptism.

BAPTISM BY DROPS OF BLOOD.

Exodus 12:7, 12, 13.

"And they shall take of the blood, and strike it on the two side posts, and on the upper door-post of the houses.

"For I will pass through the land of Egypt this night, and will smite all the first-born in the land of Egypt.

"And the blood shall be to you for a token upon the houses where ye are; and when I see the blood I will pass over you."

Interpretation.

"Pascha nostrum pro nobis immolatus est Christus Deus."

Ἔσταξε γὰρ τὸ αἷμα ἀπὸ τῆς πλευρᾶς ἐπὶ τὴν γῆν, καὶ τὸν μολυσμὸν αὐτῆς ἅπαντα ἐξεκάθηρεν. . . .

Διὰ τῆς ἐξομολογήσεως ἐκάθηρεν ἑαυτὸν τοῦ ῥύπου τῶν ἁμαρτημάτων.

"Christ the Lord, our Passover, was slain for us. Why was he slain without the city, and on a high place, and not under some roof? This was not without reason, but that he might purify the nature of the air. For this reason was he slain on high and not beneath a roof, but with the heavens stretched over him instead of a roof, that the whole heavens might be purified. Therefore the sky was purified, and the earth was purified. *For the blood from his side dropped upon the earth, and purged away all its defilement.* . . . He (the thief) did not dare to say, 'Remember me' until that by confession he purified himself from the pollution of sins. . . . For the strength of confession is great, and it has great power. For he confessed, and behold he found Paradise opened; he confessed, and he, who was a robber, received boldness to ask a kingdom."—*Chrysostom*, ii, 406, 409.

Καὶ ταῦτα βαπτισομεν; . . . ὡς δὲ καὶ ἡ τῶν φλιῶν χρίσις, διὰ τῶν ἀναισθὴτων φυλάττουσα τὰ πρωτότοκα.

"And shall we baptize these (infants)? Certainly; . . . the evidence of this is circumcision, which is a typical seal . . . . and in like manner, the smearing of the door-posts, protecting, through these insensible things, the first-born."—*Gregory Nazianzen*, ii, 400.

Βαπτισμὸν ὡς καθαρτικὸν ὄντα πάντων ἡμῶν.

"He calls his death baptism as being a purging of us all."—*Theophylact*, Matt. 22.

"Hos duo baptismos de vulnere perfossi lateris emisit."

"These two baptisms he shed forth from the wound of his pierced side."—*Tertullian*, 357; Paris, 1634.

"Baptisma publicæ confessionis et sanguinis proficere ad salutem potest. . . . Sanguine suo baptizatos et passione."

"The baptism of a public confession and of blood may avail for salvation, (but not to a heretic out of the church.) The Lord declares in the Gospel, that those baptized by his blood and passion are sanctified and attain the grace of the divine promise, when he speaks to the thief believing and trusting in the very passion, and promises that he shall be with him in Paradise."—*Cyprian*, 1123, 1124.

Τὸ αἷμα τοῦ προβάτου τύπος τοῦ αἵματος τοῦ Χριστοῦ.

"The blood of the lamb is a type of the blood of Christ."—*Basil*, M. iv, 124.

Baptism of "the First-born."

This passage, and the interpretations directly and indirectly connected with it, establishes in the most conclusive manner, that there is a class of baptisms with which neither the act of dipping, nor a covering, effected in any way, has anything to do. And more than this; it is established that the source of the baptizing power need not even be in contact with the baptized object.

Gregory Nazianzen speaks of circumcision as typical of baptism, "and in like manner" the blood smeared on the door-posts of the families of Israel. The argument which he extracts from them is this: Inasmuch as typical circumcision was able to influence the condition of the child, which was all unconscious of the transaction, and inasmuch as typical blood upon the *door-posts* destitute of all intelligence, was capable of influencing the condition of the child, unconscious of the transaction and untouched by the blood, yet on whose behalf that blood was sprinkled by parents in the way appointed by God; therefore, infant children without any intelligence as to the ordinance, may receive antitype baptism, and be changed as to their condition by receiving a more perfect purification through the antitype, than type circumcision could effect; and a more perfect salvation than the type blood of the passover lamb could bring to "the first-born." This was Patristic reasoning; and whatever else it may show, it does show conclusively, that, in their view, type baptisms shadowed forth the cleansing of the soul from sin and its redemption unto eternal life, by purifications of the body, and the preservation of the natural life, and did not shadow forth "a dipping" or "a covering."

When the root idea of all baptisms, (thorough change of condition,) is apprehended, not only can no embarrassment arise from the absence of a dipping or a covering, but, also, no embarrassment can arise from a baptism declared to be effected by a baptizing substance which does not touch the baptized object.

Whether water, blood, or ashes shall be used in divine worship is a matter of sovereign appointment. How they shall be used, and what shall be their value, are matters of the same pure sovereignty. That blood, blood of a lamb, should be used in the Passover; that it should be used by "striking;" that this striking should be against the *door-posts;* that the transaction should enure to the benefit of "the first-born," were all matters pertaining, not to the nature of things, however wise and fit they may have been, but to the good pleasure of Israel's God. It being thus determined that the condition of "the first-born" should be changed, not by dipping them into water, nor by covering them with blood; but by God-fearing parents striking the family door-posts with the bloodied hyssop branch, thus bringing them out of a condition of impending death, into a condition of unimperilled life, this change of condition, without the slightest regard to the mode of its accomplishment, is Classically as well as Patristically called *a Baptism*. They were baptized into a condition of safety by the sprinkled blood. Any attempt to solve such baptisms by "a dipping" of these little ones must be made under protest from philology and common sense; not made very loud, but enough to clear their skirts against any charge that might be made hereafter of their being guilty participants, even by silence, in such unwisdom.

It will be observed that I use the phraseology *out of* one condition *into* another condition, although there is no movement "out of" anything, or "into" anything. There is no change of position. The reason is, 1. The poverty of language. 2. Analogical fitness *in some respects.* In physical things, *change* involves movement; and movement *out of* one thing *into* another thing, involves *complete* change; when, therefore, there is "a change," not of position but condition, it may be expressed by a word immediately declaring movement, but implying, necessarily, the idea of "change;" and when the change is a *complete* one, we may introduce "out of" and "into," because of what they involve, (*thorough* change,) and not because of what they directly and of themselves express; thus giving them, in such usage, a real secondary value, while movement has disappeared.

"The first-born" *passed out of* one condition *into* another condition, as the destroying angel passed over them, without passing, for one moment, from the quiet shelter of their mother's bosom.

BAPTISM OF THE EARTH, AIR, AND SKY.

Chrysostom in speaking of the results attendant upon the sacrifice of our Passover Lamb, Christ the Lord, declares, without using directly the word, that the earth, and the air, and the sky were thereby baptized. No one, who remembers by what varied terms and descriptions the Patrists set forth baptism, will hesitate to acknowledge a baptism as taught, (though the word should not appear,) merely on the ground of the absence of that word. That a baptism is here designed is shown, 1. By the baptizing power attributed to the person of Christ. 2. By the pre-eminent power attributed to his shed blood. 3. By the sameness of phraseology employed, as when avowedly describing a baptism. 4. By the express use of the word "baptism" by other writers in connection with this transaction. 5. By the baptism ascribed to the repentant thief.

The propriety of attributing a baptism to the earth, air, and sky, by the crucifixion of Christ, on the summit of Calvary, beneath the heavens, and with his blood dropping upon the earth, is found in the claim, that their condition was thoroughly changed thereby.

Chrysostom tells us, that before this great transaction the world at large was impure and unfit for divine worship, Judea and the temple only being sanctified to this end; but by the death of Christ outside of the city, "lifted up with no covering roof, the whole earth became sanctified;" so that men could "lift up holy hands, acceptable to God, everywhere." He expounds his "lifting up" upon the cross as designed "to purify *the nature* of the air," therefore, effectually to change its condition. So, of the overhanging heavens, "purified."

As to the competency of a few drops of blood from the pierced side of the Son of God "to baptize" this whole earth, no one who reads the Patrists can have any doubt that they believed in such efficacy, or that they could consistently employ such language.

The justification of such usage is found in the true nature of βαπτίζω, which they well understood, and use in this case, as might be expected, with the utmost propriety.

It is but a short time since the friends of the theory ridiculed *a bapting* by a few blood-drops. They have learned better; and now admit that a few drops (to express it precisely in English as in Greek) can *dip*. Hippocrates says, Ἐπειδὰν ἐπιστάξῃ ἱμάτια βάπτεται. "When it *drops* upon the garments they are *dipped* (dyed)."

Chrysostom uses the same verb and the same preposition to express the dropping blood from the Redeemer's side, by which he says the world was baptized, changed as to its condition, being purified and sanctified universally to the service and worship of God.

Theorists now believe that the Father of Medicine wrote good Greek when he said "coloring drops can *dip* (dye)."

We wait for their confession that "the Golden Mouth" understood Greek as well, when he claims *the purging of the world*, by blood-drops from the cross, to be *a baptism*.

BAPTISM OF THE PENITENT THIEF.

The baptism of the penitent thief is another exemplification of the truth of the principles relied upon for the interpretation of baptisms.

In it there is neither "dipping" nor "covering," any more than in the baptism of "the earth, and air, and sky." Nor are there even a few drops of blood which hyperbole might magnify into a pool; for those blood-drops upon him are not of "a witness" for Christ, but witnesses of his guilt as a thief. Nor do "those two baptisms shed forth from the Saviour's side," of which Tertullian speaks, reach his firmly nailed body. How then, was he baptized? Chrysostom and Cyril both answer by "the baptism of *confession*." This baptism was grounded in the Saviour's declaration—"He that confesseth me before men, him will I confess before my Father in heaven." Hence the "*power*" of confession became a subject for eulogy. The former of these two writers says, that the thief "purified himself from the pollutions of sin *by confession*." He declares that "the strength of confession is great and has great power." "He confessed, and behold he found Paradise opened."

How entirely removed is the conception of these writers and their associates as to the nature of a baptism, from that presented by the theory, is manifest from their speaking of "confession," and "blood," and "water" as possessed of "*power*," and therefore competent to baptize. There is not a syllable which likens them to *pools*, *floods*, or *torrents*. No such elements of thought are introduced by them into the explanation of these baptisms. This antagonism of view between the modern theory and these Greeks is, alone, sufficient to convict of error, unless, indeed, these ancient worthies also, are to be "sent to school." Such course, in this case, might prove dangerous, for Chrysostom has the credit of having overmastered his master, (the most celebrated of his day,) while yet in his teens. That measuring-rod at Tubbermore which we are told is applied, as a matter of conscience, to the talents of every opposer of the theory might prove too short.

The "baptisma confessionis" without dipping; without "pouring *long enough to cover;*" without "washing, which may be by bathing and therefore by immersion;" without a cleansing of the feet, "which may be done by *putting them into it*, which is an immersion *as far as it goes;*" without an ark or a fishing-boat, which might then "dimly shadow forth a burial and a resurrection;" without any element of deep emotion, which then might be converted into "an overflowing torrent;" without mental solicitude, which then might be made "a burden to sink in deep waters;" without any help whereby a figure or a picture can be wrought out, this "baptisma confessionis" cannot but be a stumbling-block to the theory. "Confession," through the influence of blood-drops from the cross, baptizes the penitent sinner and fits him for Paradise!

BAPTISMS OF FIRE.

BAPTISM BY THE FLAMING SWORD.

GENESIS 3:24.

"So he drove out the man: And he placed at the east of the garden of Eden, cherubims and a flaming sword, which turned every way, to keep the way of the tree of life."

Interpretation.

"Non unum est baptisma: unum est quod hic tradit Ecclesia, per aquam et Spiritum Sanctum quo necesse est baptizari catechumenos. Est et aliud baptisma, de quo dicit Dominus Jesus: 'Baptisma habeo baptizari, quod nos nescitis,' (Luke 12:10.) Et utique jam baptizatus in Jordane fuerat, sicut superiora declarant; sed sit hoc baptismum passionis, quo etiam sanguine suo unusquisque mundatur.

"Est etiam baptismum in paradisi vestibulo, quod antea non

erat: sed posteaquam peccator exclusus est, cœpit esse romphæa ignea, quam posuit Deus, quæ antea non erat, quando peccatum non erat.

"Culpa cœpit, et baptismum cœpit: quo purificentur, qui in paradisum redire cupiebant, ut regressi dicerent: 'Transivimus per ignem et aquam.' (Ps. 66:12.) Hic per aquam, illic per ignem. Per aquam, ut abluantur peccata: per ignem ut exurantur. . . .

"Quis est qui in hoc igne baptizat? . . . Ille de quo Johannes ait: 'Ipse vos baptizabit in Spiritu sancto et igne.' . . . Veniet ergo Baptista Magnus, sic enim eum nomino quomodo nominavit Gabriel dicens, (Luc. 1:32,) 'Hic erit Magnus,' videbit multos ante paradisi stantes vestibulum, movebit romphæam versatilem, dicet iis qui a dextris sunt, non habentibus gravia peccata: 'Intrate qui præsumitis, qui ignem non timetis.' . . . Intrate in requiem meam; ut unusquisque nostrum ustus romphœa illa flammea, non exustus, introgressus in illam paradisi amœnitatem, gratias agat Domino suo, dicens: 'Induxisti nos in refrigerium.'" (Ps. 66:12.)

"Baptism is not one: that is one kind which the Church gives by water and the Holy Spirit, wherewith it is necessary that catechumens be baptized.

"And that is another Baptism, of which the Lord Jesus says: 'I have a baptism to be baptized with, which ye know not.' (Luke 12:10.) And as he had already been baptized in Jordan, as previously stated, this must be the Baptism of Passion by which, through his blood, every one of us must be cleansed.

"There is, also, a baptism at the entrance of Paradise which formerly did not exist; but after the transgressor was excluded, the flaming sword began to be, which God established, which was not, before, when sin was not. Sin began and baptism began; by which they might be purified who desired to return, that having returned they might say: 'We have passed over by fire and water. (Ps. 66: 12.) Here by water, there by fire. By water, that sins may be washed away; by fire, that they may be consumed. . . .

"Who is it that baptizes by this fire? . . . He of whom John says, 'He shall baptize with the Holy Spirit and fire.' . . . Then shall come the Great Baptizer, (for so I call him as Gabriel called him, saying, (Luke 1:32,) 'He shall be Great,') he will see many standing before the entrance of Paradise, he will wave the sword turning every way. He will say to those on the right hand, not having weighty sins, 'Enter ye, who are of good courage, who fear not the fire.' . . .

"Enter into my kingdom: So every one of us burned (purified) by that sword, not consumed, having entered into the delights of Paradise, may give thanks to his Lord, saying, (Ps. 66: 12,) '*Thou hast brought us into rest.*'"—*Ambrose*, ii, 1227, 1228.

"Statuit igneam romphœam, et cherubim custodire viam ligni vitæ. . . . Audi Salvatorem ratione ignis et ferri in duobus locis significantem. In alio loco ait: '*Non veni mittere pacem super terram, sed gladium.*' In alio vero: '*Ignem veni mittere super terram, et utinam jam ardeat.*' Igitur defert utrumque Salvator, gladium et ignem, et BAPTIZAT QUÆ non potuerunt Spiritus Sancti purificatione purgari."

"He places a flaming sword and cherubim to guard the way of the tree of life. And as if a sword, sharp and hot, be struck against the body, it causes double pain, of burning and of cutting, so, also, the sword which is mentioned as placed as a guard of Paradise, produces double torment, it burns and it cuts. Students of the medical art say that some diseases require not only the cutting of the knife, but, also, burning. Cancers require that the putrid flesh shall be cut out and their roots burned. Dost thou think that our cancer, as I may call it, has a like viciousness, so that neither the mere sharpness of the knife nor the mere burning of fire can suffice, but both must be applied, that it may be both burned and cut? Hear the Saviour showing the use of fire and knife, in two passages: In one place he says: '*I have not come to send peace on the earth but a sword.*' But in another place he says: 'I have come to send fire upon the earth, and I wish it were already kindled.' Therefore the Saviour brings both, sword and fire, and BAPTIZES THOSE THINGS WHICH could not be purged by the purification of the Holy Spirit."—*Origen* (translated by Jerome), iii, 704.

Σὺ δὲ πῶς ἐπανέλθῃς εἰς τὸν παράδεισον, μὴ σφραγισθεὶς τῷ βαπτίσματι; Ἢ οὐκ οἶδας, ὅτι φλογίνη ῥομφαία τέτακται φυλάσσειν τὴν ὁδὸν τοῦ ξύλου ζωῆς;

"But how canst thou come back again into Paradise, not being sealed by baptism? Dost thou not know that the flaming sword has been set to guard the way of the tree of life, to the unbelieving terrible and consuming, but, to the believing, easy of approach, and pleasantly shining?"—*Basil*, iii, 428.

AMBROSE.

The exposition, by Ambrose, of the import of baptism in general, and as bearing on this passage in particular, is very explicit, and very far removed from the Baptist conception of what is essential to a baptism.

"*Baptism is not one.*" In absolute contradiction of the assertion of this eminent writer, the theory declares that *baptism is one.* When the theorists take this position, they mean to say that baptism is a fixed quantity. Some say that the "quantity" consists in the form of an act, in the most marvellous disregard of facts. Others say the form of the act may vary, but a covering of the object must not vary. It is farther affirmed that this unity is such an absolute necessity, that in application to things not physical, and where neither form of act nor covering can exist, in fact, yet there must be a creation, by the force of imagination, of the one or the other, according as this or that class of theorists may attempt to defend the case. Water, wine, oil, milk, blood, marsh mud, the receiving elements, may vary; but the baptism, the dipping or the covering, cannot vary. Baptism is one. "It is mode, and nothing but mode."

If the idea of baptism is exhausted by the performance of a modal act, then no argument is needed to prove that "baptism is one." It is a self-evident proposition. Or, if the idea of baptism consists in a modal covering, departure from which is as destructive as the dashing of a crystal vase against a flinty rock, then argument is at an end, and "baptism is one." I say nothing, now, about the difficulty which these parties to the unity have among themselves in determining what the unit is; it is enough, at present, to turn the case over to Ambrose, who says: "Baptism is *not* one." But if it be "*not* one," then it is *not* a modal act, for that, as the theory claims, must ever be "one;" nor is it a modal covering, for that, too, as the theory claims, must ever be "one."

Whatever baptism may be, if Ambrose's decision is worth anything, this Janus-faced theory is worth nothing.

Lest any one should have doubts as to the extent of the repudiation of this "oneness," I would call to mind a previous declaration by this same writer: "*Multa* sunt *genera* baptismatum." The theory refuses to give baptism the dignity of a *species*. It cuts it down to a severe *individualism*. It is like nothing but itself; and when it becomes like anything else, it ceases to be itself. "It is *dip, and nothing but dip*, through all Greek literature." Now, Ambrose not merely rejects the notion that baptism is a thing simple and indivisible, always and everywhere the same, but he refuses to accept the broader idea of *species* with its individual peculiarities; he will not allow even the limitation which belongs to genus and its varying species; he insists that the "baptismata" rise up to the elevation of a *class*, and that, too, of such a breadth as to include "*multa genera*."

Were ever opposing views more thoroughly, more broadly, and more universally contradictory than those of the theorists, and this Patrist, as to the nature of baptism?

We have had already enough of facts before us to show which now is right. We have seen that "genus" of baptisms, which pertains to physics, including various differential species, such as stones, metals, coasts, uninfluenced by baptism; a bag of salt, a ship, a human being, influenced by baptism; and we have seen that "genus" of baptisms, taking in the intellect, and exhibited in varying "species," such as drunkenness, somnolence, feeble-mindedness, &c., &c. And yet another "genus," embracing the religious element, is now passing before us, revealing its varied "species" of *ceremonial* purifications, with all the varieties of *sprinklings* (water, blood, ashes), and of *washings* (body, feet, hands); and of *spiritual* purifications, mediate (water imbued with divine power, martyr blood, flaming sword), and immediate, (Holy Spirit.)

These are only some of the "Multa genera baptismatum" which make up that wide "Class," characterized by *thorough change of condition*. They are sufficient to sustain the position, "Baptism is *not* one," and to show that its contradictory

"Baptism is one," is a position neither proven nor provable. Classic Baptism is right when it says, "Baptism is a myriad-sided word."

"*Baptism by water and the Holy Spirit.*" Ambrose proceeds to cite some particular kinds of baptism, in order to sustain his assertion that "Baptism is not one." I do not enter into a discussion of this baptism. It is not within my present plan so to do. I only observe, as to its distinctive character: 1. It does not belong to the class of mere symbol baptisms; it effects a spiritual purification. 2. Whatever may have been the manner of using the water, its position in the baptism is that of *agency*. The "*power*" to effect the baptism is with the water. It is not a recipient element. This is the Patristic view.

"*Baptisma passionis.*" The baptism of passion, or of crucifixion, experienced by our adorable Lord and Saviour Jesus Christ, is declared by Ambrose to be another kind of baptism from that just mentioned, namely, Baptism by water and the Holy Spirit. We have thus specific examples furnished to illustrate the general statement, "Baptism is *not* one." What, now, is the unity, or what are the unities, which make both baptisms; and what the diversity or diversities which make them baptisms not of the same kind?

1. *As to the forms of act.* In the one case, it is applying water to the body in varying forms, and "the operation" of the Holy Spirit on the soul; in the other case, it is *striking* with a hammer and *thrusting* with a spear. 2. *As to the agencies.* In the former case it is water impregnated with a divine power, in the latter case it is the agonies of the cross. 3. *As to the results.* In the first case there is a wetting of the body and (supposedly) a purification of the soul; in the last case there is a penal death, "the just for the unjust." There is no unity in the forms of the act, none in the nature of the agency, none in the characters of the result. There is neither a dipping nor a covering to be found whereby they can be interlinked. Why then have they the common name of baptism? I answer, because a baptism is never dependent upon any specific form of action, upon any specific nature in the

instrumentality, or upon any specific character in the result; but is the production of any act, or of any agency, which is capable of thoroughly changing the condition of its object. Friends and rejecters of the dipping theory will alike admit, that the sinner baptized with water impregnated with divine influence, had (according to the Patristic faith) thereby his moral condition thoroughly changed. And all will, equally, acknowledge that the "baptism of passion" thoroughly changed the condition of the Sufferer in his relations to the law, having forever satisfied its claims; and his relations to his people, being now and thus, now in fact, thus "from the foundation of the world," the slain Lamb of God, able to take away their sins; as well as his own personal condition, changing his condition of life into a condition of death, on which changed condition all else hung suspended. By the power of this central truth, we fling off those alien elements, "dipping" and "covering," while we bring into order and harmony all those multiplied diversities which enter into the "*multa genera baptismatum.*"

The theory has ever stumbled at the unity and charity inculcated by the cross, and has thus been deservedly "broken;" the baptism of the cross now falls upon it, and it is "ground to powder." And so perish, speedily, all error which separates the people of God!

Before leaving this case of baptism, I would call attention to the form and force of the phrase "Baptisma passionis." What is the grammatical and logical relation between these two words? Very few, perhaps none, will differ in their answer to this question. For that very reason it is desirable to raise it now, as we shall meet with it hereafter, when outside influences may cause more embarrassment in its determination.

The only point to be settled, is the character of the genitive. Is it *subjective* or *objective?* Is the baptism produced by "passion," as its source, or has baptism "passion" for its end? If there should be any hesitancy in answering this inquiry, aid may, perhaps, be found in referring to a similar phrase, which has already been before us: "Baptisma confessionis." None, I presume, will regard "confession" as the end of Martyr baptism; but all will say, Martyrdom proceeds from "confession." In other words, the case is a genitive *subjective*, and not *objective*. The similar phrase, "Baptisma passionis," should, unquestionably, be determined in the same manner. The atoning sorrows of the blessed Redeemer on the cross, were the source whence his baptism came, not the end to which it tended. "Passion" baptized the atoning Redeemer into death.

I pass over this amazing baptism, now, as lightly as its presentation by Ambrose will allow. Its consideration will demand a most central position when we come to speak of Christian Baptism.

Baptism of the Flaming Sword.—A third baptism, differing from the other two, is adduced to sustain the same general position, "Baptism is *not* one." This is a baptism which takes place at the gates of Paradise.

When Aaron was baptized by Moses at the door of the congregation, Dr. Carson insisted that it must be by immersion. If Ambrose had merely said: "There is, also, a baptism at the entrance of Paradise," or, if those words only had come down to us without any explanation as to the *quo modo* of the baptism, this thrice honest believer in dipping would have gone to the stake sooner than he would have admitted, that there was or could be any other than a dipping baptism. He would have asked, in triumph, "Is there not *a river* flowing in the Paradise of God? And if one be not enough, where are the Pison, and the Gihon, and the Hiddekel, and the Euphrates?" Fortunately, however, more has been told us concerning it; and it appears that there was no dipping, no covering, no water, in the transaction. The baptism was by a "*Flaming Sword.*"

Had the statement been merely, that the baptism was by fire, all that entered Paradise would have been very promptly dipped into the fire; but, alas! the statement is "a fiery sword;" and how shall the seekers of Paradise be dipped into a *sword?* I am sure I cannot tell; but I am just as sure that the theory will cut out, to order, an explanation so plain that "any child can see it;" and if, perchance, any man should fail to do so, it must be because "he has no soul for rhetoric." Perhaps the device will be, that the strokes of the sword, descending and ascending, (like the flooding and the ebbing tide,) shall "beautifully represent *a dipping;*" while in "turning every way," its strokes come down before, behind, right, left, above, betoken a rushing torrent and a covering flood; and what could be more plain than that, (as the sword is the image of death, and burial is involved in death, while entering Paradise is proof of a resurrection,) we have "death, burial, and resurrection" as well as a dipping and a covering? Who will not justify the theorist in saying, (while standing at the gates of Paradise with the whole truth of baptism made luminous by "the Flaming Sword,") that he who will not accept its strokes for "dipping," its flashes for "covering," its emblematic character for "death and burial," and the Paradise it guards for "resurrection," "compels our charity to struggle against the conviction which forces itself upon us, that upon this subject it is not light that is most wanted, but *religious honesty.*" (Carson, xxxvii.)

Some may hesitate to receive these fruits of a warm imagination because they leave out of view the baptism of Ambrose—*the eradication of sin* which prepares for entrance through the gate into Paradise; and because they have failed to show how the "dippings" of a swordblade would fit for the kingdom of heaven; to do which thing this baptism was Patristically got up.

Others may object, that the exposition does not tally with the illustration given by Origen of the cancer, with the knife and the cautery burning its roots. This suits well with the idea of a baptism which effectually purifies the soul; but not so well with a water dipping or with a flood covering. All this may be true; but then, Ambrose and Origen may not know what a baptism is, (not having yet gone to school at Tubbermore;) or, they may not have known what sort of baptism they had in their own minds, and so may have blundered in its explication. At any rate there is so much of simplicity and good sense in the death, burial, and resurrection of Noah in the ark, of Israel in the dried-up sea, and of the Apostles in the sound like wind, that we can feel little disposition to yield anything to these Patrists, as against death, burial, and resurrection in the Flaming Sword!

In any case, however, there is much to justify the statement, that as a baptism it is not quite like either of the other two. And it is hard to resist the conclusion, that the theory is certainly scorched, if not burned up, by contact with the Flaming Sword.

I need hardly say, that inasmuch as the Patrists attribute to the sword, in its cutting character and in its fiery element, a doubly purifying power, fully competent under divine control to accomplish its mission—thoroughly to change the condition of those seeking admission into Paradise—it meets, in the most perfect manner, that which we claim to be the true and only essential characteristic of a baptism.

"*The Great Baptizer.*"

Not the least important part of this interpretation relates to the baptizer at the gates of Paradise. This is of so much importance that Ambrose, himself, raises the question: "Who is it that baptizes by this fire?" And he gives the answer: "He of whom John said, 'He shall baptize by the Holy Ghost and by fire.'" To this person is given the title of "the Great Baptizer." Now the question arises, Why was the Lord Jesus Christ called "the Great Baptizer?" We propound this question to the theorists and await their answer.

Is it replied by some one more zealous than thoughtful, "You must not obscure the truth by using untranslated words. He is called 'the Great *Dipper*,' because he dipped so many into the water." To such speech enough of his dipping friends will say: "Don't speak so fast; you blunder; Christ never dipped into water." He might, however, respond: "I thought that baptize always meant *to dip*, and if he is 'the Great Dipper' and did not dip into *water*, what did he dip into?" "Well, perhaps it means, He dipped into the Holy Ghost and into fire." Here let me interpose a word and say, 1. This latter baptism cannot now be discussed on its merits, because out of place. 2. The answer, as to the reason of this title, must be such as will meet the views of him who gives the title, not of him who undertakes to expound it. And the reason assigned will not answer; for Ambrose no more believed that the Lord Jesus dipped men into the Holy Ghost and into fire, than he believed that he dipped them into water. It is no sentiment of the Patrists, that the Holy Ghost is a receiving element into which men are to be dipped whether literally or figuratively; on the contrary, He is always represented as an agent operating on the soul and so baptizing it. It is the purest absurdity to attribute to Ambrose the giving of a title grounded on the abundant doing of that which he did not believe was ever done at all.

And as for "dipping into fire," it may be observed, 1. The use of the preposition *in* by no means determines any such idea; for it is most freely used in Patristic writings with the instrument. 2. The instrument is used subsequently without any preposition. 3. The fire, here, was not of a nature to allow of a dipping into it. 4. It is expressly stated that the act accomplishing the baptism was not a *dipping* into the flaming sword, but by *waving* it. Let it be remembered, that we are interpreting an expression not of somebody else taken up by Ambrose, and which has a value extrinsic to him, but an expression which originates with himself; and which, consequently, must be interpreted by his own sentiments as bearing upon it. And in view of them we say, the title "Great Dipper" never originated from any notion that the Lord Jesus *dipped into fire.* But supposing that there was such a phrase as "dipping into the Holy Ghost," which there is not, and "dipping into fire," which there is not, still every one not demented must admit that there is, in fact, no dipping in such expressions. Here, then, arises the question, How could the title of a "Dipper" be taken out of phrases in which no dipping exists, in fact, to be conferred on one who never dips? Is not the whole thing, (as is usual with such explanations under the theory,) full, from first to last, of conceptions untenable and unreasonable?

But this title, "the Great Baptizer," given by Ambrose to the Lord Jesus Christ means something, nay, must mean very much. What is it? If some votary of the wine cup were to call Bacchus "the Great Baptizer," would not the interpretation "Great *Dipper*" be regarded as a great joke? And would not "Great *coverer over*" prove them *tipsy* who gave such title? Could it mean anything else, in such relation, than "*the Great drunkard maker?*" Would not every native-born Greek so understand it?

But what this title means as applied to the Lord Jesus Christ, (now given for the first time and, so far as I remember, never employed but on this occasion,) we must learn from the character of him who bears it, and from the circumstances and tenor of the context out of which it originates. It would be most irrational to suppose otherwise, as it would be irrational to introduce into the text, to control the interpretation, any other element than that which is already there. Neither water nor wine, not water any more than wine, has any place in the interpretation.

What is the ruling thought of the passage? Is it not purification? Is not purification inseparable from Paradise? Is not "the flaming sword" placed at the gateway to prevent the introduction of impurity? Is not "the sword and the fire" represented as possessed of purifying power? Are not souls represented as seeking to enter Paradise, and yet "with some lighter sins" which still require purification? Is not the Lord Jesus, here and everywhere in connection with baptism, represented as a Purifier? Does he not take the flaming sword for the purpose of purifying completely, those "on his right hand?" Does he not do it, and in so doing, give them welcome into that Paradise within which "nothing that defileth" can enter? And is he not, in view of all this, and because of all this, called "the Great Baptizer?" The interpretation, I repeat, must be gathered from the passage. In that passage there is not the remotest hint of a dipping or a covering; and to introduce them as expounding elements is "a folly to be punished by the judges." It might as well be said, that nobility and a title taken from the field of battle and conferred upon a victorious soldier, must be expounded by reasons sought in the four corners of the earth and not in that hardfought field—its prisoners taken, its cannon captured, opposing standards stricken down—as to say that the title given by Ambrose, in view of the great work accomplished on earth and at the gates of Paradise, was not to be expounded by that work. Thus expounded, "the Great Baptizer" can mean nothing but "THE GREAT PURIFIER," and we offer it to Dr. Carson as an additional case where it *cannot* mean *the Great Dipper!*

I say *Dipper* and not *Immerser*, because I enter an imperative denial of the right of any under the dipping theory to make use of *immerse* or of any of its derivatives, so long as they identify *dip* and *βαπτίζω*. When they reject this error we will cheerfully give them the benefit of it, and will hold them to other responsibilities.

In the meanwhile we must affirm, that the two words, dip and immerse, differ essentially. Their power differs widely, deeply, universally; their relations to words and thoughts differ; their development, from primary thought, exhibits the same continued and magnified difference. If these statements are not true, let their error be shown. If they are not disproved, is it rational to suppose that, in a discussion turning on these differences, these terms can be allowed to be tossed about, at will, as may suit the pleasure or ends of one of the parties? If the friends of the theory have grown distrustful of *dip*, and think that *immerse* can do them more valiant service, let them frankly confess their change of ground, *and stick to it with all its consequences*, and no one will impose upon them their once trusted, but, at length, discarded favorite. But until this is done, we cannot allow a white horse and a black horse to be imposed upon us as *matches*.

ORIGEN.

What does the Great Baptizer baptize?

When the theorists have been hard pressed with the evidence against the dippings of the priests in Judaic baptisms, they have answered: "Parts of the sacrificial victims, or the utensils, may have been dipped, and such dippings would account for its being said that there were baptisms in the temple service." Dr. Halley says that he is not satisfied with the fitness of this answer, but as he cannot disprove the existence of such dippings, or demonstrate their incongruity with the baptisms designed, he will not press the argument.

This attempt to save the theory in the face of condemning facts, by the supposition of some rhetorical speech, or extraordinary figure, or some possible fact, is characteristic of the believers in "dipping, and nothing but dipping." Every one who gives attention to the subject will, at once, be aware what facilities are at hand, by large drafts on rhetoric, figure, imagination, and the rich storehouse of possibilities, for throwing back a secondary meaning on the primary, by one who is disposed, at all hazards, to reject a secondary sense. To demonstrate the impossibility of the primary sense against all these, lawful and unlawful modifying and coloring appliances, so as to compel the assent of a determined and thoroughly committed opponent, is a difficult if not impracticable task. The theorists take this double position: 1. No second meaning to βαπτίζω, dip and nothing but dip. 2. No surrender, except to blank impossibility of such meaning, after the exhaustion of all conceivable opposing appliances.

A rule in itself may not be an improper one, but the interpretation of evidence under it may be very exceptionable. Dr. Carson, who lays down this law for the opponents of the theory, refuses to govern his own action by the interpretation of the law which he would bind on others. In adducing evidence for a secondary meaning to βάπτω, there is not a case brought forward in proof, which could endure a single stroke from the machinery which he gets up to batter down, or undermine, or overtop, or circumvent, or blow up, whatever sustains a secondary meaning of βαπτίζω.

I make no protest against the rule; but I do protest against an insane judgment of the rule, or of evidence under the rule.

Proof, to the full of all rational requirement, under the

rule has already been repeatedly presented. We have such testimony renewedly furnished by the extract from Origen, and which I now present: "Igitur defert utrumque Salvator, gladium et ignem, et BAPTIZAT QUÆ non potuerunt Spiritus Sancti purificatione purgari."—"Therefore, the Saviour brings forth both the sword and the fire, and *baptizes what* (*defilements*, *faults*, *sins*) could not be purged by the purification of the Holy Spirit."

The argument from this passage is: 1. "The purification of the Holy Spirit" is, in Patristic conception, baptism *by water* impregnated with the quality of the Holy Spirit; and the object of this baptism, as stated, is to baptize the pollutions of the soul; therefore baptize cannot mean to dip, because "pollutions" *cannot be dipped.* But, no doubt, this argument, though clear as the sun, will be "puffed at," on the ground of the use of the phrase "purification of the Holy Spirit," being used instead of the word *baptize.* Well, then, as I do not believe in charging people with "wanting *Christian honesty* more than wanting light," (though they may appear to me to be madly set upon a theory,) we will pass out of the light of one sun into the light of seven suns.

2. Origen, through his translator Jerome, both of unimpeachable authority, gives us in the former part of the sentence, *totidem literis*, the very word—*baptizat.* The objection, then, on the ground of the absence of the word, is at an end. Now, as to the meaning in which the word is used. What was baptized? Priests, Levites, disciples? No. "Shoulders, breasts, legs of sacrificial victims?" No. "Basins, pots, utensils of any kind?" No. What then? *Defilements*, *faults*, *sins*, "which could not be purged by the purification by the Holy Spirit." Now test the primary meaning *attributed* to βαπτίζω, (to dip,) by the case, and we have: "Therefore the Saviour brings forth both sword and fire, and *dips* what (*defilements*, *faults*, *sins*) could not be purged by the purification of the Holy Spirit."

Is it a possibility, or an impossibility, *to dip* "defilements, faults, and sins?" Is it a possibility, or an impossibility, to dip such things by "sword and fire?"

If any friend of the theory in Europe, Asia, Africa, or America, (whom a jury under a writ *de lunatico* shall pronounce sane), will declare that it is possible "to dip defilements, faults, and sins," then I will give up the case, and pray that a like writ be taken out for myself; for if such a one be not demented, I must be. The passage furnishes an *experimentum crucis* for the theory. If Origen (the most learned and the most voluminous Greek writer of his day,) understood Greek; if Jerome (thoroughly taught in the Greek Classics before he became a Christian,) understood Greek; if these most learned men had any just understanding of what they themselves wrote; then, the theory is brought face to face with a case of usage in which the meaning "to dip," is an absolute impossibility.

That the force of this evidence may be felt, if possible, yet more deeply, I will quote an analogous case adduced by President Halley, (*Sacraments*, i, 454,) as the highest possible proof to determine a secondary meaning for βάπτω.

"Although Dr. Carson has said enough to satisfy his brethren that βάπτω has *to dye* as a secondary meaning, he has not, I think, produced the most decisive evidence which the idiom of the language supplies. *The best proof of a complete change of the meaning, is a corresponding change of the syntax accommodating itself to the deflection of sense.* . . . In the phrases to dip the wool, and to stain the wool, the syntax is the same. But if the syntax is so varied as to make not the thing colored, but *the color itself*, the object of the verb,—as when we say to dye *a purple*,—the secondary sense has then renounced all dependence upon the primary, and established itself by a new law of syntax, enacted by usage to secure its undisturbed possession. . . . This is illustrated by the passage ἐάν τέ τις ἄλλα χρώματα βάπτῃ, ἐάν τέ καὶ ταῦτα. 'Whether any one dye other *colors* or these also.' Here χρῶμα has gained in the syntax the place of the material subjected to the process; and therefore pleads a law of language that βάπτω in the passage does not, and cannot mean *to dip*, as the *color* cannot be dipped, whatever may be done with the wool. Another case is found in Lucian (*Cynic*, p. 1106), οἱ τὴν πορφύραν βάπτοντες, 'those dyeing *the purple.*' This syntax I hold to be demonstrative of a secondary meaning."

Professor Wilson, Royal College, Belfast, speaking of this principle and its value as testimony to a secondary meaning, says: "That βάπτω denotes *to dye*, without regard to mode, and even where immersion is in terms excluded, the preceding examples place beyond the pale of candid disputation. There remains, however, an additional element of proof, which, if not more convincing in its nature, is at least calculated to afford higher gratification to the mind of the true philologist. We allude to the interesting fact, that the secondary meaning, instead of hanging loosely on the outskirts of clauses and sentences, has seized upon their most intimate connections, and entered deeply into the structural fabric of the Greek language. As Dr. Halley, so far as we are aware, was the first to direct public attention to the existence and value of this branch of evidence, we shall present in his own words the statement and illustration of its character."

We have here the testimony of two most competent witnesses to the principle, that a radical change in the syntax is the highest proof of a radical change in the meaning of the word. This principle was not enunciated to meet a controversial exigency. The Baptists had already accepted a secondary meaning to βαπτω. It may, therefore, be received without suspicion, and acknowledged as a universal principle ingrained in the elements of language.

We can say, dip *wool*, but we cannot say, dip *purple*, and use the verb in the same sense in both cases; for "purple" is of such a nature as to be insusceptible of the action of which "wool" is the object. The syntax, therefore, is proof of a change of meaning. Wool may be *dipped;* purple can, only, be *dyed.*

So we may say, dip (supposing this to be, as claimed, the meaning of βαπτίζω) the *sinner;* but we cannot say, dip the *sin*, and use the word in the same sense, because "sin," by its nature, does not admit of being *dipped.* But Origen does say that the Lord Jesus dips (baptizes) *sins*, (represented in "quæ"); it follows, therefore, by a necessity of the laws of language, that he uses the verb in such case with a secondary meaning. Sins may be *purged;* they cannot be *dipped.* If proof needed to be heaped on proof, it would be found in the means used for this dipping by the Great Baptizer; "sword and fire" can no more *dip*, than "sins" can be dipped by them. "Sword and fire" can *purge;* sins can *be purged;* the Great Baptizer *does* purge; and βαπτίζω *means* TO PURGE.

The theory perishes by the Flaming Sword in the hands of the True as well as "THE GREAT BAPTIST."

BAPTISM BY A COAL OF FIRE.

ISAIAH 6:5–7.

"Then said I, Woe is me! for I am undone; because I am a man of unclean lips and I dwell in the midst of a people of unclean lips: for mine eyes have seen the King, the Lord of hosts.

"Then flew one of the Seraphim unto me, having a live coal in his hand, which he had taken with the tongs from off the altar:

"And he laid it upon my mouth and said, Lo, this hath touched thy lips; and thine iniquity is taken away, and thy sin is purged."

Interpretation.

"Lege mandata Legis, et invenies scriptum: *Quia vivens si mortuum contigerit, inquinatur* (Numb. 19:11). . . . Indigemus ergo purgatione, quia tetigimus mortuos (Numb. 19:1). . . . Omnes contigimus mortuum. Quis enim gloriabitur castum se habere cor, aut quis audebit dicere mundum se a peccatis? Sit aliquis fortasse qui in sermone non deliquerit . . . . tamen in medio peccatorum versatur, necesse habet etiam ipse purificari. Unde Esaias, cum dixisset (6:5–7), statim descendit unum de Seraphim, et contigit labia ejus carbone, et immunda ejus labia mundaret.

"14. Non unum est baptismum."

"Read the commandments of the Law, and you will find it written,—*Whosoever shall touch the dead, becomes defiled* (Numb.

19 : 11). . . . Therefore we need purgation, because we have touched the dead (Numb. 19 : 1). . . . We all touch the dead. For who will boast that he keeps his heart pure, or who will dare to say that he is clean from sins? There may be some one, possibly, who has not sinned in word, although such a one is rare, of whom God may say, as of holy Job: *He has not sinned with his lips* (Job 22 : 10); however, he could not always have the thoughts of his heart pure, the devil injects himself into the heart of man. Whoever keeps constant and vigilant guard over his heart, nevertheless lives in the midst of sinners, and even he has need to be purified. Hence Esaias, when he had said, (6 : 5–7,) immediately one of the Seraphim came down and touched his lips with a coal, and cleansed his unclean lips.

"14. Baptism is not one."—*Ambrose*, ii, 1126, 1127.

"Et sumet plenum batillum carbonibus ignis de altari, quod est contra Dominum (Leviticus 16 : 12). Legimus et in Isaia, quia igne purgatur propheta per unum ex Seraphim, quod missum est ad eum, cum accepit forcipe carbonem unum ex his qui erant super altare, et contigit labia prophetæ, et dixit: '*Ecce abstuli iniquitates tuas.*' Mihi videntur mystica hæc esse, et hoc indicare, quod unicuique secundum id quod peccat, si dignum fuerit purificari eum, inferantur carbones membris ejus. Nam quoniam dicit propheta hic: '*Immunda labia habeo, in medio quoque populi immunda labia habentis habito,*' idcirco carbo forcipe assumptus a Seraphim, labia ejus mundat, quibus solis se mundum non esse profitetur. . . . Nos autem, si redeat unusquisque ad conscientiam suam, nescio si possumus aliquod membrum corporis excusare, quod non igni indigeat."

"And he shall take a censer full of burning coals of fire from off the altar before the Lord (Leviticus 16 : 12). We read also in Isaiah, that the prophet is purged by fire by one of the Seraphim, sent to him, when he took with the tongs a live coal from those which were upon the altar, and touched the lips of the prophet and said, '*Behold I have taken away thine iniquities.*' These things seem to me to belong to the mysteries, and to indicate this, that to every one according to that which he sins, if he shall be worthy to be purified, burning coals shall be put upon his members. For since the prophet says: 'I have unclean lips, also I dwell in the midst of a people of unclean lips,' therefore, a live coal having been taken by the Seraphim with tongs, he purifies his lips, by which only he professes himself to be not clean. . . . But we, if every one would examine his conscience, I know not if we could excuse any member of our body, that *it should not need the fire*. . . . I fear lest we deserve the fire not for particular members, but for the whole body. . . . All are not purged by that fire which is taken from the altar. Aaron is purged by that fire, and Isaiah, and if there are any like them. But others who are not as they, among whom I reckon myself, will be purged by another fire. I fear lest by that of which it is written: 'A fiery stream ran before him.' (Dan. 7 : 10.) This fire is not from the altar. The fire which is from the altar is the fire of the Lord, but that which is not from the altar, is not of the Lord, but is *of the sinner himself*, concerning which it is said, 'Their worm shall not die, and *their* fire shall not be quenched.' (Isaiah 66 : 24.) Therefore, this fire is *theirs who kindled it*, as it is elsewhere written: 'Walk in the light of your fire, and in the sparks that ye have kindled.' But his own fire is not applied to Isaiah, but the fire of the altar which purged around his lips."—*Origen*, ii, 517, 519.

Βάπτισόν με, τὸν μέλλοντα βαπτίζειν τοὺς πιστεύοντας δί ὕδατος, καὶ Πνεύματος, καὶ πυρὸς· ὕδατι δυναμένῳ ἀποπλῦναι τῶν ἁμαρτιῶν τὸν βόρβορον· Πνεύματι, δυναμένῳ τοὺς χοϊκους, πνευματικοὺς ἀπεργάσασθαι· πυρὶ, πεφυκότι κατακαίειν τὰς τῶν ἀνομημάτων ἀκάνθας.

"Baptize me, who am about to baptize them that believe, by water, and Spirit, and fire; by water, possessing power to wash away the filth of sins; by Spirit, possessing power to make the earthly spiritual; by fire, possessing a nature to burn up the thorns of transgressions."—*Gregory Thaumaturgus*, x, 1188.

Σερῆνος—ὃν μετὰ πλείστην βασάνων ὑπομονὴν, κεφαλῆς ἀποτόμῇ κολοσθῆναι λογός ἔχει. Καὶ γυναικῶν δὲ Ἡραῒς ἔτι κατασχουμένη, τὸ βάπτισμα, ὥς που φησὶν αὐτὸς, τὸ διὰ πυρὸς λαβοῦσα τὸν βίον ἐξελήλυθεν.

"Serenus—who, after the endurance of great torments, is said to have been beheaded. And of women, Herais, yet a catechumen, received that baptism which is by fire, as elsewhere related, and departed out of this life."—*Eusebius*, ii, 532.

AMBROSE.

The purification from the defilement contracted by touching a dead body, required by the ceremonial law, and spoken of by Jews and Patrists as a baptism, is here applied by Ambrose to those who live among, and become defiled by contact with those who are "*dead* in trespasses and sins." As the one required baptism, so the other required baptism. Special application is made to the case of Isaiah, who confesses himself to be "a man of unclean lips, and to dwell among a people of unclean lips." The first baptism was effected by the purifying power of sprinkled heifer ashes; the second baptism was effected by the purifying power of a burning coal. In neither case is the word baptism used, but in both cases the descriptive terms identify with baptism, as proved to be held by Jew and Patrist. To make an argument on the mere absence of a word, as fatal to the existence of a baptism, is what no intelligent man will do. To deny the applicability of the term baptism to a case evidently made out for such application, and so used by competent writers, because we have not been accustomed to such application, is to rebel against supreme authority.

Suppose a child has advanced so far in the knowledge of words as to understand, among other rudimentary terms, the names and application of words to designate colors, and bringing a handful of berries from the garden, is told by a parent, not to eat them for they are *green*. The child looks up in wonder, and exclaims: "Surely they are not 'green;' they are *red* all over." When the answer is returned: "Yes, they are 'red;' but being *black*berries, they are *green* because they are *red*." With what an access of wonder and of blank incredulity will the child listen to all this. The same handful of berries are "red," and "black," and "green," at one and the same time. What shall he do? Set up his child-knowledge against the knowledge of his parent? and the testimony of his own eyes against the testimony of his parent? Shall he stoutly affirm, that *red* berries cannot be *black*-berries; but if red berries could be blackberries, certainly they could not be *green* berries; but if red could be black, or could be green, most assuredly they could not be *red*, and *black*, and *green!* And if father and mother say so, "I will order them to go to school."

The friends of the theory have learned, as they suppose, that "a baptism is a dipping, and nothing but a dipping;" and when they are told, by Jews, that a baptism is effected by the sprinkling of heifer ashes; they answer, "It cannot be." And when they are told, by Gentiles, that a baptism is effected by laying a burning coal upon the lips; they redouble their cry, "It cannot possibly be." Do we not *know* that "dipping" is baptism? How then can *sprinkling* be a baptism? But if sprinkling can be baptism, how is it possible that *laying a coal of fire on the lips* can be baptism? No; such things cannot be; and "if the Angel Gabriel, himself, were to tell us so, *we would order him to school.*"

The point made by this illustration is, not a likening of the knowledge of these ardent theorists to child-knowledge —this would be as untrue as it would be unbecoming—but it is to show the great embarrassment and strong resistance which any one must make, when a word has been fixed with a single and exclusive meaning in the mind, when that word is presented in circumstances which create meanings the most opposite and inconsistent with that meaning which we have believed to be exhaustive of the capabilities of the word.

It is not strange, that those who have put unquestioning faith in Dr. Carson's statement, "My dissertation has forever settled the meaning of βαπτίζω, if there be truth in axioms, to be *dip, and nothing but dip,*" should be startled on finding Josephus and Justin, Clement and Chrysostom, Ambrose and Gregory, Basil and Origen, and a host of others, unite in calling sprinklings, pourings, washings, coals of fire, flaming swords, &c., &c., &c., agencies effecting baptisms.

But what is best to be done under such circumstances? Is it best still to follow a leader who has shown himself to be utterly mistaken as to the meaning in question, and cry, "To school, to school, Gabriel!" or, to have faith to believe that, in some way or other, (not apprehended by us,) the same object, at the same time, may be even *red*, *black*, and *green?*

After Ambrose had spoken of the baptism, by a coal of

fire, without using the word, he shows that his mind was full of the thing, by commencing the immediately following paragraph with the words, "Baptism is not one," and introduces the baptism of the flaming sword, which has just been considered, as another illustration of fire baptism. There can then be no doubt, that this writer regarded a single coal of fire as competent, not, certainly, *to dip*, but to baptize—purifying from defilement incurred by utterances of the mouth.

While such a baptism burns up the theory, it does not leave even "the smell of fire" on the principle, that baptisms are effected by controlling influences without regard to form in the action, or covering in the condition.

ORIGEN.

Censer of Burning Coals.—Origen believed that the censer of burning coals, taken by the high priest into the holy of holies, and the burning coal applied to Isaiah's lips, were of mystical import. He interprets that meaning as teaching, a baptism of fire *applied to* whatever member of the body may be the cause of defilement through transgression. He supposes the sin of the prophet to consist in wrong utterances, and therefore the baptizing power was *applied to* the lips. Origen does not teach that the defilement was in the lips; but the whole man was defiled through the lips. Therefore he says, "Thy iniquities are taken away." So he argues afterward, that any other member—eyes, hands, feet—that should engage in doing wrong, and thus defile us, "would need the fire." This shows, conclusively, that Origen did not believe in the idea that a baptism was limited to a covering any more than to a dipping; for his doctrine *applied* fire, the baptizing agency, *to* the lips, the hand, the foot, while the baptism, the purifying influence, extended throughout the entire defiled person. He also speaks of those who give their whole bodies to sin, instead of giving them to the Lord, and of needing baptism by a different fire. This fire, he says, may be that "fiery stream" which was seen by

Daniel to run before the Lord. But here he says nothing about *dipping* into this flowing fire.

But whether the theory will, in the absence of information as to the depth of this stream, think it worth while (in view of sprinkling, and pouring, and sword baptisms) to put in a plea, "if there was a baptism the word would prove, even in a desert, that there was enough water (fire) for a dipping," or not, I cannot tell. I suppose, however, not many would volunteer "to go down into" the fiery stream, to officiate at the dipping. But in what way soever the baptism may have taken place in this fire-river, if they were put beneath the glowing flood, nothing is more certain than that such a feature had nothing to do (beyond any other accident which might or might not be present) in constituting the baptism. Origen most distinctly recognizes as baptism, the very limited application of the fire to any member of the body. This is his language: "I fear lest we deserve the fire *not for particular members*, but for the whole body." Some were baptized by fire, by a limited application, others by a general application. The character of the sins determined the extent of application of the fire.

"*Another fire.*" Not only was "baptism by fire" a distinct genus among baptisms, but there were varieties among fire-baptisms. This is distinctly taught by Origen, in making a broad distinction between baptism by "fire from off the altar," and that which was by fire not from the altar. The first is "fire of the Lord," the last is "fire of the sinner." Inasmuch as these fires are agencies, and their effect upon sin and the sinner must depend upon their own character, real or putative, it is obvious that the influence produced by fire of *the Lord* and "fire of the sinner," cannot be the same. It follows, therefore, that the resultant conditions (baptisms) produced by these alien influences, must be alien from each other. And this brings us back again to the loudly-proclaimed truth: "Baptism is not one."

GREGORY THAUMATURGUS.

Power of Baptism —The extract from Gregory Thaumaturgus, brings out vividly the truth that, in these secondary baptisms, there is no receiving element into which the baptized object passes, but the baptism is effected by, and exists in the effect of the power belonging to the agency. This is exhibited appropriately by the simple dative. But as this case is used in a local (with preposition) as well as instrumental sense, advantage has been taken of this (sometimes with unexampled violence) to insist on a conversion of the agency into a local element.

But such mischievous interpretation is effectually arrested by the substitution of the genitive in the place of the dative. That is the case here. The baptism is effected δἰ ὕδατος—πνεύματος—πυρὸς. There is no possibility of transforming this *water*, *spirit*, *fire*, into anything else than agency. Accumulate water over the baptized object until it is submerged five hundred fathom deep, and yet you have made no progress toward the conversion of δἰ ὕδατος into ἐν ὕδατι; let a diseased imagination envelop the soul and body "in the spirit" poured out and rising up around it until it out-tops the mountains, and διὰ πνεύματος is no more ἐν πνεύματι than is a circle a square; deepen the fire-river until its bed rests on the centre of the globe, and dip the hapless sinner into its lowest depths, and διὰ πυρὸς is as far removed from ἐν πυρι as *by* is from *in*. The *whence* case and the *where* case are inconvertible. This point receives additional evidence, of the strongest possible kind, by the conjunction of δυναμένῳ with these terms. To be baptized "by the *power* of water," "by the *power* of the Spirit," "by the *nature* of fire," as expressive of simple enclosure *in water*, *in Spirit*, *in fire*, is impossible and absurd phraseology. But if water, and Spirit, and fire are agencies accomplishing baptisms by their peculiar power, naturally or specially conferred, then, this qualifying term is most appropriate, and the theory is robbed of her receiving element; that palladium which being lost, all is lost.

This usage is most entirely coincident with that of the Classics. In all baptisms kindred to those which are now under consideration, they invariably use the dative, without a preposition, instrumentally. *Wine* is not the element *in which* the baptism is effected, but the means *by which*. *Drugs* are not the element *in which* the man is put to sleep (baptized), but *by which*. *Questions*, *magical arts*, *hard study*, *taxes*, *debts*, *grief*, *famine*, are not elements *in which* men are baptized, but means *by which* they are brought under their several peculiar and controlling powers.

Classic, Jewish, and Patristic writings show that the theorists, unwarned by the blunder of Gale, (in making the nude dative local, in order to make βάπτω *dip*, and so get the lake *in* the blood of the frog, instead of accepting a secondary meaning as indicated by the instrumental form, and *dyeing* the lake *by* blood), have perpetuated that error in their interpretation of these baptisms. To correct the error is to take the underpinning from the theory.

EUSEBIUS.

Baptism by the fire of martyrdom.—Herais, a female catechumen and yet unbaptized by water, was put to death by fire, as a disciple of Christ. But the historian says: "She received that baptism which is by fire." Water baptism, ordinarily, was essential to salvation, because it was believed that there was a "power" in the water to take away sin from the soul. It was, however, agreed, that this power was not limited to water, but belonged, also, to "confession" of Christ by martyrdom. This was called sometimes, generically, "baptism of martyrdom," "baptism of confession," and sometimes, specifically, "baptism of blood," "baptism of fire."

The baptism had nothing, whatever, to do with the mode or extent of the application of the blood or fire to the body. These things were only the signs, or means of death. In death by fire the body was, more or less, enveloped by the flames, perhaps never absolutely, but this was no part of the baptism; that centred in *dying* for Christ. In this same extract we have a reference to a martyr who was beheaded. How much of his body was "enveloped" by the sword? It was as much a baptism of the sword as that at the gate of Paradise. How much of his body was "covered" by his blood? If the headlesss trunk spouted forth its blood so that not one drop fell upon it, it was as much a baptism by blood, as if it had been sunk in the Nile when, under Moses' rod, its billows rolled in one crimson tide of blood.

In every aspect in which the subject is presented we find nowhere a baptism *in* a receiving element; we find everywhere, under every form of action, baptisms effected by agencies possessed of power to *control completely the condition* of their objects.

A fiery stream, or a coal of fire, is equally suitable, as agencies, to effect a baptism.

Isaiah, baptized by the seraphim with a burning coal, witnesses with pure and glowing lips that "the theory" is of earth and not from heaven.

BAPTISM BY WATER, BY SPIRIT, AND BY FIRE.

Isaiah 4:4.

"When the Lord shall have washed away the filth of the daughters of Zion, and shall have purged the blood of Jerusalem from the midst thereof, by the spirit of judgment and by the spirit of burning."

Septuagint.

Ὅτι ἐκπλυνεῖ κύριος τὸν ῥύπον τῶν υἱῶν καὶ τῶν θυγατέρων Σιών, καὶ τὸ αἷμα ἐκκαθαριεῖ ἐκ μέσου αὐτῶν, ἐν πνεύματι κρίσεως καὶ πνεύματι καύσεως.

Interpretation.

. . . . . *Ἐπεὶ γοῦν ἀμφότερα συνῆψεν ὁ Κύριος, τό τε ἐξ ὕδατος εἰς μετάνοιαν, καὶ τὸ ἐκ Πνεύματος εἰς ἀναγέννησιν, καὶ ὁ λόγος αἰνίσσεται ἀμφότερα τὰ βαπτίσματα. Μήποτε τρεῖς εἰσιν αἱ ἐπίνοιαι τοῦ βαπτίσματος, ὅ τε τοῦ ῥύπου καθαρισμὸς, καὶ ἡ διὰ τοῦ Πνεύματος ἀναγέννησις, καὶ ἡ ἐν τῷ πυρὶ τῆς κρίσεως βάσανος.*

"This passage foretells, clearly, the same things which were spoken by John concerning the Lord: 'This is he who shall baptize you by the Holy Spirit and fire;' but concerning himself, he says: 'I indeed baptize you with water into repentance.' Since then the Lord conjoined both, that from water into repentance, and that from the Spirit into regeneration, the Scripture, also, foreshadows both these baptisms. Perhaps there are three meanings of baptism: purification from defilement, regeneration by the Spirit, and trial by the fire of judgment. So that 'the washing' (v. 4) is to be understood in reference to the removal of sin now; but 'by the spirit of judgment and by the spirit of burning,' (v. 4,) the reference is to the trial by fire in the future world."—*Basil the Great*, ii, 341.

BASIL.

By the spirit of burning.—The Septuagint, in translating this passage, uses the preposition (ἐν) but once,. while Basil, following the Hebrew more closely, repeats it,—ἐν πνεύματι κρίσεως καὶ ἐν πνεύματι καύσεως.

It is admitted that ἐν has an instrumental as well as a local force; but the theory is interested to make the former meaning as near zero as possible, and especially to insist, that in all cases of baptism it must have a local meaning. It is desirable, then, to look at the matter in the light of the usage of this highly accomplished Greek writer.

1. The subject-matter embraced in these datives, is not favorable to the sense claimed. "Washing out (ἐκπλυνεῖ) and purging out (ἐκκαθαριεῖ) *in* (ἐν) a spirit of judgment and *in* (ἐν) a spirit of burning." It is not likely that the sons and daughters of Zion would be represented as put within such things, to wash them and to purge them. But such suggestions of congruity are "lighter than vanity" when they conflict with—"nothing but dip." We have seen this abundantly exemplified in Classic Baptism where, in the absence of the preposition, they have made the naked dative the occasion for putting men in a bottle of wine, in an opiate drug, and in a perplexing question. We must, then, find some other reason more imperative than the fitness of things.

2. We show then, by other phraseology in the context, that Basil had no other idea than the use of this preposition with an instrumental force.

This is manifest (1.) From his omission of the preposition; as, τὸ δὲ πνεύματι κρίσεως καὶ πνεύματι καύσεως, in the same paragraph. But as we have already seen the natural force belonging to this form of expression to be utterly set at naught, when there was nothing to encourage so doing; now, having aid and comfort from the previous use of ἐν, we can expect no voluntary concession. It must be wrung out. Basil furnishes us with material to do this.

3. The dative, with the preposition, is changed into the genitive, with its prepositions. Thus ἐν ὕδατι becomes ἐξ ὕδατος; ἐν πνεύματι becomes ἐκ Πνεύματος; ἐν τῷ πυρὶ becomes διὰ τοῦ πυρὸς, and ἐκ τοῦ πυρὸς; ἐν πνεύματι καύσεως becomes διὰ τῆς τοῦ πνεύματος καύσεως; and all this in a single paragraph.

No wonder the theory makes a hard fight here. The conversion of these datives into agencies, like the burning lightning, withers its life to the very roots. Basil does his work well.

Three meanings.—This able commentator says that baptism (as presented in this passage, not absolutely,) has three meanings or phases of development. It has been said (and I think the evidence to substantiate it given) in Classic Baptism, that "baptism is myriad-sided;" and, here, in a single passage, we are told, by a most accomplished Greek writer, that there is a threefold development of the word. And it is of this word the theory says: "It means dip, and nothing but dip, through all Greek literature."

It will be observed, in this threefold baptism, that *condition* is an ever-present element, and *dipping*, never.

1. *Purification:* a condition of purity induced, by the appropriate means, from either Judaic ceremonial impurity, or from the defilement of "lighter" sins.

2. *Regeneration:* a condition of new spiritual life; the result of a radical change in that condition pertaining to birth by nature.

3. *Trial by fire of judgment:* a final test of our condition of preparation to enter into the Paradise of God.

"Attic salt" has been freely sprinkled upon those who talked of a "religious" meaning belonging to βαπτίζω. And yet the Archbishop of Cæsarea, the first among Greek Patriarchs, furnishes us with something that looks very much like a religious meaning of this word. Certainly there is but little which resembles, in nature, that Classic use which has heretofore engaged our attention. Religious purification is the ground-thought, as presented in these three baptisms; this elementary idea receiving coloring from the specialties of each case. Religious usage has given a religious meaning, or fact is fiction.

But while there is a religious element and a religious meaning here present, it is reached without the slightest departure from the principles of language, and without laying aside the original fundamental thought of CONDITION, *characterized by completeness*. The difference exists only in the character of the agencies, and the ends to which they are addressed. Take wine, as a baptizing agency, and you have a Classic baptism of one kind. Take a drugged drink, as a baptizing agency, and you have a Classic baptism of another kind. "Baptism is not one," is a doctrine as much believed by the Classics as by the Patrists. Among the "multa genera baptismatum," the *genus* treated of by Basil and his friends, differed from that treated of by Plutarch and his associates.

These *fire* baptisms throw their light far and wide; but their light is darkness to the theory.

BAPTISMS—MENTAL AND MORAL.

BAPTISM BY HEAVY IRON AND BY HEAVIEST SINS.

II KINGS 6 : 5, 6.

"But as one was felling a beam, the axe-head fell into the water; and he cried, and said, Alas, master! for it was borrowed.

"And the man of God said, Where fell it? And he showed him the place. And he cut down a stick and cast it in thither; and the iron did swim."

Interpretation.

Ξύλον 'Ελισσαῖ.ς βαλὼν ἐις τὸν 'Ιορδάνην ποταμὸν ἀνήνεγκε τὸν σιδῆρον της ἀξίνης, ἐν ᾗ πεπορευμένοι ἦσαν δι υἱοὶ των προφητων κόψαι . . . ὡς καὶ ἡμᾶς βεβαπτισμένους ταῖς βαρυτάταις ἁμαρτίαις ἅς ἐπράξαμεν διὰ τοῦ σταυρωθῆναι ἐπὶ τοῦ ξυλου καὶ δἰ ὕδατος ἀγνίσαι ὁ Χριστὸς ἡμῶν ἐλυτρώσατο.

"Elisha casting a stick into the river Jordan, brought up the iron of the axe with which the sons of the prophets had gone forth to cut wood . . . as also Christ hath redeemed us, mersed by heaviest sins which we have committed, through the crucifixion upon the wood, and purification through water."—*Justin Martyr*, 681.

"Exiliit ferrum, et mersum est in flumine, . . . accepto ligno, et misso in eum locum, ubi submersum fuerat ferrum, statim supernatavit. . . . . Quid manifestius hujus ligni sacramento? quod duritia hujus sæculi mersa in profundo erroris, et a ligno Christi, id est passionis ejus, in baptismo, liberatur, ut quod perierat olim per lignum in Adam, id restitueretur per lignum Christi."

"Moreover we read in the book of Kings that the sacrament of this word is celebrated. For when the sons of the prophets were cutting wood with axes over the river Jordan, the iron fell off and was mersed in the river; and so the prophet Elisha, coming up, the sons of the prophets ask from him that he would draw out the iron which had been mersed in the river. Elisha having taken a piece of wood, and cast it into the place where the iron had been submersed, immediately it floated. . . . By which they understood that the spirit of Elijah was present again in him. What is more clear than the sacrament of this wood? that the hardness of this age, mersed in the depth of error, is delivered by the wood of Christ."—*Tertullian*, ii, 636.

Ὅπερ ἦν σημεῖον ἀναγωγῆς ψυχῶν διὰ ξύλου, ἐφ' οὗ πέπονθεν ὁ ψυχὰς ἀνάγειν δυνάμενος, ἀκολουθούσας ἀνόδω τῇ ἑαυτοῦ.

"Which was a sign of the bringing up of souls, through the cross, upon which he suffered, who is able to bring up souls following in the way of his ascending."—*Irenæus*, 1243.

Οὗτος (ὁ σταυρὸς) ἀπὸ τοῦ βυθοῦ τῆς κακίας ἥμας ἀνάσπάσας.

"This (the cross) drawing us up from the depth of depravity."—*Chrysostom*, ii, 407.

"Invocavit Eliseus Domini nomen, et de aqua ferrum securis ascendit quod demersum fuerat. Ecce aliud genus baptismatis. Quare? Quia omnis homo ante baptismum quasi ferrum premitur, atque demergitur, ubi baptizatus fuerit, non tanquam ferrum, sed tanquam jam levior fructuosi ligni species elevatur. . . . Vides, ergo, quod in cruce Christi omnium hominum levatur infirmitas."

"Elisha called upon the name of the Lord, and the iron of the axe which had been demersed ascends from the water. Behold, another kind of baptism! Why? Because every man before baptism, like iron, is pressed down and demersed; when baptized, not like iron, but like some lighter kind of fruitful wood, he is raised up. . . . Thou seest, therefore, that by the cross of Christ the infirmity of all men is lightened."—*Ambrose*, iii, 427.

BAPTISM OF THE AXE.

The mersion of the axe in Jordan has special interest, because it brings us back into a purely classic atmosphere. Heathen writers give us abundant cases in which heavy bodies, going down to the bottom of rivers, lakes, marshes, and seas, and remaining there unrecovered, are in a state of baptism. A ship, a fishing-spear, a breastplate, a man in armor, sunk in river or sea, is baptized, lost, in a ruined condition.

The natural, unavoidable application in secondary use, of the word expressive of such condition, would be to such things as exhibit a condition of suffering or ruin. Thus, a man who had lost the control of his intellect by hard study, or bewilderment, or idiocy; who had lost the control of his property by debt or misfortune; who had lost his happiness through some great sorrow; who had lost his health by disease; who had lost his consciousness through intoxication; was freely called a baptized man. The classic, secondary use of the word did not pass, at all or but little, beyond this range of application to conditions of injury, loss, and ruin. Josephus frequently employs the word after the usage of the classics, and also carries it into another sphere, namely, that of religion, as expressive of a condition of ceremonial purification. In doing this, he neither departs from the fundamental character of the word, nor from the principle of classic usage in its extension to cases of controlling influence, where there is no physical envelopment.

While a very large number of cases of mersion result in injury or destruction, this is not the case with every mersion. The nature of the condition resultant from a physical mersion will depend: 1. On the nature of the element within which the mersion takes place; and, 2. On the nature of the object mersed. Time of continuance cannot be introduced as an additional element determining the condition to which mersion may be applied, because mersion has no limitation of time, and to introduce such an element would be to introduce what is foreign to its nature. A mersed condition may be changed by foreign influences, but it has no element of change within itself. Baptism, therefore, can only be applied to such conditions as are either absolutely permanent, or which left to themselves would be so.

Historically we have, as elements of mersion, water, (in various forms, fresh, salt, pure, impure, hot, cold, as also impregnated with various qualities,) oil, milk, wine, blood, vinegar, mud, marsh, the human body, &c. As mersed objects we have, rocks, metals, salt, sponge, a crown, a pickle, human beings, a dolphin, an ape, clean things, unclean things, &c. &c.

Now it is obvious, that the mersion of the same object into different elements would be productive of conditions widely different. Take, for instance, a piece of limestone and immerse it, first in water and then in vinegar, and how different the resultant conditions. Take any object and immerse it in water or in oil, in milk or in blood, and how different the result. Take a vegetable and immerse it in syrup or in vinegar, and you have a preserve or a pickle. Mersion in clean water or dirty water has not the same issue. If you take different objects and use the same element, you still have a diversity of conditions. The mersion of a dolphin and an ape in water, is a condition of life in the one case and of death in the other. The mule of the fable found out, that the condition resultant from the mersion of a bag of salt or of a bag of sponge, in the same element, was widely diverse. Merse clean linen into pure water and muddy water; is the result the same?

Nothing can be more evident, than that Classic Baptism, with its wide range of elements and of objects, could never be restricted, by any necessity of its own, to the designation of condition limited by injury or ruin. It is perfectly adapted to this end; but no less so to express condition, endlessly varied, under the ruling thought of controlling influence.

When this Greek word was introduced within the sphere of revealed religion it met, everywhere, the demand for a condition of complete ceremonial purification. It met with influences proceeding, by divine enactment, from water, blood, heifer ashes, &c., competent to effect such condition. To secure such condition, modes of use—washing, pouring, sprinkling, (but never the dipping of men and women into water,) —were found divinely enacted. Under these circumstances Jewish writers took this word and applied it, without varying one jot or tittle from the principle of Classic usage, to a condition resultant from controlling influence; the specific condition being—*complete ceremonial purification.* Patristic writers, while thoroughly accepting both Classic and Jewish usage, carry on the idea through ceremonial rites and types to the consummation of a complete spiritual purification, through agencies which they believed were fully competent to control the result without dipping or covering, any more than Classic usage, in parallel cases, required dipping or covering.

Let us now attend to the manner in which this axe-baptism, so separated from Judaism and so exclusively Classical in its character, is treated by the Theorists and the Patrists respectively; as, also, to its bearing on their principles.

Dr. Carson lays hands on this transaction with a smile of joy and claims it all his own. But why, Doctor? Is this baptism to be marshalled under—"Modal act, dip and nothing but dip, through all Greek literature?" Was the axe "dipped" into the Jordan? "Although there is no exemplification of the act of dipping in the axe *falling*, yet the word expresses the act, and was designed to express it, as much as in any case of dipping, as I have proved, (to my entire satisfaction,) in the sea-coast baptism, where 'overflow' is put, by catachresis, for dipping, just as 'fall' is here put for dipping. The axe, when it fell into the water, was covered, and when it was brought up by the prophet it was uncovered, just as the sea-coast is covered and bare at high and low tide. In both cases one form of act is, by figure, put for another form of act; and any one who has a soul for poetry can see the beauty of the figure." But your friends, Fuller, and Ripley, and Conant, having read your explanation of catachristic baptism, say, they cannot see the poetry, and that "overflow" must remain *overflow*, and "fall" must remain *fall*, just as in plain prose. "Then, what are they contending for; they give up the question; baptizing is dipping, and dipping is baptizing?" Well, I have been trying to find out where they are since they have slipped anchor from the dipping ground; but I cannot say. But, Doctor, it seems that the axe was a good while under water; and if it had been a son of the prophet who got this baptism in the Jordan instead of the axe, and he had lain on the bottom until they went after the prophet, and told the story, and brought him to the spot, and he had cut a stick, and thrown it in, it would not have done him much good to have brought him up again. Like Aristobulus he would have "remained under too long."

This axe-baptism, so thoroughly Classic, confronts the theory with two projecting and very sharp horns; on the one is written—"No *dipping* in me;" on the other—"No *taking out* of Jordan by me."

This axe of the sons of the prophets cuts up the theory even on the very banks of Jordan. Perhaps it could not be put to better service. Its trenchant blows are irresistible. "Modal act," "catachresis," "*temporary* covering," can no more resist its blows, than the turbaned head of the Saracen the blows of the battle-axe of Richard. The theory is brained, and dies (with poetical justice) by the loved banks of the river.

We will now look at the theory in the light of that "other kind of baptism" which the Patrists deduce from this literal and Classic baptism.

JUSTIN MARTYR.

Justin, originally a Greek philosopher, familiar with all its schools of learning, and then, a Christian, Patrist, and Martyr, says, "So, also, we are baptized by heaviest sins." This, certainly, is "another baptism" from enveloping water, and yet it is a true baptism if we may rely upon the testimony of one who was a Greek of the Greeks. What is the resemblance between the two baptisms, and what is the justification in carrying over the name from the one to the other?

1. The baptisms resemble each other in that neither requires a modal act for its accomplishment. As a matter of fact the axe was baptized by *falling*, and "falling" is a modal act; but I have never understood that the theory took the ground that "falling was baptizing and baptizing was falling." As a matter of fact our first parents were "baptized by heaviest sin" through the *eating* of the forbidden fruit. And "eating" is a modal act; yet, I presume we will not be required to identify the modal act of *eating* with the modal act of *falling*, or be shut up to the proof that "eating is baptizing and baptizing is eating."

I think we may safely assume that Justin's baptism does not forfeit its title, because the act, by which the soul is baptized through sin, is not of the same modal form as that by which the axe passes to its baptism on the bottom of the Jordan.

2. These baptisms resemble each other in that both are characterized by completeness of condition. The one of fact, a complete water envelopment; the other not of fact, nor of imagination, but of verbal suggestion. The theory does not require that physical envelopment should be shown in sin-baptism, as a fact, but demands the ineffable absurdity that the sinner should, by a lively imagination, be dipped into *water!* There is no such rhetorical bathos in Justin's "other baptism." Verbal suggestion of envelopment, more

or less according to circumstances, is all that belongs to the word at any time in this secondary use; and oftentimes, as to the design of the writer or the fitness of the case, this suggestion has no existence. And for this there is the most substantial reason. These secondary baptisms are not deduced from those primary baptisms in which there is mere envelopment; but from a very different class, namely, those in which the envelopment is overshadowed by its result, and is of no value except as causative of that result. To illustrate: Suppose one of the sons of the prophets had picked up a pebble and thrown it into the river; there would have been a baptism, a complete envelopment, and that would have been all. The baptism would not have been causative of injury to the pebble, or of loss and grief to the son of the prophet. Now if such baptism (of mere envelopment), had been exhaustive of literal baptisms, we would never have heard of grief baptisms, and debt baptisms, and sleep baptisms, and drunken baptisms, among the Classics; nor of purification baptisms, and sin baptisms, among Jews and Patrists.

A man who would make a pebble baptism the basis of a "baptism for the soul in sin" would be a laughing-stock for the common sense of the world. What would be the resemblance? "The envelopment." But there is no envelopment in sin. "True, but we imagine it." And why, for its own sake? "No, not for the mere envelopment, but for——" Well, for what? "Why, I suppose to show how fully at every point, the soul is subject to the influence of sin." Very well; will you now be so kind as to point out the fulness of influence exerted at every point, by water, over a flint pebble? "If not made soaking wet, *it is damp outside.*"

It is unnecessary to say, that there is no more basis in baptisms of naked envelopment on which to ground secondary baptisms of influence, than there was to be found a ποῦ στῶ for Archimedes to lift the world. I repeat, therefore, that the baptism of Justin is founded on another class of baptisms, namely, the baptism of a world, of a ship, of a human being, issuing in *loss*, *ruin*, and *death*. In such baptisms envelopment is subsidiary to influence; and, therefore, in secondary baptisms based upon them, the formal cause may disappear, while correspondent influence appears in boldest relief. This truth Dr. Carson is compelled to admit. In answer to the objection, that there is no resemblance of envelopment between these secondary and primary baptisms, he replies (p. 493): "Is not the resemblance in the effects?" How this consists with the theory it is no business of ours to show; but it relieves us, by the confession of an opponent, of the necessity for showing any resemblance, or any existence of envelopment in the case of secondary baptisms, if we can show existence and resemblance of "effects."

3. I proceed, then, to show: That these baptisms resemble each other in their resultant "effects." The baptism of the axe brought it into a lost condition. There was nothing in baptism to change that condition; the son of the prophet could not recover it, and he was affected with grief, exclaiming, "Alas! master it was borrowed." The borrower cared nothing for the covering water save as it brought his axe into a lost condition. It was not the envelopment that he cared for, but the *effect* of that envelopment. Had the axe fallen into shallow water where he could see it and pick it up, effect, lost condition, would not have existed; and Justin would have lost the opportunity to ground his sin baptism upon it. It is the *lost condition* of an object lying at the bottom of a river, which suggests to this Greek, (who still wears the mantle of a philosopher,) the *lost condition* baptism of the souls of men, through sin. Now, what need, or fitness, or practicability is there of introducing envelopment in this baptism? The axe was lost, completely lost; the soul is lost, completely lost; the axe is baptized, completely under the influence of the waters as separating it from the loser; the soul is baptized, completely under the influence of sin, which separates it from God. Herein is Justin's justification in deducing sin baptism from this axe baptism.

4. There is another point of resemblance in these baptisms, which is essential. They are both without limitation in their continuance. The axe would have continued at the

bottom of Jordan, until this hour, had it been left to its baptism. The Greek word never takes its object out of that condition into which it has once placed it. Souls have continued baptized by sin through thousands of years, and, alas! some will continue "baptized by heaviest sins" through all eternity.

5. These baptisms resemble each other, in that both may be changed by *ab extra* influence. The axe may be brought out of its baptism by the prophet; the soul may be brought out of its baptism by the cross of Christ. But without foreign influence baptisms are fixed.

None can doubt but that Justin's baptism is fitly termed a baptism, not because of any form of act done, nor because of an envelopment the result of some act of any kind; but because of a condition without any self-changing element, and characterized by controlling influence.

Compare, now, with this Jordan baptism, the baptism of the theory.

1. The theory calls for a definite act. "The word, without one exception, signifies simply to dip." (Carson, p. 103.) Well, was "the axe" dipped? "In any particular instance, where this word is applied to an object lying under water, but not actually dipped, the mode essentially denoted by it, is as truly expressed as in any other instance of its occurrence. Indeed, the whole beauty of such expressions consists in the expression of a mode not really belonging to the thing expressed. The imagination," &c., (p. 21.) We will not follow Dr. Carson's "imagination." Can demonstration be more absolute in proof that Dr. C. had no just conception of the meaning of βαπτίζω? Was the axe, baptized in the Jordan, "dipped?" Will any sane "imagination" undertake the task of converting the fall of a piece of iron to the bottom of a river, into a *dipping?* Yet the theory imposes this hard task upon its disciples.

2. The theory makes no provision for *state* or *condition* of the baptized object. If the son of the prophet had "dipped" his axe into the Jordan, would he have changed its *state* or *condition?* The dipping of no object can, by any possibility,

give it a *status* within the element into which it is dipped; because it cannot be dipped without being brought out, without tarrying, from the element into which it has been introduced. But the very essence of a baptism is the bringing of an object into a new state or condition; and, without this, there can be no baptism. The *dipping* of an axe, therefore, is no baptism.

3. The theory makes no provision for complete influence. The act of dipping is, proverbially, a trivial act. The dipping of an object can produce but a trivial impression upon it. So thoroughly ingrained is this characteristic in all that pertains to the physical sphere of this word, that it forms the basis for its secondary use, to express trivial operations and influences of the mind. No word is more thoroughly removed from the sphere of βαπτίζω, whether in primary or secondary baptisms, than this dapper word "dip." And yet Dr. Carson makes this word his battle-flag, while strangely shouting, amid the din of arms, "complete subjection to influence." Hear him: "Is not the likeness between complete subjection to the influence of sleep, and the complete subjection of an object to the influence of a liquid when immersed (?) in it?" (p. 80.) One knows not whether to laugh or frown at the lawless introduction here of "immerse," heaven-wide different in meaning from *dip*, for which he avowedly contends. Its substitution, however, proves our position, that "dip" can never bring an object in "complete subjection to the influence of a liquid." It is therefore utterly incapacitated to expound secondary baptisms, which all exhibit some powerful controlling influence, or to be the basis of primary baptisms, on which secondary are grounded.

Justin would have talked more like a *scholastikos* than like a philosopher, had he deduced a sin-*dipping* from the axe lost in the river depths.

Brought face to face with this Classic-Patristic Baptism, "the theory" breaks down at all points.

Justin and Carson are at opposites in their notions of baptisms. But, alas! so much the worse for Justin. I suppose he will have to become a fellow-pupil with the Angel Gabriel.

TRANSLATION.

"Heaviest Sins."

Justin Martyr, in speaking of men as baptized by a baptism analogous to that of the lost axe, uses this language—ὡς καὶ ἡμᾶς βεβαπτισμένους ταῖς βαρυτάταις ἁμαρτίαις. This phraseology is not only of great value, as showing the true nature of baptism, by placing primary baptism and secondary baptism (the secondary being the direct offspring of the primary) side by side, but the phraseology itself has special claim to our attention. In the person of this writer, the heathen Classic and the christian Patrist meet together. The forms of expression which he employs, must therefore be of truly Grecian parentage, and any new mental conception, derived from the Christian atmosphere, into which he has been introduced, must have its fittest Grecian dress in the words with which he invests it.

In comparing the language of Justin, on this occasion, with that of other Classic Greek writers, we notice, 1. That both employ the nude dative with βαπτίζω. 2. That both employ this nude form to express the agency by which the baptism is effected, and not the element into which the object is introduced. 3. That neither, in these secondary baptisms, made any verbal statement of an enveloping element. 4. That neither, certainly, felt the need of any such suggestion, and probably, never formed any such mental conception. How, now, is this language of Justin treated by the theory? It is translated by Carson, "immersed *in* the greatest sins;" "baptized *in* the most grievous sins." The Greek word neither means "greatest" nor "most grievous," but *heaviest.* Justin employs this term because it is adapted to express, clearly and forcibly, what he wished to express, namely, an agency of baptism; and, also, because his cultivated mind enabled him to see the fitness of taking this term from the heaviness of the iron, which was causative of the baptism of the axe. Carson rejects this term because it was not adapted to express an element for a *dipping*, for which his erring theory evermore cries out.

The heavy waters of the Dead Sea are not well suited for dipping. The heaviness of the iron, certainly, was not the element into which the axe was dipped.

What must be thought of the theory of a word whose inexorable demands require the sacrifice of grammatical forms, the disregard of the evident design of a writer, and the metamorphosis of heavy iron into an element for dipping?

I bring no charge of designed wrong against Dr. Carson. His theory, conscientiously and tenaciously held, demands a dipping, and he will "make it find him one in the sands of the desert." No wonder, then, when this Classic Patristic writer gives him none, he "makes" his theory find one. It is as easy to turn heavy iron, or heavy sins, into a pool of water, as desert-sands. But Hercules may perish through exhaustion. And the theory, which amuses itself with such freaks of power, will hardly live forever.

TERTULLIAN.

"*Mersed in the Depth of Error.*"

Tertullian here introduces us to the element in which, by verbal suggestion, the baptism takes place. It is important that it should receive attention. It is as obvious that Tertullian speaks of the element, as that Justin speaks of the agency. The latter takes *weight* out of the iron agency, in the first baptism, and attributes it to "sin," the agency in the second baptism; the former takes "depth" out of the river-element, and attributes it to "error," the element, by verbal suggestion, in which the "hardness" (taken out of the axe) "of the age is mersed."

How is this language to be treated? We start out with the admission, by all, that there is no mersion in fact, and, on my own responsibility, I add, that there is no mersion in *error* possible in imagination. What process of interpretation shall be used?

The theory says: Convert "error" into a pool of water, and all runs smoothly. Let us see. If we are to have a water-pool, then all its accessories must come along with it.

We must have something to be dipped. What is it? Is it replied, "the hardness of the age?" Very well. And now that this "object" is deposited by the pool, pray tell us, as a help to our imagination, what it is like; what is its shape, color, weight, and size? "Error" having been transformed into *water*, there is now embarrassment in getting "hardness of the age" dipped into it. Into what shall this be transformed to meet the exigency? Into a stone? into a stick of wood? into a lump of iron? That would meet the "hardness" of the age; but it should not be too large, for then it would be too heavy to be dipped. Shall it be a human being? Not an infant; that could be dipped, but the theory don't like the baptism of little children. Then let it be a full-grown adult, and he can help dip himself by that peculiar mode, known to the theory, of *walking* into the water. But this Mr. "Hardness of the Age" must not walk too far into the water, for while walking will answer for dipping the feet, it will not answer for dipping the head—at least so we are told. Then we must have a dipper. Who shall it be? Will some friend of the theory answer? If not, we must apply to old Justin. He says, "sin" is the dipper. But "sin" can no more put "hardness of the age" (metamorphosed into a "*Mister*") into the water, than "hardness of the age" could get into the water without such metamorphosis. If "Sin" is to officiate as a dipper into *water* of Mr. "Hardness of the Age," then "Sin" must also take shape. What shall it be?

> "Before the gates there sat
> On either side a formidable shape:
> The one seemed woman to the waist and fair,
> But ended foul in many a scaly fold
> Voluminous and vast, a serpent arm'd
> With mortal sting: about her middle round
> A cry of Hell hounds, never ceasing, bark'd
> With wide Cerberean mouths full loud, and rung
> A hideous peal: yet when they list, would creep,
> If aught disturbed their noise, into her womb,
> And kennel there, yet there still bark'd and howl'd,
> Within unseen. . . . *and me they call'd* SIN!"

Fearful administratrix this! But, alas! none other can

officiate at the baptism of the "hardness of the age." We have now got the element, and the object, and the administratrix. What next? The baptism. What is a baptism? "The complete subjection of an object to the influence of a liquid." (Carson, p. 80.) By what act is this to be secured? Letting pass, now, the impracticable and piebald character of a union of baptism and dipping, I would inquire what is the final result of dipping Mr. Hardness of the Age, by Mistress Sin, into a pool of water? "He is completely subjected to the influence of water." In what respect? Is he drowned? "No." Is he washed? "No." Is he made very wet? "That depends upon what suit he wore." Well, I do not know what other complete influence of water there is; but make it what you will it is the full influence of *water*. Then, pray tell us what bearing the full influence of *water*, brought to bear by "sin," on a "hard age" has to do with the baptism in "*error*" spoken of by Tertullian?

Was there ever a greater rhetorical and logical blunder than the conversion of "error" into a pool of water? This "error" of Tertullian is as unalterable as the poles; around it every attendant conception must revolve. It is placed there by the writer as a despot on his throne, and every word must bow down in reverence to his sovereign power. "Sin" and "age" are, also, unalterable words. "Hardness," "heaviest," "depth," "mersion," "in," may all receive modification; but "error," "sin," and "age" must abide. When these words are used with words directly expressive of manifestly impracticable forms, it is equivalent to saying, "Be on your guard; take out from these words the thought adapted to the case."

In the phrase—"the age, by sin, is mersed in error"—we see, at a glance, that in its literality there is an impracticable statement. But it comes from an intelligent source, and we know that there is a rational thought in it. We examine the wording and perceive that "age," "sin," and "error" must be fixed quantities. This conclusion compels us to seek a solution of the thought in "mersed in." We glance over its usage in relations where its literal demand is met, and mersion, envelopment, intusposition takes place, and *nothing more.* We take our discovery and apply a mersion-envelopment to solve the difficulty. But we find that it will not answer. The nature of "error" is not such as to allow an object to get within it, so as to be enveloped by it. We try again; and find objects "mersed in" a great variety of elements in which, beside the envelopment, there is the additional feature of controlling influence proceeding from the enveloping element over its object, and, farther, that in such cases the envelopment is simply *a means to an end.* We return with our spoils and try again. Having already found that envelopment is, *ex necessitate rei*, out of the case, we apply that which is the invariable attendant upon certain mersions, and is the sole end for which certain other mersions are sought, namely, controlling influence. The phrase then reads—"the age, by sin, mersed in=*subject to the controlling influence of* error." "Mersed in" is suggestive of envelopment as the source of the influence; but envelopment is not, itself, usable, and we throw it aside for that which is demanded, namely, influence.

Is not this process simple, intelligible, satisfactory in its results, and harmonious with the laws of language development?

"*Mersos in caligine*"—"*in peccato*"—"*in blasphemia*"—"*in dementia.*" Souls mersed in *darkness*—in *sin*—in *blasphemy*—in *dementia*—are other cases of baptism spoken of by Tertullian, which demonstrate the ineptness of a water-pool for such baptism. Here are specific influences, most marked in character and most diverse from each other. Mersion in *water* is not calculated to show forth any one of them; for there is nothing in water influence which resembles *spiritual darkness*, or *sin*, or *blasphemy*, or *dementia.* If it is said that it is not because of resemblance between the influence of water and these influences that the pool is introduced, but for the sake of the mersion, then the case is, if possible, made worse; for no resemblance can be here, for no intusposition in spiritual darkness, or sin, or blasphemy, or dementia, exists in fact, or can exist in conception. There is no mersion in any one element which can shadow forth these varied baptisms. It is impracticable to get a varied element appropriate to each. We repudiate, therefore, the whole thing as a search after truth where it is not to be found; and take the grand feature of controlling influence, uncolored by any specific quality, and submit it for the stamp of character to any and every particular case, whether it be "soul darkness," "sin," in general, "blasphemy" in particular, mental "imbecility," or what not.

If in the development of language any word ever lost an element which was originally characteristic of it, such a word is βαπτίζω. And if ever βάπτω lost in the course of usage *the act of dipping*, (originally its grand and sole characteristic,) then, βαπτίζω has, as certainly, lost in the course of usage *the condition of envelopment*, which was, originally, its grand and sole characteristic. If the one word came by varied steps of progression to express, directly, *dyeing;* the other came, by a similar process, to express, directly, *controlling influence.*

"*Aliud genus Baptismatis.*"

When Ambrose speaks of "another kind of baptism," he is not speaking, like Justin, of a baptism which, while differing in nature and in all other attendant features from the mersed axe, still, resembles it in its most essential feature, namely, that of *lost* condition; but he speaks of a wholly different kind of baptism from both of these; a baptism which is grounded on the passing of the axe out of a *lost* condition into a *saved* condition. If a seal were needed to be affixed to the tomb of this thrice slain theory of "dipping and nothing but dipping through all Greek literature," we have it here furnished to our hand. The image stamped upon this seal is that of "Ambrose;" the superscription is—"Aliud genus baptismatis." Was anything ever more utterly removed from a dipping than the ascent of an axe from the bottom of a river to its surface?

But, still more, we have here the most absolute proof that

it is not act of any kind which characterizes a baptism, but condition marked by completeness and indefinite continuance. The axe by *falling* passes into a lost condition caused by enveloping waters. The axe by *rising up* passes into a saved condition not caused by any enveloping medium. Thus we see that a complete change of condition, without envelopment, is, and is well termed a baptism. Similar baptisms with this latter one may be found in Classic Baptism (pp. 325, 329). The first is like this, a baptism of iron; but of *red hot* iron, brought into a condition of *coldness* by the application of water, without envelopment. The second is a baptism of wine by pouring water into it; by which it passes out of an intoxicating into an unintoxicating condition. It is not true, then, that, even in physical things, an envelopment is essential to a baptism. Completeness of condition, with indefiniteness of continuance, is essential, in all baptisms, whether physical or unphysical. The axe is brought into a thoroughly saved condition without limitation of time, through the influence of the wood; the hot iron is brought into a thoroughly cold condition through the heat-quenching influence of water, without limitation of time; and the wine is brought into a thoroughly unintoxicant condition, without limitation of time, through the attempering influence of water.

The soul is brought out of one baptism, indefinitely long and ruinous in its nature, into another baptism, indefinitely long and saving in its nature; both of them without envelopment. Ambrose is sustained in his views by the extracts from Irenæus and Chrysostom.

BAPTISM OF POLLUTION.

Job 9: 30, 31.

"If I wash myself with snow-water, and make my hands never so clean,

"Yet shalt thou plunge me in the ditch, and mine own clothes shall abhor me."

Translation.

Καὶ τότε ἐν διαφθορᾷ βαπτίσεις με.

"Even then thou wilt baptize me with pollution."—*Aquila.*

Interpretation.

There is no Patristic interpretation of this passage, as a baptism, so far as I know. The usage, here, shows that while the Greek appropriates the word to drunkenness and the Jew to purification, its sphere embraces, no less, sobriety and pollution. Adjuncts qualify. I have given the translation of the passage, as it appears in the Greek version of the Hebrew Scriptures, by Aquila. His translation seems to have been governed more by the moral intent of the passage, than by its wording. Neither βαπτίζω nor διαφθορά is a verbal translation of the Hebrew. Yet the spirit of the passage is well represented. Rosenmüller states it thus: "Quantumvis me purum esse et innocentem ostendere voluero, Deus tamen me impurissimum et injustissimum ostendet (in loc.)." A condition "most impure and most unrighteous," is truly and forcibly represented by—"thou wilt baptize me with pollution"—make me thoroughly polluted.

It is unusual for the Classics to associate ἐν with the element within which a mersion takes place. And as it is quite common for Jewish writers to employ this preposition with a dative agency, I have regarded it as so used here.

The Hebrew verb is used both for dipping and dyeing, or smearing. It is the same as employed in expressing the staining or smearing of Joseph's coat with blood, and is there translated, in the Septuagint, by a word expressive of this latter sense, and not of a dipping. Introduction into a ditch or pit, containing mud and water, would very thoroughly "smear with filth."

The translation by the Septuagint is: Ἱκανως ἐν ῥύπῳ με ἔβαψας. Here ἱκανως seems to qualify rather an effect—that of smearing, than an act—that of dipping. The use of ἐν instead of εἰς strengthens the conclusion, that the object was not to be dipped *into* filth, but to be polluted *by* it.

BAPTISM OF DESTRUCTION.

PSALM 9:15.

"The heathen are sunk down in the pit that they made."

Translation.

. . . . ἐβαπτισθησαν.

"Demersæ sunt gentes in interitu quem fecerunt."—*Jerome*, ix, 1133.

Interpretation.

The Greek translator who here employs βαπτίζω to represent the Hebrew word, is unknown, but his translation is discriminatingly made. The Hebrew word is not the same with that which is, almost without exception, translated in the Septuagint by βάπτω.

The Hebrew has two words, טָבַל and טָבַע, more nearly resembling each other, both in form and in sound, than do βάπτω and βαπτίζω. These Hebrew words present the same parallelism of differences, in their usage, with that exhibited by the Greek words, as also with that of the Latin words *tingo* and *mergo*, and the English words *dip* and *immerse.*

It is obvious that the word in this passage could not possibly be represented by βάπτω, or *tingo*, or dip. Such words not merely fail to represent the sentiment, but they misrepresent it. They give a contradictory sentiment. What is intended to be profound, they make superficial; what is intended to be thorough, they make trivial; what is intended to issue in a condition unlimited in time of continuance, they make evanescent as the execution of the form of an act. Jerome recognizes all this when he translates—"demersæ sunt in interitu—*they were demersed in destruction.*"

Gesenius, in speaking of the relation of this word to words in other languages, says: "The primary syllable is here טָב, which, in the occidental languages, also has the signification of *depth* and of *immersing.* Compare the Gothic *diup*, the German *tief*, and the English *deep.*"

While the Hebrew, and the Greek, and the Latin, has

each two native words to express the two diverse ranges of thought, unhappily the English has not. The former Hebrew word, and the Greek βάπτω, the Latin *tingo*, and the English *dip*, are as like to each other as though they were all Shaksperian *Dromios*.

But when the latter Hebrew word is mated with βαπτίζω and *mergo*, the English language cannot offer any like-featured, native-born Antilochus, as their counterpart. Hence the embarrassment of translating βαπτίζω, especially in some aspects of its usage. To remedy this language-deficiency, we have borrowed a word from the Latin, and that, unfortunately, in a compound instead of a simple form. But, in borrowing a word, we cannot borrow its varied usage. That is made by the exigencies of a people. And it originates peculiarities of meaning among different nations, and among the same people in different ages, in the use of words having the same thought in their first use. Of all influences modifying the usage of words, none is more powerful than the religious conceptions of a people. And, of all religions, none can parallel the demand which must be made by a revealed religion introducing conceptions to which the minds of men, before, were strangers. Is it surprising, under these circumstances, that there should be some embarrassment in finding a perfect representation, in English, of a Greek word, borrowed out of heathenism, to denote Jewish religious conceptions, and then used to convey Christian religious thought, which in some respects was essentially diverse from the Jewish? If we have found it necessary to enlarge the language of common life, by borrowing *immerse* from the Latin, is it strange that we should find no usage among us of this foreign word which meets the religious application of the Greek word? And who should complain if, instead of forcing a new rôle of duty upon this Latin stranger, we should borrow, again, for religious usage, *baptize* from the Greek?

If, however, the theorists should persist in affirming, that "the suggestion of difficulty in the translation is all a pretence," we will maintain our equanimity by gazing on their desperate floundering amid dip, and plunge, and sink, and flow, and bathe, and whelm, immerse and immerge, demerge and submerge, and compassionately saying (*sotto voce*), "Poor sufferers, they are baptized in this dark abyss of words, finding no standing-place, because their mother tongue gave them no word to rest their foot upon!"

BAPTISM OF SUFFERING

PSALM 69 : 1, 2.

"Save me, O God! for the waters have come in unto my soul.

"I sink in deep mire, where there is no standing: I am come into deep waters, where the floods overflow me."

Translation.

Ἐβαπτίσθην εἰς ἀπεράντους καταδύσεις, καὶ οὐκ ἔστι στάσις.

"I am baptized into boundless depths, and there is no standing.

"I have come into the depths of the waters, and the flood has overflowed me."—*Symmachus.*

Ἐνεπάγην εἰς ἰλὺν βυθοῦ . . . καὶ καταιγὶς κατεπόντισέ με.

"I am brought into the mud of the abyss, and there is no standing-place under me.

"I have come into the depths of the sea, and a tempest has engulfed me."—*Septuagint.*

"Infixus sum in limo profundi . . . et tempestas demersit me."

"I am infixed in the mud of the deep, and there is no solid ground. I have come into the depth of the sea, and the tempest has demersed me."—*Jerome*, v, 468.

Interpretation.

The Hebrew word, with which we have to do in this passage, is the same as in the passage just considered. It is, therefore, well represented by βαπτίζω. It could, by no possibility, be represented by βαπτω.

The Septuagint does not use βαπτίζω in translating, but it repudiates βάπτω by employing a word which brings its object into a changed condition, where there is certainly every opportunity for a complete influence to be exerted over it, *and leaves it there.* In other words, the substitute does everything which the principal would have done. It performs a baptism just as well as βαπτίζω could have done, and, in addition, is so complaisant as to tell us *how* it was done, on which point βαπτίζω is ever dumb with silence. The mode used in this case is the same as that used by the theorists, who bring into the water their disciples, but who strangely say, that "this is not baptism, it is only *immersion.*" And what is baptism? "Baptism is the dipping of the nobler part (head and shoulders), with invocation of the Trinity." Indeed! I thought that the new version of the theory was, that "baptism was immersion, and that immersion was baptism;" but it seems that "immersion" has a non-religious meaning, "bringing" the more ignoble part of the body "into the water;" while "baptism" has a religious meaning, bringing the more noble part of the human form into the water, by dipping and invocation. It seems then, after all, that the Latin-English word has a vulgar meaning, and that the Greek will find his way into the religious vocabulary.

The translation by Jerome says nothing about the mode in which the baptism was accomplished; neither does he translate by *mergo* expressing condition; but he employs a word which gives *position* to the baptized object. This position βάπτω could never give, (for it can give "position" to nothing, as dipping is an unresting movement,) but βαπτίζω (primary,) always gives position to its object together with condition, which position and condition are "fixed," as Jerome says, until some foreign influence shall disturb them.

Figure.

Those friends of ours who have been so often chidden for stretching out their dipping-wand toward every object in air, and earth, and sea, and under the sea, to transmute it into *figure*, may here feast on figure, unforbidden—should it prove to their liking.

Dr. Carson, after waiting by the sea-coast twelve hours, watching the flow and reflow of its tidal waves, exclaims,

"Figure! covered and bare, a dipping." David is now in a "covered" condition of baptism; he wishes to be made "bare." What help can the theory bring him? If he is undergoing a dipping merely, his "covering" will last but a moment. If he is dipped catachrestically by the ocean tide, he will be made "bare," certainly, in twelve hours. But David has gone down to the bottom of the sea, and he is there "infixed in its mud." Will it be of much comfort to say to such a one—"You are only baptized, and to baptize is to dip and nothing but dip through all Greek literature; and to dip is to cover and make bare; therefore, don't be discouraged, you will soon be un-dipped." Whether these comforting words were drowned in the roaring of the stormy billows, or not, I cannot undertake to say; but they do not seem to have given David much comfort. In the anguish of his imperilled and helpless condition he cries, "Save me, O God, for the waters have come in unto my soul!" Because baptism in water is, of its own proper force, deadly, David employs it in figure to express his condition, by reason of troubles, as one that must speedily issue in his destruction, without Divine intervention.

The theorist who would convert this baptism into a dipping must either transcend, beyond all measuring-lines, the wisdom of the Son of David, or fall so far below, that,—well, he should not use too hot words in "sending Gabriel to school," if that angel should modestly enter a *caveat* against a too dogmatic enunciation of "the theory."

BAPTISM OF SINCERITY.

Canticles 5:12.

"His eyes are as the eyes of doves, by the rivers of waters, washed with milk and fitly set."

Interpretation.

"Baptizat in lacte Dominus, id est, in Sinceritate. Et isti sunt qui vere baptizantur in lacte, qui sine dolo credunt, et puram fidem deferunt, ut immaculatam induant gratiam. Ideo candida Sponsa ascendit ad Christum; quia in lacte baptizata est."

"The Lord baptizes with milk, that is, with Sincerity. And they are those who are truly baptized with milk, who believe without hypocrisy, and offer a pure faith, that they may put on unspotted grace. Therefore the Spouse ascends to Christ clothed in white, because she was baptized with milk."—*Ambrose*, ii, 1431.

"Denique de ipsa anima dicitur: *Quæ est hæc, quæ ascendit dealbata* (Cant. 8:5)? Antequam baptizaretur, ipsa est quæ dicebat: *Nigra sum*—Erat enim nigra, tenebrosa, peccatorum horrore deformis: sed postea . . . dealbata." . . .

"Finally, it is said of the soul, itself: 'Who is this, that ascends made white?' It is the same that said, before baptism, 'I am black.' . . . For it was black, gloomy, and deformed by the dreadfulness of sin; but after that, having been cleansed by baptism, it merited the remission of sins; made white it ascends to Christ."—*Ambrose*, i, 875.

Translation.

I have translated "in lacte," *with* milk, 1. Because the Patrists use the preposition in this sense, times without number. 2. Because it is a baptism of the soul, and therefore could not be "*in* milk." 3. Because the baptizer is the Lord, who never baptizes *in* milk, or *in* water, or *in* any other physical substance.

The use of the term "milk" is purely formal, suggested by the use in the text, and is not designed to carry the thought over to a physical fluid, but to the "*sincere milk* of the word." Irenæus (931), speaking of the corrupters of divine truth, likens them to those who mix gypsum with water and offer it for milk, deceiving through the similarity of color, and adds: "In Dei lacte gypsum male miscetur. It is a bad thing to mix gypsum (error) with God's milk (truth)." On the next page, Irenæus shows, most unmistakably, the use of the preposition "in," as here translated.

"In Christi, enim, nomine subauditur qui unxit, et ipse qui unctus est, et ipsa unctio *in* qua unctus est. Et unxit quidem

Pater, unctus est vero Filius, *in* Spiritu, qui est unctio . . . significans et unguentem Patrem, et unctum Filium, et unctionem, qui est Spiritus." If it is contrary to all reason to say, that the Messiah was inducted into his Kingly, Priestly, and Prophetical offices, by being anointed *in*, and not *with*, the anointing oil—that the Father anointed the Son *in*, not *with* the Spirit—then it is "contrary to all reason" to deny that the usage claimed does truly exist. And here, as suggested by this anointing, I may quote a passage from a more modern writer, contained in a note in Cyril of Jerusalem (597)—"refert eos non *in* aqua, sed *in* oleo baptizasse. Id Priscillianistis in Hispania forsan peculiare—he relates that they baptized, not *with* water, but *with* oil. This, perhaps, was peculiar to the Priscillianists in Spain." If it is not likely that any persons dipped, or immersed, men and women *in* oil (!), then it is likely that "in" means "with," and, rejecting water, these heretics were "baptized *with* oil." Besides, we are told (1075), that the Greek churches anointed the whole body with oil (ex oleo), while the Latin churches anointed only parts of the body, and, especially, "in Spain only the ears and the mouth—in Hispania aures et os." Now, I cannot say whether these "Spanish" heretics followed the practice of the Greek church, or of the Latin, in their use of oil in baptism, but in neither case would they find a dipping *into* oil.

Interpretation.

Milk is used (verbally) in this baptism as the fit symbol of sincerity. It is not employed because it was adapted for dipping, but because of its *color;* just as snow is referred to in Scripture because of its whiteness. Milk could not be used because of its *cleansing* qualities; for it is not so used in fact, nor is it, by its nature, adapted to such use. It is perfectly adapted by its uncolored color to represent unadulterated sincerity. "The Lord baptizes with milk, that is with sincerity, into unspotted grace." In any case it will be observed, that this baptism is intended to set forth simply and solely a complete change of condition. This is strikingly set forth by Ambrose in the second quotation. Before this baptism the soul is "black," afterwards it is "made white." The Lord is the baptizer; the absence of hypocrisy and the presence of a pure faith is the means, and the putting on of unspotted grace is the new, changed, baptized condition.

This condition is not capable of being represented by an evanescent dipping, nor a momentary covering; but is of unlimited continuance.

Whether "the Great Baptizer" employs "milk," or "the flaming sword," to effect his baptism, he brings all who are the subjects of it into a thoroughly changed condition, which, in its nature, has no limitation of time for its continuance, and which no foreign influence can change. Until some one can be found, mightier than he, to undo what he has done—able "to pluck those whom the Father has given him out of his hand"—the baptism of the Lord will bring his people into a condition of holy purity which shall never, no never, have an end.

BAPTISM OF REPENTANCE.

Isaiah 1:16, 17.

"Wash ye, make you clean; put away the evil of your doings from before mine eyes; cease to do evil;

"Learn to do well; seek judgment; relieve the oppressed; judge the fatherless; plead for the widow."

Interpretation.

Διὰ τοῦ λουτροῦ, οὖν τῆς μετανοὶας καὶ τῆς γνώσεως τοῦ θεοῦ, ὃ . . . . ὃ προηγόρευε τὸ βάπτισμα. . . . . Τί γὰρ ὄφελος ἐκείνου βαπτίσματος, ὃ . . . . Βαπτίσθητε τὴν ψυχὴν ἀπὸ ὀργῆς, καὶ ἀπὸ. . . . .

"Through the washing of repentance and of the knowledge of God, which was established on account of the transgression of the people of God, as Isaiah declares, we have believed and make known that this very baptism which he foreannounced is the only one able to cleanse the repenting; this is the water of life.

"But the cisterns which you have dug out for yourselves are

broken and are useless to you. For of what use is that baptism which cleanses the flesh and the body only? Baptize the soul from anger, and from covetousness, and from envy, and from hate, and behold the body is pure."—*Justin Martyr*, 504.

Καθὼς φησὶν Ἡσαΐας, Λούσασθε—Ἴδες, ἀγαπητὲ, πῶς προεῖπεν ὁ προφήτης τὸ τοῦ βαπτίσματος καθάρσιον;

"As Isaiah says, 'Wash ye'——. Dost thou see, beloved, how the prophet declared beforehand the purifying character of this baptism?"—*Hippolytus*, 860.

"*Lavamini, mundi estote.* Pro superioribus victimis, et . . . . Evangelii mihi placet religio: ut baptizimini in sanguine meo per lavacrum regenerationis, quod solum potest peccata dimittere."

"*Wash ye, be clean.* Instead of former victims, and burnt-offerings, and the fat of fed beasts, and the blood of bulls and of goats: and instead of incense, and new moons, the Sabbath, feast and fast days, Kalends and other solemnities, the religion of the Gospel pleases me; that ye may be baptized by my blood through the washing of regeneration, which alone can take away sins."—*Jerome*, iv, 35.

BAPTISM OF THE BODY AND OF THE SOUL.

Two baptisms are here expressly mentioned by Justin: 1. Baptism of the body. 2. Baptism of the soul. The theory remorselessly insists that the body must be dipped in fact, and that the soul must be dipped in imagination. For the word means nothing but dip and undergoes no change when used in figure.

Carson says, (in capitals,) "My position is, THAT IT ALWAYS SIGNIFIES TO DIP; NEVER EXPRESSING ANYTHING BUT MODE" (p. 55). He also says (p. 57), "I undertake to prove it has but one meaning. I blame him for giving different meanings when there is no real difference in the meaning of this word. He assigns to it figurative meanings. I maintain that in figures there is no different meaning of the word. It is only a figurative application. The meaning of the word is always the same." Dr. Carson has got into such an inveterate habit of boxing everybody's ears, that it is not at all strange that occasionally, his hand should be brought down somewhat heavily upon his own. Read alongside of the preceding, this, "Aristophanes says: '*Lest I dip you into a Sardian dye.*' The figure is but low, and is just the same as if a pugilist with us should say, *I will dip you in vermilion.* It is an allusion to the dyer's art, and means *I will beat you, till you shall be covered all over with your own blood.* It would be to no purpose to allege that when a man is beaten, he is not literally *dipped* in his blood, but the blood runs over him. This would indicate a total misconception of the figure. The likeness does not consist in the *manner* but in the *effects. I will dip you in vermilion*, is exactly the expression of the poet in English. He would be a sorry critic, who, from this, should allege that the English word dip signifies to *run over*, as blood from the wounded body."

We had just been told that βαπτίζω means to dip, and that it and every other word in figure undergoes no change of meaning, but "the meaning is always the same." And now, in a case of declared figure, we have *written down* in obedience to the law, "dip," but only to have it scratched out by being told, that it is neither in the figure of fact or of imagination; that in fact the action is "run over," and that "the meaning is *I will beat you;*" and that while there is "allusion to the dyer's art," the dyer's act of dipping has nothing whatever to do with the interpretation. To introduce it would be "a total misconception of the figure." Now, if under this manipulation both of Dr. Carson's ears do not tingle, it must be because those side appendages are in his case missing.

Self-contradiction as to theory and practice, could not be more gross.

The passage exhibits the same gross errors of translation and of interpretation, (with the addition of self-contradiction,) with those of which he convicted Dr. Gale, and for which he pulled his ears so lustily. Gale says, the lake must be dipped in the blood of a frog, because my theory says, the word has but one meaning, and is the same literal or figurative. Carson flouts at the statement as an unheard of paradox based on a misunderstanding of the word and the syntax. And yet, he falls into the same identical errors in misunderstanding the word and the syntax; and thus, is led by theory to introduce a dipping, while, with unparental hardness, he rejects his offspring as having no claim, even under the wildest imagination, to his sympathies. Under the influence of an impracticable case, the omnipresent dipping has disappeared, and in figure an act ceases to exist, and "the likeness does not consist in the *manner* but in the *effects*."

Dr. C.'s πρῶτον ψεῦδος does not consist in the position, that words in true and pure figure have the same meaning as in literal use, but in overlooking what he had pointed out to Gale, the secondary meaning of βάπτω. The remembrance of this would have saved him from the error of supposing that there was any figure in the passage. It would, also, have saved him from the necessity of violating syntactical law (Kühner, p. 403) respecting a double accusative. And this would have saved him from misleading the confiding English reader by the statement, "*I will dip you in vermilion*, is exactly the expression in English." The English counterpart of the Greek has in it neither a "dip" nor an "in," but is simply literal, "I will *dye* you a Sardian *dye*," or "I will *color* you a Sardian *color*."

It is, precisely, these same errors which vitiate, from first to last, the writings of the theorists on the subject of baptism. They insist that βαπτίζω has but one meaning, that it has the same meaning in figurative as in literal use, and that all cases where there is no dipping in fact, must be cases of figure. But when they are pointed to cases where no dipping is conceivable by imagination, or the attempt introduces a picture so grotesque, that even their rhetorical sense is shocked, why then we are told (to the baldest stultification of their theory) "the likeness does not consist in the *manner*, but in the *effects*." What has a theory to do with "effects," whose alpha and omega is the performance of a naked act? Is not the use of a word (expressive originally of an act) which is based on *effects*, a secondary and not a figurative use of such word? Is not βάπτω, *to dye*, based on the *effects* of βάπτω, *to dip*, and is not such use secondary and diverse from the former? And, yet, we are told that while βαπτίζω means "to dip, and nothing but dip," and has a usage based on, not the act, but the *effects* of the act, still it has no secondary use, and "means nothing else, through all Greek literature, but dip, and nothing but dip."

When Dr. Cox sought relief from the *manner* of Nebuchadnezzar's *dipping* in the dew, he says: "It does not imply the *manner* in which the effect was produced, but the *effect itself;* not the mode by which the body of the king was wetted, but its *condition*, as resulting from exposure to the dew of heaven." To this Carson (who assumes the office of whipping in his friends, when they overstep theory, and enter the region of truth) replies: "About what is he contending? Without doubt, the verb expresses mode here as well as anywhere else. To suppose the contrary, gives up the point at issue, as far as mode is concerned. . . . It does not literally include *wetting*, at all. . . . . Mode is as much expressed here as it is in the commission of our Lord to his apostles." Thus, *dip*, which literally expresses no "effect"—not even the "wetting," when it carries its object into water—but merely a naked act, and which, in figure, means nothing, more or less, still, in figure, is to be understood as laying aside all "manner," and to be interpreted solely by its "effects!"

This teacher of Gale, and Cox, and the Archangel Gabriel, is a study.

The "flesh and body" baptism, of which Justin speaks, is called "baptism," not because of resemblance of any act performed in its accomplishment to any other act done, but because of resemblance to certain classes of baptism characterized by controlling influence. This influence proceeded from the ritual use of the blood of bulls and goats, and the ashes of a heifer, and effected a Judaic baptism—the complete ceremonial purification of the body.

The "soul" baptism was not limited to the Jew. It was preached to the Jew, as Justin declares, by Isaiah, but it reaches over to the Christian. The "Martyr" says that he had received this baptism "through (διά) the washing of repentance and the knowledge of God." Repentance and the knowledge of God do this washing. Such agencies do thorough work. They patronize no dipping-bath. They thoroughly change the condition of the soul—as soap, a rough towel, and hard friction, change that of the body—"washing it from anger, and covetousness, and envy, and hate." And this thoroughly changed condition, is baptism of the soul, to which Isaiah calls the Jew.

This baptism, "*by* repentance and the knowledge of God," leads to the notice of the essential difference between baptism *in*, and baptism *by*, anything. The former phrase is expressive of local position, the latter is expressive only of complete influence. To illustrate: "A greasy fleece is dipped *in* a dye-vat, but it is not *dipped by* it." Is there any contradiction here? Does not the difference of phraseology clearly indicate a different sense in the words? The first dip announces the form of act by which the object is put into the dye, and the second one declares that the object was not influenced by the dye. This was the phraseology used by the Greeks, and was as intelligible to them as "dipped in, but not *dyed* by," would be to us. Christian missionaries are said "to live *immersed in* the sins of heathenism, but not to be *immersed by* them." The one expression is exhausted by expressing position without influence, and the other, influence without position. These truths may be stated in a reverse form. The hand may be *dipped by* (the juice of a berry), and not be *dipped in* (the juice of a berry). A man may be *immersed by* sin (solitary vice), and not be *immersed in* sin (iniquity abounding). Hot iron may be immersed (quenched) *by* water, and not be immersed *in* water. A man may be baptized (intusposition) *in* wine, and not be baptized (made drunk) *by* wine. A man may be baptized (made drunk) *by* wine, and not be baptized (intusposition) *in* wine.

These diversities of phraseology are constantly met with in the Classics. And it is as certain that they express differences of meaning, as that words are used to express thought, and not, according to the Prince Bishop of Autun, "to hide thought."

Jerome well understood this distinction, when he speaks, in the quotation made, of baptism by the blood of Christ—ut baptizimini in sanguine meo. "In," being here used, as in numberless cases, with the agency. Had all the scoffing murderers of the Crucified been baptized *in* his blood (as a fluid element), they would none the more have been baptized *by* his blood (received with "repentance and the knowledge of God"), which cleanses from all sin.

A word or two, before leaving this passage, with reference to the special evidence Dr. C. draws from it for a dipping. "He speaks of baptism as cleansing the *flesh* and the *body* only; this shows that the water was applied to the body in general" (p. 490). So far from showing the manner or extent of using water, it does not show the use of water at all. Justin is speaking of Jewish rites as only competent to effect the ceremonial purification of the body, leaving the soul unpurified. He refers to the sprinkling of blood, or heifer ashes, or any other thing competent to induce this condition. There was no dipping of the body into water enjoined by Jewish ritual law. Nothing is more certain than that, in Jewish rites, a sprinkling cleansed the entire "flesh and body." An argument is drawn from the mention of cisterns: "He speaks of it, also, as referring to cisterns or pits, as trenches that are *dug*. It must, then, have been an immersion." This is another of those marvellous errors of conception and representation, to which a wrong theory constringes its disciples.

When Jehovah, by Jeremiah, says: "My people have committed two evils; they have forsaken me, the fountain of living waters, and hewed them out cisterns, broken cisterns, that can hold no water," does he complain that they have "dug pits and trenches to dip themselves in, but which have failed of their purpose because the bottom had fallen out?" Just as certainly as that Justin means any such thing by his reference to this passage. Jehovah is "the fountain of living waters," not to dip in, but whence the soul may derive blessing, even life for evermore; while human devices, or divinely appointed ritual rites, abused, in being used for other purposes than those designed, are "broken cisterns," to which men apply, in vain, for blessing which accompanies salvation.

The Lord and his "Martyr" teach the same thing: Jewish rites, at the best, can but effect ceremonial purification; it is "the water of life" (repentance and the knowledge of God) which "baptizes the soul from anger, covetousness, envy, and hate." Justin has no reference to a dry dipping in a "broken" cistern; although Dr. Carson thinks that all Israel received a "dry baptism" in passing through the sea.

BAPTISM BY INIQUITY.

Isaiah 21:4.

"My heart panted, fearfulness affrighted: the night of my pleasure hath he turned into fear unto me."

Septuagint.

—— *ἡ καρδία μου πλανᾶται, καὶ ἡ ἀνομία με βαπτίζει, ἡ ψυχή μου ἐφέστηκεν εἰς φόβον.*

"My heart wanders; iniquity baptizes me; my soul is put into fear."

BAPTISM BY INIQUITY.

This passage has presented no little embarrassment to the translator and interpreter, because of want of verbal accord with the Hebrew, and because of a failure in the just appreciation of the word.

Dr. Edward Williams translates, "Iniquity pours me." Translation by this modal word must, like modal *dip*, fail through lack of support in usage. Prof. Ewing says: "The subject of baptism is viewed as having something *poured* or *brought upon* him."

Gale, Halley, Wilson, Stuart, and others, translate, "Iniquity overwhelms me." Conant, "Iniquity whelms me."

This wide consent to the introduction of "overwhelm" as the translation of a *certain class* of baptisms must have substantial ground to rest upon. Be that ground, however, what it may, it can have most obviously no sympathy with a *dipping*.

The theorists do not translate such cases by "immerse," because its primary meaning does not answer; and because its secondary meaning, *to be earnestly engaged*, as, "I am so immersed in business that I can attend to nothing else," answers just as badly. "Immerse" has no well-established secondary usage expressive of a controlling influence imparted. In this respect it fails in parallelism with the Greek word. "Overwhelm" has a secondary meaning derived from primary use which adapts it, in the absence of a more perfect word, for use in such cases. Still, as overwhelm and βάπτιζω do not represent the same form of thought in primary use, so, neither do they in the derived, secondary use. The object which is placed by the Greek word in a condition of intusposition is the quiet and unresisting recipient of influence from the encompassing medium, which seeks to interpenetrate it at all points. An object which is *overwhelmed* is brought into that condition, only, in consequence of its resistance (active or passive) having been overcome by some assailing agency. In accordance with these elements the Greek word, in secondary use, is expressive of the reception of influence which controls condition; while the English word, in secondary use, carries with it an assailing power which triumphs by overcoming resistance, active or passive.

Hannibal overcame all difficulties, and came over the Alps. Is "overcame," here, used in figure, or does it express thought directly? The swollen river whelmed over the bridge and overwhelmed the structure. Is this tautology? Is not the thought in "overwhelmed" essentially diverse from that in "whelmed over?" In the latter, the sentiment is exhausted by the physical condition of the bridge as covered by the rising and flowing waters; in the former word there is nothing to do with the covered condition of the bridge, except as a means to an end; and that which the other word throws not a ray of light upon, (the effect produced on the structure,) this states, and it is all which it states. This is its meaning. A meaning which the other form had not. And it is a meaning which has a life of its own, and is capable of being applied in any suitable case where there is no whelming flood present or conceivable. As, "the blow overwhelmed me."

"The troops came whelming over the ramparts and overwhelmed all opposition." "Whelming" is, here, clearly figure; the resemblance of men thronging upon, rising above, and passing over walls, to flowing waters rising above and flowing over obstacles, is clear and vivid. On the other hand, it is just as certain that "overwhelmed" is not figure; but expresses, directly, an effect wholly different in nature from the other. The resistance made by the garrison is not represented as overcome by a flood; but by the fighting after the walls were flooded by the troops. Napoleon was over-mastered, over-come, over-thrown, over-powered, overwhelmed, at Waterloo, by English and Prussian power. Each of these words expresses a thought directly without picture figure, and generically the same thought, to wit, a resisting power subdued by a stronger power. In each case there is a coloring from the source whence the word springs; but each has a meaning distinct from its original.

"Overwhelm" represents βαπτίζω in its controlling power, but not in its shade-color of *resistance overcome.* The Greek word, in this respect, belongs to the class of words represented by *steep*, *imbue*, &c. The influence which it exerts is quiet in its operation, penetrating in its nature, pervading in its extent, and controlling in its power.

Those friends of the theory who, in this baptism of iniquity, turn coldly away from "dip," and have no friendly recognition even for a "transient covering," but call lustily on *overwhelm* to come to their help, ought certainly to abandon or reconstruct their conceptions of a word which stands them so little in stead in the time of need. Dr. Carson, however, has not lost a jot of courage or confidence. His exposition of this baptism, laid alongside of "my position," leads one to marvel at the mental phenomenon presented.

This is his language (p. 86): "The expression, iniquity

'baptizeth me,' does not mean that iniquity comes on him either by *popping* or *dipping*, either by *pouring* or *sprinkling*: but that his sin, which originated in himself, and never was *put on him in any mode*, *sunk* him in misery. Our iniquities cause us to *sink* in deep waters. This example is, with all others in which the word occurs, whether in its literal or figurative use, completely in our favor. Iniquity is the baptizer, and instead of *popping* the subjects of its baptism, would sink them eternally in the lake that burneth with fire and brimstone, were they not delivered by that which is represented in the baptism of Christians."

If Dr. Carson had repeated the Multiplication Table backwards in proof of—"My position is, THAT IT ALWAYS SIGNIFIES TO DIP; NEVER EXPRESSING ANYTHING BUT MODE,"—"I maintain, that in figures there is no different meaning of the word,"—it would have been as creditable to him intellectually, and less damaging to his cause logically. For, to say that 12 times 12 making 144 proves, that "βαπτίζω signifies to dip both in fact and in figure," is only to adduce strangely irrelevant proof; but to adduce, as proof that βαπτίζω means to dip, a case in which it is declared to mean "to sink," is to bring not irrelevant testimony, but simple and absolute disproof. And to adduce in proof of a *dipping* ("covered and bare"), the "*sinking* of souls *eternally* in the lake that burneth with fire and brimstone," can only make the world stare at the vagaries of a distraught intellect.

Interpretation.

The general interpretation of this passage must be regulated by the capture of Babylon, to which it relates. And particular words or phrases may receive valuable light from particular facts of that transaction. There is no fact in the case which the divine record places in such bold relief as Belshazzar's feast; that was the crowning "iniquity" in which Jehovah was blasphemed and defied. And in that feast its culmination presents to view a royal figure gazing on the wall—"his countenance changed, his thoughts troubling, the joints of his loins loosed, and his knees smiting one against another,"—his sins have found him out, and "iniquity is baptizing him" with dire alarm.

The prophet is understood to speak as a Babylonian. And whom could he so aptly represent as the King of the Babylonians? And what language could more literally set forth the condition of Belshazzar, as he is passing through his baptism, in gazing upon the writing and hearing its interpretation, than that of the prophet,—"My loins are filled with pain; pangs have taken hold upon me; I was dismayed at the seeing of it?" This is the baptism of Iniquity. "Conscience makes cowards of all." And on "that night in which he was slain," conscience, aroused by the Spirit of that God against whom "he had lifted up himself," causeth his iniquities to take hold upon him, and he is baptized with unutterable terror. To introduce here a dipping, or sinking in deep waters, is impertinent bathos.

As the Septuagint differs wholly (*ad verbum*, yet not *ad sensum*) from the Hebrew, it gives fit occasion to point out the unreliability of Dr. Carson's principle in interpreting the language of the Septuagint used in connection with the baptism of Naaman. He says, (p. 315,) "That the Greek word signifies *dip*, is clear from the fact that this is the meaning of the word in the original." The meaning of the word in the original of the passage under consideration is AFFRIGHT, and the translation is βαπτίζω. Will Dr. C. vindicate his reasoning by saying, "That the Greek word signifies *affright*, is clear from the fact that this is the meaning of the word in the original?" The theorists throw their mantle of univocalism over a great many words on which it fits but queerly; is this one of them?

Identity of meaning between original and translated words is a sandy principle for a controversialist to build upon.

While this passage declares that dip and transient covering have neither part nor lot in it, it declares, as unmistakably, that *completeness of condition* is exhaustive of its thought to the very last element.

Iniquity baptizes,—*i. e.*, brings me into a complete condition of "*terror*," as shown by the case, and the context.

Very similar in form is, "Potatio quæ mergit"—"The drink which merses," brings into a complete condition "of drunkenness." Neither "iniquity" nor "wine" dips its subjects into water, shallow or deep.

The true usage of *βαπτίζω* destroys the theory as utterly as if it were sunk eternally in that lake of which Dr. Carson speaks.

BAPTISM AND MIRACLE.

We come now to the consideration of a very interesting group of baptisms. They are caused by, or accompanied with, divine power miraculously displayed. In no one of them, is there either a "dipping" or a "temporary covering." In all of them there is a controlling influence, effecting a complete change of condition, characterized by indefinitely prolonged continuance: this latter feature being as essential to the conception of a baptism as the former; while modal action, as such, of any kind, never, under any circumstances, has anything to do with effecting a baptism. The presence or absence of any particular form of action is, alike, a matter of indifference. These baptisms leave "the theory" a perfect *caput mortuum.*

RED SEA BAPTISM.

Exodus 14 : 19, 21, 28, 31.

"And the angel of God, which went before the camp of Israel, removed and went behind them; and the pillar of cloud went from before their face, and stood behind them.

"And Moses stretched out his hand over the sea; and the Lord caused the sea to go back by a strong east wind all that night, and made the sea dry land, and the waters were divided.

"And the waters returned and covered the chariots and the horsemen and all the host of Pharaoh that came into the sea after them; there remained not so much as one of them.

"And Israel saw that great work which the Lord did upon the Egyptians; and the people feared the Lord *and believed the* LORD *and his servant Moses.*"

Interpretation.

"Deinde legimus quia in virtute sua magna, et brachio suo excelso, populum suum de terra Ægypti liberavit, quando traduxit eum per mare Rubrum, in quo fecit figura baptismatis."

"Afterward we read that by his great power and his high arm, he liberated his people from the land of Egypt, when he led them through the Red Sea, in which was a figure of baptism."—*Ambrose*, i, 867.

"Denique et ipse Moyses dicit in cantico: 'Misisti Spiritum suum, et aperuit eos mare.' (Exod. 15 : 10.) Advertis quod in illo Hebræorum transitu jam tunc sacri baptismatis figura præcesserit, in quo Ægyptius interiit, et Hebræus evasit. Quid enim aliud in hoc quotidie sacramento docemur, nisi quia culpa mergitur et error aboletur; pietas autem et innocentia tuta permansit."

"Finally, even Moses himself says in his song: 'Thou didst send forth thy Spirit and opened for them the sea.' (Ex. 15 : 10.) Observe that in that passage of the Hebrews, even then, a figure of sacred baptism went before, in which the Egyptian perished and the Hebrew escaped. For what else, in this daily sacrament do we teach, except that sin is drowned and error destroyed; while piety and innocence remain safe."—*Ambrose*, iii, 393.

"In mari autem Rubro figuram istius baptismatis extitisse ait Apostolus, dicens: 'Quia patres nostri omnes baptizati sunt in nube et in mari.' (I Cor. 10 : 1, 2.) Et subdidit: 'Hæc autem omnia in figura facta sunt illis (v. 6); illis in figura, sed nobis in veritate.'"

"But the Apostle declares that a figure of this baptism shows itself in the Red Sea, saying: 'That all our fathers were baptized by the cloud and by the sea.' (I Cor. 10 : 1, 2) And added: 'But all these things were done to them in figure (v. 6); to them in figure, but to us in reality.'"—*Ambrose*, iii, 423.

"Tenebat virgam Moyses, et ducebat populum Hebræorum in nocte, in columna lucis, in die, in columna nubis. Columna lucis quid est, nisi Christus Dominus. . . . . . At vero columna nubis est Spiritus sanctus. In mari erat populus, et præibat columna lucis; deinde sequebatur columna nubis, quasi umbratio Spiritus Sancti. Vides quod per Spiritum Sanctum et per aquam typum baptismatis demonstraverit."

"Moses held the rod, and led the Hebrew people by night, with the pillar of light; by day, with the pillar of cloud. The pillar of light, what is it, but Christ the Lord. . . . But, indeed, the pillar of cloud is the Holy Spirit. The people were in the sea, and the pillar of light went before; then followed the pillar of cloud, the shadowing, as it were, of the Holy Spirit. Thou seest that by the Holy Spirit and by the water, a type of baptism may have been exhibited."—iii, 424.

"Qui non fuisti memor indignationis tuæ: sed sicut in mari mersisti omnes iniquitates nostras, sicut Ægyptium plumbum. . . . . Quod potest et ad baptismum referri, quo Ægyptius mergitur, Hebræus resurgit." . . .

"Who hast not been mindful of thy displeasure; but, as in the sea, thou hast drowned all our iniquities, like Egyptian lead. . . . . Which may also be referred to baptism, whereby the Egyptian is drowned and the Hebrew rises again."—iii, 1240.

"Filii igitur Israel, ut Pharaonem et Ægyptios evaderent, per medium sicci maris transierunt, et aquæ eis erant quasi pro muro a dextris et a sinistris. Similiter et populus gentium, ut diabolum omnesque ejus satellites evaderent, per aquam baptismatis transierunt. Et qui antea erant filii diaboli, ex aqua et Spiritu Sancto, qui per columnam ignis designabatur, renati effecti sunt filii Dei. Aqua ergo maris filios Israel salvavit. Pharaonem vero cum omnibus satellitibus suis necavit; quia aqua baptismatis imaginem Dei salvat, peccata quibus servierat, extinguit; diabolus autem unicuique, extinguitur, qui eum fideliter cum omnibus pompis ejus abrenuntiat.

"Aquæ vero quæ pro muro eis erant, a dextris et a sinistris fidem designabant nostram, quam in baptismati percipimus, quæ murus est noster ex utraque parte defendens nos et ab invisibilibus hostibus et a visibilibus."

"The children of Israel, therefore, that they might escape Pharaoh and the Eyptians, passed through the midst of the dry sea, and 'the waters were to them as a wall on the right hand and on the left.' In like manner the people of the Gentiles, that they might escape the devil and his satellites, have passed through the water of baptism. And they who, formerly, were children of the devil, born again by water and the Holy Spirit, (who was signified by the pillar of fire,) are made the sons of God. The water, therefore, of the sea saved the children of Israel. But it slew Pharaoh with all his servants. Because the water of baptism saves the likeness of God and destroys the sins which it served; but the devil is destroyed to every one who faithfully renounces him with all his pomps.

"But the waters which were to them as a wall on the right hand and on the left, designate our faith which we receive in baptism; which is our wall, on either side, defending us from enemies invisible and visible."—iv, 827.

'Η δὲ θάλασση καὶ ἡ νεφέλη πρὸς μὲν τὸ παρὸν εἰς πίστιν ἐνῆγε διὰ τῆς καταπλήξεως· πρὸς δὲ τὸ μέλλον ὡς τύπος τὴν ἐσομένην χάριν προϋπεσήμαινε.

"But the sea and the cloud, at that time, induced faith through amazement; but, as a type, it signified, for the future, the grace that should be after."—*Basil Magnus*, iv, 124.

Τὸ διὰ τῆς θαλάσσης καὶ τῆς νεφέλης.

"That baptism which is by the cloud and sea."—*John of Damascus*, i, 261. Paris, 1712.

Τά δὲ ὕδατα, μεσιτεύσαντα τῷ λαῷ τὴν ἀσφάλειαν, ἐδήλου τὸ βάπτισμα· καὶ πᾶσα δὲ ἡ ὑπόθεσις τῆς ἀπὸ Αἰγύπτιου αὐτῶν ὁδοῦ, τύπος ἦν τῆς ἐν τῷ βαπτίσματι σωτηρίας. . . . Μωϋσῆς δὲ, τύπον ἔφερεν τοῦ Χριστοῦ.

"The waters, securing safety for the people, signify baptism. . . . . And the whole material of their journey from Egypt was a type of the salvation by baptism. . . . But Moses himself was a type of Christ."—*Didymus Alex.*, 696.

A BAPTISM WITHOUT USE OF THE WORD.

The historical narrative furnished us in Exodus of the passage of the children of Israel through the divided sea, and of the drowning of Pharaoh and the Egyptians attempting to follow after them, does not furnish us with any word equivalent to βαπτίζω; nor does the Septuagint use it in its version.

But that a baptism did take place on this occasion, is accepted by all by reason of the statement of the Apostle Paul in I Cor. 10 : 2.

On the form and nature of this baptism there is a wide diversity of opinion.

It will be both interesting and instructive, to consider the different notions of baptism, held by various parties, as they are brought into contact in the attempt to resolve this historical transaction into a baptism.

Three styles of baptism are claimants for our favor: 1. That of the Theorists; 2. That of the Patrists; 3. That of the Apostle.

The nature of these several claims, with their sustaining evidences, will be considered in their order.

RED SEA BAPTISM OF THE THEORISTS.

"The passage of the children of Israel through the Red Sea is figuratively called a baptism from its external resemblance to the ordinance, and from being appointed to serve a like purpose as well as to figure the same thing. Here (I Cor. 10 : 2) they are said to have been baptized. There can be no doubt, therefore, that there is in their passage through the sea, something that represents both the external form and the purpose of Christian baptism. It was a real *immersion*—the sea stood on each side, and the cloud covered them. But it was not a literal *immersion in water*, in the same way as Christian baptism. It is, therefore, figuratively called by the name of the Christian ordinance, because of external similarity, and because of serving the like purpose as well as figuring the same event.

"The going down of the Israelites into the sea, their being covered by the cloud, and their issuing out on the other side, resembled the baptism of believers, served a like purpose as attesting their faith in Moses as a temporal Saviour, and figured the burial and resurrection of Christ and Christians as well as Christian baptism. . . . Surely there is no straining to see in this fact something that may darkly shadow a burial. . . . The baptism of Pentecost and of the Israelites in the Red Sea were dry baptisms."

Dr. Carson either writes very enigmatically or very self-contradictorily. He tells us that this passage of the Israelites was "a real immersion," and, therefore, according to his remarkable use of words, a real *dipping;* and therefore, still farther, according to his postulation, a *baptism.* But having created this real (?) baptism at the demands of theory, he very promptly, by reason of necessity in another direction, disrobes it of the real habiliment and enrobes it in the dress of figure. "It is figuratively called a baptism." One baptism may be typical of another baptism. But a real baptism cannot get its name from anything but its own reality. If the passage of the Israelites was a real baptism it takes its name from its own inherent character, and not as "a figure of the Christian ordinance."

Dr. C. also writes with a free and easy assumption, and undertakes to tell us what is the divine appointment without showing any commission on which is written—"Thus saith the Lord." "It is called a baptism from its external resemblance to the ordinance, and from being appointed to serve a like purpose as well as to figure the same thing." The writer is at liberty to imagine an "external resemblance to the ordinance" and to make out such resemblance as well as he can; but he is not at liberty to say, that God has "appointed" this Israelitish passage "to serve a like purpose and to figure the same thing" as Christian baptism, without putting his finger on the record made by higher authority than his own.

But what is the resemblance which he traces? This,—"the going down of the Israelites into the sea, their being covered by the cloud, and their issuing out on the other side, resembled the baptism of believers." That is to say, "the going down" and "the issuing out" "resemble" the act of dipping into water—*covered and bare*—our old friends of the sea-coast beyond the pillars of Hercules. The faculty for tracing a resemblance between such things reminds us of the sea story of one of our distinguished countrymen in which he represents the commander, after looking through his glass at a vessel in the far-off distance, as saying to an African sailor by his side, that "he thought it was a church," and "old Scip" promptly replied, that he thought so too.

If Dr. Carson would try his fellow-theorists who see with him a marked resemblance to a "dipping," by adding—"Now, I think it is a church," he probably would hear them respond with all alacrity—"And we think so too!"

But what "purpose" is this passage "appointed to serve?" As "attesting their faith in Moses as a temporal Saviour." Now, so far from this passage being appointed to give testimony to the faith which they had in Moses, it was appointed for the very opposite reason; namely, because they had not faith in Moses, and to the end that such faith might be begotten and established. Let us take the guidance not of theories but of the word of God. Standing on the hither side of the sea, Israel, sore afraid and full of unbelief, said unto Moses, "Because there were no graves in Egypt, hast thou taken us away to die in the wilderness? wherefore hast thou dealt thus with us, to carry us forth out of Egypt? Is not this the word that we did tell thee in Egypt, saying, Let us alone, that we may serve the Egyptians? For it had been better for us to serve the Egyptians than that we should die in the wilderness." (Exod. 14 : 11, 12.) As a result of this miraculous passage and deliverance we are told, as they stand securely on the farther side, their enemies all slain,—"And Israel saw that great work which the Lord did upon the Egyptians: and the people feared the Lord, and *believed* the Lord, and *his servant Moses.*" (v. 31.) Thus the statement of the end for which this baptism was appointed,—namely, to show the faith which they already had in Moses, is in the most absolute contradiction to Scripture statement. We are told, most expressly, that before the passage they had no faith in Moses; and we are told, as expressly, that after the passage they had faith in him; and the cause by which unbelief was removed and belief was established, was their "seeing the Egyptians dead upon the sea-shore," and "the great work which the Lord had done."

Now, unless the theory will openly set aside the word of God, this "appointment to show, by their baptism, their faith in Moses as a temporal saviour" is disposed of.

But we are farther told, that this baptism is appointed "to figure the burial and resurrection of Christ and Christians." That is to say; the march of two million men, women and children, with flocks and herds innumerable, through the divided sea, "figures the burial of Christ and Christians," while the landing on the farther side amid bleating sheep and lowing oxen "figures the resurrection." To oppose all this I confess myself unable to put my finger upon any *ipsissima verba* of Scripture. Revelation is designed to correct error and to establish truth. But it does not occupy itself with the empty fantasies or grotesque eccentricities of the human intellect. All I can say is, that this resurrection of Israel from the Red Sea burial, richly laden with all the spoils of Egypt, does not bear a very striking "resemblance" to the Scripture, which says, "We brought nothing into this world, and it is certain that we can carry nothing out."

So much for the name, and the resemblance, and the purpose, and the figure of this Red Sea baptism according to the theory.

Let us, now, look at it in some other points of view.

1. How is this baptistery constructed? What is the depth of that burial-place "down" into which these walk? Facts say, that the bottom of the sea was but little lower than the shore; not more than would allow a company on horseback to ride (as has been done) a considerable distance into the water. The "going down" into this abyss, therefore, furnished but a shallow grave. But the *lofty* water-walls may make up for the shallowness of the sea, and by inclosing and outtopping constitute an immersion for these millions with their flocks and herds. How lofty these water-walls were the Scripture does not say. There is no good reason to believe that they were any higher than the natural depth of the sea. There is good reason for believing that they

were not so high as the natural depth of the sea. The waters were divided by the blowing of the wind. If a miracle did not intervene to prevent it, the excess of waters would flow away, as they were displaced by the wind, and not become piled up in a heap. We are told that a miracle did arrest the down-flowing waters of the Jordan. We are not told of any such miracle at the Red Sea. We have no right to make miracles for ourselves. The most, then, that we are justified in affirming as to the height of these water-walls is the natural depth of the sea. But at what distance do these walls stand from each other? We are not told that any miracle was wrought to help these Israelites as to their speed. We must, therefore, allow enough of space between these walls for the ordinary march of two million men, women, and children, incumbered with flocks and herds, and tents and household goods. Now, within a very limited space it would be impossible, a few abreast, to cross this sea within a night. These millions, with flocks and herds, &c., &c., could not be put into marching condition with a less front than one mile, and make the passage. They would, then, extend back for five miles. It is more probable that these water-walls were five miles distant from each other than that they were only half a mile distant. But whether one mile or five apart, what show, for the immersion of millions, would water-walls twenty feet, more or less, high make?

But if the sea be shallow and the walls be low and afar, may not the baptistery be effectively completed by its cloud-roof? Is there not, at least, herein that vital element to an immersion—a covering? Dr. Carson evidently thinks so, and insists upon it with that positiveness and tenacity which might be expected from one who did not regard the Angel Gabriel as his peer on this matter of dipping. What evidence does he bring to show that a cloud-roof rested on these water-walls during the passage of Israel making an immersion baptistery? Why he points to two prepositions (ὑπὸ and ἐν) used by Paul, without showing that they meet together on this occasion, and without any such statement by the Apostle. And against what proof to the contrary is this adduced? Why against the statement by Moses, as explicit as language is capable of, that there was no cloud covering Israel during their passage. This is his statement: "And the angel of God, which went before the camp of Israel, *removed and went behind them;* and the pillar of the cloud went from before their face and stood behind them." (Ex. 14:19.) This was before the passage began. "And it (the pillar of cloud) came between the camp of the Egyptians and the camp of Israel; and it was a cloud and darkness to them; but it gave light by night to these: so that the one came not near the other all the night." We have here, 1. A definite position to the cloud. Not resting on the water-walls of the theoretic baptistery, but between the camps of Egypt and Israel. 2. The time of its continuance in that position. It was through the entire night,—"so that the one came not near the other all the night." 3. The functions of the cloud through that night. To invest with preternatural darkness the camp of Egypt, and to illumine the passage of Israel.

The cloud, then, was engaged in other duties, that night, than in a participation in the dipping—immersion—burial—resurrection—march—baptism—of Israel. But will these statements of Moses have any influence with the theorists, to induce them to take down their Red Sea baptistery? Surely not. Have they not studied the prepositions? Do they not know the meaning of βαπτίζω? Is it not the easiest word in the Greek language to translate? Does it not always mean dip, and nothing but dip, through all Greek literature? Why should they, who know so much, yield to Moses, who was only an eye-witness and prime actor in the scene, and inspired of God to write the record? "Either the persons referred to were immersed, on the occasions mentioned, *or the inspired writer testifies a falsehood.*" (Carson, p. 397.) And who dare mutter or peep after the inspired writer has been notified to utter the shibboleth, or to be branded as a ——. I will take the warning, at least so far as to say nothing more on this point.

2. Let us lay objection aside, and suppose the baptistery to be constructed after the Carson model. What is it worth, as to its baptizing power? Where is the element into which the baptism takes place? Confessedly there is none. There is but empty space between the walls and roof. It is a matter for admiration that this empty space was not filled with that "east wind," seeing that the wind, or the sound like wind, was employed for dipping the Apostles at Pentecost. But somehow or other this has been overlooked; and we have an empty baptistery in which some millions are to be dipped. Another thing is lacking. As there is no water, save in the walls, there can be no "figured" purification. And yet even the theory admits, that this is one of the vital features of Christian baptism, which we are told is here "figured." In fact this baptistery assumes the exclusive character of a huge sepulchre, and that night-march of men, women, and children, sheep and oxen, is a self-baptizing funeral procession, working out "the figure" of burial and resurrection.

Well, such is the baptism. Now, may we ask of the theory, which is so rich in Classic lore, and so tenacious of the heathen rights of βαπτίζω, on what cases of parallel classical usage they ground this Red Sea baptism? My limited knowledge supplies no case of heathen baptism "into empty space." It seems to me that a good deal of peculiar rhetoric will be required to make out the case, and, after all, the abandonment of the Classic side of βαπτίζω, and something, perhaps, be said, in an undertone, about "a religious use." I am afraid that the weight put on this reed will be found quite too heavy, and that, in breaking, it will pierce the hand that leans upon it.

It is something, however, to repay our study of this remarkable structure, to learn, at least, that its baptism into nothing, figuring a burial and resurrection, makes no special claim to the Classics for support.

3. Seeing, now, that this structure is repudiated by inspiration, so far as to unroof it; and is repudiated by heathenism through her Classics, so far as the "dry" baptism is

concerned; let us see what aid and comfort the theory itself is ready to extend to its offspring.

(1.) The theory demands a baptizer. The candidates for baptism are a host, before which the numbers of Pentecost dwindle into insignificance. Must this be a self-baptism—prototype, on a magnificent scale, of the self-baptism of Roger Williams? Then, along with purification, we eliminate from the "resemblances" the not unimportant feature of a baptizer.

(2.) The theory requires, that in self-baptism βάπτω shall officiate. "The person dips himself; therefore it is βάπτω, to dip, and not βαπτίζω, to cause to dip." (Carson, p. 30.) But here we have some millions "dipping" themselves, and it is βαπτίζω, and not βάπτω, that does the work. What says the theory?

(3.) The theory requires a modal act—dip, and nothing but dip. But here we have the modal act tramp, tramp, and nothing but tramp. What says the theory? All right?

(4.) The theory demands a momentary covering for its dipped object. Here was one lasting from the evening till the morning-watch. Will that answer for a dipping?

(5.) The theory requires faith in the candidate for baptism. To make these candidates suitable in their resemblance, it fills them with faith in Moses, where the Scriptures show them rampant with unbelief.

(6.) The theory repudiates infant baptism. And yet in this very remarkable baptism, it exhibits the most magnificent spectacle of infant baptism that the rolling ages have ever witnessed.

Our ear has grown familiar with the information (furnished by the theory, not the Scriptures), that there were no infant children in the family of the Jailor, or of Lydia, or of Stephanas, or of any other baptized family of the New Testament; but were there no infant children among all the families of Israel? Were these infant children taken from their parents' arms, and carried over outside the water-walls, and unshadowed by the cloud-roof? or, was their baptism put down with that of the sheep and the oxen, as of nothing worth, lest it should be supposed to be one of the "resemblances to the Christian ordinance?"

Unless the theory is prepared to take a baptism without a baptizer; unless it is willing to confess error in the distinction made between βάπτω and βαπτίζω; unless it is prepared to set aside the modal act of dipping; unless it is prepared to part with that momentary covering, with which dip only can furnish it; unless it is ready to set aside its watchword, "faith first, baptism afterward;" and, finally, unless it is prepared to recognize the baptism of little children; it must reconstruct its Red Sea baptistery, and repudiate its baptism by nobody into nothing.

There is, no doubt, surprising originality in the conception of this baptism; otherwise some mind, in the course of the three thousand years which elapsed before this theory was born, would have caught some glimpse of it. But the most brilliant originality can hardly survive repudiation by inspired writers, repudiation by classic writers, and repudiation, or suicidal acceptance, by—itself.

Such seems to be the present aspect of this "dry baptism" in the sea.

But Dr. Carson asks, more than once, "If this is not the baptism, then, what is?" Certainly not an unreasonable question. We will approach its solution by first stating what was the Patristic notion of this baptism. It will be found "another kind" of baptism from that just expounded.

PATRISTIC INTERPRETATION OF THE RED SEA BAPTISM.

AMBROSE.

First Extract.—In the first extract from Ambrose, we are told that the deliverance of Israel from the land of Egypt, by means of the passage provided for them through the Red Sea, was a figure of baptism. The baptism was the deliverance; the passage of the sea was the means whereby it was accomplished.

Second Extract.—In the second extract there is a partial development of the figure as he understands it. It is this: "The Egyptian perishes and the Hebrew escapes." The application of these historical facts to Christian baptism, he makes thus: "We teach in this sacrament that sin is drowned and error is destroyed: but piety and innocence remain." Ambrose considered the drowning of the Egyptians to be as vital a constituent in the Red Sea baptism as the escape of the Hebrews. Both had an equally vital bearing on Christian baptism as he understood it. Not so the theorists.

Third Extract.—It is only necessary, in this extract, to call attention to the use of *in* as translating ἐν, and our translation of both in an instrumental and not local sense. Some justifying reasons for this have already been assigned; more will be given hereafter.

Fourth Extract.—Here *in* makes imperative demand, by the exigency of the passage, for instrumental power. "In nocte," and "in die," may be translated "*in* the night"—"*in* the day;" yet not so well as *through* the night, *during* the night, nightly, *by* night, &c. But "in columna lucis"—"in columna nubis" cannot be translated, "*in* a pillar of light"—"*in* a pillar of cloud." Neither Moses nor the people were *in* the pillar of fire, or cloud, as a fact. But Moses did, in fact, lead the people *by* the fiery and cloudy pillar under divine direction. We must, then, allow Ambrose to state this fact though he use the preposition "in" to do it. He farther explains the figure in this baptism by interpreting "the pillar of light" as Christ the Lord; "the pillar of cloud" as the Holy Spirit; and the water as the element used in Christian baptism. He does not construct a baptistery with water-walls and cloud-roof.

Fifth Extract.—Sins pardoned are like Egyptian lead, drowned in the sea. The Egyptian is drowned; the Hebrew rises, like the axe out of Jordan.

Sixth Extract.—The special value of this extract is the clear exhibition which it makes of the passage through the sea as an agency by which something is to be effected, and not as an end in which something terminates. This is the key which unlocks the Patristic idea of baptism. Without it neither their conception nor their practice can be worthily understood.

Ambrose tells us, "The children of Israel, *that they might escape Pharaoh and the Egyptians*, passed through the midst of the dry sea." Language could not be more explicit to teach that this dry passage was an agency employed for an end, which end was "escape from Pharaoh and the Egyptians." The nail thus driven home is clinched by the statement, that those persons desirous of escaping "the devil and his satellites" employ Christian baptism as a means to this end. And herein is the resemblance between the Red Sea baptism and its Patristically understood antitype, Christian baptism. The water of the sea *saved* the Hebrews by giving them a dry passage; it *slew* Pharaoh and his servants by flowing over them. Here is agency of the most active and efficient character. So, "the water of baptism *saves* the image of God and *destroys* the sins which it served." Again, agency and nothing but agency.

Ambrose adds another explanation of the figure. "The water-walls designate our faith, which we receive in baptism." This Patrist differs from the theorists in their idea that the Israelites had faith in Moses *before* their baptism. He makes faith a consequence of baptism. He is right, and they are wrong, so far as this Israelitish baptism is concerned.

The understanding of Ambrose as to the Red Sea baptism is too clear to be mistaken. He regards the passage through "the dry sea" as the means by which Israel was delivered; which deliverance was consummated by the reflow of the waters and consequent destruction of the Egyptians.

Ambrose does not fall into the sad blunder, of mistaking an agency used to effect a baptism for the element within which the baptism takes place; nor yet, the equal blunder, of attempting to trace a resemblance between one agency and another agency; or between the agency and the element of a baptism. These patent errors belong to the theory.

Ambrose knew perfectly well, that "whatever is capable

of exercising a controlling influence over its object, thoroughly changing its condition," is capable of baptizing that object. When, therefore, he is told, that the Israelites are brought out of a condition of deadly peril, into a condition of absolute safety, by means of a miraculous passage through the sea, he does not take a line to measure the depth of the bed of the sea, or the height of the water-walls, or the extent of the cloud-roof, to find out a sepulchre for the immersion. Men who do this have lost their heads. They call midnight noon; and in proof of it kindle their rushlight and cry—"See, the sun!"

It is the same error which continually crops out in the interpretation of Classic baptisms to the violation of all rhetoric and common sense. It is the same error as that of the lake-frog dipping of Gale, and of the boxer dipped into his bloody nose by Carson. It is the dislocation of the agency in baptism, and making it fulfil the office of a receiving element.

Whatever misconception there may be in Ambrose about the interpretation, or application, of this great baptism, he makes no mistake as to the true character and proper elements of a baptism. He is in perfect accord with the Classics.

BASIL THE GREAT.

The quotation from Basil exhibits the sea and the cloud, as occupying the position of agency in this baptism. There is no debate here about prepositions, for there are none. The nominative case declares their character as agents. Faith, also, is said to be effected by them, and that through the miraculous character of their agency.

JOHN OF DAMASCUS.

This quotation is taken from President Beecher, who, also, quotes from Hilary on I Cor. 10 : 2,—"Per mare et per nubem purificati." In both cases, (cloud and sea,) the preposition used by the apostle is changed for another, more distinctively expressive of instrumentality; while the verb is changed for a word expressing, by original use, the meaning which the Greek word had secured, only, through appropriation to religious rites.

DIDYMUS ALEXANDRINUS.

In common with all others, Didymus makes "the waters" the instrumental means of salvation, and, therefore, significant of Christian baptism, which he believed to be the instrument in saving the soul. That salvation by the passage of the sea, as an instrument, without regard to mode, is the truth which allies it to Christian baptism, is conclusively shown by the additional statement, that not only this particular transaction, but "all, else, pertaining to their journey from Egypt is a type of salvation by baptism."

There is not a Patristic writer that hints at a dipping, or covering, or immersion, or burial, or resurrection, in this Red Sea baptism. With one voice they term it a baptism of salvation, in which the cloud and sea were the agencies; typifying the Holy Spirit and water, the agencies in salvation, by Christian baptism.

The conceptions of this baptism, as entertained by the theorists and the Patrists, differ from each other *toto cœlo.*

INSPIRED INTERPRETATION OF THE RED SEA BAPTISM.

"Moreover, brethren, I would not that ye should be ignorant, how that all our fathers were under the cloud, and all passed through the sea;

"And were all baptized into Moses by the cloud and by the sea."

Καὶ πάντες εἰς τὸν Μωϋσῆν ἐβαπτίσαντο ἐν τῇ νεφέλῃ καὶ ἐν τῇ θαλάσσῃ.

1 *Cor.* 10 : 2.

Baptism into Moses.

Before entering upon the interpretation of the special passage with which we are concerned, it will be well to glance at the connection in which it stands.

The apostle says: 1. All our fathers were under the cloud.

2. All passed through the sea. 3. All were baptized into Moses. 4. All ate the spiritual meat. 5. All drank the spiritual drink.

Here are five distinct facts stated in which all the Jewish fathers participated. They are all facts of successive chronological development, unless the apostle, after having carried them through the sea in the most absolute manner, (using a double διὰ, with noun and verb,) brings them back again into the sea for the purpose of baptizing them.

The historical narrative says: 1. They were under the cloud which passed over them before they commenced their march.

2. They passed from under the cloud to pass through the sea; the cloud remaining behind.

3. They are now over the sea, and being over are "baptized into Moses;" or the narrator has made a chronological slip, and has got to go back, and tell us what happened *in* the sea, before they "passed through."

If the baptism was before the "passing through," why not say so? If the baptism and the passing through were one and the same thing, why make distinct statements of them, in precisely the same form as of events in the same list, which are distinct in character and successive in development?

4. The eating spiritual meat was subsequent to the passing through the sea, and,

5. The drinking of the spiritual rock was after the eating of the spiritual meat.

It will, I think, be admitted by every one, that unless there should be a compelling necessity to place the baptism before the passing through the sea, it must stand, chronologically, as the apostle has placed it, in fact, subsequent to and, also, a result of the passage through the sea.

We will now proceed to a particular consideration of this deeply interesting statement of the Apostle.

Translation.

1. *The translation*—"and were all baptized into Moses by the cloud and by the sea"—presents all the elements which enter into a baptism of that class to which the theory says

this baptism belongs (physical), and which must appear in any formally-stated figurative baptism, based on this class of baptisms. We have: (1.) The object—"all Israel." (2.) The agency—"cloud and sea." (3.) The element (by verbal suggestion)—"into Moses."

On the other hand, the translation of the theory gives us neither the agency, nor the element; but merely an object and a locality. To secure an agency they have to resort to what, alone, is within their reach—*the act of marching.* To obtain an element, they construct a building—baptistery or sepulchre—in the sea, and fill it with the baptizing element, to wit,—*nothing at all.* Having made this provision to supplement the deficiencies of the inspired narrative, the translation reads: "And were all baptized unto Moses, in the cloud and in the sea, into nothing at all, by marching."

This is no caricature. It is no exposition of mine. It is the elaborate exposition of the sternest and ablest friend of the theory. If any one should complain—with Booth—"this makes our theory ridiculous;" it is no fault of mine.

The translation which we offer is not condemnable on the score of lacking any of the elementary features of a baptism.

2. *The translation of ἐν.*—That *with*, or *by*, may be a true translation of ἐν, is admitted by Dr. Carson: "It may be surprising that, after all that has been said on the subject, I should still lay any stress on the preposition ἐν, *in.* I may be asked, Do you deny that it may be translated *with?* I do not deny this, yet I am still disposed to lay stress upon it." (p. 121.) "The preposition is often to be translated *with*, but in the sense *by*, grammarians themselves acknowledge it to be rare." (p. 330.) Patristic writers—Greek and Latin—use ἐν, and *in*, with an instrumental sense, much more frequently than do Classic writers. The same usage is exhibited in the Septuagint. In Nehemiah 9 : 12: "Thou leddest them in the day *by* a cloudy pillar; and in the night *by* a pillar of fire." And Ps. 78 : 14: "In the daytime, also, he led them *with* a cloud, and all the night *with* a light of fire." And in Ps. 77 : 20: "Thou leddest thy people like a flock, *by* the hand of Moses and Aaron." In all these passages the

agency of the cloud and fire, of Moses and Aaron, is indicated by ἐν.

3. Unless this translation be correct, and ἐν points out the agency, there is no agency. But there can be no baptism without a baptizing agency, therefore we are shut up to this translation. I may add, that Pliny uses the phrase "in nube," when *withinness*, as to the cloud, is impossible: "*neque in nube neque in flatu cadunt rores.*" Dew never falls within a cloud. The influence of cloud and wind prevents the formation of dew. "Dews do not fall *during* a cloudy or windy night."

4. The translation accords with the historical facts. The cloud and the sea were agencies, truly magnificent agencies, employed in this transaction. The divided sea, furnishing its dry pathway, and the cloud, casting preternatural darkness over the camp of Pharaoh, while illuminating the night-march of Israel, were the miraculous agencies brought into operation. The use of miracle, to affect and to influence men, is in harmony with the steadily maintained purpose of God. To this end miracles were used in Egypt, in the wilderness, throughout the Jewish economy, during the life of the Redeemer, and in the establishment of Christianity. This agency, then, was no strange thing. The influence of these miracles on Israel could not, in the nature of things, have its development until their full consummation. And this consummation neither did, nor could, take place until Israel was placed, in safety, on the farther side of the sea, and their enemies had been swallowed up in the miraculously returning waters. Then, and not till then, does the narrative say that this influence had its development, effecting an entire change in the condition of the Israelitish mind toward Moses. That translation which usage allows, history demands. "Cloud and sea" were not elements to be dipped into. They were agencies in which was "the hiding of God's power."

5. Historical facts do not allow the adverse translation—"*in* the cloud, *in* the sea." There is no historical evidence to show that the millions of Israel were now, or were at any other time, "*in* the cloud." There is historical evidence to

the contrary. There is no historical evidence to show that Paul uses ἐν τῇ θαλάσσῃ, out of its usual sense including water, but excludes water, and limits his meaning to the *bed* of the sea. There is historical evidence to show that such cannot be his meaning.

Dr. Carson says: "He will make the word (βαπτίζω) find him water in the desert." Here he has the word, and yet he cannot find, with it, a drop of water "in the sea."

These are some of the considerations which vindicate the translation, so far as this preposition (ἐν) is concerned.

3. *The translation of* εἰς.—(1.) The translation "into," is required in order to indicate the element (verbally suggested) of the baptism. There are classes of baptism in which the mersing element is wholly lost. It has no more place in imagination than it has in fact. But in all such cases an element may be verbally introduced. In some cases this is very important in order to give precision to a statement which, otherwise, would be vague and uncertain. In other cases it is imperative, as without it we could never be certain of the nature of the baptism designed. If I am told that a man is "baptized by wine," I may conclude with much confidence, that the meaning is, *he was made drunk;* but of this I cannot be confident; for, while this is the natural and ordinary influence of wine, it also induces a condition of stupor, shame, poverty, &c. If the statement is, "baptized by wine *into drunkenness*," doubt is at an end. The verbal suggestion of the element, has settled the matter. If I do not know the nature of wine, then to be told that a man is "baptized by *wine*," conveys to me no definite information whatever. Now, the influence of a miracle is not limited, by its nature, to one result; neither are miracles always wrought for the accomplishment of one uniform result. "Baptism by miracle," therefore, is not specific in its information. What baptism would be effected by the miracles at the Red Sea, could never be known, definitely, except by specific statement. The Egyptians were baptized *into terror*, by the divine intervention troubling their chariots, and witnessing the inrolling of the waters, before they were

baptized *into the flood.* We never could have known that these miracles would issue in the baptism of Israel "into Moses," unless we had been told so; for he had wrought many miracles before without any such result. But we do know that such was the result, now, because inspiration so informs us, in terms than which language has none more explicit. "All were baptized *into Moses.*"

(2.) *Usage demands this translation.*—There is not an instance in Classic literature in which εἰς stands thus related to βαπτίζω, but that the friends of the theory translate by, *into.* We have made no objection to this. But we insist, that what was right then, cannot be wrong now. "Into" must remain *into.*

When Josephus wrote, βεβαπτισμένον εἰς ἀναισθησίαν καὶ ὕπνον—it was a "baptism *into* stupor and sleep." (Conant.) The translation must stand, though "stupor and sleep" give place to "Moses." When the Christian Patrist, Clemens Alex., wrote, εἰς πορνείαν βαπτίζουσι—the translation found a baptism "*into* fornication." (Conant.) When the inspired Apostle writes, εἰς τόν Μωσῆν ἐβαπτίσαντο,—I know of nothing in inspiration to change the force of a preposition, and therefore still read, "they were baptized *into* Moses."

(3.) The translation, "*unto* Moses," is not satisfactory. It may be so translated very frequently in other relations. It may be so interpreted, here, as to give the true sense. But it does not present the form of the original, nor lead to that method of interpretation which the form suggests. It is also objectionable, because in phrases of the same grammatical form, the subject-matter being changed, the same translation would not answer. If Eupolis must be baptized *into* the sea, and not *unto* the sea, that he may be brought under its influence—*drowned;*—then Israel must be baptized *into* Moses, and not *unto* Moses, that they may be brought thoroughly under his influence—*subject to his headship.*

(4.) To these considerations may be added the very pointed testimony of some of the Patrists.

Origen, ii, 330, says: "He calls this baptism *into Moses*"—baptismum hoc nominat in Moyse—"accomplished by the cloud and by the sea, that thou, also, who art baptized *into*

Christ, by the water and by the Holy Spirit, mayest know that the Egyptians are following after thee." . . .

Basil M., iii, 428: "That Israel was baptized *into Moses*, by the cloud and by the sea, exhibiting types and delineating for thee the truth about to be revealed in these last times; but thou dost shun baptism, not typified by the sea, but perfected by the truth; not by the cloud, but by the Spirit; *not into Moses*, a fellow-servant, *but into Christ*, the Creator—οὐκ εἰς Μωϋσῆν τὸν ὁμόδουλον, ἀλλ' εἰς Χριστὸν τὸν ποιήσαντα."

Basil M., iv, 121–5, writing of the Holy Spirit, states an objection against the equality of the Holy Spirit with the Father and the Son, thus: *Objector*, "But although we are baptized into him—βαπτιζόμεθα εἰς αὐτὸ—it is not proper that, on that account, he be ranked with God; for some were baptized into Moses: εἰς τον Μωϋσῆν τινες ἐβαπτίσθησαν." He concludes, after argument, "So, although any one be baptized into Moses—τις εἰς Μωϋσῆν ἐβαπτίσθη—the grace which is from the Spirit at baptism, is not small." "It is customary for the Scriptures to speak of Moses as the Law—thus: 'they have Moses and the prophets.' Therefore speaking of the legal baptism—τὸ νομικὸν βάπτισμα—he says: 'They were baptized into Moses'—ἐβαπτίσθησαν εἰς τὸν Μωϋσῆν." "Moses was a type, not of the Spirit, but of Christ."

No one I think can doubt but that these learned Grecians believed in a baptism *into Moses*. While there is no evidence that they had ever heard of a baptism *into empty space*, there is conclusive testimony that they were familiar with the baptism of Israel into their great Leader.

Interpretation.

But what interpretation is to be given to the phrase "baptized into Moses?"

It is obvious that the basis of the interpretation must be found in the literal use of similar phraseology. In turning to the literal use of βαπτίζω we find several classes of baptisms presenting material diversities.

1. There are baptisms of influence without intusposition whether of fact, or imagination, or verbal suggestion. The

phraseology before us cannot be grounded in baptisms of this class, because there is nothing to meet its verbal form.

2. Other baptisms are of intusposition merely; they have no attendant influence. This cannot be the baptism we wish, for we must have influence.

3. Another class of baptisms have both intusposition and influence; but the influence is an accident, unsought, uncared for. We will not take such a baptism if we can find a better.

4. A better is found in yet another class of baptisms in which intusposition is sought, solely for the sake of the influence thence resulting. For example, "They baptize *into the water* a pole covered with pitch," *for the sake* of catching floating particles of gold. "Baptizing them *into the lake*," *for the purpose* of drowning them. "Baptize it *into milk*," *for the sake* of its emollient influence. "Baptizing it *into blood*," *for the purpose* of securing the means wherewith to write. (See Classic Baptism, p. 266.) In all these cases intusposition is for the sake, and solely for the sake of influence. This influence in every case is diverse in its nature, but complete in its measure. The method of securing that influence is an accident due to the nature of the case. In applying these baptisms to that which is in hand, we reject, of course, those things in which they differ; as respects 1. The agencies in the baptism. 2. The forms of action introducing into the baptism. 3. The objects to be baptized. 4. The elements within which the baptism takes place. 5. The nature of the influence sought.

In none of these particulars do these baptisms agree. Hence we see, how patent is the error which makes baptism to consist in the performance of a form of action; and, also, the error, in interpreting figurative baptisms, by converting the source of influence into a pool of simple water. Why not convert it into water impregnated with golden particles, or into a vessel filled with milk, or into a pool of blood? The fact that intusposition in simple water, *drowns*—in gold water, *gilds*—in milk, *makes emollient*—in blood, *makes red*—is proof that figurative baptisms cannot be interpreted by making any of these things the menstruum within which its object is to be placed. All the peculiarities of any medium must be eliminated. The conception must be made abstract. We thus secure the general idea of influence from intusposition. When, with this idea, we confront the phrase εἰς Μωϋσῆν, we at once recognize the purpose to express the thought of such influence (as to its measure), as results from the intusposition of an object within an enveloping medium. It does not mean that Moses is such a medium in fact. It does not mean that we shall *imagine* Moses to be such a medium; that we shall *imagine* two million men to be put within him, or within a pool of water, milk, or blood, representing him, for the writer is not a lunatic. But it means, by the verb and the preposition, to suggest an idea inherent in these words in certain relations, and apply that idea to the peculiarities of the case with which it is here connected. In doing this we use the thought of intusposition merely to reach that of influence, and having done so, throw it aside like a scaffolding, as having served its purpose.

These suggestive words having fulfilled their function, we enter upon ours as interpreters of the Apostle, and say: He declares, that Israel was made subject to the controlling influence of Moses, by means of their miraculous deliverance; even as an object is made subject to the controlling influence of any medium by which it is enveloped through an indefinitely prolonged period of time. The resemblance is in the measure of influence, not in the mode of accomplishment.

This interpretation is precisely what the exigency of the case demands. Moses had just been appointed, as he claimed, by divine authority to be head of an unorganized nation. Their position was one of the greatest possible embarrassment and peril. They had no established confidence in him. It was essential that they should have the firmest conviction of his divine mission. Under him they were to be organized into a nation. Through him they were to receive a code of stringent laws. By him they were to be introduced into a highly developed religious system. With him they were to encounter a long series of privations, perils, marches, and battles. As no other people in this world, before or since, it was necessary that Israel should have confidence in their Moses. The infinitely wise God selected this juncture to accomplish this end, so essential to all his purposes in the future. None could be more thoroughly adapted to the purpose. The liberty and life of these millions are quivering in the balances. In their judgment the scales had already gone down on the side of bondage and death. In their anguish they cry to Jehovah. In their despair they upbraid their Leader. Then, in that hour when all hope had fled, that leader's rod is stretched over the sea and deliverance bursts upon them. The cloud-witness to their Leader plants itself between them and their enemies. The dreaded sea opens a passage for them. Safe on the farther side, (the waters closed, their enemies enclosed in them,) *baptized into Moses, through this divinely attesting miraculous deliverance by sea and cloud*, voice and timbrel proclaim JEHOVAH *to be God, and* MOSES *to be his servant!*

We are now ready to answer Dr. Carson's question: "If it was not a dry baptism into empty space, between water-walls and under cloud-roof, *what was the baptism?*" It was a baptism in which Jehovah was the baptizer; the cloud and the sea were the conjoint agency; Israel's millions were the subjects; and Moses, (as claiming to be the Legate of Jehovah,) is the verbal element. In a word, this baptism declares that Israel was, hereby, *made subject to the controlling influence of Moses in his divine mission.*

In making this declaration the apostle merely repeats, in other terms, the identical sentiment uttered by Moses himself, "And the people believed the Lord and his servant Moses."

Who would take the "dry baptism" of the theory, rather than this grand baptism of inspiration? Let others choose as they may, I will choose, with the apostle, the baptism of the fleshly Israel into the type-prophet Moses, shadowing forth the baptism of the spiritual Israel into the antitype Prophet—CHRIST THE LORD!

Such is the clear, rational and God-glorifying baptism at the Red Sea as interpreted by inspiration through Paul.

THE RIVER DIVIDED BY MIRACLE.

BAPTISM BY THE JORDAN.

II KINGS 2 : 8.

"And Elijah took his mantle, and wrapped it together and smote the waters, and they were divided hither and thither, so that they two went over on dry ground."

Interpretation.

. . . *'Εν τῷ 'Ιορδάνη βαπτισάμενος, ἐπεὶ τὴν δι' ὕδατος παραδοξοτέραν διάβασιν βάπτισμα, ὡς προπαρεθέμεθα, ὠνόμασεν ὁ Παῦλος.* . . .

"But this, also, is to be observed, that Elias, when about to be received up into heaven, having taken his mantle, and wrapped it together, he smote the water, which divided hither and thither; and they both passed through, to wit, he and Elisha; for he is made more fitted to be taken up, having baptized himself by the Jordan, seeing that Paul called, as we have before shown, a more wonderful passage through water, baptism. Through this same Jordan Elisha passes to receive the gift, by Elias, which he desired, saying: 'Let a double measure of thy spirit rest upon me.' And perhaps, for this reason, he received doubly the spirit of Elias, because he twice passed through the Jordan, once with Elias and a second time when, having received the mantle of Elias, he 'smote the water, and said, Where is the God of Elias? And he smote the waters, and they divided hither and thither.'"—*Origen*, iv, 280.

. . . *'Ηλίας ἀναλαμβάνεται, ἀλλ' ὀυ χωρὶς ὕδατος· πρῶτον γὰρ διαβαίνει τὸν 'Ιορδάνην, εἶτα ἱππηλατεῖ τὸν οὐρανὸν.* . . .

"If any one desires to know why grace is given by means of water and not by means of any other of the elements, searching the divine Scriptures he will find out. For water is some great thing and the best of the four visible elements of the world. Heaven is the dwelling-place of angels, but the heavens are of the waters. The earth is the home of men, but the earth is of the waters, and before everything, of the things which were made during the creation of the six days, the Spirit of God was upborne above the water. Water was the beginning of the world, and the Jordan was the beginning of the Gospels.

Deliverance to Israel from Pharaoh was by means of (διά) the sea, and deliverance of the world from sin is by means of (διά), the washing of water, by (ἐν) the word of God. Wherever there was a covenant with any persons, there was water. After the flood a covenant was made with Noah. A covenant was made with Israel out of Mount Sinai, but with water, and scarlet wool and hyssop. Elias was taken up, but not without water, for first he passes through (διαβαίνει) the Jordan, then rides by horses to heaven. The high priest is first washed, then sacrifices. Aaron was first washed, then was high priest. For how shall he enter in to pray for others, who is not yet purified by means of (διά) water. And the laver placed within the tabernacle was a symbol of baptism."—*Cyril*, 433.

Translation.

The translation of ἐν τῷ Ἰορδάνῃ is made "*by* the Jordan," because the case seems to demand it. 1. The baptism was effected by a peculiar influence, attributed to water, and not by water, as a simple fluid. 2. The baptism was effected by Jordan, as a whole, and not by any portion of it.

But if the translation "*in* the Jordan," be insisted upon, then, 1. The phrase ἐν τῷ Ἰορδάνῃ does not, of any necessity, involve a particle of water. 2. More than this: βαπτίζω may be conjoined with the phrase ἐν τῷ Ἰορδάνῃ, and still there be no dipping into water, no covering with water, and no application of water to the person in any form, or in any measure. 3. What is most important of all, it teaches us, that after we have been told that a person has been baptized, and after we have been told the place of his baptism, and that place a river—"*in* the Jordan"—we cannot possibly, hereby, know the *quo modo* of the baptism. If any theorist should be told that "two men were baptized in the Jordan," and asked, if he could tell *how* it was done? the answer would be prompt, and in the language of Carson, "Certainly I know *how* it was done. They were either *dipped* into the water, or whoever says 'they were baptized in the Jordan,' tells a falsehood." Unfortunately, however, for this knowing theorist and his teachers, Elias and Elisha were both "baptized in the Jordan," (as they insist,) and yet neither was "dipped" into the water, or even sprinkled with it. Classic Baptism (pp. 352. 353, *et passim*) insists upon the truth, that βαπτίζω is not a self-interpreting word, as to the *modus operandi* in effecting a baptism. And here we have that position confirmed. If Cyril does tell us that the prophets were "baptized *in* the Jordan," the statement leaves us in Egyptian night as to the mode of the baptism. If we answer in what mode they were baptized, and are guided by the Greek Archbishop of Jerusalem, this will be our reply: "They were baptized in the Jordan by walking along its dry channel, within reach of that purifying influence imparted to the element water, (and not to earth, or air, or fire,) at the beginning of the creation, when 'the Holy Spirit moved upon the face of the waters.'" And this was their mode of baptism. A new style for the theorists.

It is evident that by the translation "*in* the Jordan," you meet a local fact which is to be supplemented by the agency effecting the baptism. The translation, "by the Jordan," responds to the influential agency exerted by the Jordan in accomplishing the baptism. The first translation, if adopted, must be supplemented by the last—*in* the Jordan and *by* the Jordan influence.

Patristic Interpretation.

In speaking of the translation, we have been compelled to trespass somewhat on the interpretation. The baptism being that of Origen and Cyril, the interpretation must follow their language and sentiments. If there be any persons better qualified than these Grecians, to speak with authority as to the use of a Greek word, or to teach us the true nature of a baptism, I do not know who they are.

ORIGEN.

Origen says that Elias was baptized, and that he was baptized by passing through the Jordan. The question is, as to the nature of this baptism. Was it a dipping, or an envelopment, or by a controlling influence from which envelopment is eliminated? We must be guided in our judgment by his language and known sentiments. From his usage of the word there can be no appeal. He was a Greek of the Greeks. That there was no dipping, in fact, is unquestioned. That there was no actual envelopment, is also conceded. That there was a change in the condition of Elias, fitting him for heaven, is a matter of express statement. That this change of condition was effected, instrumentally, by passing along the dry channel of the river, is also matter of distinct statement.

We say that the baptism did not consist in any modal movement of the body, nor in any modal position occupied by the body of Elias.

Proof of this is found: 1. In the fact that the modal act, moving the body of the prophet, was walking, and not dipping.

2. In the fact that there was no *intus*position. *Inter*position there was, or rather inter*motion*. But I have never understood that the one or the other was a baptism.

3. No physical movement or position will answer for the baptism of Origen. *These things won't fit the soul for heaven.* But this was the baptism which Elias received. The baptism, then, was one of influence, changing condition. Proof of this is found:

1. In the reference to the parallel passage of the Israelites through the divided sea. Origen deduces no physical mersion from this passage; but declares, that through the influence of the miracle providing this passage, under the instrumentality of Moses, they were "baptized into Moses." So, Elias was baptized through the influence of this sacred stream, purifying him and making him meet for heaven. The holy character of the Jordan, and its power over body and soul, is developed in the paragraph following the quotation under consideration. He there argues against the "offence" which might be taken in consequence of its being stated that the Jordan was "struck." That river being a "type" of Christ, "who is our Jordan," is too sacred to be *struck* by the prophet. The difficulty is met by a reference to the smiting of the rock in the wilderness—"And that rock was Christ."

He fartner states that, "As there is none good but one, even God the Father, so there is no river good, but the Jordan, which is able to cleanse from leprosy him that washes his soul, with faith, in Jesus." This stream, of such marvellous virtue, was able to baptize for heaven, him who walked between its waters.

2. Farther evidence that this baptism was one resulting from influence, changing the condition, is found in the suggestion, that Elisha received "a double measure" of the spirit of Elias, by passing *twice* through the Jordan.

CYRIL.

Cyril's conception is the same as that of Origen. It was effected by water, as an instrumental agency, and not by water or "empty space," as capable of receiving an object dipped into it. The labored effort of Cyril to show the peculiar virtue of water above every other element, settles the character of this baptism, and at the same time settles the claims of the theory. If the idea which this Patrist had of a baptism, was a dipping or a covering, why does he assume the task of showing that water has a better quality for a dipping or a covering, than has fire, earth, or air? Why does he attempt to prove that this quality was given to it by "the Spirit of God moving upon the waters" in the beginning of creation? Was this necessary to qualify water *to cover*, or to be penetrated by an object *dipped?* Cyril believed that there was a power divinely communicated to water, to purify the soul. He believed that this power belonged to it, as water, irrespective of the mode of its use. This is clearly shown by his reasoning as to its presence in every covenant transaction; its use in the washing of the high priest; in the symbol character of the laver; and by the statement that in these transactions the water was used as an instrumental means (διά), having "magna vis"—a great virtue—and not as a fluid, for dipping into.

HARMONY WITH CLASSIC USAGE.

In this usage of βαπτίζω by these Greek writers, there is no departure, not even by a hair's-breadth, from the usage of the Classics.

In Classic Baptism (p. 316, &c.) it has been shown that baptisms are effected by controlling influences, without any conception of intusposition. This evidence has been accepted as satisfactory by competent judges. It has been neither refuted nor denied by any. The baptisms of Elias and of Elisha, are of this character. As from wine, *drunk*, there proceeds an intoxicating-baptizing influence; and as from an opiate, *eaten*, there proceeds a soporific-baptizing influence; so, from *walking* between the divided waters of the type Christ Jordan, there proceeds a purifying-baptizing influence, as from the person of the antitype Jordan.

The Theory.—What, now, is the claim which the theory presents to secure this crossing of the Jordan for her list of dippings? What can be more conclusive than her argument? "Is it not clear, that the *walking down* one side of the river, and *walking up* the other side of the river, is elegantly put, by the rhetorical figure of 'a misuse of words,' for *a dipping?*" Perhaps so. At least, I think that the argument is very evidently concluded.

I only add that, in this additional "dry dipping," the water-walls of the baptistery have lost their "cloud-roof," and the walking-dipping has to be without "a covering."

PASSAGE OF THE RIVER BY MIRACLE.

BAPTISM INTO JOSHUA.

JOSHUA 3:16, 17.

"The waters which came down from above stood and rose up upon a heap very far from the city Adam, that is beside Zaretan, and those that came down toward the sea of the plain, even the salt sea, failed and were cut off; and the people passed over right against Jericho.

"And the priests that bare the ark of the covenant of the Lord stood firm on dry ground in the midst of Jordan, and all the Israelites passed over on dry ground, until all the people were passed clean over Jordan."

Interpretation.

"Et sicut de prioribus dictum est, quia, 'omnes in Moyse baptizati sunt in nube et in mari,' ita et de Jesu dicatur, quia omnes in Jesu baptizati sunt in Spiritu sancto et aqua."

"And as it was said concerning the fathers, that 'all were baptized into Moses by the cloud and by the sea,' so, also, it may be said of Jesus (Joshua), that all were baptized into Joshua by the Holy Spirit and water."—*Origen*, ii, 743.

"De iis quidem qui Mare Rubrum transierunt . . . . quod per baptismum celebratur."

"Of those who passed over the Red Sea, the Apostle says, that 'all were baptized into Moses by the cloud and by the sea.' But of those who passed over the Jordan we may also declare in like manner, that 'all were baptized into Jesus (Joshua) by the Jordan.' So that those things which are related as done in the Jordan, possess the form of a Sacrament, which is celebrated by baptism."—*Origen*, ii, 847.

Ὅτι εἶπεν ἂν καὶ περί ταύτης ὁ Παῦλος· Οὐ θέλω ὑμᾶς ἀγνοεῖν, ἀδελφοι, ὅτι οἱ πατέρες ἡμῶν πάντες διὰ τοῦ Ἰορδάνου διῆλθον, καὶ πάντες εἰς τὸν Ἰησοῦν ἐβαπτίσαντο ἐν τῷ πνεῦματι, καὶ ποταμῷ.

"Paul might say of this: 'I do not wish you, brethren, to be ignorant that all our fathers passed over *through the Jordan*, and all were baptized into Jesus (Joshua) *by the Spirit and the river*.'"—*Origen*, iv, 276.

. . . . *Τὸ δὲ εἰς Ἰησοῦν βάπτισμα, ἐν τῷ ἀληθῶς γλυκεῖ καὶ ποτίμῳ ποταμῷ, πολλὰ ἔχει παρ᾽ ἐκεῖνο ἐξαίρετα. . . . Ἐν γάρ τῷ βαπτίσασθαι εἰς Ἰησοῦν γνωσόμεθα, ὅτι θεὸς ζῶν ἐν ἡμῖν ἐστι.*

"But Jesus (Joshua) who succeeded Moses, was a type of Jesus Christ who succeeded the economy of the law by the preaching of the Gospel. Wherefore, though they all were baptized into Moses by the cloud and the sea, their baptism has something bitter and unpleasant, because still fearing their enemies. . . . But the baptism into Jesus (Joshua) by a truly sweet and potable river, has many choice things above that. . . . And Joshua said to the people, 'Sanctify yourselves, for to-morrow the Lord will do wonders among you.' . . . And the Lord said to Jesus (Joshua), 'This day will I begin to magnify thee in the sight of all Israel, *that they may know that as I was with Moses, so I will be with thee.*' 'Come hither and hear the word of the Lord our God; by this shall ye know that the living God is among you.' For by the baptism into Jesus, we know that the living God is in us. And the Lord acknowledges the reproach of Egypt to be taken away in the day of the baptism into Jesus (Joshua), when Jesus (Joshua) thoroughly purified (περιεκάθαιρεν) the children of Israel."—*Origen*, iv, 277.

LIKENESS AND UNLIKENESS TO THE RED SEA BAPTISM.

There are very obvious points of similarity, and some of dissimilarity, between this Jordan baptism and the Red Sea baptism. By considering the two, both in their agreement and disagreement, we shall find valuable aid in determining the question—What is the real character of the baptism?

Let us look at some of the points of difference which most concern us.

Dr. Carson insists, (without historical statement to sustain him, and contrary to facts so far as related,) that Israel was *in* the cloud, on the ground of a possible meaning of a preposition used by the apostle in connection with this transaction. And this, to get that for which his theory makes inexorable demand—"immersion in the cloud." He, also, insists (contrary to express historical statement,) in roofing the water-walls with the cloud, because of another preposition used by the apostle, without giving the shadow of proof that Paul had any reference to this particular occasion. And this to secure a *quasi* "immersion in water."

Every one must feel that such absolute resting on (not to say wresting of) doubtful words, and such antagonism to an historical record, would never be ventured upon except in the direst extremity. What shall be done, then, in the case of an otherwise *ditto* baptism, to meet the demands of a theory, which (like a famished ogre that can feed on nothing else) is ever crying for *dipping*, *dipping*, when there is no "*in* nube" or "*sub* nube" out of which to construct a dipping?

There is one water-wall which "heaped up" looks down

upon this baptism of Israel, and by its miracle character is instrumental in its accomplishment; but the other has run away and "immersed itself in the abysses of the sea—*maris gurgitibus fuisset immersa.*" There is then a lack of wall whereon to rest the cloud-roof, even if any cloud were present. The Red Sea baptistery, then, must be dispensed with. And with it, I suppose, must go "death, burial, and resurrection." And well they may, for this is a joyous baptism into Joshua Jesus. No enemies are pressing on from behind. The privations of the wilderness have all ceased. The land of promise is before them. How different this baptism at high noon, from that baptism by deep midnight! How different is baptismal subjection to the stern representative of Law, from the baptismal influence proceeding from the lovely type of a Gospel Saviour! But the question returns: Seeing that the baptistery is gone, what shall be done for a dipping? I cannot tell; unless, indeed, after the hard experience of the theory, it should conclude to share in that, only, immersion of which Origen speaks, and float down with the onflowing waters until it should find welcome rest,—"*Salsi maris gurgitibus immersa.*" No little specific gravity is required for a baptism in those heavy waters; but there is quite enough of leaden error in this theory to give it an honest immersion in the deepest depths of a sympathizing Dead Sea.

N. B. This Greekly immersion of the theory, by Origen, will give to it "death and burial," but will allow of no "resurrection." No dipping can be found in this "immersa."

THE BAPTISM TAUGHT BY ORIGEN.

We will now seek for some better baptism than that of the theory.

Inspiration does not speak of this transaction as a baptism. But any one who should reflect upon the perfect accord between the leading features of the passage of the Red Sea under the leadership of Moses, and the passage of the Jordan under the leadership of Joshua, would feel that if the former were a baptism into Moses, the latter must be a baptism into

Joshua. As the exigencies of the case demanded divine intervention to baptize Israel into—make thoroughly subject unto—Moses, so, like exigencies demand that they shall be baptized into—be brought thoroughly under the influence of his divinely appointed successor. And this is done by affixing the divine seal to his commission, through a most stupendous miracle wrought under his instrumentality. The object, "to magnify thee in the sight of all Israel, that they may know that as I was with Moses, so will I be with thee," and the means, "to-morrow the Lord will do wonders among you," were distinctly stated. History shows that the means were adequate to the result—"And Israel served the Lord all the days of Joshua." After reflecting on the language of Paul interpreting the passage of the Red Sea as issuing in a baptism into Moses, it occurred to me, that by parity of reasoning Israel might be said to have been baptized into Joshua at the crossing of the Jordan. The conviction of the propriety of using such language in the case, was not diminished when I found, subsequently, that Origen had been led to the same conclusion a thousand years before me. He declares, a dozen times over, that the baptism was "into Joshua." The theory, and everybody else, admits that no language is more competent to point out the element of baptism than βαπτίζω εἰς. And, unless the most satisfactory reasons to the contrary can be given, it must be regarded as pointing it out in fact.

If any one objects to Joshua being the element into which two million men are "dipped," my reply is: I object, also, to any such nonsense. Such *brobdignagian* figures belong to the theory. I claim "no soul for poetry" like this. It belongs to the lake frog class. But I do claim, that Joshua is the verbally suggested element, as pointing out the source whence influence, under God, is to proceed, bringing these millions into subjection to all the rights of his heaven-given and divinely-attested commission. And as illustrative of this verbally suggested inness, I may refer to the language of Origen in the last quotation,—"For by (ἐν) the baptism into Jesus we know that *the living God* is *in* us." Now, is it any easier for Him who fills all space to get within these bodies of ours than it is for all Israel to get within Joshua? It will be time enough to object to Origen's "baptism into Joshua," when objection is made to his—"living God entering into us." And whoever objects to the one, or the other, will probably be set down as belonging to the *crassissima Minerva* class.

Take a more modern parallel passage which happens to be under my eye.

Professor Tholuck, speaking of John Calvin says, "In the Pauline Epistles he *merges himself* in the spirit of the Apostle, and becoming one with him," &c. Now, although Calvin was not a very stout man, yet as Paul is reputed to be a very short one, it would be a tax upon the imagination to conceive how the Genevese reformer could merse himself inside of the Apostle to the Gentiles. Most probably, any who undertake the feat will give it up unaccomplished. Those for whom the German Professor wrote will be content to understand (by this verbal suggestion of sources of influence and a mode by which that influence is developed) that the more modern Paul came thoroughly under the influence of the inspired Paul—was baptized into Paul—came so controllingly under his influence as to "become one with him."

This baptism will answer quite well for the "baptism of Israel into Joshua." If they are so subjected to his influence as to "become one with him," Origen will not ask for the millions to get either inside of him, or of a pool of water.

But there is other phraseology than that employed at the Red Sea baptism, in connection with the instrumental means, which gives additional evidence to the correctness of the view now presented.

THE INSTRUMENTAL AGENCY.

1. It may be remarked, in general, that the expression βαπτίζω ἐν is not the usual form for indicating the element within which baptism takes place. I do not remember an instance among Classic writers where, with the uncompounded verb, it is so employed in connection with a fluid.

It is used, I believe, twice indicating the body as that in which the soul is mersed.

2. This phrase, βαπτίζω ἐν, is employed with varied significance. (1.) In the rare use just indicated,—"the soul baptized in (ἐν) the body." (2.) Expressing locality, place where the action occurred. Origen speaks in this connection, of a baptism "in (ἐν) Bethabara," simple locality. (3.) It expresses a period of time within which a baptism took place. Hippolytus speaks of a baptism "*in* (ἐν) that very night."

3. It marks the condition of things during the continuance of which a baptism occurred. Thus we are told of a baptism "in (ἐν) a calm."

4. It indicates the agency or instrumentality by which a baptism is effected.

Origen says, the baptism under consideration was "by (ἐν) the Holy Spirit and water."

This last statement is, of course, denied by friends of the theory. It must then be sustained by evidence. As it is admitted that ἐν may have the force attributed to it, proof in that direction is unnecessary. We are required to show that a general possibility becomes concrete in a particular necessity.

In attempting this task we remark, that the only antagonistic senses to that claimed are, 1. Locality, 2. Inness. If these are disproved, then the other, *agency*, is established.

1. The matter of locality is settled at once. "The Holy Spirit" is not a locality. "Water," the abstract element, is no more so. We have done then with ἐν as representing the place where.

2. As to "*inness*," I remark that this confronts us with these trifling embarrassments. (1.) Making two baptisms out of one "in *the Holy Spirit*" and "in *water*." (2.) One in a *person* and the other in a *thing*. (3.) The one a spiritual baptism, the other a physical baptism. This is absurd. It is farther absurd to attribute such a statement to Origen. (1.) Because there was nothing to call for a baptism of Israel "in the Holy Ghost." (2.) Because Origen did not believe in any such baptism in Old Testament times. (3.) Because

it makes Origen talk, I will not say like a theorist, but certainly like one bereft of his reason, to say, that all Israel were baptized *in water*, when the miracle was wrought to keep them out of the water.

If such are the results of attributing to ἐν the duty of pointing out the element within which the baptism takes place, we must excuse this particle from any such duty.

The field, then, is left unoccupied for ἐν, instrumental.

In this sense Origen uses it in close connection with this transaction. "Elisha desired to receive a gift *through* Elias—χάρισμα διὰ Ἠλίου;" and it is added, "he received the gift *by* the spirit of Elias upon him—χάρισμα ἐν πνεύματι Ἠλίου ἐφ' ἑαυτόν." Here διὰ and ἐν seem to be used, substantially, with the same force. And this suggests the perfectly parallel passage respecting χαρίσματα, given by the Holy Spirit—Ὧι διὰ τοῦ Πνεύματος δίδοται λόγος σοφίας . . . ἄλλῳ δὲ χαρίσματα ἰαμάτων, ἐν τῷ αὐτῷ Πνεύματι. Here, again, we have διὰ and ἐν interchanged, and expressive of the same idea of agency in bestowing "gifts."

If, now, agency suits the passage, we have a possible sense converted into an imperative sense, by the exigency of the case. And, 1. There is no embarrassment in saying, "Israel was baptized into Joshua by the Holy Spirit and water," because these two agencies can cooperate, under this miraculous working, in accomplishing this great result. 2. Divine power was not only necessary to work the miracle, but to influence the minds of the people to secure the result. "The Holy Spirit," then, and the miraculously heaped up "water" were necessary—conjoined—agencies in effecting the baptism.

In another passage Origen says, "by the Spirit and *the river*." The whole "river" was employed in this baptism, without one drop being used, even so much as to sprinkle. It was a "dry baptism," by a river of "heaped up waters." And as they passed over Jordan, gazing upon that crystal monument, ever rising higher and higher, witness from God, magnifying their new Leader, its influence brought them out of that condition of forty years' subjection to their great Moses, and brought them into a like condition of lifelong subjection to his illustrious successor.

The "baptism into Joshua, by the Spirit and the river," "by the Holy Spirit and the water," was complete.

Whatever specific difference there may be between this baptism and Classic baptisms, the principle governing the use of the word is essentially the same.

SACRIFICE CONSUMED BY MIRACLE.

BAPTISM OF THE ALTAR.

I Kings 18 : 32–38.

"And with the stones he built an altar in the name of the Lord; and he made a trench about the altar, as great as would contain two measures of seed.

"And he put the wood in order, and cut the bullock in pieces, and laid him on the wood, and said, Fill four barrels with water, and pour it on the burnt sacrifice and on the wood.

"And he said, Do it the second time. And they did it the second time. And he said, Do it the third time. And they did it the third time.

"And the water ran round about the altar; and he filled the trench, also, with water. . . .

"Then the fire of the Lord fell and consumed the burnt sacrifice, and the wood, and the stones, and the dust, and licked up the water that was in the trench."

Πόθεν δὲ ὑμῖν πεπίστευεται Ἠλίαν βαπτίσειν τὸν ἐλευσόμενον, ουδὲ τὰ ἐπὶ τὰ τοῦ θυσιαστηρίου ξύλα, κατὰ τοὺς τοῦ Ἀχαὰβ χρόνους, δεόμενα λουτροῦ, ἵνα ἐκκαυθῇ ἐπιφανέντος ἐν πυρὶ τοῦ Κυρίου, βαπτισαντος; Ἐπικελεύεται γὰρ τοῖς ἱερεῦσι τοῦτο ποιῆσαι. . . .

Ὁ τοίνυν μὴ αὐτὸς βαπτίσας τότε, . . . πῶς βαπτίζειν ἔμελλε; Χριστὸς οὖν ουκ ἐν ὕδατι βαπτίζει, ἀλλ' οἱ μαθηταὶ αὐτοῦ· ἑαυτῷ δὲ τηρεῖ τὸ ἁγίῳ Πνεύματι βαπτίζειν καὶ πυρί.

"But why do you believe that the Elias to come will baptize, when he did not, in the time of Ahab, baptize the victim upon the wood of the altar, which needed cleansing, at the appearing of the Lord by fire? For he commands the priests to do this. . . . How, then, is he, coming according to the words of Malachi, to baptize, since he did not baptize then, but committed the work to others? Christ, therefore, did not baptize with water, but his disciples. He reserves to himself the baptizing by the Holy Spirit and fire."—*Origen*, iv, 241.

Ἔδειξεν Ἠλίας τοῦ βαπτίσματος τὴν ἰσχὺν ἐπὶ τοῦ βωμοῦ τῶν ὁλοκαυτωμάτων ὀυ διὰ τοῦ πυρὸς, ἀλλὰ δι᾽ ὕδατος τὴν θυσίαν ὁλοκαυτώσας. . . .

"Elias has shown the power of baptism by burning the sacrifice upon the altar of burnt-offerings, not by means of fire, but by means of water. For although the nature of fire is opposed to that of water, yet when the water is mystically poured, thrice, upon the altar, the fire begins, and kindles a flame, as though it were oil."—*Basil Magnus*, iii, 428.

Ἔχω τρεῖς ἐπικλύσεις κατὰ τῶν σχιδάκων, αἷς καθιερώσω τὴν θυσίαν, ὕδατι πῦρ ἐγείρων, τὸ παραδοξότατον; καὶ τοὺς προφήτας καταβαλῶ τῆς αἰσχύνης, μυστηρίου δυνάμει χρώμενος.

"I have three overpourings upon the wood, with which I will hallow the sacrifice, kindling fire by water, which is most wonderful; and I will cast down the false prophets, using the power of the mystery."—*Gregory Naz.*, ii, 421.

"Siquidem baptismus velut ignis quidam peccata consumit; quia Christus in igne et Spiritu baptizat. Denique hunc typum legis in Regnorum libris, ubi Elias super altare ligna imposuit, et dixit ut mitterent super de hydriis aquam et dixit: . . . . et cum manaret aqua, precatus est Elias, et ignis descendit de cœlo. Tu es homo super altare, qui ablueris aqua, cujus exuritur culpa, ut vita renovetur. . . .

"Typum baptismatis demonstravit Elias, et cœlum aperuit. . . . Nemo enim nisi per aquam et Spiritum ascendit in regnum cœlorum."

"Since baptism, like a fire, consumes sins, for Christ baptizes by fire and Spirit. Finally, thou readest this type in the books of the Kings, where Elias placed wood upon the altar, and directed that they should cast over it water from water-pots, . . . and when the water flowed, Elias prayed, and fire descended from heaven. Thou, O man! art upon the altar, who shalt be cleansed by water, whose sin is burned up that thy life may be renewed.

"Elias showed a type of baptism, and opened heaven, which had been shut three years and six months. . . . For no one can ascend into the kingdom of heaven except by (*per*) water and the Spirit."—*Ambrose*, i, 727, 728.

EXPERIMENTUM CRUCIS.

This baptism of the altar furnishes a crucial test for the theory. I have never known a friend of the theory voluntarily to speak of this baptism. Whenever their attention is called to it by others, they approach it as reluctantly as the victim comes to the altar where death glitters in the edge of the sacrificial axe.

There is a painful foreboding of some fatal blow.

True, there are scores of cases which do as fatally brain the theory; but some word, or thought, or thing, by its presence or absence, or some figure, rational or irrational, gives material out of which to raise a cloud, under whose shadow there may be a way of escape. Here, from the nature of the transaction, from the locality where it takes place, and from the fulness and explicitness of language, there is less opportunity to mystify the statement, or to elude the damaging blow. At the sea-coast baptism, where "dip, and nothing but dip," seemed hopelessly to perish, he was charmingly revived by a potion of poetry applied through "covered and bare!" At the Red Sea baptism, where there was no dipping, and no chance for poetry through a tidal wave, two prepositions (ἐν and ὑπὸ) are converted into architects, and lo! in a trice, a baptistery arises, within which "death, burial, and resurrection" are enacted *secundum artem*. In the baptism of Elijah the roof is taken from the baptistery, but then there is the going down and the coming up, which answers, in poetry, for "dip," just as well as "covered and bare." And, in the baptism under Joshua, although the baptistery is still farther dilapidated by the loss of one of its walls, still there is the bed of the river left, and that will still "darkly shadow" a grave and burial. All this being admitted to be unanswerable (and, in all good conscience, I can say that I do most sincerely think that it is very embarrassing to answer such flights of poetry, and such feats of architecture), we come to the case in hand.

Here we have no tidal wave to poetize this altar baptism. We have no prepositions wherewith to build water-houses without any water in them. We have no bed of the sea to convert into a sepulchre. We have no channel of a river into which we may "go down," and out of which we may "come up." We are not even at the edge of a pool where a baptism must be by dipping, or the inspired writer "tells a falsehood." We are not introduced to a baptism by "washing" at a tent door to be silenced by the revelation, that "washing may be by dipping, and that baptism washing must be by dipping." We have not a baptism by sprinkling, to be pointed to "a washing" at some other time and place as the baptism, for "sprinkling cannot baptize." We have not the case of hot iron baptized by cold water poured upon it, to hear the smiling solution—"the pouring was long enough to cover it, and the covering was the baptism." We have no one baptized by an opiate pill, to be schooled in that rhetoric which dips sleepers, by figure, into pools of water. We are on the top of old Carmel. Seas, rivers, pools, water-walls, clouds, dry channels, goings down and comings up, have all disappeared from the scene. We have indeed a washing; but we are expressly told that it was without a dipping. And we have a pouring; but we are as explicitly told that it was *not* "continued long enough to cover."

What is to be done with this Carmel baptism?

Let the friends of the theory answer:

"*Any child can understand it means a dipping.*"—Carson.

On this very remarkable baptism Dr. Carson has the following paragraph:

"Dr. Miller (of Princeton) tells us that Origen was contemporary with Cyprian, and that he, in commenting on I Kings 18:33, tells us that 'Elijah baptized the wood on the altar.' This proceeds on a principle I have often explained and illustrated. Every child knows that our word immerse may be used in the same way."

And this is all that Dr. Carson has tc say on a case which, on the face of it, utterly destroys his theory as to the meaning of βαπτίζω, and nullifies the "demonstration" which sums up his life labor.

It seems impossible that Dr. C. could ever have read the passage which he so cavalierly expounds. There is not the shadow of evidence for the baptism turning on the quantity of water used. The amount of water was to satisfy all, that there was no concealed fire. The use of the word baptize contemplates a wholly different aspect of the altar and sacrifice. They needed "cleansing" (λουτροῦ) to be acceptable to God.

But let us look at that "principle" so often explained that it has become too wearisome even to state.

It is probable that he refers to the explanation given of the sea-coast baptism, in which he says,—"When this word (βαπτίζω) is applied to an object lying under water, but not actually dipped, the mode essentially denoted by it is as truly expressed as in any other instance of its occurrence—figuring the object which is successively bare and buried under water, as being dipped when it is covered, and as emerging when it is bare. Can any child, then, be at a loss to learn from this that baptism means to lay under water?"

The Academiciens of Paris having been asked by Dr. Franklin, "why, when a fish was put into a vessel filled with water it would not overflow?" very learned answers were given, based on the nature of the fish, to show that it must be so; but they were declared to be unsatisfactory. Being asked for the solution of the phenomenon, he gave them this piece of advice: "Gentlemen, before giving reasons for a fact be sure of the existence of the fact. *I think the vessel will run over.*" Before Dr. C. accounts so learnedly for βαπτίζω being used in a covered and bare figure dipping, it might be well to inquire whether there is any such conception in the word. I think that there is none. But even if there were any such idea ever associated with this word, the altar is not "lying under water," and therefore the application fails. But we have another exposition of this "open sesame" principle to which all obstacles to the theory must give way.

It is called upon in the case of Nebuchadnezzar and the

dew. He says, "It will be of importance to settle the question though it should occupy some pages." After "some pages" we have this result: "Without doubt the verb expresses, here, mode as well as anywhere else. . . . The Holy Spirit by Daniel used the word signifying to immerse, when speaking of the wetting of Nebuchadnezzar by the dew, to enliven the style. . . . Wetting by the gentlest distillation in nature, is here, in the liveliest and most imaginative language, figured as an immersion." . . . "Can any child then be at a loss," &c.

Whether, in this application of the principle, this "lively and imaginative language" extends to figuring the king as "lying under water," when the dew was on him, and as "bare" when the beams of the sun had dried up the moisture, we are not told. And having "no soul for poetry," I am not able to throw any light upon the matter. However, we have "the principle often explained and illustrated," which is to illuminate the Carmel baptism. We are by "a lively imagination" to conceive of the altar as "lying under water," while the water is poured, and "bare" when the pouring stops. Then convert the action of pouring into the action of dipping, and you have a lively and imaginative expression for an immersion.

Now, "can any child fail to understand" from this *flowing* tide, *falling* dew, and *pouring* water, that "βαπτίζω means to dip, and nothing but dip, through all Greek literature?"

So long as the appeal is made to children, (and this is quite a favorite refrain with Dr. C.,) I have nothing to say. The audience and the ratiocination seem to be very well adapted to each other.

One remark, however, I may be permitted to make:—When an object is said to be baptized, and the manner of the baptism is not stated, Dr. C. will not listen to the suggestion of any other mode of baptizing than by dipping. No "principle," no "figure," no "beautiful play of the imagination" is tolerated. It is all plain, prose, dipping. If instead of an altar "a couch" is to be baptized, no "flow of water," no "gentle distillation," no "pouring" can have a hearing.

The couch must be "lifted up by pulleys," or must be "taken to pieces" by a bed-screw, and carried forth for a dipping. If a man is to be baptized in a desert, no pouring, no dewy sprinkling, must be mentioned. "The word shall find the water and do the dipping."

Such statements fully justify us in saying: "If this Carmel altar had been declared to be baptized, without the historical statement of the mode, Dr. C. would have insisted, either that there was a pool on the top of the mountain, into which the altar was dipped, or that it was 'taken to pieces,' like the couch, and carried down the mountain to the shore of the sea, and dipped into the Mediterranean."

If objection should be raised that such a baptism would be a heavy task for the prophet, the answer would be at hand, "Where were the tribes of Israel?" Such "demonstrations" of dipping, the Baptist world receives with exultant joy, and laments that "it is not light that is most wanted, but religious honesty," on the part of those that cannot see it.

Such extravagant interpretations ignore the laws of language, modifying the meanings of words; conflict with Carson's own judgment, in assigning to the word "enlighten" (Figurative Language, p. 278) a secondary meaning; and condemns his own condemnation of Gale on the ground of bad rhetoric.

"*It is a drench, surround, steep-baptism.*"—FULLER.

We pass on to Dr. Fuller's treatment of this baptism.

"Our opponents tell us that Origen says, of the wood and sacrifice of Elijah's altar, that they were baptized. But as we are inquiring into the meaning of βαπτίζω at the time the Saviour used it, and as Origen lived two hundred years after this period, I have not thought it worth while to examine this case. (!) Suffice it to say, that Origen's meaning is plain. . . Origen was one of the most impassionate of men; dealing in bold metaphors and allegories; and who but sees the force of his words? . . . What was the idea in Origen's mind? It was an immersion. . . . In the case of Elijah's altar, the twelve barrels of water were first poured, and the trenches all around filled, and it is the effect of this, it is the thus being drenched, surrounded, and steeped, which Origen figuratively calls a baptism."

Dr. Fuller is evidently preparing for some sad catastrophe, as with funereal step he approaches Elijah's altar. His "two hundred years after Christ;" "most impassionate of men;" "allegories and metaphors;" "who but sees?" "I have not thought it worth while to examine the case;" sound very much like a requiem at the death and burial of the theory. The dénouement explains it all. He was invited to a baptism by the great Grecian Instructor of the Alexandrian school, and instead of taking him down a river's bank, he conducts him up a mountain's side; and there he witnesses the rite administered, not by "going down into the water and coming up," not by "dipping or covering," but by the simple outpouring of water. Now, it will not answer for the Baptist to come to open war with the Greek, so he makes the best terms possible, and very affably says: "Your misuse of terms is quite excusable; nay, highly rhetorical. Who cannot see the impassioned poetry which converts the *act* of dipping into '*a drenching, surrounding, and steeping* EFFECT?'"

To argue or expostulate with those who can originate or accept such figures, is all in vain. Gale will still dip his lake in the frog's blood, and the theorists will still dip Carmel's altar by "drenching, surrounding, and steeping." We must be content, with the rest of the "enlightened but dishonest" world, to believe that Origen meant just what he said, and that the altar was baptized by pouring water upon it.

I do not know whether we should most rejoice or regret, that the theorists are tending steadily toward those regions (abounding in light, but void of honesty) which we inhabit. There is this comfort, however, we will try and keep our "light," while they will bring "honesty" enough for us all. Thus we can live with a fair fame and in goodly fellowship. In the meantime we will mark the progress of Dr. Fuller, as the representative man of the coming theorists.

1. He once wrote on this wise, making baptism centre in

the performance of a *definite* act: "In commanding his disciples to be baptized, Jesus knew *what act* he enjoined, and he could have been at no loss to express his meaning."

2. He eviscerates baptism, subsequently, of all definite act, thus: "*It matters not how* the baptism is effected."

3. He again stretches out his wand, and lo! all act has disappeared from the essence of the word, and it is turned into a *condition:* "Suppose a man should lie in the baptistery while it is filling by water poured into it. The pouring would not be an immersion (baptism), yet an immersion (baptism) would take place if he remained long enough."

4. And now condition, in turn, disappears, and *effect* takes its place: "It is the *effect* of this; it is the thus being drenched, surrounded, and steeped, which Origen figuratively calls a baptism."

But the marvel is, that having thus passed from definite act to general act, and from general act to condition, and from condition to effect, he should talk of an opponent after this manner: "One of the latest and most prominent of our opponents, drops altogether the *act*, and assures us that βαπτίζω means"—an effect. . . . "It is appalling to think how many receive the sentiments of these authors, and quiet themselves by their assertions. One consolation, however, is left: it is plain from this last feeble attempt to defend"—an effect—"that the case is becoming desperate; that God is causing error to culminate, and show itself on an eminence, and thus be exposed before all."

Strongly said, for one who has brought baptism to the issue of "effect," on this mountain top. The "eminence" to which God has brought the "error" of this theory, for its culmination, is that same old Carmel where the "error" of Baal's worshippers was exposed. There, at the feet of the grand old prophet, (solitary but glorious and triumphant defender of Jehovah and his truth,) do these good brethren, "exposed before all," lay down their error, which affirms that the Lord Jesus Christ commanded "nothing but *an act*." As surely as Baal was no God; so surely is "the theory" no truth.

One more illustration of the treatment of this baptism, and I will leave it. R. Ingham (Handbook on Christian Baptism, London, octavo, pp. 620) says, (p. 530): "Origen, who died A.D. 254, is quoted as saying, that 'Elias did not baptize the wood upon the altar, but commanded the priests to do that.' When our friends begin thus to baptize the dear babes brought to them, to have a good work wrought on them, we believe that 'the right of election' will lead to the choice of a single immersion as more convenient than such a trine pouring as caused the water to run 'round about the altar,' and 'filled the trench also with water.' And we rather opine that such a practice would help in perceiving that the baptism enjoined in God's word is nothing else than immersion."

Well, I suppose that when good argument has ceased, and bad rhetoric will no longer answer, we must take the best jokes that can be got up. And if this joke about "the dear babes," is the very best that "R. Ingham" can get off, we must accept it, excusing its heaviness on the ground of a naturally dolorous spirit, in view of the failure of the theory under the *experimentum crucis* of Mount Carmel.

The theorists having been allowed to interpret this baptism according to their own conceptions, we find that their methods for escape under difficulties are both various and inconsistent. This we would expect from fundamental error in the conception of the nature of a baptism. Error is multiform. Truth is uniform. Not only are their interpretations discordant and disregardful of the principles of language, but some of them, at least, bear internal evidence that the passage in the original had never been examined.

ORIGEN.

We will, now, let the Patrists speak and expound this baptism by their own language and principles.

1. The word *βαπτίζω* as used by Origen in this case has nothing to do with a "dipping" as claimed by Carson.

The conversion of the acts of "flowing,' "falling," "pouring," by figure, into the act of *dipping*, Dr. C.'s own friends unite to repudiate.

It has nothing to do with "passion," "metaphor," "allegory," "drenching," "surrounding," "steeping," (Fuller.)

Origen is making a cool, critical examination as to the justness of Jewish opinion in relation to the administrators of baptism, and grounds his argument, largely, on the leading feature of this baptism, viz., that it was not effected by Elias personally. We do not look for passion, or metaphor, or allegory, in a critical argument. The word has as little to do with "drenching," "surrounding," and "steeping." The logical and grammatical relation of the word is in an entirely different direction. Its relation is with τὰ δεόμενα λουτροῦ, "that which needed *cleansing*." A newly built altar was required to be "cleansed and purged" (Ezekiel 43 : 18–20). The appointed mode of cleansing was not adopted by the prophet; nor does the Scripture say that he used the water for cleansing; but our business is with Origen and his conceptions, who uses the word. He believed, for he expressly declares, that a "cleansing was necessary." Now it is, precisely, to meet this exigency that Origen uses the word. With the form employed to effect this cleansing βαπτίζω has nothing to do either by intrinsic force or grammatical relation. This conclusion, reached by the study of this particular passage, is in harmony with all other writings of this Patrist. The force of βαπτίζω is expounded by τὰ δεόμενα λουτροῦ,—"he did not, himself, baptize (cleanse) that which needed cleansing."

2. Origen's use of the word has no more to do with "*twelve* barrels of water" and their "soaking effect," than it has to do with the act of pouring.

According to the phraseology there were three baptisms. The priests were commanded, (according to Origen,) "to baptize the altar by pouring four barrels, or pitchers, of water upon it." This command they obeyed, and the altar was baptized. They were commanded to baptize it a second time and in the same way. This, also, they did, and the altar was baptized a second time. The command was repeated yet again, and again it was obeyed, and the altar was baptized a third time. This is the only just interpretation of the language employed. And it is sustained by the well-known Patristic trine baptism. If, then, this be a "soaking" baptism, it must be made out of *four* pitchers of water poured over a slain bullock, wood and stones. But such a baptism, laid at the door of this learned Greek, is enough to wake him from the dead to defend his fair fame.

3. Since "the twelve barrels" have been transformed into "four pitchers," and one-fourth of one would have answered just as well for Origen's baptism, (although not so well to prove that the prophet had "put no fire under,") "the dear children brought to have a good work wrought upon them" need not feel so very much alarmed.

BASIL MAGNUS.

The "effect" which Dr. Fuller attributes to this baptism,—"drenching and steeping," is not much like the effect attributed to it by Basil. The one thinks it is called a baptism because the altar becomes watersoaked; the other says it is in fact a baptism, because it brings its own credentials in "the power" to kindle a devouring fire. There is "power" in baptism, (that is, in the water used in baptism mystically poured thrice,) not to make very wet (!), but to burn up sacrifice and altar stones, or to burn up the sins of the soul. Those who do not like Patristic theology are at full liberty to reject it; but those who do not like their philology must first show, that the Greeks did not understand Greek, before they can be allowed to thrust a "drenching" into the place of a *purification*, or a "soaking" into the place of a *burning*.

GREGORY NAZIANZEN.

"*Three* OVERPOURINGS." This language is used without the slightest hesitation by Gregory, and in accordance with all Patristic usage and sentiment, to denote baptism.

"*With which I will hallow the sacrifice.*" Again, we have evidence that the Patrists attributed to water "a power" not to make wet, but "to make holy" by "three *pourings*." Water of baptism is, with them, an agency.

"*The* POWER *of the mystery.*" If anything has been established by these multiplied examples of baptism which have engaged our attention, it has been proved, that "the power of the mystery" has nothing to do with the manner in which the element (in which this "power" resides) is used. Three overpourings irrespective of quantity, or, once walking through the dried Jordan, will equally well baptize.

They equally well baptize, not because of the action in pouring or walking; not because of the effect, wet or dry; but because of a development of "the power" *changing the condition*, either of the victim on the altar, making it hallowed for God's acceptance in sacrifice, or of Elijah, making him hallowed for God's fellowship in heaven.

AMBROSE.

Ambrose says, the water of baptism burns up sin, and, that the baptism on Carmel, by which the sin offering was burned up, was a type baptism.

He also likens the person about to be baptized by himself, to the victim laid upon Carmel's altar, and declares that he shall be "cleansed by water—*qui ablueris aqua*" (the Latin daguerreotype of Origen's statement—τὰ δεόμενα λουτροῦ) "and his sins burned up."

It will, I think, be admitted by the theorists themselves, that there is no little difference between their conceptions of this baptism and that entertained by the Patrists; while doubtless they will think—so much the worse for the Greeks. For has it not been discovered in these latter days, that "βαπτίζω means dip and nothing but dip through all Greek literature?" Something which Origen, and Basil, and Gregory, and Ambrose never knew.

THE ERROR.

Baptist writers find themselves involved in inextricable difficulties in the interpretation of this and kindred baptisms, by reason, 1. Of a fundamental misconception of the meaning of βαπτίζω, supposing it to express *action* rather than to make demand for *condition*. 2. From supposing that it has no secondary meaning. They involve themselves in precisely the same difficulties which they did so long as they denied to βάπτω a secondary meaning. Then, when a berry was pressed in the hand and the hand was said to be *bapted* (dipped), of course, as there is but one meaning to the word, it was necessary to make out a *dipping*. This must be done in the Carson style by making one act (press) figure in the place of another act (dip); or, in the Fuller method, making the *wetness* caused by the juice of the berry to figure (by its likeness in effect) a dipping. So, the hand wet by blackberry-juice is figuratively dipped into it, under the patronage of "poetry" and "passion." By the assignment of a secondary meaning to βάπτω—(to dye), this swollen balloon filled with poetry, passion, and figure, has been pricked, and has collapsed into plain prose. All this, *mutatis mutandis*, applies to their interpretation of βαπτίζω. They can never interpret the usage of this word by the laws of language and common sense, without a fundamental modification of their conception as to its meaning.

This baptism must be interpreted from a Patristic-Judaic point of view. The altar and the sacrifice are Judaic; the interpretation of the water used as effecting a baptism, is Patristic. There is no baptism resultant from the ordinary physical qualities of water. There is no act by which the altar and victim are "put into and under water." There is no act by which the water is brought upon the altar and sacrifice "long enough" to cover it over. These are admitted facts.

To make out a baptism, where there is no baptism according to their "axioms," the theorists resort, as we have seen, to all sorts of devices. And the result is, that no one of their writers seems to satisfy any other, and, indeed, not to satisfy himself. And no wonder, for there is no satisfaction to be found in the direction in which they are looking. One might as well look toward the Southern Cross for the North Star.

This baptism is not one of primary physical baptism. It is not one of intusposition simply, nor of intusposition with or for influence; but it is a baptism without intusposition—

a change of condition effected through the influence of the baptizing agency. The water is the baptizing agency. Origen, Basil, Gregory, and Ambrose, believed that there was a "power" in water "mystically poured thrice," to change thoroughly the condition of the object to which it was applied. They believed that the condition of this slain bullock was thoroughly changed ("purified," "hallowed," "made meet for the Lord at his coming by fire") through the "mystery" of the water poured upon it. Therefore they said it was baptized.

In this use of the word there is the sternest adherence to the principle regulating the word in Classic usage.

It is the natural, not mystical, "power" of water which changes the condition, baptizes hot iron when poured over it. It is the natural, not mystical, "power" of water which changes the condition, baptizes wine when poured into it. It is the natural, not mystical, "power" of wine which changes the condition, baptizes a man when it is poured into him. But it is the mystical, and not natural, "power" of water which changes the condition, baptizes the sacrifice upon the altar. The baptism is Judaic in its character. It introduces its object into a condition of ceremonial purification.

Could any interpretation meet more absolutely the demands of a case? Could any interpretation be in more absolute harmony with the laws of language? Could any interpretation be more fully vindicated by Classic usage? Could any interpretation be more crucially fatal to "the theory?"

We, now, close the testimony of Grecian and Latin writers in applying βαπτίζω to the facts and ceremonials of Old Testament history. That testimony is given so abundantly, so uniformly, so explicitly, and so authoritatively, that few will, henceforth, hold in much regard the theory which proclaims "a dipping and nothing but a dipping, or at least a covering, through all Greek literature."

APOCRYPHA.

BAPTISM AND MIRACLE.

ALTAR BAPTIZED BY SPRINKLING.

II Maccabees 1: 19–36.

"For when our fathers were led into Persia, the priests that were then devout, took the fire of the altar privily, and hid it in an hollow place of a pit without water, where they kept it sure, so that the place was unknown to all men.

"Now after many years, when it pleased God, Neemias being sent from the King of Persia, did send of the posterity of those priests that had hid it, to the fire: but where they told us they found no fire, but thick water;

"Then commanded he them to draw it up (ἀπο βαψάντας·), and to bring it; and when the sacrifices were laid on, Neemias commanded the priests to sprinkle (ἐπιῤῥᾶναι τῷ ὕδατι) with the water, the wood and the things laid thereupon.

"When this was done, and the time came that the sun shone, which afore was hid in the cloud, there was a great fire kindled, so that every man marvelled.

. . . "Now when the sacrifice was consumed, Neemias commanded the water that was left to be poured on the great stones.

"When this was done, there was kindled a flame; but it was consumed by the light that shined from the altar.

"So when this matter was known, it was told the King of Persia, that in the place where the priests that were led away had hid the fire, there appeared water, and that Neemias had purified (ἥγνισαν) the sacrifices therewith. . . . . . And Neemias called this thing Naphthar, which is as much as to say a cleansing (καθαρισμός)."

Interpretation.

"Superioris eventus ac potissimum oblati a Neemias sacrificii narratione, Sanctum Spiritum, Christianorumque baptisma significari;

"Arbitror quod nec ignem istum possimus ignorare, cum legerimus quia baptizat Dominus Jesus in Spiritu Sancto et igni.

"Quid ergo sibi vult esse quod ignis aqua factus est, et aqua ignem excitavit; nisi quia spiritalis gratia per ignem exurit, per aquam mundat peccata nostra?

. . . "Eliæ quoque tempore descendit ignis, . . . hostiam suam tertio ipse perfudit aqua, et manabat aqua in circuitu altaris, et exclamant, et cecidit ignis a Domino de cœlo, et consumpsit holocaustum.

"Hostia illa tu es."

"The narrative of the preceding event (see Levit. 9:24), and especially of the sacrifice offered by Nehemiah, betokens the Holy Spirit and the baptism of Christians.

"I think that we cannot be ignorant as to this fire, since we learn that the Lord Jesus baptizes by the Holy Spirit and fire.

"What then means the fire was made water, and the water kindling the fire, except that spiritual grace, by fire, burns, and by water, cleanses our sins?

. . . "Fire also in the time of Elias descended, . . . he bathed the victim with water thrice, and the water flowed around the altar, and they cry out, and fire fell from the Lord out of heaven, and consumed the burnt-offering.

"Thou art that victim."—*Ambrose*, iii, 174.

SPRINKLING BAPTISM.

It was stated in Classic Baptism (p. 346), "that *a state of complete purification* induced by the sprinkling of Ibis water, is as legitimate and true a baptism, interpreted by Classic Greek, as would be *a state of complete covering* of the body sunk to the bottom of the Nile."

"Sprinkling demands, not as of grace but as of absolute right, the acknowledgment of its power to baptize."

This statement we re-affirm, after having largely considered Judaic and Patristic usage. Unnumbered examples sustain the position. The case before us furnishes yet another. It teaches us, immediately, through Ambrose, and with the unanimous consent of every Classic, Jewish, and Patristic writer, that a sprinkling which is capable of thoroughly changing the condition of its object, is capable of baptizing that object.

Every sprinkling will not baptize; because a baptism does not result from the mere act, or, from the sprinkling of any and every fluid or substance. It is essential that the thing sprinkling should have a controlling power over the condition of the object sprinkled, which power finds development by such action. In all such cases I maintain, that a most Greekly baptism (without any help from figure and without favor from any quarter) is effected. Thus Nehemiah's altar and sacrifice were baptized by water sprinkled upon them, being purified through a special "virtue" belonging to the fire-water.

"BAPTISM (IMMERSION) BY SPRINKLING, ABSURD."

Dr. Conant (p. 99) quotes Alex. de Stourdza, Russian State Councillor of the Greek Church, as saying: "It is an abuse of words and of ideas, to practise *baptism* by *aspersion*, this very term being, in itself, a derisive contradiction. The verb *βαπτίζω*, *immergo*, has in fact but one sole acceptation. It signifies, literally and always, *to plunge*. Baptism and immersion are, therefore, identical, and to say, *baptism by aspersion*, is as if one should say, *immersion by aspersion*, or any other absurdity of the same nature."

As Dr. Conant declines to be bound by his own quoted authority, as to the defining of *βαπτίζω* "literally and always *to plunge*," and feels at liberty, or feels the necessity for nullifying that "literally and always," by adding six other defining words, showing that, in his judgment, his friend was quite at fault in his definition; and as Booth thinks that "plunge, literally and always," "would make our sentiments ridiculous," I do not know why we should be required to strait-jacket ourselves in the Stourdza opinion, as to the absurdity of a baptism, or immersion, by aspersion.

The Greek Councillor forgot his Greek, when he said, that there was any essential absurdity in the phrase, (to take it in the strongest and baldest form in which the case can be put,) "*immersion* by *sprinkling*."

The Septuagint says: "Nebuchadnezzar was *dipped* by the *falling* dew-*drops*."—"Ah! yes," replies the theorist, "it does seem to be absurd to talk of *dipping* by *dropping;* but it is not so in fact. There is a lofty vein of poetry, and highly wrought figure in such expressions, which not only imbue it with all that is rational, but invest it with a sparkling, rhetorical beauty."

Well, and what do you say of the Father of Medicine speaking of "garments *dipped* by *drops* falling on them?"—"In good sooth, the absurdity is, on the face of the statement, the same; but we expound the absurdity out of it in another way. We now lay aside poetry and figure (which we once used in this case), and take the statement as literal. It might be thought that, in doing so, we would certainly run against 'the absurdity.' But we do not. We turn a sharp corner, by the help of a secondary meaning, and find this 'absurd' phraseology to be most rational."

And how do you treat the same "absurdity" as uttered by the Romans, *e. g.*, "pastures *dipped* by dew-*drops?*"—"As we have not yet agreed to allow the Latins a secondary meaning for 'dip' when used with pure water, we again fall back on poetry, and are lost in admiration of the beautiful figure by which the grassy plains, and hills, and valleys are, by the giants of rhetoric, picked up and *dipped.* Thus the absurd vanishes and the rational appears."

And is the elimination effected in the same way when Ovid speaks of "the body *dipped* by *sprinkled* water?"—"Not exactly. We do not think it prudent to resort to these highest flights of poetry and rhetoric except under pinching necessity. We seek, then, first to change the word *tingere* to *tangere*, but in case of failure we fall back on our reserved poetry and figure, which takes away all 'absurdity.'"

And are English writers, who use the same absurd language as do the Romans and the Greeks, converted into sensible men by the same process? What of Comus, whom "dew-drops *dip* all over?"—"We are highly favored in that case. Spirits and nymphs abound. We have only to imagine the dew to be some elfin sprite which picks up the Leader of fun and 'dips him all over' in some convenient pool, and all is rational. Some might suppose that it would be better to get rid of the 'absurdity' by allowing a secondary meaning to dip (*wet*), but having once refused any secondary meaning to the Greek 'dip,' and having been compelled to give that up and to admit *dye* as a true meaning, it would look too bad to have to concede, still farther, the meaning *to wet.* In refusing this meaning to the Greek word, we must do the same to the Latin, and the English word, and rely solely upon poetry and rhetoric to help us out."

And what do you say of the "immersion by sprinkling" of Triptolemus?—"Oh! Sir Walter Scott, you know, was a poet. And although this statement is made in very plain prose, yet the 'absurdity' must be taken out of it by putting into it a strong poetic afflatus. He was figuratively *dipped.*"

It would seem, then, that this very "absurd" mode of expression has been very widely adopted by Greek, and Latin, and English writers. And if we should choose to speak of a *dipping*, or an *immersion*, by *sprinkling*, we shall use language with just the same "absurdity" as that with which it has been used by the learned and the wise among all cultivated nations for some thousands of years.—"Ah! but they used dip and immerse with a modified meaning."

And can you not give us the benefit of a like license of usage?—"No; for, then, we must abandon the theory—'one meaning, *dip*, *plunge*, *sink*, *immerse*, *immerge*, *submerge*, *bathe*, *whelm*, *overwhelm*, &c., &c., through all Greek literature.'"

Well; keep this very remarkable "one meaning," which is so free from "absurdity;" but do spare us, in the interpretation of our language, the sublimities of poetry or the profundities of rhetoric. We mean to speak in the most unadorned prose. And with our hand upon the garment which Hippocrates "dips" by *sprinkled* coloring drops, we will venture to defend the altar *baptized* by sprinkled napthar, even though somebody should think it very "absurd" to contradict their theory by talking like the classic Greeks and Romans.

Napthar = Καθαρίσμος

In the term, "purification," applied by Nehemiah to this fire-water after he had purified the altar with it, we see how words obtain wider extensions of meaning.

Purification, properly, denotes an effect produced by some agency. But, here, that term denotes the agency itself.

In precisely the same manner, that which produces a condition of cleansing (βαπτίσμα) takes its name from the condition effected. Thus Anastasius speaks of *water* as "baptism," because it effects a baptism. "*Baptism* is poured into water-pots, and they are baptized by the *baptism* poured into them." (Bibl. Patr., v, 958.) Baptism, here, cannot mean immersion, because there is no immersion effected. That which is employed to effect the thorough cleansing peculiar to baptism, has obtained the name of the effect produced.

So, "two baptisms," water and blood, come from the Saviour's side.

Napthar, *wine*, *sanctified water*, *heifer ashes*, were agencies which, severally, had "power," "virtue," "force" to BAPTIZE *by sprinkling* and otherwise, Stourdza to the contrary, notwithstanding.

AMBROSE.

Ambrose says: "This baptism was especially significant of Christian baptism." It is not Christian baptism, but it is a baptism; and by reason of the agencies operating, and the nature of the effect produced, it had a vividness of significance beyond ordinary type baptisms. The sacrifice of Abel's lamb was significant of the great atoning sacrifice of Calvary; but the sacrifice of Isaac, by his father, was a far more significant type of the sacrifice of "the only begotten Son of the Father."

The resemblance between the baptism of Nehemiah and Christian baptism is expressly declared by Ambrose. It is not found in any *form of act* done, nor in any resultant *covered* condition. It consists in the use of fire and water, as agencies, and in the purified condition consequent upon their influence. "I think that we cannot be ignorant as to this fire, since we learn that the Lord Jesus baptizes by the Holy Spirit and fire. What, then, means the fire made water, and the water kindling the fire, except, that spiritual grace by fire, burns, and by water, cleanses our sins."

This is Ambrose's own exposition; and how utterly it ignores a *dipping*, I need not say.

COMMON FEATURE.

This is the last of those baptisms with which miracle is (really or supposedly) associated. In glancing back over them we see many diversities in them, and some points of resemblance. Their common fitness to shadow forth the baptism of Christianity cannot be in the things in which they differ; nor can it be in minor points in which they agree. There must be some one, bold, outstanding point of agreement by which they are fitted to fulfil the same duty. There is one, and but one, such point of agreement. It is found in a change of condition inducing purification. The action in the baptisms is diverse without, in any case, approaching to the form of DIPPING. The mode of using the water is diverse without any approach to a *covering*. The point in which they agree, without exception as Patristically interpreted, is the resultant condition of purification.

No one has studied Patristic baptism to any purpose who has not learned, upon its very threshold, that purification was its *sine qua non* feature. How they used the water is not included in the present discussion. The business, in hand, is to prove that the transactions passed in review were called by them baptisms, and the ground on which they were so designated. The evidence determining these points may be found within the domain of Judaic baptisms, without trespassing on that of Christian baptism. We claim that they were called *baptisms*, because they exhibit a thorough change of condition; and TYPES *of Christian* baptism, because the change was from impurity to purity.

This napthar baptism makes a clear path for Dr. Fuller to make farther progress in the right direction. Having abandoned modal dip for "immerse in any way," even by "pouring if continued long enough *to cover;*" and having yielded up pouring long enough to cover, for "pouring long enough to *drench;*" he may now drop the "drenching," and change the pouring into *sprinkling.*

We may, also, congratulate "R. Ingham" on the very great relief which he must experience by the discovery, that the "dear babes brought to have a good work wrought on them" will not require "twelve barrels" of water to be poured over them. A sprinkle will suffice.

BAPTISM BY SPRING WATER.

CEREMONIAL PURIFICATION.

JUDITH 12: 5–9.

"And the servants of Holofernes brought her into the tent, and she slept until midnight; and she arose at the morning watch.

"And she sent to Holofernes, saying, Let my lord, now, command that thy handmaid may go out for prayer.

"And Holofernes commanded his body-guard not to hinder her; and she remained in the tent three days, and went out nightly into the valley of Bethulia, and baptized herself in the camp at the fountain of water.

"And as she went up, she besought of the Lord God of Israel to direct her way to the raising up of the children of her people.

"And entering in pure, she remained in the tent." . . .

Septuagint.

Καὶ εξεπορεύετο κατὰ νύκτα εἰς τὴν φάραγγα Βετυλούα, καὶ ἐβαπτίζετο ἐν τῇ παρεμβολῇ ἐπὶ τῆς πηγῆς τοῦ ὕδατος.

Καὶ ὡς ἀνέβη, ἐδέετο τοῦ Κυρίου Θεοῦ Ἰσραήλ. . . . Καὶ εἰσπορευομένη καθαρὰ παρέμενε τῇ σκηνῇ . . . .

What the Theory says.

CARSON.

"This ought here to have been translated *she dipped herself.* . . . It is evident that though she was in a camp, she was in such a part of it as afforded her the necessary seclusion. . . . We neither *imagine* nor *assume* that Judith was immersed in water. It is from the established meaning of the word, not from views of independent probability, that we must derive our knowledge of the fact. Even were the fact improbable in itself, the testimony of the word would establish it. . . . I care not if there had not been a fountain at all in Bethulia, she might have been immersed without it. If from other places I prove that *immerse* is the meaning of the word, this, in every situation, will provide the water. We refuse, then, to be gauger of the fountain of Bethulia; let them dip it who need the evidence. . . .

"I care not whether she was immersed in the fountain, or in a cistern, or bath beside it. The historian understands that it was in the fountain. The preposition, indeed, does not designate this, but it is often used when *in* might have been used. That the historian meant that she was immersed *in* the fountain, is plain from his speaking of her praying immediately on *ascending*. . . . It cannot be known, or rationally admitted, that she was dipped, but on the testimony of this word. . . .

"Was it not usual to have stone troughs at fountains, for the purpose of watering cattle? . . The immersion is proved, not by the preposition, but by the verb; and though *at a fountain* does not signify *in a fountain*, yet it is consistent with it. . . . Is it not evident, on the face of the document, that Judith went out from the camp to the fountain at Bethulia, for the purpose of bathing, or washing her whole person? . . . Why did she go to the fountain? Why did she leave the tent? Could not a small basin of water have served the purpose of successive washing? . . .

"All my opponents endeavor to take advantage of my candor in proving the secondary meaning of βάπτω, taking it for granted that this equally applies to βαπτίζω. Let βαπτίζω show as good evidence of a secondary meaning, as I have shown on the part of βάπτω, and I will, without controversy, admit the fact."

FULLER.

"She bathed in the fountain. She was, of course, dressed in proper apparel. . . . As if to leave no doubt, however, as to her bathing, it is expressly said, that 'she came out of the water.' The pretence, that bathing would have been indelicate, is absurd."

CONANT.

"According to the common Greek text, this was done '*at the fountain*,' to which she went, because she had there the means of immersing herself. Any other use of water, for purification, could have been made in her tent. . . . There was evidently no lack of water for the immersion of the body, after the Jewish manner, namely, by walking into the water to the proper depth, and then sinking down till the whole body was immersed."

ARGUMENT OF THE THEORY.

Admissions.

It is admitted by the friends of the theory, that there are no incidental circumstances connected with this baptism of Judith, which show that a dipping did, in fact, take place.

One of the most marvellous things connected with this cast-iron theory, is the utter failure to show, by incidental facts, that a dipping or a covering of the body in water ever took place. There is no such evidence to show, that in a single instance, for fifteen hundred years, the body was dipped into water in effecting a Jewish purification.

This marvel is only paralleled by that other marvel, to wit, the courageous conflict with facts, which declare that no such dipping took place, in the hope that some weapon in the armory of poetry or rhetoric may win a triumph for *quasi* dipping. It is of no consequence whether the facts are, washing at a tent-door in the sight of all Israel, pouring on a lofty mountain summit, sprinkling a temple altar, or walking across the dry channel of a river, the theorist, without the winking of an eye, undertakes to *rosecrucianize* these base materials into dipping gold.

It is admitted that, in this case, no favor for dipping can be got from the prepositions. These prepositions are εἰς, ἐν and ἐπὶ. The εἰς, however, does not take down into the water, but "into a valley." And although Dr. Carson says, going into a valley will answer very well for an immersion (when you cannot get anything better), still, he does not insist upon it on this occasion. We have also ἐν in connection with βαπτίζω—ἐβαπτίζετω ἐν baptized in—yet this is not here insisted upon as pointing out a dipping, and indicating the element in which the dipping takes place, for the dipping would, then, be not in the water but in *the camp*. Might it not be worth while, here, to review the argument which derives evidence for a dipping from ἐν θαλάσσῃ and ἐν νεφέλῃ? If instrumental force be not allowed to the preposition, why go beyond naked locality? The sea was dry, and the miracle-cloud was just as dry. If an enclosure was made by the remote water-walls, there was, perhaps, as lofty and certainly a more closely investing enclosure of army tents, to say nothing of the valley-walls. Indeed, we are only saved from having these army tents and deep valley sides flung in our faces as charming elements of a poetical dipping, by the fortunate presence of "a fountain."

A baptism "in the camp" is felt to be not the most favorable position for dipping the entire person of Judith. Therefore Carson says: "It is evident, that though she was in a camp, she was in such a part of it as afforded her the necessary seclusion." Where the "evidence for seclusion" is, I do not know. It is in evidence that these fountains of Bethulia were captured; and the great hope for capturing the city was in holding securely the fountains whence the supply of water for the inhabitants was derived. It is in evidence that Holofernes, after he "took the fountains of their waters, *set garrisons of men of war over them*." (7 : 7.) And it is in evidence, that the camp was just as close unto, or as deeply in, this fountain, as was the baptism of Judith. The very identical terms which bring her baptism into relation with the fountain, are employed to denote the relation of the camp to the fountain. "They encamped in the valley near Bethulia, *at the fountain*—ἐπὶ τῆς πηγῆς." What now becomes of the, "It is evident, that though she was in the camp, she was in such a part of it as afforded her the necessary seclusion?" It is worth just as much as ninety-nine parts out of a hundred of all the utterances of the theory, in attempting to get rid of facts, and to thrust in a dipping into Jewish purifications. That is, it is worth just nothing at all.

But Dr. Carson is not satisfied with the repudiation of these facts, in order to secure a secluded place within the camp. He takes the lady "out of the camp" entirely. "Is it not evident that Judith *went out from the camp* to the fountain of Bethulia, for the purpose of bathing or washing her whole person?" (p. 459.) Why, yes; it is just as evident that Judith "went out of the camp," in going to that point which was specially garrisoned, as that the millions of Israel were "*dipped* in the sea," or that the sea-coast was "*dipped* in the tide," or that the altar on Carmel was "*dipped* in the on-poured water." Yes, just as "evident!"

If Judith had "gone out of the camp" from the tent of Holofernes, she would have had a long night-walk. The army and its followers made up about a quarter of a million men. "And they camped in the valley, near unto Bethulia, by the fountain, and they spread themselves in breadth over Dothaim, even to Belmaim, and in length from Bethulia unto Cyamon, which is over against Esdrælon. And the children of Israel said, 'Now will these men lick up the face of the earth; for neither the high mountains, nor the valleys, nor the hills, are able to bear their weight.'" (7:3, 4.) We dismiss, then, this—"it is evident" that she was in a secluded place, and *out of the camp*, and could therefore without embarrassment engage in "bathing or washing her whole person." Does "*out of* the camp" translate ἐν παρεμβολῇ?

Dr. Fuller does not take this heroine out of the camp, nor is he very solicitous for a secluded place, seeing that "she was, of course, dressed in proper apparel."

This "of course," of Dr. Fuller, wakes up as quiet a smile as the "it is evident," of Dr. Carson. Why "of course," Doctor? Are spectators from "the garrison" admitted to this baptism? And of what did this "proper apparel" consist? Was an orthodox "bathing robe" provided for these nightly dippings? When did the enrobement take place, before leaving the tent, or at the fountain? When did the disrobement take place, after going back to the tent, or on coming out of the dipping? Would not the putting on and off this "proper apparel" require as much seclusion as the use of none at all? The "of course she was dressed in proper apparel" does not help much "the washing of her entire person in the camp." This "in the camp" is a thorn in the side of the theory.

It is admitted, that the preposition ἐπὶ has neither aid nor comfort for the theory. Still, this is but a gnat compared with the camels which the theory has become familiar with swallowing. And, after all, it is about as good as if it were ἐν, for "the historian understands that it was *in* the fountain." It is a little odd, to be sure, that Dr. Carson should know that the historian understands one thing, when he says quite a different thing. But, I suppose, the same figure of speech which converts one act into some other act, will suffice to convert an historical statement into a very different conception in the mind of the historian. It is freely admitted by Carson that "*at a fountain* does not signify *in a fountain;*" yet Dr. Fuller very dogmatically affirms (p. 39), "she bathed *in* a fountain." Perhaps he thought that the discovery made by his friend ought to be made use of. And it was very natural for him to conclude, that "in the fountain" would be of more practical value if incorporated in the text, than by remaining "in the understanding of the historian," since few persons would have the wit to find it in the latter place, unless they were deep in the mysteries of the theory. Thus we have the amended text—"she bathed *in* a fountain." This ἐπὶ is an annoyance. The camp was pitched—ἐπὶ τῆς πηγῆς—"at the fountain," and every one is willing for them to remain outside of the fountain. Judith was baptized—ἐπὶ τῆς πηγῆς—"at the fountain," and the theorists insist that she must be put inside of the fountain.

It is admitted that the dimensions of this fountain are unknown. Yet every theorist seems ready to declare, if needs be, under oath, that it was large enough for Judith to go into it and "immerse her entire person." As this point, in which alone he feels any interest, is fully settled to Dr. Carson's satisfaction, he refuses "to be the gauger of it," and bids those "dip it" who care to do so.

Dr. Conant knows why she went to the fountain, although the narrative is silent on the subject.

"She went because she had, there, the means of immersing herself." He says, that he knows this because he knows something else, touching which the narrative gives no information to any one else—"any other use of water for purification, could have been made in her tent." Does Dr. Conant know, that water for *immersion* could not have been used in her tent? And is Dr. Conant quite sure that *Judith* believed with him, that water "for purification" (furnished by unclean heathen men in unclean vessels) could have been used in her tent in any form, with propriety? Why did she refuse to share in the meat and drink brought from the table of Holofernes? "And Judith said, I will not eat thereof, lest there be an offence; but provision shall be made for me of the things that I have brought." Now, if this Jewess could not partake of the food from Holofernes' own table because it was "unclean," is it well considered in Dr. Conant to say, "any other use of water for *purification* could have been made in her tent?" How could she use *in a religious rite* the water furnished by heathen, when she could not use their food for an ordinary meal? Without caring to say, that I have special knowledge on this point, may I not ask—If this is common sense, what becomes of the exclusive knowledge, that she went to the fountain for the purpose of *immersing* herself? Why not *for water free from heathenish pollution?*

But Dr. Carson knows that she *dipped* herself, and Dr. Fuller knows that she *bathed* herself, and Dr. Conant knows that she *immersed* herself,—where? Why, in the fountain from which the Bethulians got their drinking-water, and from which "the garrison" guarding that fountain, got their water. Well, this is certainly a little remarkable, that a lady should go and "wash her entire person" in a drinking fountain! However, these learned men say, that they know that she did it. We must, then, set down this lady Judith as remarkably solicitous for her own "purification," and remarkably regardless of the purification of the waters for those who drank after her nightly washings!

But there is another item of assured knowledge furnished us by Dr. Fuller—"As if to leave no doubt, however, as to her bathing, it is expressly said that she 'came out' of the water."

No wonder dippings, and bathings, and immersings, are furnished to order, when they are accepted on authority like this.

By whom is it "expressly said that she came out of the water?" Why really by no one. For it takes two to make up this statement. First, the English translator, who is responsible for the "come out," and second, Dr. Fuller, who is responsible for the addendum "of the water." Then it should read—"It is expressly said by the English translator, *and by me*, that she came out of the water." Is it not amusing to hear a conclusion builded on such a foundation, which is to relieve the subject of all doubt? No one knows better than Dr. Fuller that the translation of ἀνέβη by "come out" is without the shadow of authority. And when Dr. F. adds—"it is expressly said that she came out *of the water*," no one knows better than he, that neither in the English translation, nor in the Greek original, is there any such "express" statement. And this is Dr. Fuller's "best card," which is to leave "no doubt as to her bathing!"

What shall be said of such a statement? Why, we must say, that it is pure fiction, and will sadly mislead every one who trusts in it. And what shall be said of Dr. F.? Why, that he is just as honest and true as any other thoroughly mistaken Christian man. He will promptly acknowledge his error when his attention is called to it, and, doubtless, will say—"My statement was made incautiously and erroneously. I should have said, It is expressly stated—'and when she went up,'"—and to this should have been added, "*I do most confidently believe*, that this refers to her 'going up out of the water.'" Had it been "expressly" said, "she came out of the water," it would have mattered very little what Dr. F., or I, might have believed as to the matter; but in the absence of any such statement, I have as much right to "believe confidently" that no such fact ever took place, as he to believe the contrary. And if I can give better reasons for my faith, then my confidence is better justified.

As to these reasons let me appeal to facts. 1. Judith went out, of her tent, into the valley of Bethulia. She could not go into a valley, without going down from a higher to a lower position. 2. This descent brought her "by the fountain" where she baptized herself. 3. After her baptism she went up out of the valley to her tent. 4. She entered into her tent. These are the facts as to the movements of this Jewish lady. I cannot say, that it is expressly stated that she did *not* "come out of the water," for there is not a syllable said as to her going in or coming out. But I can say, that the word relied upon to prove such movement has other duty to perform. It is in proof that Judith went down *into the valley;* and it is in proof that she went up *out of the valley.* We need ἀνέβη to effect a movement the existence of which is in proof. If any other movement is introduced into the case, through exigencies of the theory, words must be found outside of the history to meet the new demand.

To enforce this interdict against pressing ἀνέβη into this water service, I would refer to Genesis 24:15, 16,—"And behold Rebecca went out (ἐξεπορέυετο) and went down (καταβᾶσα) by the fountain (ἐπὶ τῆν πηγην), and filled her water-pot, and went up (ἀνέβη)." All the leading words in this reference are identical with those in the passage under consideration. The preposition indicating the proximity of Judith and Rebecca is precisely the same. The verb which expresses the movement of these females, after their respective missions to the fountain were accomplished, is the same. If that word did not bring Rebecca "out of the water," how will it bring Judith? If that word carried Rebecca up out of the lower ground of the fountain, why shall it not do the same kind office for her sister Jewess?

I would, also, refer to chap. 7:8, 12, 17, 18, of the same book, in which this baptism is related. We, there, find the record of a transaction in connection with this same fountain. It is proposed to take possession "of the fountain of water which flows from the foot of the mountain." In the execution of this project "they pitched their camp in the valley, and took the waters, and the fountains of the waters of the children of Israel." Having effected this object, "the children of Esau went up—ἀνέβησαν—and encamped in the hill country." I presume no one will contend that these sons of Esau went up *out of the water* to reach the hill country. And very few, I presume, will care to say,—"It is expressly stated that Judith *came out of the water*," and, thus, prove her bathing beyond doubt. The assumptions of the friends of the theory are very abundant; their facts are very deficient.

"*At the Fountain.*"

It is insisted upon, that going to *a fountain* for baptism necessarily carries with it a dipping of the person into the waters of the fountain.

"Why did she go to the fountain? That she was immersed in the fountain is plain." (*Carson.*) "She bathed in the fountain." (*Fuller.*) "She went because she had there the means of immersing herself." (*Conant.*)

Let us test this assertion, also, to see whether it be anything more than an assumption.

In Classic Baptism (p. 330) we have the account of a person who was baptized at a fountain without being dipped, bathed, or immersed in its waters. He neither "went into it" nor "came out of it." Had he gone into it, and dipped, or bathed, or immersed himself in its waters, *he would not have been baptized by it.*

Baptism, at this fountain, was effected, not by *dipping* into it, but by *drinking* of it. Thus, "the virtue" of this fountain was developed. Silenus, the special friend of Bacchus, "took possession of" the drinker. Brought under his controlling influence, the condition of the drinker is thoroughly changed. He is baptized by the Silenic fount, and resembles one who is made "heavy-headed and baptized" by Bacchus. These baptisms of Silenus and of Bacchus "resemble" each other as closely in their mode and nature, as do the "jolly god" and his "tipsy follower" resemble each other in character. The one baptizes at the banquetting-table, the other at the fountain. But whether at the festive board or at the bubbling spring, the baptism is effected by *drinking.* A man dipped into a wine cask does not receive the baptism of Bacchus. A man dipped into this fabled fountain does not receive the baptism of Silenus. These drunken deities do not, after such mode, "take possession" of their votaries. We have here the most absolute proof of a baptism "at a fountain," without any dipping, bathing, or immersing *in the fountain.* Thus we estop the reasoning which makes *at* a fountain equivalent to *in* a fountain. Thus, also, we arrest the reasoning which makes a *fountain*-baptism necessarily a *dipping*-baptism.

To this it may be replied: "Although a fountain appears in each of these baptisms, still, the cases are not parallel. The fountain of Silenus was imbued with a peculiar quality, the controlling influence of which was developed only by drinking; but the fountain of Bethulia had no such quality, and therefore a baptism at this fountain must be by dipping into its waters." Truth and error mingle together in this objection. It is true that this fountain of Classic story did possess a peculiar quality which could not be developed by dipping, (and therefore disproves the theory—"no dipping no baptism,") but was developed by drinking. It is also true that the fountain of Bethulia had no *such* quality as the fountain of Silenus. And it is farther true, that we cannot reason conclusively from baptism by drinking at one fountain, to baptism by drinking at another fountain. For every fountain may not yield up its virtue through the same channel. But it is error to conclude because the fountain of Bethulia is not imbued with the *same* "virtue" as that of the fountain of Silenus, therefore it is not imbued with *any* "virtue" at all. It is also error to conclude, because the "virtue" of this fountain is not developed by *drinking*, therefore it must be developed by *dipping.*

The "virtue" which belonged to this fountain in the valley, was a specially purifying quality. The Jews were taught to regard living water, running water, spring water, as having a purifying power above standing or dead water. The use of "living water" was especially enjoined in their ritual purification. (Levit. 13: 50–52; Numb. 19: 17, &c.)

Josephus designates this "living water," of the Hebrew and the Septuagint, by the same word which is used in the passage before us—τῆς πηγῆς—*spring* water. (*Ant. Jud.*, iv, 4.)

While, therefore, this fountain had no *intoxicating* quality, it had, in the estimation of all Jews, and especially of this very religious lady, an eminently *purifying* quality. It was to secure the purifying quality of this spring water that Judith "went down into the valley to the fountain." If the old man, at the fountain of Silenus, was baptized by drinking its waters, (their "virtue" thus taking possession of him, and thoroughly changing his condition,) then, the youthful Jewess was baptized at the fountain of Bethulia, by using its waters in any such way as would develop their "virtue" so as to "take possession" of her, thoroughly changing her condition. And this is as certain as the mathematical axiom, "things that are equal to the same thing, are equal to each other." Saratoga Springs yield their "virtue" to drinking.

Thus Classic baptism utterly repudiates the assumption, that because a baptism took place "at a fountain," there must have been a *dipping in* the fountain.

But Dr. Carson will not confide the cause of dipping in the fountain to such unfriendly auspices as ἐπὶ τῆς πηγῆς. "I care not whether she was immersed in the fountain, or in a cistern or bath beside it. . . Was it not usual to have stone troughs at fountains for the purpose of watering cattle?"

Alas! is the theory so merciless, that, rather than spare this Jewish lady a dipping, they will make her lie down in "a trough for watering cattle?"

It is hard to tell which to admire most, "the washing of her entire person" *in* the fountain of which others were to drink, or the purifying of herself "*at* the fountain" in a horse-trough!

SHE BAPTIZED HERSELF.

But the apology for all this extravagance, is "the word," "*the word!*"

"It cannot be known, or rationally admitted, that she was dipped, but on the testimony of this word. The immersion is proved, not by the preposition, but by the verb." She was baptized. And βαπτίζω means dip, and nothing but dip, through all Greek literature.

As the friends of the theory confess that a dipping cannot be got out of this transaction, except through the naked word βαπτίζω, it becomes a necessity to follow them into this last retreat.

In their conclusion, that the phrase—"she baptized herself in the camp at the fountain of water"—can give them no help except it be found "in the word," I think all will agree.

The hope to secure a dipping, through "the word," will be found, by bitter experience, "to feed on ashes."

Meaning Obscure to the Theory.

It is obvious, that when three different meanings are assigned to a word by three intelligent men, each affirming that the word has but one meaning, the meaning of that word is, probably, but obscurely apprehended by any of them.

Drs. Carson, Fuller, and Conant, all declare that βαπτίζω has but one meaning. Each one claims to know, as well as he knows his own name, what that meaning is; and each, writing with declared critical accuracy of the same transaction in which that word appears, gives to it a different meaning.

One (Carson) says, it means *to dip;* which meaning it never has. Another (Fuller) says, it means *to bathe;* which meaning it never has. A third (Conant) says, it means to immerse; which meaning (carrying with it the idea of limitation of time) it never has. There must be some radical defect, when critical scholars, starting from the same premises, cannot walk together in the same path; but one turns off to the right hand, another to the left hand, and a third thinks—*in medio tutissime ibis.*

It is not pertinent but trifling with their readers to say, that although none of these words expresses the meaning of the original word, yet that meaning underlies all these words; and we know very well what it is, and it is very easy to state it, and our object in writing elaborate treatises is to translate it, and to tell all about it; yet we will not say what it is, but we will state a dozen words which it is not, and out of them you may find the meaning as well as you can. We should be chided "with bated breath," if we fail to find out the meaning, seeing that, of these scholars, one says: "I have found it, it is *dip.*" And a second cries, "I have found it, it is *bathe.*" And a third responds, "You must be mistaken, I have found it, it is *immerse.*" Is there no fourth to arise, (like the umpire in the chameleon dispute,) who shall say, "Good friends, you all are wrong; I have found it, and have it here, and if, when brought forth, you do not find it *plunge*, I will eat it!" Yes, Stourdza will do this.

Condition, not Act, Expressed.

In the phraseology, "she baptized herself," there is no form of act expressed; and all the theorists on earth might spend a lifetime in guessing, and they could no more determine the question as to the act performed, than they could tell, by like guessing, what kind of a spade Adam used, or what kind of a spinning-wheel Eve employed, in those days when "Adam delved and Eve span."

Let me state other cases of baptism expressed by similar phraseology: "Seeing him baptized." "I am one of those yesterday baptized." "Whom having baptized." "Whom it were better to baptize."

In all of these cases βαπτίζω is used absolutely, as here expressed. If the word is capable of expounding itself, and making known, in the clearest and most definite manner, a form of act, then there will be no difficulty for any one initiated into the mysteries of this word, to tell us what was the one modal act performed in these several baptisms. If the wealth of all the Indies were offered as the prize, it could not be done. If Webster's last quarto should be taken, and all the forms of act between A and Z were gone over, there would be no approximation to the truth. For there is no definite act expressed.

In the first case, the word expresses a condition of mental bewilderment. The second case, expresses a condition of drunkenness. The third, expresses a condition of drugged stupor. The fourth, is the condition of drowning in the sea.

Such facts of usage show that the statement—"Judith baptized herself"—might mean, she brought herself into a condition of bewilderment—or drunkenness—or stupor—or drowning.

What shall be thought, then, of the bold promise to find out by this naked "word," a definite act done?

Is relief sought by assuming the position, that this is a case of literal baptism, and such baptisms can only be by one definite act?

I answer, 1. It is nothing but naked assumption to pronounce this a case of literal, physical baptism. To appeal to the word, is to go back on a track which has just been found to be barren of all friendly results. To call upon "fountain"—"ἐπὶ"—"ἀνέβη"—is to call for reeds which have already been broken and can yield no support. To appeal to facts of usage in such cases, is to attempt to prove a proposition by a result which is itself yet to be proved. Also, it is an appeal to that which has no existence. There is no evidence of Jewish ritual purification through all the period of the law—fifteen hundred years—by dipping the entire person in water. Judith sought purification; and it is nothing but an absolute assumption to say, that this required her person to be put under the water.

I answer, 2. It is not true, by the showing of the theorists, that the covering of the entire person by water is necessary to a physical baptism. It is declared that Noah was literally and physically baptized in the ark; while it is admitted that he was not covered by the water. It is affirmed that the Israelites were literally and physically baptized at the Red Sea; yet it is admitted that they were not covered by the water. It is affirmed that Elijah's altar was physically baptized; yet it is admitted that it was not covered by the water.

How does it happen, that under all these diversities there is a most cast-iron certainty as to the manner of Judith's baptism? Would not "the *pouring* of twelve barrels of water" suffice?

I answer, 3. A physical baptism is precluded because there is no case of similar phraseology in physical baptisms, except in such as involve destruction of life. Baptism always expresses unlimited duration in its continuance. That duration never terminates by the force of "the word." This is a vital, nay, the most vital, and universally present element in all the usage of the word. To take it out of the word, and make it express limitation of time, would be giving it a secondary meaning with a vengeance. This idea of unlimited continuance, (so far as the word is concerned,) appears in every case of secondary usage, and grows out of that grand and essential characteristic of the primary use. Therefore,

I answer, 4. This was a case belonging to secondary baptism. Proof of this is found (1.) In the fact that spring water can purify, ritually, without covering the body. The Classic and the Jewish world, alike, are filled with exemplifications of this statement. Sprinkling purifies, ritually, as completely as pouring, bathing, or any other use of water.

Because of this quality, (enabling it to change the condition of the person on whom it was sprinkled,) it was capable by sprinkling, of baptizing. Any one who will deny this, "kicks against the pricks" of all Greek literature.

(2.) Judith came to the fountain for purification. She came to be baptized by the ritually purifying power of spring water. That is to say, she came to have her present condition of ceremonial impurity changed to one of thorough ceremonial purity. Does not this state the facts of the case in the fullest and most definite manner? Now remember that when the phrase—"she came to be baptized by the ritually purifying power of spring water," is abbreviated into the phrase—"she came to be baptized"—the whole force of the omitted words become merged in the one word "baptized;" and that word by such addition, by the laws of language, now expresses the idea of purification in its representative character.

(3.) This change of condition, the baptism effected by the spring water, was not evanescent. She went up from the fountain purified. She prayed to God for imperilled Israel, purified. She entered into her tent, purified.

Here is that vital and universally present feature of baptism—a continuance of condition without any self-limitation of that continuance.

There is no such feature in the dipping, or the covering of "the theory;" and therefore it is an error. A dipping into water neither is nor can be a baptism.

Israel "baptized into Moses" did not emerge from their baptism for the space of forty years. Israel "baptized into Joshua" did not emerge from their baptism during "all the days of his life." Judith baptized into ceremonial purity at the fountain of Bethulia, did not emerge from her baptism until taken out of it by some defiling influence.

This is the teaching of the Classics. There is no limit of time when the lost ship shall emerge from its baptism, or when the drunken man, or the bewildered man, or the opiately stupefied man shall emerge from his baptism.

Secondary Meaning.

Dr. Carson makes this complaint: "All my opponents endeavor to take advantage of my candor in proving the secondary meaning of *βάπτω*, taking it for granted that this equally applies to *βαπτίζω*. Let *βαπτίζω* show as good evidence of a secondary meaning, as I have shown on the part of *βάπτω*, and I will without controversy admit the fact."

If this complaint is well grounded, Methuselah must have been young in years compared with Dr. Carson. The proof of a secondary meaning to *βάπτω* has been in existence for some centuries beyond a thousand years. It only remained for Dr. C.'s friends to profit by his "candor" in accepting the meaning urged by his opponents.

As to the evidence of a secondary meaning to βαπτίζω, (the primary meaning being, the change of the condition of an object by its intusposition within a closely investing medium without limitation of time, the secondary meaning being, the thorough change of condition, without limitation of time, of an object by some controlling influence, without intusposition,) a limited portion of this evidence may be found in the following facts:

1. The condition of heated iron is represented as changed (baptized) into a condition of coldness *by* water. Water is, here, represented as an agency effecting this change of condition by its quality of coldness. If it should be objected, "This change might be effected by the immersion of the hot iron *in* cold water." I grant it; but reply, this is not what is said. And demand in turn the admission, that the *quality of coldness* in water is capable of controlling and changing thoroughly the condition of *hot* iron without any immersion.

2. It is said, that the condition of a sober man is changed (baptized) into the condition of a drunken man by means of wine-drinking. It cannot be objected, in this case, that the same change of condition may be effected by the immersion of a man *in* a hogshead of wine; for it is obviously and confessedly untrue. Such an immersion would produce a baptism, but as different from the other as light from darkness, or as life from death. It is most irrational, therefore, to say that these baptisms have any relation, in kind, to each other. It follows, consequently, by necessity, that there is a baptism in which no intusposition exists in fact or by imagination.

3. It is said, that a man who drinks of the fountain of Silenus is like to a "baptized" man. But there is no conceivable resemblance between such a one and an *immersed* man. There is a resemblance to a drunken man. "Baptized," therefore, is here employed to denote, directly, a

drunken condition. The change of condition, in one case, is likened to the change of condition, in the other case. In neither case is there any possibility of immersion.

Such proof of a secondary meaning is absolute.

4. It is said, that Bacchus is baptized by water poured into wine. It is impossible that wine should be immersed by water poured into it. For the same reason it is impossible that the word, here, can mean "immersed." The condition of wine is thoroughly changed by water poured into it, and this condition, (without immersion,) is expressed by *βαπτίζω*. It has, therefore, a secondary meaning.

5. Josephus says, a man ceremonially impure is baptized by heifer-ashes sprinkled upon him. It is impossible that he should be immersed by these ashes. The word, therefore, cannot possibly mean, here, "immersed." But these ashes do, by their purifying quality, thoroughly change the condition of those upon whom they are sprinkled. They are brought out of a condition of ceremonial impurity into a condition of complete ceremonial purity. This change of condition is expressed by *βαπτίζω*; and being without intusposition it has passed to a secondary meaning.

6. Origen says, the altar, with its sacrifice, was baptized by water poured upon it. The altar and holocaust were not immersed in water. The Greek word, therefore, does not, here, mean "immersed." The condition of the altar and sacrifice was thoroughly changed. They passed out of a condition of ceremonial impurity into a condition of ceremonial purity. This change of condition is expressed by *βαπτίζω*; and being without intusposition exhibits, again, its secondary meaning.

These instances of usage representative of many others, Classic, Jewish, and Patristic, prove a secondary meaning for *βαπτίζω*, as unanswerably as the "candor" of Dr. Carson has succeeded in showing, to his unbelieving friends, to belong to *βάπτω*.

The principle of development, in the two cases, is not merely the same, but the form of development is almost identical.

The object of βάπτω is dipped into fluids colorless or colored.

In the former case the secondary meaning which would result must be a state of *wetness*. This is exemplified in the wet state of Nebuchadnezzar produced by the night-dew. But to this secondary meaning the "candor" of Dr. C. did not attain. But certain objects dipped into colored liquids became, thereby, colored. Hence the word which caused the coloring by its act of dipping, was applied to the coloring of objects when the act of dipping was not present. Thus arose the secondary meaning *to dye*, without dipping.

The object of βαπτίζω is brought into a condition of intusposition within a fluid element, not by the transient act of dipping, but by any competent act, and never removing its object out of this new condition into which it has been introduced. Some objects (rocks and other impenetrable masses) are not affected by this change of condition. Other objects, (human beings, penetrable and soluble substances,) are powerfully affected, according to their nature, and the characteristics of the investing element. From the effects thus produced, by intusposition, on this class of objects, proceeds that secondary meaning of βαπτίζω, which is expressive of controlling influence, without intusposition as the inducing cause. The word, out of whose demand the controlling influence originally proceeded, is still retained to express the condition resultant from influence when exerted under modes of development other than that with which it was originally associated.

If the friends of the theory seek to take the life of this word in secondary development, by the aid of monster beauties in poesy and rhetoric, the answer is: The same troop of "beauties" will as readily murder βάπτω, second, or any other word that has passed to a secondary meaning.

What proves too much, proves nothing.

The condition of Judith was changed from that of ceremonial impurity to one of ceremonial purity, by the influence of "living water;" and this change, without intusposition, βαπτίζω is competent, and is, in fact, used to express. The circumstances and the phraseology of the statement unite to declare that the word is so used here.

To enforce this conclusion against the dogmatic assertion of Dr. Carson and friends, I will adduce an exemplification of the unreliability of his judgment as to words, in attributing to them one unswerving meaning.

Περικλύζω.

There was a washing of Judith previous and preparatory to her going to the camp of Holofernes. This washing is expressed by the word περικλύζω. It is the same word used to express the washing of Tobias at the river Tigris: "And when the young man went down (to the river) (περικλύσασθαι) to wash himself." (Tobit 6:2.)

This passage having been quoted by President Beecher, Dr. Carson thus comments (p. 445): "But Mr. B.'s criticism on the Greek word κλύζω, here employed for washing, is entirely false. He expounds the word as signifying a washing all round, just as a man stands in a stream and throws the water all over his body, and washes himself by friction. Mr. B. criticizes from imagination, not from a knowledge of the language. Has he justified his criticism by a single example? He seems better acquainted with the different circumstances in the operation of bathing, than with the occurrences of the word on which he undertakes to criticize. The simple word signifies to deluge, to overwhelm, to inundate, to flow over anything, and is generally applied to water flowing or rolling in a horizontal manner. . . . There is no friction nor hand washing in this word. It performs its purpose by running over, either gently or with violence. The word does not signify that the young man, in bathing, splashed about like a duck, or rubbed himself like a collier, but that he threw himself into the river that the stream might flow over him. He was then baptized, indeed, and much more than baptized."

This criticism is in the usual Carsonic style: supercilious

toward the utterances of others; self-complacent in his own, as the embodiment of absolute truth.

In reply, Dr. Beecher refers, among other quotations, to the washing of a child—ὕδατι περικλύζειν (Aristotle); and the wetting by spray—ἀφρῷ περικλυζόμενον. (Lucian.) Such passages do effectually take the underpinning from beneath the claims of Dr. C. to critical accuracy.

No less so does this washing of Judith, related 10 : 2: "She rose and went down" (not into the river or fountain, but) "into the house, and washed her body all around with water—περιεκλύσατο τὸ σῶμα ὕδατι—and anointed herself with precious ointment."

Now, what becomes, in the presence of this statement, of the dictum, that it is "entirely false" to expound the word as meaning a "washing all around?" What is the worth of the declaration, "the word signifies that he threw himself into the river, that the stream might flow over him?" Does this same word, also, signify that Judith, in her house, "threw herself into the river, that the water might flow over her?" Or, does the word "signify" that the water "deluged, overwhelmed, inundated, flowed or rolled over her in a horizontal manner?" Does it "signify" that Judith was in the water (ὕδατι, with water) at all? "Most assuredly; ignorance itself should know that the word will supply the water." Well, when the word cries out, under the tutorage of Dr. C., for water to deluge and roll over the lady Judith, what is the response from the Bethulians? Here it is: "All the vessels of water fail all the inhabitants of Bethulia. And the cisterns are emptied; and we have not water to drink our fill for one day; for we give drink by measure. Therefore our young children are out of heart, and our women and young men faint for thirst, and fall down in the streets of the city and by the passages of the gates, and there is no longer any strength in them. And all the people assemble, both young men and women and children, and cry with a loud voice, and say, 'Deliver the whole city for a spoil to Holofernes and to all his army. For it is better for us to be made a spoil unto them, than to die for thirst.'"

And, in the midst of this wailing from parched lips and tongues cleaving to the roofs of their mouths, Dr. C. would have us believe, that this Jewess "throws herself into a water-bath, that the water may flow horizontally over her!"

The Jew Apelles may believe this; the Bethulian Jew will not.

Dr. Carson may "make βαπτίζω find water in a desert," but he cannot make περικλύζω find "a deluge, and an inundation, and an overwhelming, and a flowing over" of water in Bethulia, whose people are dying of thirst.

Judith must be left quietly in her house, "to wash her body all around with water," using so much as she may be able to get, notwithstanding the faith of Carson should declare all such action, under περικλύζω, to be "entirely false."

WASHING FOR PRAYER.

This washing having been stained by the defilements of the idolatrous camp, Judith goes to renew her purification at the fountain of Bethulia. At her previous washing, *in her house*, we are expressly told, that "she *pulled off* the sackcloth which she had on, and *put off* the garments of her widowhood, and washed, . . . and *put on* the garments of gladness."

Here is the whole process of disrobing and enrobing. Where is all this, or anything like this, at the theory *dipping*, when "she baptized, *in the camp*, at the fountain?"

Homer makes Telemachus "wash his hands, of the hoary sea, before prayer to Minerva." Hesiod inculcates "the washing of hands, in pure water, before prayer." Ovid teaches "the washing of hands, and the sprinkling of the head with water, before prayer." The Jewish priesthood washed their hands and feet before engaging in religious worship. Aristeas says: "It is customary for all Jews to wash their hands with sea-water, when they would pray to God." Philo declares, "It is the custom of nearly all others to sprinkle themselves for purification with pure water, many with that of the sea, some with that of rivers, and some with that which, in vessels, they have drawn up from wells." But when this Jewish heroine comes to the running water to *baptize* (purify) *herself for prayer*, she finds encamped there a troop, under the bold leadership of "the theory," who defend the passage, and refuse to recognize any permit from Holofernes, or from "an angel from heaven," except the shibboleth—"no dipping no baptism"—be first accepted, and the lady be pledged "to wash her entire person in the fountain," (or, at her option, purify(?) herself in the horse-trough,) the garrison of heathen soldiery being witnesses to the faithful performance of the requirement!

The theory is more pitiless than the Assyrian Holofernes.

And, now, having gone through, in detail, the features of this last case of baptism in the Apocryphal writings of the Jews, it might be well asked, (if the theory were not full of castles in the air,) Could anything be more foundationless than the attempt to dip this fair Jewess, nightly, in the camp, at a fountain surrounded by its special garrison of soldiers?

But, where interpretation is so generally phenomenal, any new case ceases to awaken surprise.

The Apocryphal writers fully agree with the interpreters of the Canonical Scriptures as to the usage of *ΒΑΠΤΙΖΩ*.

NEW TESTAMENT.

JEWISH BAPTISMS.

It was my purpose to have introduced, here, all the cases of Judaic baptism mentioned in the New Testament; but have concluded to defer those practised during John's ministry until his baptism shall be under consideration.

Paul interprets the Jewish ordinances, and calls them "baptisms," just as do the Patrists, without the slightest regard to any modal act of dipping into or covering over with water, or anything else.

An illustration of this statement will now engage our attention. And although more than a century has elapsed since the record of Judith's baptism, we will find the usage of the Greek word unchanged.

"VARIOUS KINDS OF BAPTIZINGS."

HEBREWS 9: 9, 10.

"Which was a figure for the time then present, in which were offered both gifts and sacrifices, that could not make him that did the service perfect as pertaining to the conscience;

"Which stood only in meats and drinks and diverse baptizings; carnal ordinances, imposed on them until the time of reformation."

Μόνον ἐπὶ βρώμασι καὶ πόμασι, καὶ διαφόροις βαπτισμοίς, δικαιώματα σαρκὸς.

Diverse Baptisms.

After having examined the endless variety presented in the baptisms passed in review we are well prepared to hear the inspired Apostle speak of "various kinds of baptizings."

But such language must have a painful and ominous sound to the ear of the theory. It compels it, once again, to assume an apologetic attitude. We have been chidden for speaking of the mode of baptizing. "To speak of the mode of baptizing was as absurd as to speak of the mode of dipping. The word expressed mode and nothing but mode." The theory, then, has the embarrassing task to explain how it happens that Paul speaks of "diversity" in that which is nothing but mode, and the most wonderful example of uniformity in mode which the history of language presents. I do not say that the theory cannot show, that what the Apostle says is *diverse*, and what it says is *uniform*, agree perfectly together. After having witnessed demonstrations that baptism by *pouring* means baptism by *dipping*, I am quite prepared to listen to another demonstration proving that *diversity* is *uniformity*.

PATRISTS.

Diversity of baptisms was a truth quite familiar to Patristic writers.

Hilary, i, 519, under the heading "Baptismata sunt diversa," speaks of the baptism of John, the second baptism of the Saviour (*alio baptismo baptizari*), the baptism of the Spirit, baptism of fire, of judgment, and the baptism of martyrdom. These baptisms are all diverse in manner and matter.

Ambrose, iii, 424: "Multa sunt genera baptismatum," (1248,) "plurima baptismatum genera præmissa sunt." Among these "many, very many kinds of baptisms," he enumerates as "one kind, the healing of the leprosy of Naaman; another kind was the purging of the world by the deluge; a third kind, when our fathers were baptized in the Red Sea; a fourth kind, in the pool (Bethesda), when the water was troubled; a fifth kind was the ascent of the axe out of the water; and a sixth kind was the casting wood into the fountain and the sweetening of the waters."

The diverse character of these baptisms is obvious at a glance.

Basil, ii, 632, *ed. Ven.*: "John the Baptist says, I indeed baptize you with water into repentance, but he shall baptize you by the Holy Spirit, and many such things. But as much as the Holy Spirit *differs* from water so much, evidently, also he who baptizes by the Holy Spirit excels him who baptizes with water, and the baptism itself."

The Apostle uses the same word to point out the differences among Jewish baptisms, as Basil uses to indicate the difference between water baptism and baptism by the Holy Spirit. The difference between these latter baptisms cannot be a difference in the dipping or the covering; for in baptism by the Spirit there is neither dipping nor covering. Nor can it be a difference as to the objects baptized—"cups, pots, skins"—for the objects are the same, human beings.

III, 1532: "I think that we should learn, in brief, the diversity between the baptism of Moses and that of John—τὴν διαφορὰν τοῦ κατὰ Μωϋσέα βαπτίσματος πρὸς τὸ τοῦ Ἰωάννου." It is obvious that if a baptism begins and ends with a modal act or covering, there can be no difference between such act or covering under the direction of Moses or of John. The exposition of these baptisms, therefore, cannot be found in any such direction.

IV, 125: "Why then compare baptisms which have nothing in common but the name, while the difference of things—ἡ δὲ τῶν πραγμάτων διαφορὰ τοσαύτη—is as great as between a dream and the truth, or a shadow and the substance?"

How diverse was the view of Basil of baptism from that of the theorists! He declares that between Jewish and Christian baptism there is nothing in common but a name; while they labor, in ways most extravagant, to show the most perfect uniformity.

Chrysostom, ii, 366: "John exhorted the Jews not to cherish hopes of salvation through diverse baptisms and purifications of waters,—οὐκ ἐν βαπτισμοῖς διαφόροις καὶ καθαρμοῖς ὑδάτων."

The distinction made by Chrysostom between "diverse baptisms" and "purifications of water" leads directly to the conclusion, that among the diversities of baptisms there were some not effected by water. And this is true, for some baptisms were by the sprinkling of blood, of heifer-ashes, &c.

Justin Martyr (Op. Sp.), 1340: "The law released from blame, daily, transgressors, by certain sprinklings, and sacrifices of animals, and diverse kinds of baptisms—διαφοραῖς βαπτισμάτων—but grace grants only one baptism." It is probable that the writer intended to include the "sprinklings" and "the sacrifices" among the diversities of baptism. This is the understanding of Matthies (Baptismatis Expositio, p. 17): "Verum enim vero apud Judæos tota vocis," baptizare seu baptismus "potestas istis purgandi ritibus continetur iisque prorsus concluditur, ita ut quævis lustrationes dici possint baptismi—But truly among the Jews the whole force of the word *baptize* or *baptism* is thoroughly expressed by those rites of purification, so that any lustrations whatever may be called baptisms."

Gregory Nazianzen, ii, 353: "Come let us inquire somewhat concerning the differences of baptisms,—περὶ διαφορᾶς βαπτισμάτων—that we may go hence purified. Moses baptized, but with water, and previously with the cloud and sea. And John baptized, but not Judaically, nor yet with water only, but, also, into repentance; but not wholly spiritually, for he does not add, 'with the Spirit.' And Jesus baptizes, but with the Spirit. And this is perfect. . . . I know a fourth kind of baptism, that which is by martyrdom and blood, with which Christ himself was baptized. And I know yet a fifth, the baptism of tears,—washing—λούων—nightly, his bed with tears. . . . Perhaps, then, they will be baptized with fire—τῷ πυρὶ—harder to bear and longer in duration, the final baptism."

If any value is to be attached to the judgment of these Greek writers as to the meaning of βαπτίζω, in such relations, it is a point made out, that so far from a dipping or a water covering constituting the *alpha* and the *omega*, neither of these things entered into the conception of the word at all in such use. Baptism was a conception myriad-sided, presenting multiplied diversities as to nature, and no less multiplied diversities in the modes of accomplishment. Amid these diversities there is this one element, which is always to be found,—*a thorough change of condition*. The nature of the condition may vary endlessly, as may the cause inducing it and the mode of its operation; but, still, condition as a present element is a *sine qua non*.

The use of λούω, by Gregory, reminds us of the statement by Dr. Carson, that this word is limited in use to animal bodies, and requires that its object shall be covered with water. Neither of these features is present in the case related. The "bed" is not an *animal body*, nor is the bed "washed" by being "covered over" with tears. It is wholly insufficient to talk about hyperbole. It is quite enough of extravagance to imagine the bed to be superficially wet all over with tears. To be asked to imagine the bed to be enveloped in a watery covering of tears is insufferable. Nor does the literal use of the word justify any such extravagant figure. A baptism is sought to be got out of every case of "washing." Water may be found to cover "the couches;" but tears will not be found in the actual world, or in the world of imagination, to *immerse* this bed. But it is no greater blunder to seek a solution of this "tears baptism" in a hyperbolic immersion of this bed, than to seek a solution of the "altar baptism" in a hyperbolic immersion of the bullock, wood, and stones. Dr. Fuller says, Origen, "one of the most impassionate of men," figuratively calls the effect of pouring the water, a baptism.

He defends the interpretation by quoting from Hamlet:

> "What would he do,
> Had he the motive and the cue for passion
> That I have? He would *drown* the stage with tears."

Whether Gregory was "one of the most impassionate of men" I do not know; but if Dr. Fuller will take the altar poured upon, the bed washed, and the penitent sinner sprinkled with tear-drops, as honestly baptized, we shall certainly be making progress.

However, when an author writes a book entitled "*the act* of baptism," and opens it with the portentous words, "Saved or Damned," and then expounds a baptism in which "the act" is left out, it reminds one of the adage associated with the play which the Doctor has quoted: "Hamlet, with the part of Hamlet left out."

CLASSICS.

The Patrists, in their view of diverse baptisms, differ, in no respect, from the Classics. They say that Mosaic, Johannic, and Christian baptisms, are diverse, on the ground that the agencies inducing them are of diverse "power," and therefore induce diverse conditions. The Classic writers teach us precisely the same truth in connection with wine, opiates, and cold water. The power of these agencies is diverse, and they induce diverse conditions—baptisms. A condition of intoxication, a condition of stupefaction, and a condition of coldness, are all diverse conditions. And these diverse conditions the Classics call baptisms, "diverse baptisms."

The manner of using these agencies to effect these baptisms, was endlessly diverse; yet this fact is not singled out for discussion or explanation, because it does not appear to have entered into the mind of Classic or Patristic writers, as needing either discussion or explanation. The only vital idea in a baptism, is *thorough change of condition.* This was effected, primarily, by intusposition within a closely investing medium. The manner in which such intusposition was accomplished, was a thing wholly extraneous. This change of condition was effected, secondarily, without intusposition, by any agency competent to the end.

And as every Classic and Patristic writer knew, that to raise the question, *how* intusposition, primary, was effected, was to raise a question wholly foreign to the case; so, also, they knew that there was no place for the *quo modo* of baptism, secondary. *Drinking* wine, *eating* an opiate, *pouring* cold water, *sprinkling* sacrificial blood, had the same equal and absolute right to appear for duty on such occasions. They, therefore, do not discuss any such diversities. They are recognized and spoken of as accidents, which are indifferently present or absent. The word baptism has nothing to do with modes of action. But baptism has to do, first and last, with condition. And the conditions to which it is applied are so diverse, and so alien from each other, that, as Basil says, "they have nothing in common but the name."

These diverse baptisms (conditions effected by agencies greatly diverse in their powers, and applied in modes unlimited in their diversity) are largely discussed by Patristic writers.

Judaic baptism belongs, exclusively, to baptisms of the secondary class. It is causative, distinctively, of a condition of ceremonial purification. The diversities which enter into it, are due to the diverse *causes*—"dead body," "bone," "leprous person," "market," &c.,—inducing defilement; and the diverse *agencies*,—simple water, water and heifer ashes, blood, &c.,—employed to remove these defilements; as also to the diverse *modes*—washing, pouring, sprinkling —in which these agencies were employed to develop their baptizing power.

The diverse baptizings of the Apostle, and the diverse baptisms of the Patrists, are in the most absolute accord with the diverse baptisms of the Classics. That the former differ in kind from the latter, is only confirmatory of the diversity of baptisms, and establishes the statement of Ambrose, "plurima baptismatum genera."

CARSON.

That the "diverse baptizings" are included in the "carnal ordinances," (ordinances of the flesh,) is a matter of universal acknowledgment. It is also certain, that "the blood of bulls and of goats, and the ashes of a heifer sprinkling the unclean, sanctifying to the *purifying* of the *flesh*," is an exposition of the "ordinances of the *flesh*." Now, the "ordinances of the flesh" embrace "meats, and drinks, and diverse baptizings;" and if "the sprinkling of the blood of bulls and of goats, and the ashes of a heifer," does not enter into "meats and drinks," it must be found in "diverse baptizings."

This, however, is strenuously objected to by friends of the theory, and, as usual, with special vehemence by Dr. Carson. He says, "the sprinklings under the law cannot be included under the baptisms, but might be included in the carnal ordinances." True, "the sprinklings" are in the carnal ordinances, but only because "the baptisms" are there.

The sprinklings and the baptizings are the same thing under diversity of designation. The *sprinkling* expresses the mode in which the agency was employed, and the *baptizing* indicates the controlling influence attendant upon the agency so applied.

Dr. Carson farther asks: "How do we know that what are here called 'divers baptisms,' were performed by sprinkling and effusion? Can this be done in any other way than by ascertaining the meaning of the word baptism by the usage of the language?" And then to determine this usage, he appeals to case after case of use, as far removed in character from the case in hand, as the poles are in distance from each other. As well might Dr. Gale repudiate Carson's plea for *dyeing* the lake, on the ground that usage has settled the meaning of βάπτω, and proceed, in vindication of his position, to adduce cases in which it does, unquestionably, mean *to dip*. The position of the theorists, now, in relation to βαπτίζω, is just the same with that which they formerly assumed with respect to βάπτω. The same shifts of "figure," which are appealed to under embarrassment, now, were used, under like circumstances, then.

Dr. Carson goes on to ask: "Does he refer to the baptisms what was done with the sprinkling of the blood? There is not the semblance of truth for the assertion. The subtilty of Satan himself cannot plausibly contrive to force these sprinklings into the divers baptisms."

Notwithstanding the Doctor's opinion as to what "the subtilty of Satan" can accomplish, there are very many who believe that Paul, without any such aid, has quite "plausibly contrived to force these sprinklings into the divers baptisms."

But Paul does not stand alone in this achievement. Ambrose has been no less successful. This is his language: "Per hyssopi fasciculum aspergebatur agni sanguine qui mundari volebat typico baptismate." (i, 875.) "He who wished to be purified with typical *baptism* was *sprinkled* with the blood of the lamb by a bunch of hyssop."

I do not know how much of "subtilty" or "force" there

may be in this statement, but I do know that, by very direct statement, *sprinklings* are brought into unity with *baptisms.* The same writer (iii, 399) says again: "Qui enim baptizatur, et secundum legem et secundum evangelium videtur esse mundatus; secundum legem quia hyssopi fasciculo Moyses aspergebat sanguinem agni." "For he who is *baptized*, both according to the law and according to the gospel, is seen to be made pure; according to the law, because Moses, with a bunch of hyssop, *sprinkled* the blood of the lamb."

If language be designed to express thought, and not to conceal it, then Ambrose has placed, not "plausibly," but absolutely, "the *sprinkling* of the blood of the lamb" among the diverse baptizings.

Let us note the success of another in this same impossible (according to the theory) direction.

Josephus (Jew. Ant., iv, 4) says: "*βαπτίσαντες τε καὶ τῆς τέφρας ταύτης εἰς πηγὴν, ἔρραινον τρίτῃ καὶ ἑβδόμῃ τῶν ἡμερῶν*—and also *baptizing* by this ashes put into spring water, they *sprinkled* on the third and seventh day."

This embraces the other sprinkling—ashes of the heifer—mentioned by Paul. Now, with such help from Ambrose and Josephus, I do not see why any one (with subtilty far less than that usually attributed to Satan) might not be able, without force, to identify these *sprinklings* with those "divers baptizings."

Let it be observed, that neither Ambrose nor Josephus confounds sprinkling and baptism, so as to make the sprinkling the baptism and the baptism the sprinkling. They make the baptism to depend, in the one case, on the influence of the *blood of the lamb*, which is applied (not of necessity but of fact) by sprinkling. In the other case, the baptism is effected through *the ashes of a heifer;* the influence of which, also, is developed, in fact, by the act of sprinkling. The blood, the sprinkling, and the purification, are as distinct as are the wine, the drinking, and the intoxication.

Because the sprinkling is not a dipping, or because it is not "continued long enough" to produce a covering *in* blood or *in* ashes and water, it is concluded that there is no baptism. But such forget that there are baptisms *by* influential agencies, as well as mersions *in* physical substances.

Sacrificial blood, and emblematical ashes and water, *sprinkled* have as much power to baptize, as the intoxicating or drugged cup *drunk*, has power to baptize. If wine drunk, baptizes (without mersion) into intoxication, the blood of the lamb sprinkled, baptizes (without mersion) into purification.

If Satyrus could baptize (without mersion) into stupefaction, by means of a few opiate drops mixed with wine, why could not Moses baptize (without mersion) into ceremonial purity, by means of a few drops of ashes mixed with spring water?

If clean linen may be *bapted* (dyed) by *sprinkling* blood upon it, as truly as by dipping it into blood, why may not an unclean man be baptized (made ceremonially clean) by the sprinkling of clean water upon him, as truly as by his being dipped into clean water? If βάπτω can lay aside a dipping, why cannot βαπτίζω lay aside a mersion?

Dr. Carson will not deny, that sacrificial blood, and the ashes of a heifer sprinkling the unclean, were competent thoroughly to change the condition of the ceremonially unclean, making them thoroughly ceremonially clean; for by such denial he would place himself in direct antagonism with the clearest teachings, and ritual provisions, of the word of God. But should he deny, that this thoroughly controlling influence of blood, and ashes, over the condition of those upon whom they were sprinkled, can be justly termed baptism; then, he places himself in antagonism with the teachings of all profane Greek literature. And if he denies, that this influence, controlling condition, is in fact called baptism; then, he places himself in antagonism with all Patristic literature which treats of Jewish purifications; as, also, with the Jewish historian who was personally conversant with, and a participant in those observances.

The "subtilty of Satan" will be more severely taxed to get these sprinklings out of the "divers baptisms," than to force them into them.

Will "the theory" venture to make the trial?

JUDAIC AND JOHANNIC BAPTISM.

SYMBOL BAPTISM.

. . . *βαπτισμῷ συνίεναι· οὕτω γὰρ τὴν βάπτισιν ἀποδεκτὴν αὐτῷ φανεῖσθαι, μὴ ἐπὶ τινῶν ἁμαρτάδων παραιτήσει χρωμένων, αλλ' ἐφ' ἁγνέιᾳ τοῦ σώματος, ἅτε δὴ καὶ τῆς ψυχῆς δικαιοσύνῃ προεκκεκαθαρμένης*. . . .

"For Herod slew him (John the Baptist), a good man, and exhorting the Jews to cultivate virtue, and observing uprightness toward one another and piety toward God, to come for baptizing (purifying); for thus the baptism would appear acceptable to him, not using it for the remission of sins, but for purity of the body, provided that the soul has been, previously, purged by righteousness."—*Josephus, Jew. Ant.*, xviii, 6. 2.

The Latin translation of this passage by Valesius, in his edition of Eusebius (ii, 116), is as follows: "Quippe hunc Herodes obtruncaverat, cum esset vir bonus, Judæosque ad virtutis studium excitaret, præcipiens ut juste quidem inter se, erga Deum autem pie agentes, ad lavacrum accederent. Tunc enim demum acceptum Deo fore lavacrum aiebat, cum eo non ad expiationem criminum uterentur, sed ad corporis munditiem, ut mentibus jam ante per justitiam expurgatis, corporis quoque adderent puritatem."

BAPTISM OF JUDAISM AND OF JOHN MET TOGETHER.

This quotation shows very clearly that Josephus, as well as the Patrists and the apostle, believed in "divers baptisms." This diversity, as between Judaic and Johannic baptisms, is made both distinct and broad. The one baptism is a purification of the body; the other is a purification of the soul. In the one case the agency effecting the purification is *water;* in the other it is *righteousness.* "Righteousness" is not represented as an element within which the soul is to be immersed; but the agency by which the purified condition of the soul is to be accomplished. The same must be true of the water used in effecting the other purified condition, that of the body. Water, as ritually used by the Jew, was not used to remove physical pollution, but ceremonial. Its competence for this duty did not depend upon any natural quality; but upon a communicated quality dependent upon its appointment to this use. In view of such appointment it was possessed of a "power," when used by sprinkling or otherwise, to change the condition of the body, removing it out of ceremonial pollution into ceremonial purity; as truly, as "righteousness" had power to change the condition of the soul, removing it out of a condition of spiritual pollution into a condition of spiritual purity.

DIVERSITY.

Josephus, in common with all other writers quoted, represents the water used in Jewish purifications as an *efficient agency*, and *not as an element within which* mersion is to take place. But in his view water no longer occupies the position of an efficient agency in John's baptism. John's baptism is of the soul and not of the body. Water is used in this baptism; but not as having power to control spiritual results.

The historian still represents water in its Jewish aspect, as having power to purify the body; which becomes a symbol of, or complementary to, the full purification of the entire man, when the soul is purified by "righteousness."

I do not now enter upon the discussion as to the perfect correctness of the view of John's baptism as entertained by Josephus. That will come up hereafter. It is enough, in passing, to indicate the fact recognized by him as to the essential difference in their nature, and the no less essential difference in the agencies by which they were effected.

But Josephus could have no misconception as to Judaic baptism. And he tells us, that it consisted in *a condition of physical ceremonial purity induced by the ritual agency of water, ashes, &c., used in sprinkling.*

Having, now, passed in review all the evidence within our reach as to the nature of Judaic baptism, together with the agencies and their manner of use in its accomplishment, and having heard from Jewish lips the announcement of another baptism, a higher and better, even than that of the Forerunner; we will here pause to look back upon our course and gather up some of its results, in order to our better preparation to determine the question, which is next in order, *What was* JOHN'S *baptism?*

RESULTS.

Material for Judgment.

1. We have before us adequate material for an intelligent determination as to the distinctive character of Judaic baptism, as well as for the confirmation of conclusions previously reached in Classic Baptism.

The number of facts embraced in the investigation is not less than fifty, and the number of times in which the Greek word, in one form or another, appears, is more than three times fifty.

The facts are all taken from Jewish sources, from writings both inspired and uninspired. Ten Jewish writers employ the word in application to their religious rites and to matters apart from religion.

Christian writers, with one consent, interpret these facts of Jewish religious history as cases of baptism.

The time embraced by the usage of this word by Jewish writers, in application to their religious rites, extends through several centuries.

Such varied and abundant material leaves nothing to be desired for the intelligent determination of the meaning of this word from usage.

Usage, of Jew and Greek, harmonious.

2. The usage of this word by Jewish writers is in the most perfect accord with the usage of Greek *Classic writers.*

By this statement I do not mean to affirm that the Jew uses βαπτίζω only in the same applications as the Greek; but I mean to say, that whatever application they make of the word, religious or otherwise, they are governed by the same principles and in recognition of the same fundamental meaning.

(1.) There is no *dipping* in the Jewish use of the word. In all the instances cited from the writings of Josephus and Philo, in the translations of Symmachus and Aquila, in the facts of the Old Testament and of the Apocrypha, there is not a single case in which it is stated that the baptism was by dipping, or in which there is any adequate inferential evidence to show that the baptism was effected by the modal act of dipping.

Jewish and Greek usage are, here, at one.

(2.) The Jew recognizes baptisms of intusposition without limit of time as to their continuance. These baptisms are of two kinds. Those in which *no influence is exerted* over the baptized object. As in the case of the sword of Simon baptized into his own body. The sword exerts a destructive influence, but no influence is exerted over the sword by its mersion. So, in the case of the axe fallen into the Jordan. The iron is not affected by its watery envelopment. Those in which *controlling influence is exerted* over the baptized object. Such cases are those of ships sunk to the bottom of the sea; and of the human race baptized in the waters of the deluge. These baptisms are attended with influences absolutely controlling in their power. And, herein, they are most essentially distinguished from the preceding cases of baptism, and give origin to the secondary usage of the word in which mersion disappears, and a changed condition stands alone.

(3.) The Jew employs verbal figure to indicate the source and nature of the baptizing influence, without demand for, or allowance of, intusposition.

Thus, Josephus speaks of "baptism *into* insensibility and sleep." This phraseology is modelled after the form which is expressive of the introduction of an object within a physical substance for the purpose of securing the full influence of the enveloping material. Cases of this character may be found in Classic Baptism, p. 266. Objects are introduced, baptized, "into the water (εἰς τὸ ὕδωρ,") "into the lake (εἰς τὴν λίμνην"), "into milk (εἰς γάλα γυναικὸς"), "into the blood (εἰς τὸ αἷμα"). In all these cases there is intusposition for an indefinitely prolonged time of the object within the water, the lake, the milk, and the blood; and in all of these cases the intusposition is not an end, but a means to an end, namely, to secure a full development of influence; and in each case the influence developed is peculiar. The pole smeared with pitch, mersed into water impregnated with an auriferous quality, becomes incrusted with gold. Human beings mersed, in simple water of the lake, are drowned. A medical prescription mersed, in woman's milk, becomes emollient. A hand mersed, in the bloody pool of the battle-field, becomes fitted to write, in gory characters, "vanquished, not conquered." It is most obvious, that there can be no interchange among these enveloping elements, substituting the one for the other. "Woman's milk" cannot be substituted for "gold impregnated with water," into which a pitch-smeared pole may be mersed in order that it may be gilded. Nor can gold-water be substituted for woman's milk, in order that a mersed blister or pessary may be made more soothing. Lake-water cannot be substituted for blood, that a hand mersed into it may write a battle record. Nor can the crimson flowings of gory .wounds be substituted for lake waters, in which a vanquished host may be mersed, and drowned. No more can the ἐις ἀναισθησίαν καὶ ὕπνον of Josephus (into which Gedaliah was baptized) be transformed into gold-water, lake-water, woman's milk, human blood, or anything else whatever. There is as much of irrationality in putting Gedaliah, by imagination, into a water-pool, as there is in putting a pitched pole into woman's milk to extract gold. "Insensibility and sleep" must remain *insensibility and sleep;* just as "gold-water" must remain *gold-water;* and "woman's milk" must remain *woman's milk.*

But it may be said, a man cannot be put within "insensibility and sleep;" must we not then convert (in imagination) these things into *fluids,* that Gedaliah may be put within them? I answer, no; (1.) Because it is beyond the power of imagination to convert "insensibility" or "sleep" into *distinctive* fluids. (2.) To imagine them to be fluids without a distinctive character, would be as irrational as to confound gold-water and woman's milk. (3.) To put Gedaliah within any fluid would never answer Josephus's purpose; but would put him into that sleep "which knows no waking."

Josephus never meant to put the imagination under bonds to accomplish the impossible absurdity of putting a man within a liquefied insensibility and sleep; nor yet the impossible conception of putting him within them under any condition.

Is it asked, "Why then does Josephus use the phraseology, '*baptized into* insensibility and sleep'?" I answer, because he means to express a condition characterized by the controlling influences of "insensibility and sleep." For this purpose he conjoins these things with βαπτίζω εἰς; phraseology used in physics to secure the development of any distinctive influence belonging to its adjunct. Thus βαπτίζω εἰς with gold-water, with lake-water, with woman's milk, with human blood, indicates the full influence distinctively attaching to these several elements over an object *mersed in them* for an indefinitely prolonged period. And when conjoined with "insensibility and sleep," it denotes the full influence distinctively belonging to these elements over the object *brought within their control*, not by mersion within them, (for this is impossible whether of reality or of imagination,) but in that way which is appropriate to the case, and which is expressly stated by Josephus, namely, *by excessive wine-drinking.*

The office, then, of the phrase βαπτίζω εἰς, is to conduct us, in thought, to those cases where influence is sought as the end, and mersion is used as the means; while its adjunct, "insensibility and sleep," teaches us that the end only is to be retained, and the form for securing that end is to be rejected as unsuited to the case.

In all this, the Jew is in perfect accord with the Greek. It has been abundantly shown in Classic Baptism, that condition resultant from controlling influence, and secured without mersion, was placed, without hesitation or discrimination, among baptisms. Josephus exhibits this truth in the clearest and strongest manner, by using the complete phraseology of verbal figure. The hand is *bapted*, not by dipping, (the mode is rejected,) but by *pressing* a berry; the body and the mind are *baptized*, not by mersion, (the mode is rejected,) but by *drinking* wine.

(4.) The Jew employs this Greek word, like Classic writers, absolutely, and appropriatedly, to denote a specific baptism.

The Greeks thus used it to express a condition of drunkenness; the Jew used it, on the same principles, to express a condition of ceremonial religious purity. There was the same right to appropriate to the one use or the other. Alien as is drunkenness from purity, the word, in itself, was equally susceptible of application in the one direction or the other. The baptism of the god Bacchus (C. B., p. 324), and of the demi-god Silenus (p. 330), was effected by drinking, and not by mersion. The baptism of Jehovah was effected by sprinkling ashes, blood, and water, and not by mersion. This baptism was, by eminence, Judaic baptism.

Jewish Baptisms not Dippings.

3. Jewish baptisms were effected generally neither by dippings nor by envelopings, but by influential agencies, variously applied, usually by sprinkling.

This fact stands out in the boldest relief, and governs the whole course of Patristic interpretation. This development is only a repetition of that in Classic Baptism. There, in score after score of baptisms, there is not one word said of dipping or of envelopment. Nothing appears but an influential agency, changing the condition, after its own nature, and thus effecting a baptism.

The Classics recognized a "power" in wine, and in a drug, and in a thousand other things, to baptize. They speak of water impregnated with a quality—"*incerto medicamine*"—by which it was able to change the condition of those coming in contact with it, just as Bethesda's water received a "quality," by which it was able to change the condition of those coming under its power.

Let it be pointedly noted, *that it was not the fluid, as such,* which effected the baptism, but a foreign "quality," imparted to it, whose "power" to baptize was not restricted to any modal use.

While the Classics use one class of agencies to effect their baptisms, the Jews use those of a different character to effect their distinctive baptism. The ashes of a red heifer, sacrificial blood, and living water, have, with them, a power to baptize (to change the ceremonial condition from defilement to purity), so as other ashes, blood, or water, have not. This shows, demonstrably, that the baptism does not consist in a dipping, or in an envelopment, but in an effect produced. The Patrists, in like manner, make the baptism to depend not on the receptivity of the element, but on a "vis," or "qualitas," not inherent in it and not dependent on any modal use of it, for its development. A coal of fire, or a flaming sword, therefore, can baptize as readily and as legitimately, as any or as any amount of fluid element.

A Jew, *ritually sprinkled by ashes*, (to which, by divine appointment, was communicated a power to cleanse from ceremonial defilement,) was as truly baptized, as was Aristobulus *drowned in the fish-pool.*

The evidence is overwhelming, in support of the position, that JEWISH BAPTISMS *were effected by influential agencies, usually, developing their power over the object baptized by the act of* SPRINKLING.

The Theorists made Apologists.

4. The facts of these Jewish baptisms, and their interpretation by most learned Grecians, force the theorists into an unvarying apologetic attitude.

Any one who has passed over the course through which we have been led, by Jew and Patrist, must profoundly feel, that nowhere along the route is aid or comfort to be found for the theory which ascribes to βαπτίζω "one meaning, dip, and nothing but dip, through all Greek literature."

In the baptism of the sword, mersed into Simon's body, there is no dipping. In the baptism of the ship, sunk into the sea, there is no dipping. In the baptism of Aristobulus, drowned by the Galatians, there is no dipping. In the baptism of the human race in the deluge waters, there is no dipping. In the baptisms by washing, by sprinkling, and by pouring, there is no dipping. In the baptism by the waving sword, and by the touch of the coal of fire, there is no dipping. In the baptism by suffering, and terror, there is no dipping.

Everywhere the theory is called upon to apologize for the absence of "the only meaning," and to construct, by some extravagance of rhetoric or imagination, a grotesque substitute for it.

On the other hand, we confidently appeal to the theorist himself, who may think our view to be but a counterfeit of the truth, and ask him, Whether counterfeit was ever more like the truth? Whether the truth itself ever met more squarely every fact, resolved every difficulty, and moved on more harmoniously with the laws of language?

If the theory is to be sustained, it must be on some other ground than that which is covered by Judaic baptism. Here, there is but repudiation of its postulations, and a deaf ear for its apologies.

Classic Baptism Confirmed.

5. The farther investigation, now instituted, confirms the conclusion reached in Classic Baptism, that condition of intusposition involving complete influence, and not modal act, is the fundamental idea of the word; while it advances to a secondary use, in which intusposition (as the form by which the influence is effected) is lost, and influence, in whatsoever way operative, (if capable of thoroughly changing the condition of its object and subjecting it to itself,) takes the place of intusposition.

The illustrations vindicating these positions furnished by Judaic Baptism, are, if possible, more explicit and more utterly concluding reply, than those found in Classic Baptism. What can be more out of the reach of all rational opposition, than the baptism by the sprinkling of heifer ashes, as announced by Josephus? or by the sprinkling of the blood of the lamb, as declared by Ambrose? What should be more conclusive of all controversy as to a dipping or an envelopment being essential to a baptism, than a baptism effected by the *waving of a flaming sword*, or by *the pouring of water* upon an altar, or *the baptism* of SIN itself?

I cannot venture to believe that these conclusions will be accepted by the present friends of the theory; but I do dare to believe that there is such a self-evidencing power in truth, that those who come after them, with minds less preoccupied with mistaken conceptions, will accept them as truths from which there is no escape, and from which, I am happy to believe, they will not wish to escape.

Appropriation—Ceremonial Purification.

6. Finally, in connection with Jewish ritual purifications, βαπτίζω secures the meaning *to purify ceremonially.*

Whether, in other relations, it ever expresses a purification broader and higher than that which is merely ceremonial, is not now a question. Dr. Edward Williams, more than a century since, and President Beecher and Professor Godwin, more recently, have argued with eminent ability and accomplished scholarship, to show that this word means *to purify.* They failed to establish, fully, their views in the minds of thoughtful persons, not because there was not great and evident truth in many of their positions, but because the fundamental idea of the word not having been clearly traced out, and the development of this specific meaning thence deduced, the truth, while seen, was not seen without a penumbra, and its boundaries not always accurately indicated. They, consequently, put in claim for this meaning, in some cases where such claim could not be satisfactorily established, and thus threw doubt over those claims which were well grounded. If I were to say, βαπτίζω means *to make drunk*, and then were to apply this meaning to all cases of *stupefaction*, an opponent, who should show that some particular case of stupefaction was produced, not by an intoxicant, but by an opiate, might shake confidence, not merely in that particular application, but in the general position.

It is essential, to intelligent conviction, that the origin of meanings claimed, should be clearly traced, and the limits of their dominion be rightfully defined. When this is done, conviction of the truth sooner or later is sure to follow. In claiming that this word means "to purify ceremonially," we acknowledge our obligation to show how this meaning may originate under the laws of language, and to show its actual development by facts of usage. This obligation we have attempted to meet.

No one questions, but that a sentence of many words, each with a distinct thought, may be absorbed by some single word of such sentence, which word will express a thought the result of the whole. Thus: "He drinks intoxicating liquor until he becomes drunk," is abbreviated into, "He drinks intoxicating liquor;" and then into, "He drinks;" when "drinks" has absorbed the entire sentence, and expresses the resultant condensed thought of the whole, viz.: "He gets drunk."

And when I say of one: "He is like a drinking man;" *drinking* does not express the act of swallowing a liquid, but the condition of a man who is in the habit of *getting drunk.* A new meaning has been secured for the word. So in the sentence, "Baptized by wine into drunkenness," abbreviation drops "into drunkenness," and then "by wine;" while "baptized" remains the sole representative of the whole, and expresses the entire resultant thought. Thus: "I am one of those *baptized,*" (C. B., p. 317,) means, "I am one of those *made drunk.*" And, "He is like one *baptized,*" (C. B., p. 330,) means, "He is like one *made drunk.*" The word has secured a new meaning.

Under precisely the same conditions of the laws of language and the facts of usage, frequent in occurrence, and reaching through centuries of continuance, βαπτίζω secures the meaning *to purify ceremonially.*

No theorist can deny the fitness of the language, "Baptized by heifer ashes, by sacrificial blood, by living water, into ceremonial purity." Neither can he deny the lawful abbreviation, "baptized by heifer ashes," or that of the single word, "baptized;" which word shall embody, within itself, the one thought which is the joint product of the several parts of the sentence, to wit, *made ceremonially pure.* And when Josephus speaks of "*baptizing* by heifer ashes," he speaks of *making ceremonially pure* by this agency. And when the Son of Sirach speaks of one "*baptized* from the dead," he speaks of one *made ceremonially pure.* And when, two centuries afterward, the Jew wondered that the Saviour did not "first *baptize* before eating," he expressed his wonder that he did not *ceremonially purify* himself. Such had become the direct meaning of the word, as shown by its absolute use, for centuries, in connection with ritual purifications.

The conclusion, then, of our inquiry is this:

JUDAIC BAPTISM *is a condition of* CEREMONIAL PURIFICATION *effected by the* WASHING *of the hands or feet, by the* SPRINKLING *of sacrificial blood or heifer ashes, by the* POURING *upon of water, by the* TOUCH *of a coal of fire, by the* WAVING *of a flaming sword, and by divers other modes and agencies, dependent, in no wise, on any form of act or on the covering of the object.*

With such evidence, deduced from language development, sustaining the previous conclusion of Classic Baptism, that the word makes demand for a condition and not for a modal act; and with such varied, explicit, and authoritative evidence sustaining the present conclusion of Judaic Baptism, that the word makes demand for a condition of ceremonial purity; any attempt to overthrow these conclusions can have but little happier issue than an attempt to overturn this solid globe of ours, while no answer comes to the despairing cry—

"*ΔΟΣ ΜΟΙ ΠΟΥ ΣΤΩ.*"